Arbitration Act 2010 and Model Law: A Commentary

Arbitration Act 2010 and Model Law: A Commentary

BARRY MANSFIELD
BCL (NUI), LLM (Georgetown),
Barrister-at-Law, Attorney-at-Law

CLARUS
PRESS

Published by
Clarus Press Ltd,
Griffith Campus,
South Circular Road,
Dublin 8,
Ireland.

Typeset by
Deanta Global Publishing Services

Printed by
CPI Group (UK) Ltd.,
Croydon,
CR0 4YY

ISBN
978-1-905536-47-4

Foreword

Law books can come in many different forms. At one end of the spectrum lies the simple guide designed to outline basic principles for the benefit of students in their early years or, indeed, members of the public with an interest in the subject at hand. Where books are designed, at least in part, for practitioners, same can range from the textbook model, which goes through the subject on a topic by topic basis, to the commentary on an important piece of relevant legislation. This excellent work falls into the latter category.

While the textbook model may have some advantages for those who are venturing into a field with which they are not familiar, there can be little doubt that the practitioner, who has at least a broad general familiarity with an area, finds great assistance in a comprehensive commentary book most particularly where, as now applies in relation to arbitration, most of the relevant law can be found either in a single piece of legislation or the cases decided under that legislation.

It is, of course, the case that the backdrop to the legislation on which this book is a commentary is the adoption, through the 2010 Act, of the UNCITRAL Model Law as the basis for both domestic and international arbitrations in Ireland. It follows that interpretations of that Model Law from other jurisdictions which have adopted it, either in whole or in part, as the basis for their domestic arbitration law, are of particular relevance in this field.

The author has not only provided a comprehensive internal account of the 2010 Act which makes cross referencing between sections an easy task, but also has provided useful and informative background information together with comprehensive reference both to relevant case law and the work of other authors on the topic. For the practitioner with some general familiarity with the structure of arbitration law this book will, in my view, provide a one stop shop which will give a comprehensive guide to all materials necessary for a proper understanding of any of the relevant provisions of the 2010 Act.

As the author points out the UNCITRAL Model Law is designed for adoption in respect of international arbitrations with a view to seeking to harmonise the law relevant to international arbitrations across jurisdictions. However, Ireland has chosen to apply the same Model Law not only to international arbitration but also to domestic ones. The 2010 Act is, therefore, the code by reference to which all future issues concerning arbitration will be determined in this jurisdiction. A knowledge of the Act and how it operates is an essential prerequisite for any practitioner who may have need to advise on or participate in the arbitral process in Ireland. The author has done all such persons a great service by bringing together, in one comprehensive commentary, all of the materials which anyone dealing with problems in the arbitral process or its review may require. This book will undoubtedly prove to become the standard work of reference for all practitioners (and in that regard I would include judges). The author is worthy, therefore, of both our thanks and our congratulations.

Frank Clarke
The Supreme Court
3 April 2012

Preface

The genesis of this work was at the 18th Willem C Vis International Commercial Arbitration Moot in Vienna, which I attended during Easter week 2011 with a team of students from Trinity College Dublin. Amidst legal scholars and scholarship from across the globe, it was a source of surprise to me that no Irish work existed to provide commentary on our arbitration law and practice since the commencement of the Arbitration Act 2010.

Although it would be an exaggeration to suggest that the Act has revolutionised arbitration practice in Ireland — particularly as the United Nations Commission on International Trade Law (UNCITRAL) Model Law, which the Arbitration Act 2010 adopts as the substantive law governing arbitration in Ireland, has been applicable to international commercial arbitrations seated in Ireland since 1998. However, in deciding to write this work I believed that an academic lacuna existed in respect to current arbitration law and practice in Ireland, not only in respect of those new provisions of law introduced by the Arbitration Act 2010 but also in respect of an analysis of the UNCITRAL Model Law specific to an Irish legal audience. Indeed, in writing this work, my twin goals were to provide commentary on the new provisions of the Arbitration Act 2010 and also to disseminate at least some of the vast international sources on the UNCITRAL Model Law to a mainstream Irish legal audience. These international sources include not only case-law but also secondary materials from leading academic commentators. In this regard, although I hope this work will be of value, any comparison of my contribution to the subject with the contribution of those commentators is meaningless; the oft-used metaphor about 'standing on the shoulders of giants' does not do justice at all.

Although writing is a solitary process I have received much assistance from others. I extend my thanks and gratitude to my editor and publisher, David McCartney of Clarus Press for his encouragement and diligence; to Dr Daniel Simms BL, who was an constant advisor on the structure of the work; to Joseph Garvey Esq, a student of mine at Trinity College Dublin who conducted invaluable research on international case-law in Model Law jurisdictions — I hope he will have a fine career in international dispute resolution; and to Hugh B Byrne BL, Dr Oran Doyle BL, Máire Mullarkey BL, Colm Ó hOisín SC, Klaus Reichert SC and Rory White BL who have all provided guidance on various aspects of the work. I also extend my thanks and gratitude generally to Flavia Mange Esq, an International Bar Association colleague, whose enthusiasm for arbitration proved infectious; and to Andrew Walker BL, my former pupil master, and Nigel Wilson Esq, my former (unofficial) mentor at Davis Polk & Wardwell LLP, for their patience with me during the infancy of my legal career.

I wish to thank Mr Justice Frank Clarke of the Supreme Court for kindly agreeing to write the foreword to the work and, furthermore, for his kind words — to receive praise from a judge of his stature is humbling indeed.

Finally, I, of course, express my love and thanks to my parents Jim and Patricia; my brother Cían (who also provided comments and suggestions on a number of sections); and my sister Kate for their continued support.

I have attempted to state the law as it stands on 3 April 2012. However, some errors or omissions are inevitable and I accept responsibility for the same. Any suggestions for improvement or addition to the work will be greatly welcomed.

Barry Mansfield
3 April 2012

Contents

Table of Legislation

Primary Legislation

Secondary Legislation

Rules of Court

EU Legislation

Other Jurisdictions

International Materials

Table of Cases

I

J

K

L

M

R

S

T

Introduction

This aim of this work is to provide a section-by-section commentary on the Arbitration Act 2010 (the "Act") and the United Nations Commission on International Trade Law (UNCITRAL) Model Law (the "Model Law"). Each section of the Act (and article of the Model Law) is reproduced in full with commentary, which is highlighted in grey, immediately following. Like most legal commentaries, readers are not expected to read the entire work and each separate commentary is a standalone entry. To this effect, where material is relevant to more than one section, it is reproduced in full in each relevant commentary.

The work seeks to set out the current law governing arbitration in Ireland and it includes materials that may be helpful to a future Irish court called upon to interpret the provisions of the Act and the Model Law. These materials include not only domestic materials such as case-law decided under the Act and, where relevant, case-law decided under the previous legislation governing arbitration in Ireland, but also international materials including UNCITRAL's *travaux préparatoires*, which are the official record of the negotiations in preparation for the adoption of the Model Law;[1] case-law from other jurisdictions that have adopted the Model Law, which is made available by UNCITRAL at its CLOUT database[2]; and secondary materials from leading international commentators. Given the vast quantity of international sources, this work cannot hope to be definitive in its selection of materials. However, it is hoped that the most persuasive and authoritative materials have been collated and that, where necessary, those in need of further detail will be directed to more specialised sources.

The Act and the Model Law

The Act was passed on 8 March 2010 and commenced operation on 8 June 2010.[3] The Act applies to all arbitrations commenced on or after 8 June 2010[4] while the provisions of the Arbitration Acts 1954-1998, the previous legislation governing arbitration in Ireland, continue to apply to arbitrations commenced before that date. This definite time limit on the continued application of the Arbitration Acts 1954-1998 represents an attempt to minimise the potential confusion occasioned by the concurrent application of different arbitration legislation and to regulate the transition from the application of the previous legislation governing arbitration in Ireland to the application of the Act. If, instead, the date on which an arbitration agreement was entered into was to determine whether the Act is to apply then the potential application of the provisions of the Arbitration Acts 1954-1998 would continue indefinitely as disputes that are the

---

[1] The *travaux préparatoires* are available in their entirety from the UNCITRAL website at: http://www.uncitral.org/uncitral/en/uncitral_texts/arbitration/1985Model_arbitration_travaux.htModel Law.

[2] That is collated by UNCITRAL on its CLOUT database, which is available at: http://www.uncitral.org/uncitral/en/case_law.htModel Law.

[3] Arbitration Act 2010, s 1(2).

[4] Arbitration Act 2010, s 3(1).

subject matter of an arbitration agreement may arise long after the arbitration agreement is entered into.[5]

The Act adopts the Model Law for all arbitrations both domestic and international,[6] which take place in Ireland.[7] Prior to the commencement of the Act, the Model Law applied only to international commercial arbitrations taking place in Ireland.[8] The Model Law means the law as adopted by the United Nations Commission on International Trade Law on 21 June 1985, with amendments as adopted by that Commission at its thirty-ninth session on 7 June 2006. While the Model Law has no legislative force on its own, it is designed to serve as a template for national arbitration legislation. Although the Model Law has been drafted with flexibility in mind permitting states which adopt it to complete the detail without departing from the spirit of the Model Law,[9] the Act encourages an interpretation of the Model Law uniform with those other jurisdictions that have adopted its provisions through judicial notice of UNCITRAL's *travaux préparatoires.*[10]

Irish Case-law Decided under the Act

To date, case-law decided under the Act, though limited, confirms the willingness of the Irish judiciary to consider international materials when called upon to interpret the provisions of the Model Law.[11] In *Barnmore Demolition and Civil Engineering Ltd v Alandale Logistics Ltd,*[12] the High Court (Feeney J) was asked to consider the appropriate standard of judicial review to be applied when considering whether or not a valid arbitration agreement. Although the High Court declined to definitively establish the appropriate standard to be applied as it was held that under either standard the defendant had failed to establish that a valid arbitration agreement had been concluded, the High Court examined international case-law and the views expressed by leading international commentators noting that both seemed to favour full judicial review. Similarly, in *Danish Polish Telecommunication Group I/S v Telekomunikacja Polska SA,*[13] the High Court (Finlay Geoghegan J) examined international case-law from UNCITRAL's CLOUT database before it held that it had no jurisdiction to give leave to enforce a partial award in circumstances where there was no order of the arbitral tribunal separately directing payment of

[5] Arbitration Bill 2008: Hearing before Select Committee on Justice, Equality, Defence and Women's Rights, Dáil Debate, 23 April 2009 (statement of Dermot Ahern, the then Minister for Justice, Equality and Law Reform).

[6] Therefore, an almost identical regime governs both international and domestic arbitration in Ireland; the only legislative distinction between an international commercial arbitration and a domestic arbitration under Irish law concerns a party's ability to demand the taxation of costs, which is only applicable in a domestic arbitration (Arbitration Act 2010, s 21(4)).

[7] Arbitration Act 2010, s 6.

[8] A(IC)A 1998, s 4.

[9] Brekoulakis and Shore in Mistelis, *Concise International Arbitration, UNCITRAL Model Law* (1st ed, Kluwer Law International, Alphen Arbitration Act n den Rijn, 2010) p 584.

[10] Arbitration Act 2010, s 8(1).

[11] The very fact that the quantum of case-law decided under the Act has been limited is an indication not only of clear and coherent legislative drafting but also of the limited role of the courts under the Act and, consequently, the Model Law.

[12] Unreported, High Court (Feeney J), 11 November 2010.

[13] [2011] IEHC 369.

the partial amount sought. There is little doubt that the Irish judiciary will continue to analyse international materials when called upon to interpret provisions of the Model Law.

Changes from the Provisions of the Arbitration Acts 1954-1998

For those familiar with the previous law governing domestic arbitrations in Ireland, the adoption of the Model Law introduces many changes. Founded on the concept of party autonomy, the changes introduced by the Model Law mostly strengthen the powers of an arbitral tribunal while limiting the ability of the High Court, the Irish court which fulfils the requisite supervisory functions under the Act,[14] to intervene in arbitral proceedings. For example, the increased powers of an arbitral tribunal now include the ability of an arbitral tribunal to rule on its own jurisdiction (the doctrine of 'competence-competence');[15] the ability of an arbitral tribunal to award interim measures of protection akin to interim and interlocutory injunctive relief under Irish law;[16] and the potential to given an interpretation of a specific point raised by an award.[17] The limitation on High Court intervention now means that, unless otherwise agreed by the parties to an arbitration agreement, the High Court cannot order security for costs of the discovery of documents in connection with arbitral proceedings.[18]

In addition, while some concepts that were a feature of the Arbitration Acts 1954-1998 remain, their application differs. For example, although a party may still seek recourse from the High Court against an award under the Model Law, recourse is now permitted only in very limited grounds circumstances which are definitively set out under the Model Law.[19] Crucially, the High Court no longer has an ability to set aside an award merely because there is an error of law.[20] In addition, although both the Modal Law and the Arbitration Acts 1954-1998 require a court to refer to arbitration litigation commenced in violation of an arbitration agreement, the Model Law, unlike the previous law,[21] does not require that there be facts in dispute before a matter must be so referred. That a matter is the subject of an arbitration agreement and not that there is a factual dispute between the parties is the critical issue for whether the courts are required to refer a matter to arbitration.[22]

Benefits of the Act

As Irish public policy has long dictated that "parties should be encouraged as far as possible to settle their disputes without recourse to litigation",[23] it is desirable that, where some dispute resolution mechanism other than litigation is chosen, then it is permitted to operate in an efficient and effective manner with only confined judicial supervision as is necessary to protect the fundamental tenets of the legal system. Where the chosen dispute resolution mechanism is

---

[14] Arbitration Act 2010, s 9.

[15] Arbitration Act 2010, s 8(3) and MODEL LAW, Art 16.

[16] Model Law, Art 17.

[17] Model Law, Art 33(1)(b), which requires that the parties agree to the exercise of this power.

[18] Arbitration Act 2010, s 10(2).

[19] Model Law, Art 34.

[20] Model Law, Art 5.

[21] Arbitration Act 1980, s 5.

[22] Model Law, Art 8(1).

[23] *Greencore Group plc v Murphy* [1995] 3 IR 520 at 525, which is a decision of the Irish Supreme Court.

arbitration, which is intended to be a binding process, it is important that the parties' agreement to prosecute arbitral proceedings is not lightly undone through recourse against an award through the courts. In particular, parties should not see their investment of time and expense in arbitral proceedings undone merely because a court believes that some outcome alternative to the arbitral tribunal's award could have been achieved. Only where an alleged breach of procedures has surpassed the boundaries of legitimate expectation and propriety should the courts be permitted be intervene overturn an arbitral tribunal's award. The Act achieves each of these policy goals, and more, by ensuring that the correct equilibrium between the courts and arbitration is maintained. There is little doubt that the operation of the Act will strengthen and encourage arbitration, both domestic and international, in Ireland.

Arbitration Act 2010

Number 1 of 2010

PART 1

PRELIMINARY AND GENERAL

Schedule 5

Text of 1923 Protocol on Arbitration Clauses

Schedule 6

Consequential Amendments to Other Acts

Acts Referred to

Arbitration Act 1954	1954, No. 26
Arbitration Acts 1954 to 1998	
Copyright and Related Rights Act 2000	2000, No. 28
Industrial Relations Act 1946	1946, No. 26
Landlord and Tenant (Ground Rents) Act 1967	1967, No. 3
Legal Practitioners (Ireland) Act 1876	39 & 40 Vict., c. 44
Merchant Shipping Act 1894	57 & 58 Vict., c. 60
Patents Act 1992	1992, No. 1
Property Values (Arbitration and Appeals) Act 1960	1960, No. 45
Statute of Limitations 1957	1957, No. 6

Arbitration Act 2010

AN ACT TO FURTHER AND BETTER FACILITATE RESOLUTION OF DISPUTES BY ARBITRATION; TO GIVE THE FORCE OF LAW TO THE UNCITRAL MODEL LAW ON INTERNATIONAL COMMERCIAL ARBITRATION (AS AMENDED BY THE UNITED NATIONS COMMISSION ON INTERNATIONAL TRADE LAW ON 7 JULY 2006) IN RESPECT OF BOTH INTERNATIONAL COMMERCIAL ARBITRATION AND OTHER ARBITRATION; TO GIVE THE FORCE OF LAW TO THE PROTOCOL ON ARBITRATION CLAUSES OPENED AT GENEVA ON THE 24TH DAY OF SEPTEMBER 1923, THE CONVENTION ON THE EXECUTION OF FOREIGN ARBITRAL AWARDS DONE AT NEW YORK ON 10 JUNE 1958 AND TO THE CONVENTION ON THE SETTLEMENT OF INVESTMENT DISPUTES BETWEEN STATES AND NATIONALS OF OTHER STATES OPENED FOR SIGNATURE IN WASHINGTON ON 18 MARCH 1965; TO REPEAL THE ARBITRATION ACTS 1954 TO 1998; AND TO PROVIDE FOR RELATED MATTERS.

[*8th March,* 2010]

BE IT ENACTED BY THE OIREACHTAS AS FOLLOWS:

Part 1

Preliminary and General

1.—Short title and commencement

(1) This Act may be cited as the Arbitration Act 2010.

(2) This Act shall come into operation 3 months after its passing.

Definitions

'months': Interpretation Act 2005, sch, pt 1.

Notes

Short title of the Act: The Act is formally cited as the Arbitration Act 2010.[1]

[1] Arbitration Act 2010, s 1(1).

Commencement of the Act: This section provides for the commencement of the Act. Under Irish law an act is passed on the day on which the bill for the act is signed by the President.[1] The bill for the Act was signed on 8 March 2010 and, accordingly, the Act was passed on that date. The Act commenced operation three months[2] after its passing on 8 June 2010.[3]

[1] Interpretation Act 2005, s 15(1).

[2] Interpretation Act 2005, sch, pt 1 defines 'month' as a calendar month.

[3] Arbitration Act 2010, s 1(2).

2.—Interpretation

(1) In this Act:

"arbitration" means—

(a) an international commercial arbitration, or

(b) an arbitration which is not an international commercial arbitration;

"arbitration agreement" shall be construed in accordance with Option I of Article 7;

"award" includes a partial award;

"consumer" means a natural person, whether in the State or not, who is acting for purposes outside the person's trade, business or profession;

"Geneva Convention" means the Convention on the Execution of Foreign Arbitral Awards done at Geneva on the 26th day of September, 1927, the text of which is set out in Schedule 4;

"Geneva Protocol" means the Protocol on Arbitration Clauses opened at Geneva on the 24th day of September, 1923, the text of which is set out in Schedule 5;

"Minister" means the Minister for Justice, Equality and Law Reform;

"Model Law " means the UNCITRAL Model Law on International Commercial Arbitration (as adopted by the United Nations Commission on International Trade Law on 21 June 1985, with amendments as adopted by that Commission at its thirty-ninth session on 7 July 2006), the text of which is set out in Schedule 1;

"New York Convention" means the Convention on the Recognition and Enforcement of Foreign Arbitral Awards, done at New York on 10 June 1958, the text of which is set out in Schedule 2;

"State authority" means—

(*a*) a Minister of the Government,

(*b*) the Commissioners of Public Works in Ireland,

(*c*) the Irish Land Commission,

(*d*) the Revenue Commissioners,

(*e*) a body established by or under any enactment, and financed wholly or partly, whether directly or indirectly, by moneys provided, or loans made or guaranteed, by a Minister of the Government or the issue of shares held by or on behalf of any Minister of the Government;

"Washington Convention" means the Convention on the Settlement of Investment Disputes between States and Nationals of Other States opened for signature in Washington on 18 March 1965, the text of which is set out in Schedule 3.

(2) In this Act—

(a) a word or expression that is used in this Act and that is also used in the Model Law has, unless the context otherwise requires, the same meaning in this Act as it has in the Model Law, and

(*b*) a reference to an Article is a reference to an Article of the Model Law.

Definitions

'arbitration': Arbitration Act 2010, s 2(1) and Model Law, Art 2(a); 'arbitration agreement': Arbitration Act 2010, s 2(1) and Model Law, Art 7(1) (Option I); 'award': Arbitration Act 2010, s 2(1); 'consumer': Arbitration Act 2010, s 2(1); 'Geneva Convention': Arbitration Act 2010, s 2(1); 'Geneva Protocol': Arbitration Act 2010, s 2(1); 'Government': Interpretation Act 2005, sch, pt 1; 'Minister': Arbitration Act 2010, s 2(1); 'Model Law': Arbitration Act 2010, s 2(1); 'New York Convention': Arbitration Act 2010, s 2(1); 'State Authority': Arbitration Act 2010, s 2(1); 'Washington Convention': Arbitration Act 2010, s 2(1).

Notes

***Interpretation of the Act*:** This section provides definitions of certain terms used in the Act and in the Model Law.[1] Terms used in both the Act and the Model Law have the same meaning in the Act as in the Model Law.[2]

[1] Arbitration Act 2010, s 2(1).
[2] Arbitration Act 2010, s 2(2).

***Definition of 'arbitration'*:** The definition of 'arbitration' merely provides clarification that an arbitration includes both an international commercial arbitration and a domestic arbitration (which is any arbitration other than an international commercial arbitration).[1] The definition does not explain what the term means nor does it describe what constitutes an arbitration. This approach is deliberate and follows the approach adopted by much other arbitration legislation worldwide, which either decline to define what arbitration means[2] or provide only a circular definition.[3] However, definitions of arbitration have been provided by the courts and by commentators. An early judicial definition of arbitration defined it as "a reference to the decision of one or more persons, either with or without an umpire, of some matters or matter in difference between the parties".[4] A more recent judicial observation stated "the hallmark of the arbitration process is that it is a procedure to determine the legal rights and obligations of parties judicially, with binding effect, which is enforceable in law, thus reflecting in private proceedings the role of a civil court of law".[5] Definitions of arbitration from commentators include "an effective way of obtaining a final and binding decision on a dispute or series of dispute, without reference to a court of law",[6] and "a device whereby the settlement of a question, which is of interest for two or more persons, is entrusted to one or more other persons—the arbitrator or arbitrators—who derive their powers from a private agreement, not from the authorities of a State, and who are to proceed and decide the same on the basis of such an agreement".[7]

[1] Under the Arbitration Acts 1954-1998, the Model Law was adopted for international commercial arbitrations only. As Arbitration Act 2010, s 6 now adopts the Model Law for both international commercial arbitrations and domestic arbitrations, the only legislative distinction between an international commercial arbitration and a domestic arbitration is contained at Arbitration Act 2010, s 21(4) and concerns a party's ability to demand the taxation of costs, which is only applicable in a domestic arbitrations.
[2] See, for example, the English Arbitration Act 1996; the German ZPO; and the US Federal Arbitration Act, 9 USC.

(*Continued*)

[3] See, for example, Model Law, Art 2(a), which specifies that "'arbitration' means any arbitration whether or not administered by a permanent arbitral institution".

[4] *Per* Romilly MR in *Collins v Collins* (1858) 26 Beav 306, 312.

[5] Per Hirst LJ in *O'Callaghan v Coral Racing Ltd*, unreported, English Court of Appeal (Hirst LJ, May LJ, Sir Christopher Slade) 19 November 1998 at p 5.

[6] Blackaby, Partasides, Redfern and Hunter, *Redfern and Hunter on International Arbitration* (5th ed, Oxford University Press, Oxford, 2009) p 2.

[7] Gaillard and Savage, *Fouchard Gaillard Goldman on International Arbitration* (1st ed, Kluwer Law International, The Hague, 1999) p 9.

Definition of 'arbitration agreement': The Model Law provides for two distinct definitions of the term 'arbitration agreement', either of which can be adopted by a State enacting the provisions of the Model Law: Option I, which requires an arbitration agreement to in writing; and Option II, which does not.[1] Both Options I and Option II provide that an arbitration agreement can relate to existing or future disputes resulting in no distinction being made between a submission agreement to refer an existing dispute to arbitration and an arbitration clause to refer any future disputes that may arise between the parties to arbitration.[2] In Ireland, the Act has adopted Option I of the Model Law resulting in a requirement that an arbitration agreement be in writing.[3] This requirement is consistent with the arbitration legislation of most arbitration regimes worldwide.[4]

[1] Model Law, Art 7.

[2] Roth in Weigand, *Practitioner's Handbook on International Commercial Arbitration, UNCITRAL Model Law on International Commercial Arbitration* (2nd ed, Oxford University Press, Oxford, 2009) pp 983-984.

[3] Arbitration Act 2010, s 2(1).

[4] See, for example, the English Arbitration Act 1996, s 5; the German ZPO, s 1031; the Singapore Arbitration Act 1996, s 4(3); and the US Federal Arbitration Act, 9 USC, s 2. Arbitration statutes that do not include a formal requirement for a written arbitration agreement include the New Zealand Arbitration Act 1996, 1st sch, Art 7(1); and the Swedish Arbitration Act (SFS 1999:116), Art 1. Similarly, the New York Convention, Art II provides that contracting States are only required to recognise and enforce arbitral awards issued in other contracting States where an arbitration agreement is made in writing.

Definition of 'award': The definition of the term 'award' merely provides that an 'award' includes a partial award. What constitutes a 'partial award' is not specified and neither the Act nor the Model Law uses the term 'partial award' at any other instance in the text. However, a 'partial award' should be contrasted with a 'final award', which the *travaux préparatoires* (of which Irish courts are permitted to take judicial notice when interpreting provisions of the Model Law)[1] suggest is an award intended "to settle the dispute in full".[2] A similar concept of an 'interim award' disposing of a single issue existed in the context of a domestic arbitration (which is any arbitration other than an international commercial arbitration) under the Arbitration Acts 1954-1998.[3] Commentators have noted that under the Arbitration Acts 1954-1998 an interim award was distinguishable from a final award on the basis that it disposed of only a single issue whereas a final award conclusively disposes of all remaining disputes between the parties.[4]

(*Continued*)

An award, whether partial or final, must be made in writing and must be signed by at least a majority of the arbitral tribunal.[5] It must be reasoned.[6] It must state the date on which and place where it is made[7] and, after it is made, a signed copy must be delivered to each of the parties.[8]

[1] Arbitration Act 2010, s 8(1).
[2] UNCITRAL First Working Group Report First Draft, A/CN.9/WP.38, Art 25 [*incorporated in part into Model Law, Art 32 in the final text*].
[3] Arbitration Act 1954, s 25.
[4] Dowling-Hussey and Dunne, *Arbitration Law* (1st ed, Thomson Round Hall, Dublin, 2008) p 169.
[5] Model Law, Art 31(1).
[6] Model Law, Art 31(2).
[7] Model Law, Art 31(3).
[8] Model Law, Art 31(4).

***Definition of 'consumer'*:** The definition of 'consumer' is based upon Council Directive 93/13 EEC on Unfair Terms in Consumer Contracts, which defines a 'consumer' as "any natural person who . . . is acting for purposes which are outside his trade, business or profession".[1] The Act provides that the following restrictions apply to an arbitration where one party is a consumer:

1. An arbitration agreement providing that each party bear its own costs is deemed to be an unfair term[2] and is unenforceable against the consumer;[3] and

2. A consumer is not bound by an arbitration agreement where the value of a claim is less than €5,000.00, unless the arbitration agreement has been individually negotiated.[4] A term is regarded as having not been individually negotiated where it has been drafted in advance and where the consumer has not been able to influence its substance (*i.e.*, a standard form contract).[5]

An amateur sportsperson, who in that capacity is party to an arbitration agreement, is not a consumer simply because he or she is an amateur.[6]

[1] EC 93/13, Art 2.
[2] As defined by European Communities (Unfair Terms in Consumer Contracts) Regulations 1995 (SI No 27/1995), reg 2.
[3] Arbitration Act 2010, s 21(6).
[4] Arbitration Act 2010, s 31(1).
[5] European Communities (Unfair Terms in Consumer Contracts) Regulations 1995 (SI No 27 of 1995), reg 3(4).
[6] Arbitration Act 2010, s 31(2).

***The Geneva Convention*:** The Geneva Convention was done on 26 September 1927 at Geneva to provide for the recognition and enforcement of foreign awards. The Geneva Convention has the force of law in Ireland.[1] The Geneva Convention has been superseded by the New York Convention and it only applies where recognition and enforcement of an award made in a non-New York Convention State is sought.

(*Continued*)

[1] Arbitration Act 2010, s 24(1)(b). The text of the Geneva Convention is set out at Arbitration Act 2010, sch 4. As this work is concerned only with the Model Law in Ireland, detailed consideration of the Geneva Convention is outside the scope of this work.

The Geneva Protocol: The Geneva Protocol was opened on 24 September 1923 at Geneva to provide for the recognition and enforcement of foreign awards. The Geneva Protocol has the force of law in Ireland.[1] The Geneva Protocol has been superseded by the Geneva Convention and the New York Convention and it only applies where recognition and enforcement of an award made in a non-Geneva Convention/non-New York Convention State is sought.

[1] Arbitration Act 2010, s 24(1)(c). The text of the Geneva Protocol is set out at Arbitration Act 2010, sch 5. As this work is concerned only with Model Law in Ireland, detailed consideration of the Geneva Protocol is outside the scope of this work.

Definition of 'Minister': The definition of 'Minister' refers to the Minister for Justice, Equality and Law Reform. A minister means a member of the Irish government having charge of a department of State.[1]

[1] Interpretation Act 2005, sch, pt 1.

The Model Law: The Model Law means the law as adopted by the United Nations Commission on International Trade Law on 21 June 1985, with amendments as adopted by that Commission at its thirty-ninth session on 7 June 2006. While the Model Law has no legislative force on its own, it is designed to serve as a template for national arbitration legislation. The Model Law has been drafted with flexibility in mind permitting States which adopt it, or which use it as a template for arbitration legislation, to complete the detail without departing from the spirit of the Model Law.[1]

Although the Act purports to adopt the provisions of the Model Law in full for arbitral proceedings where Ireland is the place of arbitration,[2] Art 2 A of the Model Law is not included in the text of the Model Law as set out at sch 1 to the Act.[3] The effect of this omission most likely means that Art 2 A is not included in the Act. However, in practice, the omission of Art 2 A is unlikely to present a difficulty as commentators have noted that the provisions of Art 2 A are "little more than hortatory".[4]

[1] Brekoulakis and Shore in Mistelis, *Concise International Arbitration, UNCITRAL Model Law* (1st ed, Kluwer Law International, Alphen aan den Rijn, 2010) p 584.

[2] Arbitration Act 2010, s 6.

[3] Model Law, Art 2 A is entitled 'International origin and general principles' and provides that: "(1) In the interpretation of this Law, regard is to be had to its international origin and to the need to promote uniformity in its application and the observance of good faith. (2) Questions concerning matters governed by this Law which are not expressly settled in it are to be settled in conformity with the general principles on which this Law is based".

(*Continued*)

[4] Brekoulakis and Shore in Mistelis, *Concise International Arbitration, UNCITRAL Model Law* (1st ed, Kluwer Law International, Alphen aan den Rijn, 2010) p 591. Furthermore, it has been noted that Arbitration Act 2010, s 8 already encourages a uniform interpretation of the Model Law, which is the principle promoted by Model Law, Art 2 A. See Walsh, "2006 UNCITRAL Model Law: Are States Adopting the Law in Letter and Spirit?" (2010) *Arbitration and ADR Review* p 215.

The New York Convention: The New York Convention was done on 10 June 1958 at New York to provide for the recognition and enforcement of foreign awards. The New York Convention has the force of law in Ireland.[1]

[1] Arbitration Act 2010, s 24(1)(a). The text of the New York Convention is set out at Arbitration Act 2010, sch 2. As this work concerns only with the Model Law in Ireland, detailed consideration of the New York Convention is outside the scope of this work.

Definition of 'State authority': The definition of 'State authority' provides a list of bodies that are to be regarded as State authorities. The bodies listed at (a), (b), (c) and (d) of the definition are substantially identical to the bodies listed within the definition of a 'State authority' under the Arbitration Acts 1954-1998.[1] However, the inclusion at (e) of "a body established by or under any enactment, and financed wholly or partly, whether directly or indirectly, by moneys provided, or loans made or guaranteed, by a Minister of the Government or the issue of shares held by or on behalf of any Minister of the Government" has the effect of including certain State-sponsored bodies within the definition of 'State authority' which would not have been included under the Arbitration Acts 1954-1998. The Act and, consequently, the Model Law are fully applicable to State authorities.[2]

[1] Arbitration Act 1954, s 2.
[2] Arbitration Act 2010, s 28.

The Washington Convention: The Washington Convention was opened for signature on 18 March 1965 at Washington, DC to establish the International Centre for the Settlement of Investment Disputes (ICSID). The Washington Convention provides private individuals and corporations who are investors in a foreign State the right to bring legal proceedings against that foreign State before an international arbitral tribunal. The Washington Convention has the force of law in Ireland.[1]

[1] Arbitration Act 2010, s 25(3). The text of the Washington Convention is set out at Arbitration Act 2010, sch 3. As this work concerns only with the Model Law in Ireland, detailed consideration of the Washington Convention is outside the scope of this work.

3.—Application of Act

(1) This Act shall not apply to an arbitration under an arbitration agreement concerning an arbitration which has commenced before the operative date but shall apply to an arbitration commenced on or after the operative date.

(2) In this section, "operative date" means the date on which this Act comes into operation pursuant to section 1.

Definitions

'arbitration': Arbitration Act 2010, s 2(1) and Model Law, Art 2(a); 'arbitration agreement': Arbitration Act 2010, s 2(1) and Model Law, Art 7(1) (Option I).

Notes

Application of the Act and the continued application of the Arbitration Acts 1954-1998: In an attempt to minimise the potential confusion occasioned by the concurrent application of different arbitration legislation and in an attempt to regulate the transition from the application of the previous legislation governing arbitration in Ireland[1] to the application of the Act, this section provides a definite time limit on the continued application of the Arbitration Acts 1954-1998.[2] The Arbitration Acts 1954-1998 continue to apply all arbitrations commenced before 8 June 2010 while the Act and, consequently, the Model Law apply only to arbitrations commenced[3] on or after 8 June 2010.[4] Where civil proceedings were commenced before 8 June 2010 but a request to refer the dispute to arbitration was received on or after 8 June 2010, the Act and the Model Law apply.[5]

---

[1] Prior to the enactment of Arbitration Act 2010, an international commercial arbitration which had taken place in Ireland was governed by the provisions of parts I and II of the Arbitration (International Commercial) Act 1998 and a domestic arbitration (which is any arbitration other than an international commercial arbitration) which had taken place in Ireland was were governed by the Arbitration Acts 1954-1980 and the provisions of parts I and III of the Arbitration (International Commercial) Act 1998.

[2] Arbitration Bill 2008: Hearing before Select Committee on Justice, Equality, Defence and Women's Rights, Dáil Debate, 23 April 2009 (statement of Dermot Ahern, the then Minister for Justice, Equality and Law Reform). If the date on which an arbitration agreement was entered into was to determine which arbitration legislation would apply then the potential application of the provisions of the Arbitration Acts 1954-1998 would continue indefinitely as disputes that are the subject matter of an arbitration agreement may arise long after the arbitration agreement is entered into.

[3] The parties to an arbitration agreement may agree on the date of commencement, but in absence of agreement an arbitration is deemed to commence on the date on which a request for the dispute to be referred to arbitration is received by the respondent. Arbitration Act 2010, s 7(1).

[4] Arbitration Act 2010, s 3(1). For judicial consideration of the effect of this provisions see *FBD Insurance plc v Connors* [2011] IEHC 184; *On-Site Welding Services Ltd v Quinn Insurance Ltd (in administration)* [2011] IEHC 215; and *Winthrop Engineering & Contracting Ltd v Cleary & Doyle Contracting Ltd* [2011] IEHC 249.

[5] *Osmond Ireland On Farm Business v McFarland* [2010] IEHC 295.

4.—Repeals and effect of repeals

(1) Subject to subsection (2), the Arbitration Acts 1954 to 1998 are repealed.

(2) Subject to section 3, the repeal of the Acts referred to in subsection (1) shall not prejudice or affect any proceedings, whether or not pending at the time of the repeal, in respect of any

right, privilege, obligation or liability and any proceedings taken under those Acts in respect of any such right, privilege, obligation or liability acquired, accrued or incurred under the Acts may be instituted, continued or enforced as if the Acts concerned had not been repealed.

(3) In this section "proceedings" includes arbitral proceedings and civil or criminal proceedings.

Notes

***Repeal of existing legislation and the continued application of the Arbitration Acts 1954-1998*:** This section repeals the Arbitration Acts 1954-1998, the previous legislation governing arbitration in Ireland.[1] However, the Arbitration Acts 1954-1998 continue to apply to all proceedings, including arbitral proceedings and civil proceedings concerning an arbitration, commenced before 8 June 2010.[2] Where a right accrued under the Arbitration Acts 1954-1998 before 8 June 2010, then their repeal does not prejudice an application in respect of that right, even where it was not pending at the time of the repeal.[3]

[1] Prior to the enactment of Arbitration Act 2010, an international commercial arbitration which had taken place in Ireland was governed by the provisions of parts I and II of the Arbitration (International Commercial) Act 1998 and a domestic arbitration (which is any arbitration other than an international commercial arbitration) which had taken place in Ireland was were governed by the Arbitration Acts 1954-1980 and the provisions of parts I and III of the Arbitration (International Commercial) Act 1998.

[2] Arbitration Act 2010, s 3(1). The primary purpose for the continued application of the provisions of the Arbitration Acts 1954-1998 was the practical desire to minimise the potential confusion occasioned by amending the laws governing pending proceedings. In addition, where the effect of the amendment is substantive in nature, a secondary consideration is the desire to avoid a potential violation of the constitutional prohibition against legislative interference with pending judicial proceedings. *See Buckley & ors (Sinn Féin) v AG* [1950] 1 IR 67, where the Supreme Court (O'Byrne J) stated that "the effect of [the Constitution] is to vest in the Courts the exclusive right to determine justiciable controversies between citizens . . . In bringing these proceedings the plaintiffs were exercising a constitutional right and they were, and are, entitled to have the matter in dispute determined by the judicial organ of the State. The substantial effect of the Act [amending the law governing the pending proceedings] is that the dispute is determined by the Oireachtas and the Court is required and directed by the Oireachtas to dismiss the plaintiffs' claim without any hearing and without forming any opinion as to the rights of the respective parties to the dispute. In our opinion this is clearly repugnant to the provisions of the Constitution, as being an unwarranted interference by the Oireachtas with the operations of the Courts in a purely judicial domain". However, retroactive amendments which are purely procedural may apply to pending proceedings. See Dodd, *Statutory Interpretation in Ireland* (1st ed, Tottel Publishing, Dublin, 2008) p 105.

[3] Arbitration Act 2010, s 4(2). See *On-Site Welding Services Ltd v Quinn Insurance Ltd* (*in administration*) [2011] IEHC 215, where the High Court (Laffoy J) permitted an extension of the contractual time limit in which to bring an application in circumstances where the right which the applicant sought to enforce had accrued before 8 June 2010. Therefore, the repeal of the Arbitration Acts 1954-1998 did not prejudice or affect the right to extend the contractual time limit in which to commence an application under Arbitration Act 1954, s 45, notwithstanding that any arbitral proceedings commenced would be governed by Arbitration Act 2010.

5.—Expenses

The expenses incurred by the Minister in the administration of this Act shall, to such extent as may be sanctioned by the Minister for Finance, be paid out of moneys provided by the Oireachtas.

Definitions

'Minister': Arbitration Act 2010, s 2(1); 'Oireachtas': Interpretation Act 2005, sch, pt 1.

Notes

Payment of expenses: This section provides that the expenses incurred by the Minister in the administration of the Act are to be paid out of moneys provided by the Oireachtas.[1] This is similar to provisions contained in much contemporary legislation.[2]

---

[1] Central Fund (Permanent Provisions) Act 1965, s 2 provides that moneys are provided by the Oireachtas to the Minister and other State bodies each financial year out of the central fund by the enactment of the Appropriation Act for a relevant year.

[2] See, for example, Student Support Act 2011, s 3; Criminal Justice (Money Laundering and Terrorist Financing) Act 2010, s 5; Health (Miscellaneous Provisions) Act 2010, s 4; Adoption Act 2010, s 8; and Criminal Justice (Psychoactive Substances) Act 2010, s 24.

PART 2

ARBITRATION

6.—Adoption of Model Law

Subject to this Act, the Model Law shall have the force of law in the State and shall apply to arbitrations under arbitration agreements concerning—

(a) international commercial arbitrations, or

(b) arbitrations which are not international commercial arbitrations.

Definitions

'arbitration(s)': Arbitration Act 2010, s 2(1) and Model Law, Art 2(a); 'arbitration agreement(s)': Arbitration Act 2010, s 2(1) and Model Law, Art 7(1) (Option I); Model Law': Arbitration Act 2010, s 2(1).

Notes

***Adoption of the Model Law*:** The Model Law means the law as adopted by the United Nations Commission on International Trade Law on 21 June 1985, with amendments as adopted by that Commission at its thirty-ninth session on 7 June 2006. While the Model Law has no legislative force on its own, it is designed to serve as a template for national arbitration legislation. The Model Law has been drafted with flexibility in mind permitting States which adopt it, or which use it as a template for arbitration legislation, to complete the detail without departing from the spirit of the Model Law.[1]

Although the Act purports to adopt the provisions of the Model Law in full for arbitral proceedings where Ireland is the place of arbitration,[2] Art 2A of the Model Law is not included in the text of the Model Law as set out at sch 1 to the Act.[3] The effect of this omission most likely means that Art 2A is not included in the Act. However, in practice, the omission of Art 2A is unlikely to present a difficulty as commentators have noted that the provisions of Art 2A are "little more than hortatory".[4]

---

[1] Brekoulakis and Shore in Mistelis, *Concise International Arbitration, UNCITRAL Model Law* (1st ed, Kluwer Law International, Alphen aan den Rijn, 2010) p 584.

[2] Arbitration Act 2010, s 6.

[3] Model Law, Art 2 A is entitled 'International origin and general principles' and provides that: "(1) In the interpretation of this Law, regard is to be had to its international origin and to the need to promote uniformity in its application and the observance of good faith. (2) Questions concerning matters governed by this Law which are not expressly settled in it are to be settled in conformity with the general principles on which this Law is based".

[4] Brekoulakis and Shore in Mistelis, *Concise International Arbitration, UNCITRAL Model Law* (1st ed, Kluwer Law International, Alphen aan den Rijn, 2010) p 591. Furthermore, it has been noted that Arbitration Act 2010, s 8 already encourages a uniform interpretation of the Model Law, which is the principle promoted by Model Law, Art 2 A. See Walsh, "2006 UNCITRAL Model Law: Are States Adopting the Law in Letter and Spirit?" (2010) *Arbitration and ADR Review* p 215.

(*Continued*)

***The adoption of the Model Law for both international commercial arbitrations and domestic arbitrations*:** While the Model Law itself provides that it applies only to international commercial arbitrations,[1] the Act adopts the Model Law both for international commercial arbitrations[2] and for domestic arbitrations (which are any arbitrations other than international commercial arbitrations) where Ireland is the place of arbitration.[3] Therefore, the only legislative distinction between an international commercial arbitration and a domestic arbitration concerns a party's ability to demand the taxation of costs, which is only applicable in a domestic arbitration.[4]

[1] Model Law, Art 1(1).
[2] Arbitration Act 2010, s 6(a).
[3] Arbitration Act 2010, s 6(b).
[4] Arbitration Act 2010, s 21(4).

***Amendments to the Model Law*:** The Act amends and supplements the Model Law through the following sections for arbitrations where Ireland is the place of arbitration:

1. Section 7, which provides that arbitral proceedings commence on either the date on which the parties to an arbitration agreement agree as being the commencement date or, where no date has been agreed, the date on which a written communication containing a request for the dispute to be referred to arbitration is received by the respondent. This is a clarification of the Model Law, which provides that, unless otherwise agreed by the parties, arbitral proceedings commence on the date on which a request for the dispute to be referred to arbitration is received by the respondent[1] but leaves unspecified whether or not such a request for must be in writing;[2]

2. Section 10(2), which provides that, unless otherwise agreed by the parties, the High Court may not make an order for security for costs or an order for discovery. This is a clarification of the Model Law, which provides that a party to an arbitration may request an interim measure of protection from a national court but it does not specify whether security for costs is included in such a measure.[3] The Model Law also provides that an arbitral tribunal or a party to an arbitration may request assistance from a national court in taking evidence but it does not specify whether discovery can be sought;[4]

3. Section 12, which provides that an application to annul set aside an award on the grounds of public policy must be made within 56 days from the date on which the circumstances giving rise to the application became known or ought reasonably to have become known, rather than within three months from the date on which the party making the application had received the award as provided by the Model Law;[5]

4. Section 13, which provides that, unless otherwise agreed by the parties, the default number of arbitrators is one. The Model Law provides that the default number of arbitrators is three;[6]

(*Continued*)

5. Section 19, which provides that, unless otherwise agreed by the parties, an arbitral tribunal may order a party to provide security for costs. This is a clarification of the Model Law, which permits an arbitral tribunal to conduct arbitral proceedings in such manner as it considers appropriate;[7]
6. Section 20, which provides that unless otherwise agreed by the parties, an arbitral tribunal has the power to make an award requiring specific performance (other than a contract for the sale of land). This is a clarification of the Model Law, which is silent on an arbitral tribunal's power to award specific performance; and
7. Section 23(4), which provides that the provisions of the Model Law concerning recognition and enforcement of awards[8] are not applicable to an award made in a domestic arbitration (which is any arbitration other than an international commercial arbitration).

---

[1] Model Law, Art 21.
[2] Binder, *International Commercial Arbitration and Conciliation in UNCITRAL Model Law Jurisdictions* (3rd ed, Sweet & Maxwell, London, 2010) p 295.
[3] Model Law, Art 9.
[4] Model Law, Art 27.
[5] Model Law, Art 34(3).
[6] Model Law, Art 10(2).
[7] Model Law, Art 19(2).
[8] Model Law, Arts 35; and 36.

***Prior adoption of the Model Law for international commercial arbitrations which have taken place in Ireland*:** Prior to the enactment of the Act, international commercial arbitrations where Ireland was the place of arbitration were governed by the provisions of parts I and II of the Arbitration (International Commercial) Act 1998, which adopted the Model Law, albeit without the amendments as adopted by the United Nations Commission on International Trade Law at its thirty-ninth session of 7 July 2006.[1] Prior to the enactment of the Act, domestic arbitrations (which are any arbitrations other than international commercial arbitrations), where Ireland was the place of arbitration were governed by the Arbitration Acts 1954-1980 and by parts I and II of the Arbitration (International Commercial) Act 1998, which did not adopt the Model Law.

---

[1] Arbitration (International Commercial) Act 1998, s 4.

***Non-application of the Act to certain employment arbitrations*:** The Act and, consequently, the Model Law do not apply to arbitrations relating to the terms and conditions of employment or the remuneration of employees[1] or arbitrations under s 70 of the Industrial Relations Act 1946.[2]

---

[1] Arbitration Act 2010, s 30(1)(a).
[2] Arbitration Act 2010, s 30(1)(b).

7.—Commencement of arbitral proceedings

(1) For the purposes of this Act and for the purposes of section 496 of the Merchant Shipping Act 1894 (as amended by section 29) arbitral proceedings shall be deemed to be commenced on—

(a) the date on which the parties to an arbitration agreement so provide as being the commencement date for the purposes of the commencement of arbitral proceedings under the agreement, or

(b) where no provision has been made by the parties as to commencement of proceedings as referred to in paragraph (a), the date on which a written communication containing a request for the dispute to be referred to arbitration is received by the respondent.

(2) The Statute of Limitations 1957 is amended by substituting the following section for section 74:

"74.— (1) For the purposes of this Act and for the purposes of any other limitation enactment, arbitral proceedings shall be deemed to be commenced on—

(a) the date on which the parties to an arbitration agreement so provide as being the commencement date for the purposes of the commencement of arbitral proceedings under the agreement, or

(b) where no provision has been made by the parties as to commencement as referred to in paragraph (a), the date on which a written communication containing a request for the dispute to be referred to arbitration is received by the respondent.

(2) For the purposes of subsection (1)(b), unless the parties otherwise agree, a written communication is deemed to have been received if it is served or given to the respondent in one or more of the following ways:

(a) by delivering it to the respondent personally;

(b) by delivering it to the respondent's place of business, habitual residence or postal address;

(c) where none of the addresses referred to in paragraph (b) can be found after making reasonable inquiry, by sending it by pre-paid registered post or by any other form of recorded delivery service addressed to the respondent at his or her last known place of business, habitual residence or postal address.

(3) Unless the parties otherwise agree, where a written communication under this section has been delivered to a respondent in accordance with subsection (2), the communication is deemed to have been received on the day it was so delivered.

(4) For the purposes of subsection (2), a company registered under the Companies Acts shall be deemed to be habitually resident at its registered office in the State and every other body corporate (wherever it is incorporated) and every unincorporated body (wherever it carries out its activities) shall be deemed to be habitually resident at its principal office or place of business."

Definitions

'arbitration': Arbitration Act 2010, s 2(1) and Model Law, Art 2(a); 'arbitration agreement': Arbitration Act 2010, s 2(1) and Model Law, Art 7(1) (Option I).

Notes

***Commencement of arbitral proceedings*:** The Model Law provides that, unless otherwise agreed by the parties, arbitral proceedings commence on the date on which a request for the dispute to be referred to arbitration is received by the respondent.[1] The effect of the Model Law has been superseded by this section, which provides that arbitral proceedings commence on either the date on which the parties to an arbitration agreement agree as being the commencement date or, where no date has been agreed, the date on which a written communication containing a request for the dispute to be referred to arbitration is received by the respondent.[2] This amendment to the Model Law clarifies that a request for arbitration must be in written form as the Model Law leaves unspecified whether or not such a request for must be in writing.[3]

---

[1] Model Law, Art 21.

[2] Arbitration Act 2010, s 7(1).

[3] Binder, *International Commercial Arbitration and Conciliation in UNCITRAL Model Law Jurisdictions* (3rd ed, Sweet & Maxwell, London, 2010) p 295.

***Service of a written communication*:** The requirements for service of written communications under the Act are based on similar provisions of the Model Law.[1] A written communication is deemed to have been received on the day it was delivered to a respondent where delivered to the respondent by personal delivery; to the respondent's place of business, habitual residence or postal address; or where any of those places cannot be found after reasonable inquiry, by sending it by pre-paid registered post or by any other form of recorded delivery service addressed to the respondent at his or her last known place of business, habitual residence or postal address.[2]

What constitutes 'reasonable inquiry' is not specified and neither the Model Law nor the *travaux préparatoires* (of which Irish courts are permitted to take judicial notice when interpreting provisions of the Model Law)[3] provide clarification. Although international case-law decided under the Model Law on what constitutes reasonable inquiry is limited, the delivery of written communications to all known addresses of a company within a jurisdiction has been held to satisfy the requirements of reasonable inquiry and permitted an arbitral tribunal to proceed to make an award in the absence of a respondent.[4] However, some proof of reasonable inquiry must be demonstrated.[5]

---

[1] Model Law, Art 3.

[2] Arbitration Act 2010, s 7(2).

[3] Arbitration Act 2010, s 8(1).

[4] CLOUT CASE 384 – Canada/Ontario Court of Justice: *Skorimpex Foreign Trade Co v Lelovic Co* (26 April 1991).

[5] CLOUT CASE 402 – Germany/Highest Regional Court of Bavaria: *4Z Sch 50/99* (16 March 2000).

Requirement that the dispute and the claimant are identified adequately and the effect of errors in written communications: Although not specified, it is axiomatic that a written communication containing a request for the dispute to be referred to arbitration must adequately identify the dispute in question to permit the proposed respondent to ascertain the nature of the case against it.[1] English case-law has held that the written communication must identify an existing dispute not a potential future dispute.[2] The effect of an error in a written communication delivered is uncertain under Irish law, however English case-law, which is likely to be persuasive to a future Irish court, has held that a written communication to be valid provided that any error contained therein was a result of oversight rather than a fundamental error.[3]

---

[1] English case-law in particular deems that a degree of flexibility is necessary when determining whether a written communication adequately identifies a dispute. See *Atlanska Plovidba & anor v Consignaciones Asturianas SA* (*The "Lapad"*) [2004] 2 Lloyd's Rep 109, which is a decision of the English High Court, where it was held that while a notice identifying the dispute was required to commence arbitral proceedings, where a written communication identifies the wrong document as evidencing a contract or an arbitration agreement a court should be slow to hold that the written communication is ineffective if the dispute is otherwise sufficiently identified.

[2] *Interbulk Ltd v Ponte de Sospiri Shipping Co ("The Standard Ardour")* [1988] 2 Lloyd's Rep. 159, which is a decision of the English High Court.

[3] *Harper Versicherungs AG v Indemnity Maine Assurance Co Ltd* [2005] 2 All ER (Comm) 225, where a written communication was valid notwithstanding that it was commenced by the wrong claimant.

Limitation periods for arbitral proceedings: The date of commencement of arbitral proceedings is significant for the application of relevant limitation periods, which apply to arbitral proceedings as they do to civil proceedings.[1] The limitation period governing specific arbitral proceedings depends on the substantive nature of the claim but as the substance of most arbitral proceedings concern claims for breach of contract, the limitation period is typically six years.[2]

---

[1] Statute of Limitations 1957, s 75.

[2] *ibid*, s 11.

Effect of the Act's amendment to the Statute of Limitations 1957: The Act amends the provisions of the Statute of Limitations 1957.[1] Prior to its amendment, the Statute of Limitations 1957 provided that an arbitration was deemed to commence:

> "when one party to the arbitration agreement serves on the other party or parties a written notice requiring him or them to appoint or concur in appointing an arbitrator or, where the arbitration agreement provides that reference shall be to a person named or designating the agreement, requiring him or their to submit the dispute to the person so named or designated".[2]

The effect of the amendment to the Statute of Limitations 1957 is to require less formality as a claimant needs now only to request that a dispute be referred to arbitration rather

(*Continued*)

than request that an arbitrator be appointed.[3] This is consistent with international case-law decided under the Model Law, which has held that an opening letter requesting that a dispute be referred to arbitration was sufficient to commence arbitral proceedings.[4]

[1] Arbitration Act 2010, s 7(2).
[2] Statute of Limitations 1957, s 74.
[3] The amendment reflects modern English case-law on the commencement of arbitral proceedings, which permits a certain degree of flexibility. See *Nea Agrex SA v Baltic Shipping Co Ltd ("The Agios Lazaros")* [1976] QB 933, which is a decision of the English High Court, where a communication by the claimant asking the respondent to "advise your proposals in order to settle this matter, or name our arbitrators" was deemed sufficient to commence an arbitration notwithstanding that the communication did not name a specific arbitrator. See also *Atlanska Plovidba & anor v Consignaciones Asturianas SA (The "Lapad")* [2004] 2 Lloyd's Rep 109, which is a decision of the English High Court, where it was held that the only requirement for arbitral proceedings to be adequately commenced was a notice identifying the dispute and specifying the intention to refer to the dispute to arbitration.
[4] CLOUT CASE 706 – Hong Kong/High Court of Hong Kong: *Fustar Chemicals Ltd v Sinochem Liaoning Hong Kong Ltd v Sinochem Liaoning Hong Kong Ltd* (5 June 1996).

Contractual time limits: The parties to an arbitration agreement may agree contractual time limits that require arbitral proceedings to be commenced within a certain time period that is shorter than the Statute of Limitations 1957.[1] Contractual time limits are used to promote efficiency and certainty in order that a party is made aware of the extent of any claims against it within a specific period of time.[2] However, neither the Act nor the Model Law makes provision for contractual time limits. Under the Arbitration Acts 1954-1998, where a party failed to commence arbitral proceedings within that agreed period, the High Court had power to extent any contractual time limit on such terms as the justice of the case required.[3] As neither the Act nor the Model Law provides the High Court with a comparative power to extend the time permitted to commence arbitral proceedings, a party who fails to comply with a contractual time limit will not be permitted to commence arbitral proceedings where there is a failure to comply with a contractual time limit.[4]

The failure of the Act to provide for a mechanism to extend contractual time limits may occasion harshness by prohibiting a party from commencing proceedings to resolve a dispute notwithstanding that the relevant limitation period under the Statute of Limitations 1957 has not expired. Some solutions to this potential harshness suggested by commentators include permitting a party to commence civil proceedings despite the existence of the arbitration agreement where a contractual time limit has expired;[5] or permitting an arbitral tribunal to exercise an implied power to extend any contractual time limit.[6] As yet, there is no Irish case law to support either of these views. However, recent Irish case law has held that where the right to extend a contractual time limit has accrued under the Arbitration Acts 1954-1998 then the repeal of the Arbitration Acts 1954-1998 does not prejudice or affect an application in respect of that right, notwithstanding that any arbitral proceedings commenced will be governed by the Act and the Model Law.[7] While this judicial solution is entirely consistent with the provisions of the Act, it is only temporary in nature as rights will not continue to accrues under the Arbitration Acts 1954-1998 forever and, ultimately, a permanent solution may be required to alleviate the

(*Continued*)

potential harshness occasioned by the failure of the Act to provide for a mechanism to extend contractual time limits.

---

[1] For a discussion on contractual time limits under English law see Mustill and Boyd, *Commercial Arbitration* (2nd ed, Butterworths, London, 1989) pp 200-215.

[2] Stewart, *Arbitration: Commentary and Sources* (1st ed, First Law, Dublin, 2003) p 139.

[3] Arbitration Act 1954, s 45.

[4] As the Act and the Model Law are silent on the court's power to extend time to commence arbitral proceedings, no power exists. In this regard, Model Law, Art 5 provides "[i]n matters governed by this Law, no court shall intervene except where so provided in this Law". However, where the right to extend a contractual time limit has accrued under the Arbitration Acts 1954-1998 then the repeal of the Arbitration Acts 1954-1998 does not prejudice or affect an application in respect of that right, notwithstanding that any arbitral proceedings commenced will be governed by the Act and the Model Law. See *On-Site Welding Services Ltd v Quinn Insurance Ltd (in administration)* [2011] IEHC 215, where the High Court (Laffoy J) permitted an extension of the contractual time limit in which to bring an application in circumstances where the right which the applicant sought to enforce had accrued before 8 June 2010. Therefore, the repeal of the Arbitration Acts 1954-1998 did not prejudice or affect the right to extend the contractual time limit in which to commence an application under Arbitration Act 1954, s 45, notwithstanding that any arbitral proceedings commenced would be governed by the Act and the Model Law.

[5] Carey, "Contractual limitation periods in arbitration agreements" (2007) *Commercial Law Practitioner* p 3.

[6] Hutchinson, *Arbitration and ADR in Construction Disputes* (1st ed, Round Hall, Dublin, 2010) p 42.

[7] *On-Site Welding Services Ltd v Quinn Insurance Ltd (in administration)* [2011] IEHC 215, where the High Court (Laffoy J) permitted an extension of the contractual time limit in which to bring an application in circumstances where the right which the applicant sought to enforce had accrued before 8 June 2010. Therefore, the repeal of the Arbitration Acts 1954-1998 did not prejudice or affect the right to extend the contractual time limit in which to commence an application under Arbitration Act 1954, s 45, notwithstanding that any arbitral proceedings commenced would be governed by the Act and the Model Law.

8.—Construction of Model Law and construction of arbitration clauses

(1) Judicial notice shall be taken of the *travaux préparatoires* of the United Nations Commission on International Trade Law and its working group relating to the preparation of the Model Law.

(2) The *travaux préparatoires* referred to in subsection (1) may be considered when interpreting the meaning of any provision of the Model Law and shall be given such weight as is appropriate in the circumstances.

(3) Where parties agree that disputes under a contract or agreement or disputes arising out of a contract or agreement shall be submitted to arbitration, this shall include disputes as to the existence or validity of the contract or agreement.

Definitions

'arbitration': Arbitration Act 2010, s 2(1) and Model Law, Art 2(a); 'Model Law': Arbitration Act 2010, s 2(1).

Notes

Construction of the Model Law and construction of arbitration agreements: This section provides for two distinct and unrelated scenarios relating to construction and interpretation of the Model Law and of arbitration agreements, respectively. First, it provides that the courts are permitted to take judicial notice of UNCITRAL's *travaux préparatoires* when interpreting provisions of the Model Law.[1] Second, it provides that where parties to an agreement agree that disputes shall be resolved by arbitration, any disputes as to the existence or validity of the arbitration agreement may be submitted to arbitration.[2]

---

[1] Arbitration Act 2010, s 8(1).
[2] Arbitration Act 2010, s 8(3).

Judicial notice of the travaux préparatoires: In general, *travaux préparatoires* or 'preparatory works' are the official record of the negotiations in preparation for the adoption of international treaties or international statutes such as the Model Law. UNICTRAL's *travaux préparatoires* refer to the official record of the negotiations in preparation for the adoption of the Model Law on 21 June 1985 and in the preparation for the amendment of the Model Law as adopted on 7 July 2006.[1]

Judicial notice permits a court to take into account a source without its formal proof as an aid to statutory interpretation.[2] Although the courts in Ireland are not generally permitted to look to parliamentary history and explanatory memoranda as an aid to interpretation of domestic legislation, the courts are permitted to take judicial notice of external sources such as *travaux préparatoires* when interpreting domestic legislation that gives effect to international treaties.[3] The rationale for judicial notice of external sources such as *travaux préparatoires* is to ensure that the treaty is interpreted consistently with the interpretation of the treaty in other countries:

> "For a very long time principles of common law concerning the interpretation of statutes which give effect to international treaties permit the courts to interpret such a statute in the light of the meaning of relevant provisions of the treaty concerned. No doubt this is in part because the intention of the national legislature is clear - to give effect to provisions of the treaty in domestic law - and the objective consequence of that intent can be clarified or ascertained, where necessary, by reference to the meaning of the relevant provisions of the treaty, itself a legal instrument. There is also the consideration that contracting parties to international agreements should seek, as far as possible, to give uniform effect to its provision in domestic law. Furthermore, with this latter objective in mind, international treaties are interpreted in accordance with the principles of international law according to which the *travaux préparatoires* may be consulted for the purposes of their interpretation (unless such an approach is excluded, expressly, or by implication by the terms of the treaty itself or if there are no *travaux préparatoires* available)".[4]

(*Continued*)

This section provides that Irish courts are permitted to take judicial notice of the *travaux préparatoires* "as is appropriate in the circumstances".[5] However, there is no requirement for a court to take judicial notice of the *travaux préparatoires* and Irish case-law has held that use of external materials should be rare even when interpreting international treaties or statutes.[6]

---

[1] The *travaux préparatoires* are available in their entirety from the UNCITRAL website at: http://www.uncitral.org/uncitral/en/uncitral_texts/arbitration/1985Model_arbitration_travaux.html.
[2] See Dodd, *Statutory Interpretation in Ireland* (1st ed, Tottel Publishing, Dublin, 2008) p 243.
[3] *Crilly v T & J Farrington Ltd* [2001] 3 IR 251.
[4] *ibid*, at 291.
[5] Arbitration Act 2010, s 8(2).
[6] *Crilly v T & J Farrington Ltd* [2001] 3 IR 251.

***Disputes as to the existence or validity of the contract or agreement and the doctrine of 'competence-competence'*:** The doctrine of 'competence-competence' (which is also referred to as 'Kompetenz-Kompetenz' or 'jurisdiction to decided jurisdiction'), which permits an arbitral tribunal to decide upon its own jurisdiction, is a fundamental concept of arbitration under the Model Law.[1] The Act clarifies that where an arbitration agreement exists, an arbitral tribunal may determine whether the arbitration agreement is applicable to the dispute that has arisen. Therefore, a party will not permitted be to evade the effect of an arbitration agreement merely by alleging its non-existence or non-validity.[2]

A full discussion on the doctrine of 'competence-competence' is contained at Art 16 of the Model Law.

---

[1] Model Law, Art 16.
[2] Where arbitral proceedings are commenced but one party has disputed the existence of a valid arbitration agreement, the arbitral tribunal has the power to decide whether the arbitration agreement is valid. However, where civil proceedings are commenced and one party asserts the existence of a valid arbitration agreement which the other party denies, then some form of judicial review by the courts is required. The standard of judicial review to be applied by the courts under Irish law is currently uncertain. See *Barnmore Demolition and Civil Engineering Ltd v Alandale Logistics Ltd*, unreported, High Court (Feeney J), 11 November 2010.

9.—Functions of High Court

(1) The High Court is—

(a) specified for the purposes of Article 6,

(b) the relevant court for the purposes of Article 9, and

(c) the court of competent jurisdiction for the purposes of Articles 17 H, 17 I, 17 J, 27, 35 and 36.

(2) The functions of the High Court—

(a) under an Article referred to in subsection (1), or

(b) under sections 10, 23 or 25,

shall be performed by the President or by such other judge of the High Court as may be nominated by the President, subject to any rules of court made in that behalf.

(3) An application may be made in summary manner to the President or to such other judge of the High Court as may be nominated by the President under subsection (2).

(4) In this section "President" means the President of the High Court.

Definitions

'functions': Interpretation Act 2005, sch, pt 2; 'High Court': Interpretation Act 2005, sch, pt 1.

Notes

***Functions of the High Court*:** This section provides that, other than applications to refer pending civil proceedings to arbitration, which are heard in the court in which the proceedings themselves are commenced,[1] and the limited power of the Circuit Court to adjourn pending civil proceedings to enable the parties to consider whether the matters in dispute might be determined by arbitration,[2] all judicial supervisory functions in connection with arbitral proceedings under the Act and the Model Law are to be performed by the High Court. The High Court's supervisory functions are:

1. To provide interim measures of protection before or during arbitral proceedings;[3]
2. To appoint an arbitrator or arbitrators in the absence of agreement of the parties;[4]
3. To appoint an arbitrator or arbitrators where there has been a failure in the agreement of the parties;[5]
4. To decide on a challenge to the appointment of an arbitrator;[6]
5. To appoint an arbitrator where there has been a failure or an impossibility in an arbitrator who had been appointed acting;[7]
6. To rule on the jurisdiction of an arbitral tribunal where requested to do so by a party within 30 days of the arbitral tribunal's own ruling;[8]
7. To recognise interim measures issued by an arbitral tribunal;[9]
8. To refuse to recognise interim measures issued by an arbitral tribunal;[10]
9. To order interim measures in relation to arbitral proceedings;[11]
10. To assist in the taking evidence at the request of an arbitral tribunal or a party;[12]
11. To recognise and enforce an award where Ireland was not the place of arbitration;[13]
12. To refuse to recognise and enforce an award where Ireland was not the place of arbitration;[14]
13. To enforce an award where Ireland was the place of arbitration;[15] and
14. To enforce the pecuniary obligations of an award rendered pursuant to the Washington Convention.[16]

(*Continued*)

Unless the Act or the Model Law expressly provides that the parties may agree otherwise, any agreement of the parties which purports to oust the supervisory functions of the High Court is likely to be void as being contrary to public policy.[17]

---

[1] Model Law, Art 8.
[2] Arbitration Act 2010, s 32(1).
[3] Model Law, Art 9; and Arbitration Act 2010, s 10(1).
[4] Model Law, Art 11(3).
[5] Model Law, Art 11(4).
[6] Model Law, Art 13(3).
[7] Model Law, Art 14.
[8] Model Law, Art 16(3).
[9] Model Law, Art 17 H.
[10] Model Law, Art 17 I.
[11] Model Law, Art 17 J.
[12] Model Law, Art 27; and Arbitration Act 2010, s 10(1).
[13] Model Law, Art 35.
[14] Model Law, Art 36.
[15] Arbitration Act 2010, s 23(1).
[16] Arbitration Act 2010, s 25(5).
[17] *Czarnikow v Roth, Schmidt & Co* [1922] 2 KB 478, which is a decision of the English Court of Appeal where the parties had agreed that they would not invoke the special case stated procedure under the English Arbitration Act 1889, s 7 after an award was issued by the arbitral tribunal. This agreement was held to be an ouster of the jurisdiction of the courts and was void as being contrary to public policy. Scrutton LJ stated at p 488 that: "Arbitrators, unless expressly otherwise authorized, have to apply the laws of England . . . This is done in order that the Courts may insure the proper administration of the law by inferior tribunals. In my view to allow English citizens to agree to exclude this safeguard for the administration of the law is contrary to public policy. There must be no Alsatia in England where the King's writ does not run". The decision in *Czarnikow v Roth, Schmidt & Co* has received judicial approval in Ireland in *Uniform Construction Ltd v Cappawhite Contractors Ltd* [2007] IEHC 295; and *John Mowlem Construction Ltd t/a Irishenco Construction v Dublin City Council* [2009] IEHC 225.

***Supervisory functions of the High Court to be performed by the President of the High Court or his nominee*:** All supervisory functions in connection with arbitral proceedings under the Act and the Model Law are to be performed by the President of the High Court or his nominee.[1] At present, the High Court's supervisory functions are performed in the Chancery list or in the Commercial list where a matter has been adopted into it.

---

[1] Arbitration Act 2010, s 9(2).

***Procedure for application to the High Court in connection with arbitral proceedings*:** An application made to the High Court to fulfil its supervisory functions in connection with arbitral proceedings is made in a summary manner[1] and must be commenced by originating notice of motion grounded on affidavit.[2] Such summary procedure "is provided in order to enable speedy justice to be done in particular cases where there is either no issue to be tried or the issues involved are simple and capable of being easily determined".[3]

(*Continued*)

Where arbitral proceedings have been commenced, an application must be entitled in the matter of the arbitral proceedings to which it relates and in the matter of the Act.[4] Where no arbitral proceedings have been commenced, an application must be entitled in the matter of an intended arbitral proceedings and in the matter of the Act.[5] An application must name as respondent the party or intended party to the arbitral proceedings[6] or intended arbitral proceedings.[7] An arbitrator or arbitral tribunal should not be joined as a party to any application to the High Court to fulfil its supervisory functions in connection with arbitral proceedings.[8] However, Irish case-law has held that an error in procedure may not be fatal to an application to the High Court for it to fulfil its supervisory functions.[9]

1 Arbitration Act 2010, s 9(3).
2 Rules of the Superior Courts, Ord 56, r 3(1).
3 *Prendergast v Biddle*, unreported, Supreme Court (Maguire CJ, Lavery J, O'Dalaigh J), 31 July 1957, per Lavery J at 12, in the context of a summary summons.
4 Rules of the Superior Courts, Ord 56, r (2)1.
5 Rules of the Superior Courts, Ord 56, r (2)2.
6 Rules of the Superior Courts, Ord 56, r 2(1).
7 Rules of the Superior Courts, Ord 56, r 2(2).
8 *FBD Insurance plc v Connors* [2011] IEHC 184.
9 *ibid*, where the applicant commenced an application by special summons rather than originating notice of motion. The High Court (Laffoy J) held that it was appropriate to hear the application notwithstanding the defect in the procedure adopted, particularly as the respondents offered no opposition to the approach adopted.

10.—Court powers exercisable in support of arbitral proceedings

(1) Subject to subsection (2), the High Court shall have the same powers in relation to Articles 9 and 27 as it has in any other action or matter before the Court.

(2) When exercising any powers in relation to Articles 9 or 27, the High Court shall not, unless otherwise agreed by the parties, make any order relating to security for costs of the arbitration or make any order for discovery of documents.

Definitions

'arbitration': Arbitration Act 2010, s 2(1) and Model Law, Art 2(a); 'High Court': Interpretation Act 2005, sch, pt 1.

Notes

***Court power in support of arbitral proceedings*:** This section provides that the High Court has the same power to order interim measures of protection and to provide assistance in taking evidence in respect of arbitral proceedings as it does in civil proceedings.[1] However, unless otherwise agreed by the parties, the High Court cannot order security for costs or order discovery of documents.[2]

1 Arbitration Act 2010, s 10(1).
2 Arbitration Act 2010, s 10(2).

***High Court's power to order interim measures in support of arbitral proceedings*:** This section reaffirms certain provisions of the Model Law[1] and provides that the High Court has the same powers to order interim measures in respect of arbitral proceedings as it does in any civil proceedings pending before it, irrespective of whether or not the arbitral proceedings are taking place in Ireland.[2] Although the term 'interim relief' under Irish law typically refers to urgent injunctive relief sought on an *ex parte* basis to maintain the status quo for a short period until an interlocutory application is heard,[3] in arbitration the term 'interim measures' has a broader meaning and includes injunctive relief, which under Irish law would be classified as both 'interim' and 'interlocutory' relief.[4]

[1] Model Law, Arts 9; and 17 J.
[2] Arbitration Act 2010, s 10(1).
[3] Kirwan, Injunctions Law *& Practice* (1st ed, Thomson Round Hall, Dublin, 2008) p 240.
[4] *Shelbourne Hotel Holdings Ltd v Torriam Hotel Operating Company Ltd* [2010] 2 IR 52. Model Law, Art 17(2) defines an 'interim measure' as "any temporary measure . . . by which, at any time prior to the issuance of the award by which the dispute is finally decided, the arbitral tribunal orders a party to: (a) Maintain or restore the status quo pending determination of the dispute; (b) Take action that would prevent, or refrain from taking action that is likely to cause current or imminent harm or prejudice to the arbitral process itself; (c) Provide a means of preserving assets out of which a subsequent award may be satisfied; or (d) Preserve evidence that may be relevant and material to the resolution of the dispute".

***Test for interim or interlocutory injunctive relief at Irish law*:** Under Irish law the test for whether or not injunction relief will be granted at an interim or interlocutory stage is based on the so-called '*Campus Oil* guidelines'.[1] The *Campus Oil* guidelines comprise a multi-stage test requiring, in summary: first, that there is a *bona fide* question to be tried; second, that damages would not be an adequate remedy for a party if it was refused injunctive relief at an interim or interlocutory stage but was later successful at the trial of the action; and finally, that the balance of convenience favours the granting of the injunction.[2]

[1] Named after the seminal case of *Campus Oil Ltd v Minister for Industry and Energy (No 2)* [1983] 1 IR 88, where the principles established by the House of Lords (as it then was) in determining whether to grant interlocutory relied in *American Cyanamid Co v Ethicon Ltd* [1975] AC 396 were adopted by the Supreme Court.
[2] *Osmond Ireland On Farm Business v McFarland* [2010] IEHC 295, where the High Court (Laffoy J) approved the application of the Campus Oil guidelines in the context of an arbitration.

***High Court's power to order anti-suit injunctions*:** In arbitration, an anti-suit injunction is an order directed against the parties or intended parties to foreign litigation prohibiting the commencement or prosecution of litigation where the matter in dispute is the subject of an arbitration agreement.[1] Although the power to prohibit the commencement or prosecution of foreign litigation brought in violation of an arbitration agreement has long been exercised by courts in certain common law jurisdictions,[2] Irish commentators have noted that "[t]here is a dearth of [modern] case-law in this jurisdiction on anti-suit injunctions".[3] However, it is likely that, as in other common law

(*Continued*)

jurisdictions, an anti-suit injunction may be ordered in appropriate circumstances.[4] However, where a court within the European Union has been seised of civil proceedings within the meaning of Council Regulation (EC) No 44/2001 of 22 December 2000 on Jurisdiction and the Recognition and Enforcement of Judgments in Civil and Commercial Matters (the Brussels Regulation),[5] the court of another European Union Member State cannot order an anti-suit injunction to prohibit the prosecution of foreign litigation, even where the initial civil proceedings have been brought in violation of an arbitration agreement.[6]

---

[1] Born, *International Commercial Arbitration* (1st ed, Kluwer Law International, Alphen aan den Rijn, 2009) p 1036.

[2] See *Lett v Lett* [1906] 1 IR 618, where the pre-independence High Court granted an injunction restraining the prosecution of family law proceedings in Argentina in violation of an agreement of the parties not to proceed with the suit. The High Court's decision was upheld on appeal. See also *Pena Copper Mines Ltd v Rio Tinto Co Ltd* [1911-1913] All ER Rep 209, where the English Court of Appeal enjoined an English company not to proceed with litigation in the Spanish courts in violation of an arbitration agreement. Courts in Australia, Bermuda, Canada, Singapore and the United States have also ordered anti-suit injunctions to prevent a party from commencing or prosecuting foreign litigation. For a discussion on anti-suit injunctions in common law jurisdictions, see Born, *International Commercial Arbitration* (1st ed, Kluwer Law International, Alphen aan den Rijn, 2009) pp 1036-1041.

[3] Kirwan, *Injunctions Law & Practice* (1st ed, Thomson Round Hall, Dublin, 2008) p 68.

[4] Guidelines for what may be considered 'appropriate circumstances' were set out in the case of *Airbus Indus GIE v Patel* [1999] 1 AC 119, where the House of Lords (as it then was) refused to grant an anti-suit injunction as the English forum did not have a sufficient interest in, or connection with, the matter in question to justify such interference. It was held that for an anti-suit injunction to be ordered the party seeking the injunction must demonstrate that: first, the forum in which the anti-suit injunction is sought must have a sufficient interest in, or in connection with the dispute in question; second, the foreign proceedings would cause prejudice to the party seeking the anti-suit injunction; and, finally, the anti-suit injunction would not unfairly deprive the plaintiff in the foreign litigation of a legitimate advantage.

[5] EC No 44/2001.

[6] *Allianz SpA v West Tankers Inc* [2009] 1 AC 1138, where the European Court of Justice held that an order restraining a party from commencing or continuing proceedings before a court of another Member State on the ground that those proceedings would be contrary to an arbitration agreement was in violation of the provisions of the Brussels Regulation. The decision has been met with near-universal criticism and it has been proposed by the European Commission that its effect will be neutralised by a proposed amendment to the Brussels Regulation, which includes a specific rule on the relation between arbitration and civil proceedings obliging a court seised of a dispute to stay proceedings where its jurisdiction is contested on the basis of an arbitration agreement.

***High Court's power to order interim measures prior to the commencement of arbitral proceedings*:** As any civil proceedings pending before a court that are the subject of a valid arbitration agreement must be referred to arbitration where a party so requests "not later than when submitting his first statement on the substance of the dispute",[1] it is uncertain whether a party that commences civil proceedings to obtain interim or interlocutory injunctive relief loses its right to have the proceedings referred to arbitration. In particular, where an interim measure is requested from the High Court, it is uncertain whether

(*Continued*)

unconditional documents filed in support or opposition to the interim measures sought are a statement on the substance of the dispute such as to jeopardise a party's ability to request that pending civil proceedings be referred to arbitration.[2] The question must be bifurcated depending on whether it is a plaintiff or a defendant to the injunctive relief that requests that pending proceedings be referred to arbitration. Where a plaintiff has attempted to refer its own proceedings to arbitration, case-law decided under the Arbitration Acts 1954-1998 has held that a plaintiff should not be permitted to issue proceedings and subsequently refer those proceedings to arbitration.[3] The likelihood of an Irish court reaching a similar result under the Model Law is uncertain as the Model Law expressly contemplates court-ordered interim measures[4] and, in matters of extreme urgency, it may be prudent for a potential plaintiff to obtain interim measures from the High Court prior to the commencement of arbitral proceedings in circumstances where the plaintiff is concerned about the possibility of the dissipation of assets or destruction of evidence by the proposed defendant. Where a defendant has attempted to refer proceedings to arbitration, case-law decided under the Arbitration Acts 1954-1998 has held a defendant should be permitted to have proceedings referred to arbitration after interlocutory injunctive relief had been obtained by a plaintiff[5] and it is highly likely that an Irish court would reach a similar result under Model Law.

---

[1] Model Law, Art 8(1).

[2] Where a party makes clear that an affidavit is filed without prejudice to the entitlement to refer arbitration, the entitlement shall not be lost. *Gleeson v Grimes & anor* [2007] 4 IR 417; and *Dublin Docklands Development Authority v Jermyn Street Ltd & anor* [2010] IEHC 217.

[3] *MacCormac Products Ltd v Monaghan Co-Operative Agricultural and Diary Society Ltd* [1988] 1 IR 304, in which the High Court (O'Hanlon J) refused to refer proceedings to arbitration under Arbitration Act 1980, s 5 where the plaintiff sought to refer proceedings that he had commenced. The High Court held that the obtaining of interlocutory injunctive relief was a 'step' in the proceedings notwithstanding that only a plenary summons had been issued.

[4] Model Law, Art 17 J.

[5] *Telenor Invest AS v IIU Nominees Ltd* [1999] IEHC 188, where the plaintiff commenced proceedings and sought interlocutory injunctive relief. The High Court (O'Sullivan J) granted the relief sought and referred the proceedings to arbitration.

***Security for costs in arbitration*:** The provisions of security for costs balances the right of a party against whom proceedings are commenced to recover costs in the event that it successfully defends the claim against the right of a party commencing proceedings to vindicate its legal rights.[1] Where arbitral proceedings have been commenced, unless otherwise agreed by the parties, it is an arbitral tribunal[2] and not the High Court that has the power to order a party to arbitral proceedings to provide security for costs.[3] This represents a change from the Arbitration Acts 1954-1998, which provided that only the High Court had power to order security for costs in respect of arbitral proceedings.[4] Commentators have noted that by empowering an arbitral tribunal to order security for costs, this section "puts in place the correct equilibrium, namely that the arbitral tribunal should have control of the process, particularly with something as important and as far-reaching as the ordering of security for costs. Satellite litigation in the High Court on such issues distorts the equilibrium".[5]

---

[1] For a discussion on security for costs in Irish civil proceedings, see Delany and McGrath, *Civil Procedure in the Superior Courts* (3rd ed, Round Hall Thomson Reuters, Dublin, 2012) pp 485-525.

(*Continued*)

[2] Arbitration Act 2010, s 19(1).
[3] Arbitration Act 2010, s 10(2).
[4] Arbitration Act 1954, s 22(1)(a).
[5] Reichert, "Security for Costs in Arbitration – A New Landscape in Ireland" (2010) *Arbitration and ADR Review*, p 130.

***Court assistance in the taking of evidence*:** The High Court has the same powers in relation to the assistance in the taking of evidence as it does in any other action before it.[1] The assistance which may be offered by the High Court is governed by the Rules of the Superior Courts[2] and includes the examination of witnesses and the issue of *subpoenas* for the attendance of witnesses. A request for assistance in the taking of evidence is made *ex parte* to the High Court and must be grounded on affidavit.[3]

A full discussion on the provisions governing court assistance in the taking of evidence is contained at Art 27 of the Model Law.

[1] Arbitration Act 2010, s 10(1).
[2] Rules of the Superior Courts, Ord 56, r 4(4).
[3] Rules of the Superior Courts, Ord 56, r 4(4).

***Discovery of documents*:** In Ireland, as in most common law jurisdictions, parties to civil proceedings can obtain 'discovery' of documents relevant to the issues that are in the possession or control of another party prior to the trial of an action.[1] The basic purpose of discovery "is to ensure as far as possible that the full facts concerning any matter in dispute before the court are capable of being presented to the court by the parties concerned, so that justice on full information, rather than on a limited or partial revelation of the facts arising in a particular action, may be done".[2] However, discovery can be a cumbersome and expensive process which serves to delay the resolution of an action. The courts have attempted to minimise discovery "where enormous volumes of documents were swamping parties to litigation in giving rise seemingly endless interlocutor speeds thereby delaying trials".[3] Therefore, although discovery will be granted in Irish civil proceedings where a party can demonstrate that some other party has a document within its possession that is necessary for disposing fairly of the matter or for saving costs,[4] "an applicant is not entitled discovery based on mere speculation on the basis of what has been traditionally characterised as a fishing expedition".[5]

Discovery is not a feature of international arbitration and it has been noted that "[t]he word/expression 'discovery' is a term of art used in . . . some common law countries . . . to describe a process whereby the parties (and their lawyers) are legally obliged to produce documents that are 'relevant to the pleaded issues', even if they are prejudicial to that parties' case. Subject to any mandatory rules of the *lex arbitri*, or agreement of the parties, the process known as 'discovery' has no place in international arbitration".[6] In an attempt to harmonise Irish arbitration practice with international standards, arbitral proceedings are no longer governed

(*Continued*)

by the rules of court procedure concerning discovery. Unless the parties expressly agree otherwise, the High Court cannot order the discovery of documents in arbitral proceedings.[7] This is in contrast to the Arbitration Acts 1954-1998, which provided the High Court with the same power to order discovery in arbitral proceedings as it did in civil proceedings.[8]

---

[1] For a discussion on discovery in the Irish superior courts, see Delany and McGrath, *Civil Procedure in the Superior Courts* (3rd ed, Round Hall Thomson Reuters, Dublin, 2012) pp 396-460.
[2] *Per* Finlay CJ in *Allied Irish Banks plc v Ernst & Whinney* [1993] 1 IR 375, 390.
[3] *Per* Kelly J in *Sheehy v Government of Ireland*, unreported High Court (Kelly J), 30 July 2002 at 5.
[4] Rules of the Superior Courts, Ord 31, r 12(1)(a).
[5] *Per* Murray J in *Aquatechnologie Ltd v National Standards Authority of Ireland* [2010] IESC 209.
[6] Blackaby, Partasides, Redfern and Hunter, *Redfern and Hunter on International Arbitration* (5th ed, Oxford University Press, Oxford, 2009) p 393, fn 65.
[7] Arbitration Act 2010, s 10(2).
[8] Arbitration Act 1954, s 22(1)(b).

11.—Determination of court to be final

There shall be no appeal from—

(a) any court determination of a stay application, pursuant to Article 8(1) of the Model Law or Article II(3) of the New York Convention,

(b) any determination by the High Court—

(i) of an application for setting aside an award under Article 34 of the Model Law, or

(ii) of an application under Chapter VIII of the Model Law for the recognition and enforcement of an award made in an international commercial arbitration,

or

(c) any determination by the High Court in relation to an application to recognise or enforce an arbitral award pursuant to the Geneva Convention, New York Convention or Washington Convention.

Definitions

'award': Arbitration Act 2010, s 2(1); 'Geneva Convention': Arbitration Act 2010, s 2(1); 'High Court': Interpretation Act 2005, sch, pt 1; 'Model Law': Arbitration Act 2010, s 2(1); 'New York Convention': Arbitration Act 2010, s 2(1); 'Washington Convention': Arbitration Act 2010, s 2(1).

Notes

***Limitation on right of appeal from determinations of the High Court*:** In order to ensure finality in arbitration matters and to prevent delay, the right of appeal is expressly removed from any determination by a court to refer pending civil proceedings to arbitration;[1] to

(*Continued*)

set aside an award;[2] to recognise or enforce an award;[3] or to recognise an award pursuant to the Geneva Convention, the New York Convention or the Washington Convention.[4]

The Constitution of Ireland provides that "[t]he Supreme Court shall, with such exceptions and subject to such regulations as may be prescribed by law, have appellate jurisdiction from all decisions of the High Court, and shall also have appellate jurisdiction from such decisions of other courts as may be prescribed by law".[5] Any statutory provision which removes decisions of the High Court from the appellate jurisdiction of the Supreme Court must be "clear and unambiguous"[6] and "restricted or regulated by legislation clearly intended to have this effect".[7] As the language used in this section is clear and unambiguous and has the clear intent of restricting the right of appeal, it is highly unlikely that any constitutional issues will arise as a result of this section.

[1] Arbitration Act 2010, s 11(a).
[2] Arbitration Act 2010, s 11(b)(i).
[3] Arbitration Act 2010, s 11(b)(ii).
[4] Arbitration Act 2010, s 11(c).
[5] Art 34.4.3.
[6] *People (AG) v Conmey* [1975] 1 IR 341 at 360, where the Supreme Court held that the establishment of the Court of Criminal Appeal as a court of appeal was not invalid having regard to the provisions of the Constitution of Ireland since Art 34.3.4 contemplates the establishment of courts with appellate jurisdiction other than the Supreme Court.
[7] *ibid*, at 354.

***Preservation of right of appeal from determinations of the High Court in certain matters*:** Although the right of appeal is expressly removed from any determination by a court to refer pending civil proceedings to arbitration;[1] to set aside an award;[2] to recognise or enforce an award;[3] or to recognise an award pursuant to the Geneva Convention, the New York Convention or the Washington Convention,[4] the High Court has power the make other determinations under the Act and the Model Law[5] from which a right of appeal has not expressly been removed. Therefore, the appellate jurisdiction of the Supreme Court remains for the following functions:

1. The provision of interim protection before or during arbitral proceedings;[6]
2. The ordering of interim measures in relation to arbitral proceedings;[7] and
3. The assistance in the taking evidence at the request of an arbitral tribunal or a party.[8]

[1] Arbitration Act 2010, s 11(a).
[2] Arbitration Act 2010, s 11(b)(i).
[3] Arbitration Act 2010, s 11(b)(ii).
[4] Arbitration Act 2010, s 11(c).
[5] Arbitration Act 2010, s 9, which provides for a full list of the High Court's powers and functions.
[6] Arbitration Act 2010, s 10(1) and Model Law, Art 9.
[7] Model Law, Art 17 J.
[8] Model Law, Art 27.

***Mandatory nature of the section*:** This section is mandatory in nature and the parties may not circumvent its effect by agreeing otherwise.

12.—Time limits for setting aside awards on grounds of public policy

Notwithstanding Article 34(3), an application to the High Court to set aside an award on the grounds that the award is in conflict with the public policy of the State shall be made within a period of 56 days from the date on which the circumstances giving rise to the application became known or ought reasonably to have become known to the party concerned.

Definitions

'award': Arbitration Act 2010, s 2(1); 'High Court': Interpretation Act 2005, sch, pt 1.

Notes

Time limit for setting aside an award on public policy grounds: This section amends the time limit provided by the Model Law within which a party can apply to set aside an award on public policy grounds from three months from the date of receipt of the award[1] to 56 days from date on which the circumstances giving rise to the application became known or ought reasonably to have become known to the party concerned.[2] The rationale for this amendment is to ensure that a party may seek redress where circumstances giving rise to challenge on public policy grounds become apparent only some time after an award is received.[3]

[1] Model Law, Art 34(3).
[2] Arbitration Act 2010, s 12.
[3] Arbitration Bill 2008: Hearing before Select Committee on Justice, Equality, Defence and Women's Rights, Dáil Debate, 23 April 2009 (statement of Dermot Ahern, the then Minister for Justice, Equality and Law Reform).

Mandatory nature of the section: This section is mandatory in nature and the parties may not circumvent its effect by agreeing otherwise.

13.—Default number of arbitrators

Unless otherwise agreed by the parties, the arbitral tribunal shall consist of one arbitrator only.

Definitions

'arbitral tribunal': Model Law, Art 2(b).

Notes

The default number of arbitrators: This section amends the Model Law and provides that the default number of arbitrators on an arbitral tribunal is one.[1] The Model Law provides that the default number of arbitrators on an arbitral tribunal is three.[2] In international commercial arbitration the modern preference is for disputes to be referred

(*Continued*)

to an arbitral tribunal of three arbitrators, unless the amount in dispute is small.[3] However, arbitral tribunals in Ireland have traditionally consisted of a single arbitrator. The default number of arbitrators under the Arbitration Acts 1954-1998 was one.[4]

---

[1] Arbitration Act 2010, s 13.

[2] Model Law, Art 10(2).

[3] See Blackaby, Partasides, Redfern and Hunter, *Redfern and Hunter on International Arbitration* (5th ed, Oxford University Press, Oxford, 2009) p 250. Examples of institutional rules which reflect this preference include: the International Chamber of Commerce's Rules of Arbitration, Art 12.1; the London Court of International Arbitration's Arbitration Rules, Art 5.4; and the International Center for Dispute Resolution's International Arbitration Rules, Art 5.

[4] Arbitration Act 1954, s 14.

***Rationale for amendment of default number of arbitrators*:** The section amends the default number of arbitrators from three to one in order to minimise the costs of arbitral proceedings as it is axiomatic that it is more economic to appoint a single arbitrator rather than three arbitrators. In addition, the amendment to the default number of arbitrators ensures consistency with existing arbitration practice in Ireland as the default number of arbitrators under the Arbitration Acts 1954-1998 was one.[1] This is particular importance as the Act applies to many arbitration agreements that were entered into prior to the Act's enactment.[2] It would be undesirable to impose increased costs associated with a three-person arbitral tribunal on parties that had entered into an arbitration agreement when the default number of arbitrators was one.[3]

---

[1] Arbitration Act 1954, s 14.

[2] Arbitration Act 2010, s 3(1).

[3] Arbitration Bill 2008: Second Hearing before Dáil, Dáil Debate, 19 November 2008 (statement of Dermot Ahern, the then Minister for Justice, Equality and Law Reform).

***Applicability to international commercial arbitration*:** As the default number of arbitrators in international commercial arbitration is typically three, it may have been preferably for the Oireachtas to draw a distinction between international commercial arbitrations and domestic arbitrations (which are any arbitrations other than international commercial arbitrations) concerning the default number of arbitrators.[1] However, in practice, the departure from the provisions of the Model Law is unlikely to present a difficulty as most international commercial arbitrations are conducted under the auspices of an arbitral institution and will typically adopt that arbitral institution's rules on the composition of an arbitral tribunal.

---

[1] For example, a distinction has been drawn between international commercial arbitrations and domestic arbitrations (which are any arbitrations other than international commercial arbitrations) concerning taxation of costs by Arbitration Act 2010, s 21(4).

***Non-mandatory nature of the section*:** This section is non-mandatory in nature and the parties may circumvent its effect by agreeing otherwise.

14.—Examination of witnesses

Unless otherwise agreed by the parties, the arbitral tribunal may for the purposes of the arbitral proceedings concerned—

(a) direct that a party to an arbitration agreement or a witness who gives evidence in proceedings before the arbitral tribunal be examined on oath or on affirmation, and

(b) administer oaths or affirmations for the purposes of the examination.

Definitions

'arbitral tribunal': Model Law, Art 2(b); 'arbitration agreement': Arbitration Act 2010, s 2(1) and Model Law, Art 7(1) (Option I); 'oath': Interpretation Act 2005, sch, pt 1.

Notes

***No requirement for evidence in arbitral proceedings to be given on oath*:** This section clarifies the provisions of the Model Law[1] and provides that an arbitral tribunal has discretion over whether or not it requires a witness to give evidence under oath.[2] This section, which is based on a similar provision of English arbitration legislation,[3] is in contrast both with the provisions of the Arbitration Acts 1954-1998, which, unless the contrary intention was expressed in the arbitration agreement, required that witnesses give evidence in arbitral proceedings on oath or affirmation[4] and with civil proceedings in Ireland, where it is a fundamental principle of the common law that *viva voce* evidence must be given on oath or affirmation.[5]

---

[1] The Model Law contains no requirement that a witness be examined on oath or affirmation. Unless otherwise agreed by the parties, Model Law, Art 19(2) provides that the arbitral tribunal may conduct arbitral proceedings in such manner as it considers appropriate, which would seem to include the power to determine whether or not evidence must be given on oath.

[2] Arbitration Act 2010, s 14(a).

[3] The English Arbitration Act 1996, s 38(5), which provides that "[t]he tribunal may direct that a party or witness shall be examined on oath or affirmation, and may for that purpose administer any necessary oath or take any necessary affirmation".

[4] Arbitration Act 1954, s 19.

[5] *Mapp (a minor) v Gilhooley* [1991] 2 IR 253.

***Non-mandatory nature of the section*:** This section is non-mandatory in nature and the parties may circumvent its effect by agreeing otherwise.

15.—Taking evidence in State in aid of foreign arbitration

The reference in Article 27 to an arbitral tribunal includes a reference to an arbitral tribunal conducting arbitral proceedings in a place other than the State.

Definitions

'arbitral tribunal': Model Law, Art 2(b).

Notes

***Extension of court assistance in taking evidence to foreign arbitrations*:** The Model Law provides that an arbitral tribunal, or a party with the approval of an arbitral tribunal, may request assistance in the taking of evidence in arbitral proceedings from the competent court of the place of arbitration.[1] In Ireland, the court of competent jurisdiction is the High Court.[2] However, the Model Law is silent on whether assistance may be given to an arbitration where the place of arbitration is outside the State adopting the Model Law (*i.e.*, a 'foreign arbitration').[3] In Ireland, this section expressly permits the High Court to provide assistance in the taking of evidence in arbitral proceedings even where Ireland is not the place of arbitration.

[1] Model Law, Art 27.

[2] Arbitration Act 2010, s 9(1)(c); and Model Law, Art 6.

[3] In fact, international case-law decided under the Model Law has held that requests for assistance in taking evidence may only be made to courts in the State of the place of arbitration. See CLOUT Case 391 – Canada/Superior Court of Justice: *Re Corporación Transnacional de Inversiones, SA de CV and STE International SpA et al* (22 September 1999) This view is shared by commentators, see Holtzmann and Neuhaus, *A Guide to the UNCITRAL Model Law on International Commercial Arbitration* (1st ed, Kluwer Law and Taxation Publishers, The Hague, 1989) p 738.

***Provisions of the Model Law on court assistance in taking evidence*:** As the Model Law governs court assistance on taking evidence,[1] a full discussion on these provisions is contained at Art 27 of the Model Law.

[1] Model Law, Art 27.

16.—Consolidation of and concurrent arbitrations

(1) Where the parties to an arbitration agreement so agree—

(a) arbitral proceedings shall be consolidated with other arbitral proceedings, including arbitral proceedings involving a different party or parties with the agreement of that party or parties,

(b) concurrent hearings shall be held,

on such terms as may be agreed between the parties concerned.

(2) The arbitral tribunal shall not order the consolidation of proceedings or concurrent hearings unless the parties agree to the making of such an order.

Definitions

'arbitral tribunal': Model Law, Art 2(b); 'arbitration agreement': Arbitration Act 2010, s 2(1) and Model Law, Art 7(1) (Option I).

Notes

***Consolidation of arbitrations and concurrent hearings*:** This section supplements the Model Law and provides for the consolidation of arbitral proceedings[1] and the holding of concurrent hearings.[2] However, the agreement of all parties to each of the constituent arbitral proceedings is required for consolidation of arbitral proceedings.[3]

[1] Arbitration Act 2010, s 16(1)(a).
[2] Arbitration Act 2010, s 16(1)(b).
[3] Arbitration Act 2010, s 16(2).

***Consolidation of arbitral proceedings*:** Consolidation of arbitral proceedings may only take place where all the parties to each of the constituent arbitral proceedings agree to consolidate the matters into a single set of arbitral proceedings.[1] The rationale for this approach is the principle of party autonomy, which dictates that the parties to an arbitration agreement are to decide upon a mechanism for resolving disputes arising; it would be inconsistent with this principle for an arbitral tribunal to order the consolidation of proceedings arising from separate arbitration agreements in the absence of all parties' consent.

[1] Arbitration Act 2010, s 16(1).

***Concurrent hearings*:** As there is no conjunction between parts (a) and (b) of sub-section (1),[1] it is unclear whether concurrent hearings can take place without consolidation of arbitral proceedings. This section is based on English arbitration legislation, which contains the conjunction 'or' between similar text with the express effect of expressly permitting either the consolidation of arbitral proceedings or the holding of concurrent hearings without consolidation.[2] While it is uncertain whether arbitral tribunals in Ireland will permit concurrent hearings without consolidation of arbitral proceedings, in practice, it is unlikely that the interpretation of this section will present a difficulty as the consent of all parties is required to either consolidate arbitral proceedings or to hold concurrent hearings.

[1] Arbitration Act 2010, s 16(1).
[2] The English Arbitration Act 1996, s 35.

17.—Reference of interpleader to arbitration

(1) Subject to subsection (2), where in legal proceedings relief by way of interpleader is granted by a court and it appears to the court that the issue between the claimants is one in respect of which there is an arbitration agreement between the claimants, the court shall direct that the issue between the claimants be determined in accordance with the agreement.

(2) A court shall not direct that the issue between the claimants referred to in subsection (1) be determined in accordance with the arbitration agreement concerned where the court finds that the arbitration agreement is null and void, inoperative or incapable of being performed.

(3) Where subsection (1) applies but the court does not direct that the issue be determined in accordance with the arbitration agreement, any provision that an award is a condition precedent to the bringing of legal proceedings in respect of any matter shall not affect the determination of that issue by the court.

Definitions

arbitration agreement': Arbitration Act 2010, s 2(1) and Model Law, Art 7(1) (Option I).

Notes

***Relief by way of interpleader*:** Interpleader is a civil process whereby a person in possession of property or owing money that is or may be claimed adversely by two or more persons (to one or other of whom alone he can be liable) is enabled, subject to certain conditions, to be relieved from liability to the claimants or either of them with regard to the disposition of property or money.[1] Relief by way of interpleader is given to two classes of persons:

1. Persons who are under liability for any debt, money, goods or chattels for or in respect of which they are, or expect to be, sued by two or more persons making adverse claims thereto;[2] and
2. Sheriffs and other officers charged with the execution of a process by or under the authority of the courts and a claim is made to any money, goods or chattels taken or intended to be taken in execution under the process.[3]

[1] *State (Murphy) v Deale* [1964] 1 IR 40.
[2] Rules of the Superior Courts, Ord 57, r 1(a).
[3] Rules of the Superior Courts, Ord 57, r 1(b).

***Interpleader and arbitration*:** This section supplements the Model Law and provides that where relief is sought by way of interpleader in a matter that is the subject of an arbitration agreement, a court must refer the matter to arbitration,[1] unless it finds that the arbitration agreement is null and void, inoperative or incapable of being performed.[2]

[1] Arbitration Act 2010, s 17(1).
[2] Arbitration Act 2010, s 17(2).

Interpleader and 'Scott v Avery clauses': A clause which provides that an award is a condition precedent to the right to bring a court action is known as a '*Scott v Avery* clause'.[1] Where relief by way of interpleader is sought and the court finds that the alleged arbitration agreement is null and void, inoperative or incapable of being performed, a *Scott v Avery* clause has no effect and a party will be permitted to commence civil proceedings notwithstanding the existence of the clause.[2]

---

[1] Named after the seminal case of *Scott v Avery* (1865) 5 HL Cas 811, which is a decision of the House of Lords (as it then was).
[2] Arbitration Act 2010, s 17(3).

18.—Interest

(1) The parties to an arbitration agreement may agree on the arbitral tribunal's powers regarding the award of interest.

(2) Unless otherwise agreed by the parties, the arbitral tribunal may award simple or compound interest from the dates, at the rates and with the rests that it considers fair and reasonable—

(a) on all or part of any amount awarded by the arbitral tribunal, in respect of any period up to the date of the award, or

(b) on all or part of any amount claimed in the arbitration and outstanding at the commencement of the arbitration but paid before the award was made, in respect of any period up to the date of payment.

(3) Unless otherwise agreed by the parties, the arbitral tribunal may award simple or compound interest from the date of the award (or any later date) until payment, at the rates and with the rests that it considers fair and reasonable, on the outstanding amount of any award (including any award of interest under subsection (2) and any award of costs).

(4) References in this section to an amount awarded by the arbitral tribunal include an amount payable in consequence of a declaratory award by the arbitral tribunal.

(5) This section is without prejudice to any other power of the arbitral tribunal to award interest.

Definitions

'arbitration': Arbitration Act 2010, s 2(1) and Model Law, Art 2(a); 'arbitration agreement': Arbitration Act 2010, s 2(1) and Model Law, Art 7(1) (Option I); 'arbitral tribunal': Model Law, Art 2(b); 'award': Arbitration Act 2010, s 2(1).

Notes

Power of arbitral tribunals to award interest under the Act: This section provides that the parties may agree on the power of an arbitral tribunal to award interest on any amount awarded.[1] In the absence of agreement, an arbitral tribunal has a broad discretion to

(*Continued*)

award simple or compound interest at the rate it considers fair and reasonable,[2] both for any period prior to the date of the award[3] and from the date of the award to the date of payment.[4] As the Model Law provides very limited grounds for setting aside an award it is difficult to see any basis for interference by the courts with this discretion.[5] Although the parties to an arbitration agreement may agree to modify or supplant an arbitral tribunal's power to award interest,[6] under a similar provision of English arbitration legislation[7] it has been held that express agreement is required to modify or supplant an arbitral tribunal's power to award interest and that an implied agreement to modify the power of an arbitral tribunal to award interest is insufficient.[8]

---

[1] Arbitration Act 2010, s 18(1). At common law, an arbitral tribunal was not permitted to award interest in the absence of express provision of such a power by the parties to an arbitration agreement. *London, Chatham & Dover Railway Co v South Eastern Railway Co* [1893] AC 429. The common law position was first amended by Arbitration Act 1954, s 34, which permitted an arbitral tribunal to award interest from the date of an award until the date of payment at a simple rate of interest equal to the judgment debt rate. However, no power was provided to permit an arbitral tribunal to award interest for any period prior to the date of an award. As Courts Act 1981, s 22 permitted the courts in civil proceedings to award interest from the date of an accrual of a cause of action to the date of judgment, the power of arbitral tribunals was incomplete. For example, in *McStay v Assicurazioni Generali SpA* [1991] ILRM 237, the Supreme Court held that an arbitral tribunal required express power to adjudicate on the question of a party's entitlement to interest in respect of the period prior to the award by virtue of the terms of the arbitration agreement and that Courts Act 1981, s 22 was not relevant in the context of arbitral proceedings. Consequently, Arbitration (International Commercial) Act 1998, s 17 permitted an arbitral tribunal to award simple or compound interest at the rate it considered met the justice of the case both for any period prior to the date of the award and from the date of the award to the date of payment.

[2] Arbitration Act 2010, s 18(2).

[3] Arbitration Act 2010, s 18(2)(a).

[4] Arbitration Act 2010, s 18(2)(b). However, under a similar provision of English arbitration legislation, it has been held that an arbitral tribunal cannot award interest for a period prior to the accrual of a cause of action. See *Durham County Council v Darlington Borough Council* [2003] EWHC 2598 (Admin), which is a decision of the English High Court.

[5] Similarly, case-law decided under English arbitration legislation, which provides for wider grounds for challenge of awards than under Model Law has held that an arbitral tribunal's discretion to award interest will not be lightly interfered with by the courts. See *AMEC Building Ltd v Cadmus Investment Co Ltd* (1996) 51 ConLR 105 which is a decision of the English High Court.

[6] Arbitration Act 2010, s 18(1).

[7] The English Arbitration Act 1996, s 49.

[8] See *Lesotho Highlands Development Authority v Impregilo SpA* [2006] 1 AC 221, where the House of Lords (as it then was) held that the parties' choice of the law of Lesotho, which did not permit the award of pre-award interest, as the governing law of an underlying contract was not an agreement sufficient to displace the arbitral tribunal's power to order pre-award interest. This decision is in contrast to the views of some commentators who state "[w]here parties to a contract have chosen (or are deemed to have chosen) as the substantive law of their agreement a law that prohibits the payment of interest, they can scarcely complain if interest is not payable". Blackaby, Partasides, Redfern and Hunter, *Redfern and Hunter on International Arbitration* (5th ed, Oxford University Press, Oxford, 2009) p 544.

***Declaratory judgments*:** Where an arbitral tribunal makes a declaration that a sum of money is owed by one party to another, it may also declare an award interest as if it were ordering the payment of a sum of money.[1] However, under a similar provision of English arbitration legislation,[2] it has been held that an arbitral tribunal may only award interest if the sum declared owing pre-dates the award. Interest cannot be ordered where the award itself gives rise to the liability.[3]

---

[1] Arbitration Act 2010, s 18(4).

[2] The English Arbitration Act 1996, s 49.

[3] *Durham County Council v Darlington Borough Council* [2003] EWHC 2598 (Admin), which is a decision of the English High Court.

***Arbitral tribunal's other powers to award interest*:** The provisions of the Act are in addition to, and not instead of, any other powers an arbitral tribunal may have to award interest. Other powers may include powers agreed by parties pursuant to contract; and the power to award interest under European Communities (Late Payment in Commercial Transactions) Regulations 2002.[1]

---

[1] European Communities (Late Payment in Commercial Transactions) Regulations 2002 (SI No 388 of 2002).

***Enforcing awards that carry interest in international commercial arbitrations*:** The award of interest is prohibited in some jurisdictions,[1] which may occasionally prevent the enforcement of awards that carry interest in international commercial arbitrations. However, as an arbitral tribunal are unlikely to know in advance where enforcement of an award will be sought, the fact that the award of interest is prohibited in certain jurisdictions should not prevent an arbitral tribunal from awarding interest. In this regard, commentators have noted that "in deciding whether or not to award interest, an arbitral tribunal cannot be expected to take into account the likely consequences of such an award in a potential place of enforcement, unless the point is expressly brought to its attention by one or both of the parties".[2]

---

[1] The law of some Middle Eastern States precludes the award of interest by either courts or arbitral tribunals. See Born, *International Commercial Arbitration* (1st ed, Kluwer Law International, Alphen aan den Rijn, 2009) p 2504, fn 460.

[2] Blackaby, Partasides, Redfern and Hunter, *Redfern and Hunter on International Arbitration* (5th ed, Oxford University Press, Oxford, 2009) p 544.

19.—Security for costs

(1) Without prejudice to the generality of Article 19, the arbitral tribunal may, unless otherwise agreed by the parties, order a party to provide security for the costs of the arbitration.

(2) A party shall not be ordered by an arbitral tribunal to provide security for the costs of the arbitration solely on the ground that the party is—

(a) an individual who is domiciled, habitually resident, or carrying on business outside the State, or

(b) a body corporate established under a law of a place other than the State or whose central management and control is situated outside the State.

Definitions

'arbitral tribunal': Model Law, Art 2(b); 'arbitration': Arbitration Act 2010, s 2(1) and Model Law, Art 2(a).

Notes

***Security for costs*:** The requirement that security for costs be provided balances the right of a party against whom legal proceedings are commenced to recover costs in the event that it successfully defends the claim against the right of a party commencing proceedings to vindicate its legal rights.[1] While the provision of security for costs protects parties against whom speculative claims are commenced, if ordered too readily it may also defeat meritorious claims. This section supplements the provisions of the Model Law and provides that an arbitral tribunal may order a party to provide security for costs of the arbitral proceedings.[2]

[1] For a discussion on security for costs in Irish civil proceedings, see Delany and McGrath, *Civil Procedure in the Superior Courts* (3rd ed, Round Hall Thomson Reuters, Dublin, 2012) pp 485-525.

[2] Arbitration Act 2010, s 19(1).

***Security for costs in arbitration*:** The Model Law provides that, unless the parties otherwise agree, an arbitral tribunal may only grant an interim measure to provide a means of preserving assets out of which a subsequent award may be satisfied.[1] However, this section supplements the Model Law and provides that, unless otherwise agreed by the parties, an arbitral tribunal may order that a party to provide security for costs of arbitral proceedings.[2] That an arbitral tribunal and not the High Court that may order a party to provide security for costs of arbitral proceedings[3] represents a change from the Arbitration Acts 1954-1998, which provided that only the High Court had power to order security for costs in respect of arbitral proceedings.[4] Commentators have noted that by providing an arbitral tribunal and not the High Court to order security for costs "puts in place the correct equilibrium, namely that the arbitral tribunal should have control of the process, particularly with something as important and as far-reaching as the ordering of security for costs. Satellite litigation in the High Court on such issues distorts the equilibrium".[5]

[1] Model Law, Art 17(2)(c).

[2] Arbitration Act 2010, s 19.

[3] Arbitration Act 2010, s 10(2).

[4] Arbitration Act 1954, s 22(1)(a).

[5] Reichert, "Security for Costs in Arbitration—A New Landscape in Ireland" (2010) *Arbitration and ADR Review*, p 130.

Circumstances where security for costs may be ordered in arbitral proceedings: In Irish civil proceedings security for costs may be ordered against individual parties who reside outside the European Union[1] or against corporate parties.[2] The High Court summarised the test under Irish law where an order for security for costs is sought as requiring the party seeking the order to establish that:

> "(a) [That it] has a *prima facie* defence to the plaintiff's claim, and (b) that the plaintiff will not be able to pay [its] costs if [it] be successful . . . In the event that the above two facts are established, then security ought to be required unless it can be shown that there are specific circumstances in the case with ought to cause the court to exercise its discretion not the make the order sought. In this regard the onus rests upon the party resisting the order. The most common examples of such special circumstances include cases where a plaintiff's liability to discharge the defendant's costs of successfully defending the action concerned flow from the wrong allegedly committed by the moving party or where there has been delay by the moving party in seeking the order sought. The list of special circumstances referred to is not of course, exhaustive".[3]

In arbitral proceedings, the Act clarifies that security for costs may not be ordered against a party solely because it resides outside the jurisdiction.[4] As no guidance is provided as to when security for costs may be ordered in arbitral proceedings arbitral tribunals enjoy a broad discretion to order security for costs on a case-by-case basis. However, while noting that "security for costs in arbitration is a rarity", commentators have identified the following principles which may assist an arbitral tribunal when determining whether to order security for costs against a party:

1. Where the party seeking an order for security for costs had concerns about the enforceability of claims against the other party at time the arbitration agreement was entered, security for costs should not be granted as the party should have ascertained the possibility of not recovering costs before entering the arbitration agreement;
2. Where the party seeking an order for security for costs did not have concerns about the enforceability of claims against the other party at time the arbitration agreement was entered, it must demonstrate sustainable evidence that the other party is now in a perilous financial position; and
3. Where the party seeking an order for security for costs demonstrates that the other party is now in a perilous financial position, broad factors to be examined by an arbitral tribunal include whether the party's perilous financial position was brought on by the actions of the party seeking an order for security for costs; the timing of the application; and some analysis of the merits of the claims; and the potential impact an order for security for costs might have on stifling a *bona fide* cause of action.[5]

Although security for costs may be ordered against any party to arbitral proceedings, in practice, it will typically be ordered against a claimant and will only be ordered against a respondent for the claimant's costs in defending any counterclaim pursed.[6]

---

[1] Rules of the Superior Courts, Ord 29.

[2] Companies Act 1963, s 390.

(*Continued*)

[3] *Connaughton Road Construction Ltd v Laing O'Rourke Ireland Ltd* [2009] IEHC 7. This test was approved by the High Court in context of the exercise of its power to order security for costs in arbitral proceedings commenced under the Arbitration Acts 1954-1998 in *Frank McGrath Construction Ltd v One Pery Square Hotel Ltd* [2010] IEHC 524.

[4] Arbitration Act 2010, s 19(2).

[5] See Reichert, "Security for Costs in Arbitration – A New Landscape in Ireland" (2010) *Arbitration and ADR Review* p 130.

[6] Dowling-Hussey and Dunne, *Arbitration Law* (1st ed, Thomson Round Hall, Dublin, 2008) p 257.

Non-mandatory nature of the section: This section is non-mandatory in nature and the parties may circumvent its effect by agreeing otherwise.

20.—Specific performance

Without prejudice to the generality of the Model Law, an arbitral tribunal shall, unless otherwise agreed by the parties, have the power to make an award requiring specific performance of a contract (other than a contract for the sale of land).

Definitions

'arbitral tribunal': Model Law, Art 2(b); 'award': Arbitration Act 2010, s 2(1); 'land'; Interpretation Act 2005, sch, pt 1; 'Model Law': Arbitration Act 2010, s 2(1).

Notes

Specific performance generally: Specific performance is a discretionary remedy by which a party to a contract is compelled to carry out his or her contractual obligations.[1] The traditional view is that specific performance will not be granted where damages are an adequate remedy.[2] Damages will not be an adequate remedy where the contractual obligation in question is in some way unique.[3] Like all equitable remedies, specific performance is granted only on a discretionary basis even where a plaintiff can demonstrate that there has been a breach of contract and that damages are not an adequate remedy.[4] Defences to an action for specific performance include: a lack of mutuality;[5] misrepresentation;[6] mistake;[7] delay;[8] illegality;[9] and impossibility.[10] An order for specific performance will not be ordered for contracts involving personal service;[11] contracts which require constant supervision;[12] and contracts that are too vague.[13]

This section, which is based on English arbitration legislation,[14] clarifies that the Model Law permits an arbitral tribunal to order specific performance of a contract, other than a contract for sale of land. This section is also similar to a provision of the Arbitration Acts 1954-1998, which permitted an arbitral tribunal to order specific performance of a contract, other than a contract relating to land or any interest in land.[15]

---

[1] For a general discussion on the doctrine of specific performance in Ireland, see Delaney, *Equity and the Law of Trusts in Ireland* (5th ed, Round Hall Thomson Reuters, Dublin, 2011) pp 653-699.

(*Continued*)

[2] *Wilson v Northampton and Banbury Junction Railway Co* (1874) 9 Ch App 279.
[3] *Keating v Bank of Ireland* [1983] 1 ILRM 295, where it was held that a purchaser of land would not be adequately compensated by damages and, therefore, could obtain an order for specific performance.
[4] *Murphy & anor v Ryan* [2009] IEHC 305.
[5] *O'Regan v White* [1919] 2 IR 339 at 393.
[6] *Smelter Corporation v O'Driscoll* [1977] IR 305.
[7] *Ferguson v Merchant Banking Ltd* [1993] 3 IR 382.
[8] *Guerin v Heffernan* [1925] 1 IR 57 at 68.
[9] *Starling Securities Ltd v Woods*, unreported, High Court (McWilliam J), 24 May 1977.
[10] *Aranbel Ltd v Darcy* [2010] 3 IR 769.
[11] *Ahmed v Health Service Executive* [2007] IEHC 312.
[12] *Co-Operative Insurance Society v Argyll Stores (Holdings) Ltd* [1998] AC 1. In an Irish context see the *Dakota Packaging Ltd v APH Manufacturing BV* [2005] 2 IR 54, where the High Court (Peart J), *obiter dicta*, refused to grant an order requiring business to be carried on.
[13] *Tito v Waddell (No 2)* [1977] Ch 106.
[14] English Arbitration Act 1996, s 48(5)(b).
[15] Arbitration Act 1954, s 26. For a discussion on the differences between Arbitration Act 2010, s 26 and Arbitration Act 1954, s 26, see Carrigan, "Arbitration act spells radical changes" (2010) *Law Society Gazette* (Nov) p 14.

***Specific performance of contracts for the sale of land*:** Notwithstanding that an arbitral tribunal may not grant specific performance of a contract for sale of land, where a contract for the sale of land contains an arbitration agreement, the matter must be referred to arbitration and civil proceedings may not be commenced or prosecuted. Although the arbitral tribunal will not be permitted to order specific performance it may order some other remedy *in lieu*.[1]

[1] *O'Dwyer v Boyd* [2002] IESC 54.

***Non-mandatory nature of the section*:** This section is non-mandatory in nature and the parties may circumvent its effect by agreeing otherwise.

21.—Recoverability of costs, fees and expenses of tribunal

(1) The parties to an arbitration agreement may make such provision as to the costs of the arbitration as they see fit.

(2) An agreement of the parties to arbitrate subject to the rules of an arbitral institution shall be deemed to be an agreement to abide by the rules of that institution as to the costs of the arbitration.

(3) Where no provision for costs is made as referred to in subsection (1) or where a consumer is not bound by an agreement as to costs pursuant to subsection (6), the arbitral tribunal shall, subject to subsection (4), determine by award those costs as it sees fit.

(4) In the case of an arbitration (other than an international commercial arbitration) the arbitral tribunal shall, on the request of any of the parties to the proceedings made not later than 21 working days after the determination by the tribunal in relation to costs, make an order for the

taxation of costs of the arbitration by a Taxing Master of the High Court, or as the case may be, the County Registrar; and the Taxing Master, or as the case may be, the County Registrar, shall in relation to any such taxation, have (with any necessary modifications) all the functions for the time being conferred on him or her under any enactment or in any rules of court in relation to the taxation of costs to be paid by one party to another in proceedings before a court.

(5) Where the arbitral tribunal makes a determination under subsection (3), it shall specify—

(a) the grounds on which it acted,

(b) the items of recoverable costs, fees or expenses, as appropriate, and the amount referable to each, and

(c) by and to whom they shall be paid.

(6) Without prejudice to the generality of the European Communities (Unfair Terms in Consumer Contracts) Regulations 1995 and 2000, an arbitration agreement—

(a) to which one of the parties to the agreement is a consumer, and

(b) a term of which provides that each party shall bear his or her own costs,

shall be deemed to be an unfair term for the purposes of those Regulations.

(7) Section 3 of the Legal Practitioners (Ireland) Act 1876 shall apply as if an arbitration were a proceeding in the High Court and the Court may make declarations and orders accordingly.

(8) In this section references to—

"costs" include costs as between the parties and the fees and expenses of the arbitral tribunal;

"fees and expenses of the arbitral tribunal" include the fees and expenses of any expert appointed by the tribunal.

Definitions

'arbitration': Arbitration Act 2010, s 2(1) and Model Law, Art 2(a); 'arbitration agreement': Arbitration Act 2010, s 2(1) and Model Law, Art 7(1) (Option I); 'arbitral tribunal': Model Law, Art 2(b); 'award': Arbitration Act 2010, s 2(1); 'consumer': Arbitration Act 2010, s 2(1); 'court': Model Law, Art 2(c); 'High Court': Interpretation Act 2005, sch, pt 1.

Notes

Recoverability of costs, fees and expenses: This section provides for the recoverability of parties' costs and fees and for the expenses of an arbitral tribunal. The parties to an arbitration agreement may make any provision for the costs of arbitral proceedings as they see fit,[1] subject to the proviso that where one party is a consumer any term that requires each party to bear its own costs is to be regarded as an unfair term and will not bind the

(*Continued*)

consumer.[2] Costs include the parties' legal fees, the fees and expenses of an arbitral tribunal and the fees and expenses of any experts appointed by the arbitral tribunal.[3]

The power of the parties to agree the basis upon which costs are awarded represents a change from the Arbitration Acts 1954-1998, which only permitted the parties to make any provision for costs they see fit in respect of an international commercial arbitration.[4] In respect of a domestic arbitration (which is any arbitration other than an international commercial arbitration), any term in an arbitration agreement, other than a submission agreement,[5] to the effect that a party be required to pay its own costs was void.[6]

---

[1] Arbitration Act 2010, s 21(1).
[2] Arbitration Act 2010, s 21(6).
[3] Arbitration Act 2010, s 21(8).
[4] Arbitration (International Commercial) Act 1998, s 11(1).
[5] Arbitration Act 1954, s 30(2).
[6] Arbitration Act 1954, s 30(1).

***Rules of arbitral institutions as to costs*:** Where arbitral proceedings are conducted under the rules of an arbitral institution, its rules on costs will apply.[1] Although the rules of most arbitration institutions consider the costs of an arbitral tribunal only,[2] some arbitration institutions rules consider the costs of both the arbitral tribunal and of the parties.[3] Typically, the rules of arbitral institutions provide arbitral tribunals with discretion to determine how the costs of arbitral proceedings be allocated.[4]

---

[1] Arbitration Act 2010, s 21(2).
[2] See, for example, the International Center for Dispute Resolution's International Arbitration Rules, Art 31; and the International Chamber of Commerce's Rules of Arbitration, Art 37.
[3] The London Court of International Arbitration's Arbitration Rules, Art 28.
[4] See, for example, the International Center for Dispute Resolution's International Arbitration Rules, Art 31; and the International Chamber of Commerce's Rules of Arbitration, Art 37. However, the London Court of International Arbitration's Arbitration Rules, Art 28, provides the arbitral tribunal with discretion but requires that the discretion be exercised "on the general principle that costs should reflect the parties' relative success and failure in the award or arbitration".

***Scope of an arbitral tribunal's discretion when awarding costs*:** In Irish civil proceedings the general rule is that the costs of every action, question or issue are to 'follow the event'.[1] This means that "the winning party is to obtain an order for costs to be paid by the other party, unless the court for special cause otherwise directs".[2] While exceptions to the general rule exist for challenges in the public interest, or in circumstances where there has been improper conduct by a party,[3] the burden of persuading the court to depart from the general rule is on the party arguing the costs should not follow the event.[4]

Case-law decided under the Arbitration Acts 1954-1980 has held that, notwithstanding the discretion afforded to an arbitral tribunal when determining an award of costs,[5] "[t] he usual order in arbitration [was] that costs follow the event . . . If there is a departure from the usual order then it should be clear and reasons should be given".[6] The 'event' in

(*Continued*)

arbitration is the outcome of the arbitral proceedings.[7] Under the Arbitration Acts 1954-1998 a failure to provide sufficient reasons for departing from the general rule could result in an award being remitted or set aside.[8] However, as the Model Law provides only limited grounds to set aside an award on its merits,[9] which includes an award on costs, it is likely that arbitral tribunals are no longer obliged to follow the general rules of Irish civil procedure when determining an award of costs. Although it remains likely that in the absence of improper conduct by a party most arbitral tribunals will continue to apply the general rule that costs follow the event, there should be no obligation to do so. Full discretion for an arbitral tribunal when awarding costs is consistent with best practice in international arbitration, as has been noted by commentators:

> "The practice of national courts in following their own rules in relation to awarding costs hardly seems to provide compelling guidelines for the way in which an international tribunal should exercise the discretion granted to it either by the relevant set of rules of by the *lex arbitri*. It is suggested that international tribunals, wherever the seat of arbitration, should be guided by the *lex arbitri* and the substantive laws as to the scope of its discretion, and by the applicable arbitration rules (if any) as to the exercise of that discretion".[10]

---

[1] Rules of the Superior Courts, Ord 99, r 1(3). In complex litigation where a number of relatively discreet issues may arise by way of interlocutory application during the course of proceedings, the 'event' is the issue which is determined by the interlocutory application. See *Veolia Water UK plc v Fingal County Council (No 2)* [2007] 2 IR 81.

[2] *Per* Morris P in *Cooper-Flynn v RTE* [2004] 2 IR 72 at 79.

[3] See Delany and McGrath, *Civil Procedure in the Superior Courts* (3rd ed, Round Hall Thomson Reuters, Dublin, 2012) pp 724-732.

[4] *Grimes v Punchestown Developments Co Ltd* [2002] 4 IR 515.

[5] Arbitration Act 1954, s 29(1).

[6] *Per* Denham J in *Horan v Quilter* [2004] 1 IR 431 at 442.

[7] Dowling-Hussey and Dunne, "Arbitration: The Award on Costs" (2009) *Irish Law Times,* p 316.

[8] *Office and Industrial Cleaners Ltd v John Paul Construction Ltd* [2008] IEHC 38.

[9] Model Law, Art 5 provides that "no court shall intervene except where so provided in this Law" and Model Law, Art 34(2)(b) provides only very limited grounds to set aside an award on its merits where "(i) the subject-matter of the dispute is not capable of settlement by arbitration under the law of this State or (ii) the award is in conflict with the public policy of this State".

[10] Blackaby, Partasides, Redfern and Hunter, *Redfern and Hunter on International Arbitration* (5th ed, Oxford University Press, Oxford, 2009) p 549.

Requirement to hear parties' submissions on costs: Despite the broad scope of the discretion afforded to an arbitral tribunal when determining an award of costs, fair procedures must be adhered to when exercising this discretion. Irish case-law decided pursuant to the Arbitration Acts 1954-1980 has held that an award on costs made in the absence of submissions from the parties would typically be remitted to the arbitral tribunal for reconsideration or would be set aside.[1] It is likely that the Irish courts would make a similar decision under the Model Law where an arbitral tribunal prevents a party from making submissions on costs.

---

[1] *Office and Industrial Cleaners Ltd v John Paul Construction Ltd* [2008] IEHC 38.

***Requirement for an arbitral tribunal to specify the grounds upon which it acted and to provide a detailed analysis of costs, fees and expenses*:** Where no provision on costs is made by the parties or where the parties' provision on costs is ineffective as one party is a consumer, an arbitral tribunal will have discretion to determine costs as part of the award.[1] However, notwithstanding this broad discretion where the arbitral tribunal makes a determination on costs it must specify:

1. The grounds on which it acted;[2]
2. The items of recoverable costs, fee and expenses;[3] and
3. By whom and to whom they shall be paid.[4]

These requirements are mandatory and the failure of an arbitral tribunal to specify the basis of its determination may lead to an award being set aside[5] or recognition of the award being refused.[6]

[1] Arbitration Act 2010, s 21(3).
[2] Arbitration Act 2010, s 21(5)(a).
[3] Arbitration Act 2010, s 21(5)(b).
[4] Arbitration Act 2010, s 21(5)(c).
[5] Model Law, Art 34(2)(a)(iv).
[6] Model Law, Art 36(1)(a)(iv); and the New York Convention, Art V(1)(d).

***Applicability of an agreement that each party shall bear own costs to consumers*:** Where one party to an arbitration agreement is a consumer any term that requires each party to bear its own costs is to be regarded as an unfair term and will not bind the consumer.[1] This is the case even where the term has been individually negotiated. However, a non-consumer continues to be bound by the term and a non-consumer cannot obtain an award of costs against a consumer where such a term is included in an arbitration agreement.[2]

[1] Arbitration Act 2010, s 21(6).
[2] European Communities (Unfair Terms in Consumer Contracts) Regulations 1995 (SI No 27 of 1995), reg 6(1) provides that "[a]n unfair term in a contract concluded with a consumer by a seller or supplier shall not be binding on the consumer".

***Taxation of costs in a domestic arbitration*:** In a domestic arbitration (which is any arbitration other than an international commercial arbitration), an arbitral tribunal must make an order for taxation of the costs by either a Taxing Master of the High Court or by a County Registrar, where requested to do so by any party within 21 working days after any determination by the arbitral tribunal in relation to costs.[1] This provision is mandatory in any instance where an arbitral tribunal makes a determination in relation to costs and it would seem that it may only be superseded by an agreement of the parties that removes in its entirety an arbitral tribunal's discretion to make a determination in relation to costs. No guidance is provided by the Act as to when an arbitral tribunal is to make an order for the taxation of costs by a Taxing Master or when an arbitral tribunal is to make an order

(*Continued*)

for the taxation of costs by a County Registrar.[2] However, while the Rules of the Superior Courts provide that a Taxing Master has power to tax "any costs which are the subject of an order made by an arbitral tribunal in accordance with section 21(4) of the Act for the taxation of the costs of the arbitration by a Taxing Master",[3] the Circuit Court Rules provide no comparative power to a County Registrar.[4] Therefore, it is suggested that any order for the taxation of costs made by an arbitral tribunal should be made to a Taxing Master, other than in the limited circumstances where an award is enforced by action in the Circuit Court.[5] Under the Arbitration Acts 1954-1998, the costs of an arbitration could be taxed by a Taxing Master of the High Court only.[6]

---

[1] Arbitration Act 2010, s 21(4). The Legal Services Regulation Bill 2011 proposes to replace the system of taxation of legal costs with adjudication of legal costs by a Chief Legal Costs Adjudicator.
[2] As the High Court is the court of competent jurisdiction under the Act and the Model Law, it seems more appropriate that the costs of arbitral proceedings be taxed by a Taxing Master of the High Court rather than by a County Register of the Circuit Court.
[3] Rules of the Superior Courts, Ord 99, r 14(b), as inserted by The Rules of the Superior Courts (Arbitration) Regulations 2010 (SI No 361 of 2010).
[4] Circuit Court Rules, Ord 18, r 6 provides that a County Registrar "shall have power, when directed by the Judge or empowered by these Rules, to tax all Bills of Costs".
[5] Arbitration Act 2010, s 23(1) provides that enforcement of awards may be sought either by action upon the award or by leave of the High Court. In practice, the overwhelming majority of awards are enforced by leave of the High Court.
[6] Arbitration Act 1954, s 29(2)(a).

Taxation of costs in an international arbitration: There is no provision for the taxation of costs in an international commercial arbitration.[1] Therefore, the costs of arbitral proceedings must be measured by an arbitral tribunal.[2]

---

[1] Arbitration Act 2010, s 21(4).
[2] Born, *International Commercial Arbitration* (1st ed, Kluwer Law International, Alphen aan den Rijn, 2009) p 2490.

Application of section 3 of the Legal Practitioners (Ireland) Act 1876 to arbitral proceedings: Section 3 of the Legal Practitioners (Ireland) Act 1876, which permits a court before which any proceeding has been heard or is pending to charge property recovered or preserved in the proceeding for the benefit of a party's solicitor until the payment of the solicitor's costs are discharged,[1] applies to arbitral proceedings.[2] There is no apparent defence to an application by a solicitor for a declaration that a charge exists pursuant to s 3 of the Legal Practitioners (Ireland) Act 1876 and the declaration sought should be made accordingly.[3] Application may be made to the High Court by way of originating notice of motion[4] or by notice of motion where an order in relation to the arbitral proceedings has been previously made by the High Court.[5]

---

[1] Legal Practitioners (Ireland) Act 1876, s 3 provides that: "[i]n every case in which an attorney or solicitor shall be employed to prosecute or defend any suit, matter, or proceeding in any court of justice, it shall be lawful for the court or judge before whom any such suit, matter, or proceeding

(*Continued*)

has been heard or shall be depending to declare such attorney or solicitor entitled to a charge upon the property recovered or preserved, and upon such declaration being made such attorney or solicitor shall have a charge upon and against and a right to payment out of the property, of whatsoever nature, tenure, or kind the same may be, which shall have been recovered or preserved through the instrumentality of any such attorney or solicitor, for the taxed costs, charges, and expenses of or in reference to such suit, matter, or proceeding; and it shall be lawful for such court or judge to make such order or orders for taxation of and for raising and payment of such costs, charges, and expenses out of the said property as to such court or judge shall appear just and proper; and all conveyances and acts done to defeat or which shall operate to defeat such charge or right shall, unless made to a bona fide purchaser for value without notice, be absolutely void and of no effect as against such charge or right: Provided always, that no such order shall be made by any such court or judge in any case in which the right to recover payment of such costs, charges, and expenses is barred by any Statute of Limitations".

[2] Arbitration Act 2010, s 21(7). A substantially identical provision existed at Arbitration Act 1954, s 32.

[3] For an example of the application of Legal Practitioners (Ireland) Act 1876, s 3 in the context of arbitral proceedings, see *J & G McGowan Roofing Contractors Ltd v Manley Construction Ltd* [2011] IEHC 317.

[4] Rules of the Superior Courts, Ord 56, r 3(1)(m).

[5] Rules of the Superior Courts, Ord 56, r 3(2).

22.—Restriction on liability of arbitrators, etc.

(1) An arbitrator shall not be liable in any proceedings for anything done or omitted in the discharge or purported discharge of his or her functions.

(2) Subsection (1) shall apply to an employee, agent or advisor of an arbitrator and to an expert appointed under Article 26, as it applies to the arbitrator.

(3) An arbitral or other institution or person designated or requested by the parties to appoint or nominate an arbitrator shall not be liable for anything done or omitted in the discharge or purported discharge of that function.

(4) An arbitral or other institution or person by whom an arbitrator is appointed or nominated shall not be liable for anything done or omitted by the arbitrator (or his or her employees or agents) in the discharge or purported discharge of his or her functions as arbitrator.

(5) Subsections (3) and (4) shall apply to an employee or agent of an arbitral or other institution or person as they apply to that arbitral or other institution or that person mentioned in those subsections.

Definitions

'functions': Interpretation Act 2005, sch, pt 2.

Notes

***Immunity of an arbitrator*:** This section extends the common law immunity of an arbitrator from liability for negligence[1] to a complete immunity from all civil liability.[2] This complete immunity also extends to persons engaged by arbitrators[3] and arbitral institutions.[4] The immunity applies even where an arbitrator or other person acts in 'bad faith'.[5] As a consequence of this immunity, an arbitrator or arbitral tribunal should not be joined as a party to any application to the High Court to fulfil its supervisory functions in connection with arbitral proceedings.[6]

---

[1] *Redahan v Minister for Education & Science* [2005] 3 IR 64. The rules of many arbitral institutions also provide an immunity from civil liability for arbitrators, persons engaged by arbitral tribunals and arbitral institutions. See, for example, the International Chamber of Commerce's Rules of Arbitration, Art 40 provides complete immunity for arbitral tribunals, the institution itself and its employees. The London Court of International Arbitration's Arbitration Rules, Art 31 provides a similar immunity as do the SIMI and Travel Schemes, Arts 18 operated by the Chartered Institute of Arbitrators — Irish Branch. The International Center for Dispute Resolution's International Arbitration Rules, Art 35 provides an immunity other than for "conscious and deliberate wrongdoing".

[2] Arbitration Act 2010, s 22(1).

[3] Arbitration Act 2010, s 22(2).

[4] Arbitration Act 2010, s 22(3).

[5] This was a matter of some debate in the Oireachtas. See Arbitration Bill 2008: Hearing before Select Committee on Justice, Equality, Defence and Women's Rights, Dáil Debate, 23 April 2009 (statement of Dermot Ahern, the then Minister for Justice, Equality and Law Reform). An immunity from suit where an arbitrator acts in bad faith has been criticised by some commentators. See Stewart, "Arbitration in 2010 and the Arbitration Bill 2008" (2010) *Arbitration and ADR Review* p 2. However, it has also been noted that the likelihood of an arbitrator acting in bad faith is "hopefully remote". See Carey, "Arbitrators' Immunity from Suit in the New Order" (2010) *Arbitration and ADR Review* p 206.

[6] *FBD Insurance plc v Connors* [2011] IEHC 184.

***Parties' immunity from civil liability for defamation*:** The parties to arbitral proceedings enjoy a defence of absolute privilege to a claim for defamation over statements made in the course of those arbitral proceedings where the statement is connected to those proceedings and, therefore, have an immunity from civil liability for defamation.[1]

---

[1] Defamation Act 2009, s 17(2)(v).

23.—Effect of award

(1) An award (other than an award within the meaning of section 25) made by an arbitral tribunal under an arbitration agreement shall be enforceable in the State either by action or, by leave of the High Court, in the same manner as a judgment or order of that Court with the same effect and where leave is given, judgment may be entered in terms of the award.

(2) An award that is referred to in subsection (1) shall, unless otherwise agreed by the parties, be treated as binding for all purposes on the parties between whom it was made, and may accordingly be relied on by any of those parties by way of defence, set-off or otherwise in any legal proceedings in the State.

(3) Nothing in this section shall be construed as affecting the recognition or enforcement of an award under the Geneva Convention, the New York Convention or the Washington Convention.

(4) Articles 35 and 36 shall not apply in respect of an award in arbitral proceedings which took place in the State.

Definitions

'arbitration agreement': Arbitration Act 2010, s 2(1) and Model Law, Art 7(1) (Option I); 'arbitral tribunal': Model Law, Art 2(b); 'award': Arbitration Act 2010, s 2(1); 'Geneva Convention': Arbitration Act 2010, s 2(1); 'High Court': Interpretation Act 2005, sch, pt 1; 'New York Convention': Arbitration Act 2010, s 2(1); 'Washington Convention': Arbitration Act 2010, s 2(1).

Notes

Enforcement of awards: This section provides for the enforcement of awards. Irrespective of whether arbitral proceedings have taken place in Ireland or have taken place outside Ireland,[1] where an unsuccessful party to arbitral proceedings does not meet its obligations under an award, the successful party may seek to enforce the award either:

1. As an independent cause of action,[2] arising from the breach of an implied term in the arbitration agreement that the award would be honoured;[3] or
2. By leave of the High Court.[4]

In practice, the overwhelming majority of awards are enforced by leave of the High Court rather than as an independent cause of action.

[1] Where arbitral proceedings have taken place outside the Ireland, enforcement may also be sought pursuant to the terms of the New York Convention or the Geneva Convention.

[2] Arbitration Act 2010, s 23(1).

[3] *Bremer Oeltransport GmbH v Drewry* [1933] 1 KB 753, which is a decision of the English Court of Appeal; and *Agromet Motoimport v Maulden Engineering Co (Beds) Ltd* [1985] 1 WLR 762, which is a decision of the English High Court (Queen's Bench Division). At common law, every contract that contained an arbitration agreement also contains an implied term that any award made pursuant to the arbitration agreement can be enforced by action. Arbitration Act 1954, s 27 merely gave statutory effect to this implied term. Although the Arbitration Act 1954 has been repealed, there is no reason to suspect that the common law implied term does not continue to exist.

[4] Arbitration Act 2010, s 23(1).

The procedure for enforcement by action: The procedure for enforcing an award by action depends on the nature of the relief sought. Where enforcement is sought for judgment in the amount of the award as a liquidated sum, an action may be commenced by summary summons.[1] Otherwise, an action must be commenced by plenary summons.[2] An action may be commenced in the District Court, the Circuit Court or the High Court

(*Continued*)

depending on the monetary value of the relief sought. Commentators have noted that in order to succeed in an action to enforce an award, a plaintiff is required to prove:

1. The arbitration agreement;
2. That the arbitrator was duly appointed in accordance with the terms of the arbitration agreement;
3. That the subject matter of the dispute between the parties was within the scope of the arbitration agreement;
4. The arbitration award; and
5. That the unsuccessful party has defaulted in the obligations imposed upon him by the arbitration award.[3]

[1] Rules of the Superior Courts, Ord 2, r 1(1).
[2] Rules of the Superior Courts, Ord 1, r 1.
[3] Dowling-Hussey & Dunne, *Arbitration Law* (1st ed, Round Hall, Dublin 2008) p 363.

***Procedure for enforcement by leave*:** Enforcement by leave of the High Court is sought by originating notice of motion[1] grounded upon affidavit, which must set out the basis upon which the moving party alleges that the High Court has jurisdiction to grant the relief sought in the notice of motion.[2] A respondent may deliver a replying affidavit within seven days of the service by the moving party of the originating notice of motion upon the said respondent.[3] Any replying affidavit must set out concisely the grounds relied upon by the respondent to resist the moving party's claim for the reliefs set out in the originating notice of motion.[4] The moving party is at liberty to file a further affidavit replying to any matter raised by a respondent in a replying affidavit within seven days after the service upon the moving party of the respondent's replying affidavit.[5]

Where leave to enforce is granted the High Court will enter a judgment 'in the terms of the award'.[6] Where enforcement of a partial award is sought there must be an order of an arbitral tribunal separately disposing of the partial award.[7]

[1] Rules of the Superior Courts, Ord. 56, r 3(1)(j).
[2] Rules of the Superior Courts, Ord. 56, r 6(2).
[3] Rules of the Superior Courts, Ord. 56, r 6(4).
[4] Rules of the Superior Courts, Ord. 56, r 6(5).
[5] Rules of the Superior Courts, Ord. 56, r 6(6).
[6] Arbitration Act 2010, s 23(1).
[7] *Danish Polish Telecommunication Group I/S v Telekomunikacja Polska SA* [2011] IEHC 369.

***Limitation period for enforcement of awards*:** The limitation period to enforce an award begins to run from the date of the failure to honour the award rather than from the date of the breach of the matrix contract, which had been the subject of the arbitration.[1] Enforcement must be commenced with six years from the date of the failure to honour the award.[2]

[1] *Agromet Motoimport v Maulden Engineering Co (Beds) Ltd* [1985] 1 WLR 762, which is a decision of the English High Court (Queen's Bench Division).
[2] Statute of Limitations 1957, s 11.

***Grounds for refusing recognition and enforcement of an award*:** At common law, certain grounds for refusing recognition and enforcement of an award existed as a result of the inherent jurisdiction of the courts, including:

1. That the award was made without, or in excess of, an arbitral tribunal's jurisdiction;
2. That the arbitral proceedings were conducted in the name of a wrong party;
3. That the arbitration agreement was not binding;
4. That the award was incomplete;
5. That the subject matter of the award is *res judicata*;
6. That enforcement of the award would be contrary to public policy; and
7. That the award was statute-barred.[1]

However, the Model Law provides that the national courts of a State adopting the Model Law are permitted to intervene in matters governed by the Model Law to fulfil certain supervisory functions only where they are expressly authorised to do so by the Model Law.[2] Commentators have noted that "[t]his means that unless the High Court has been accorded a specific role by the [Model Law], then it cannot intervene; inherent jurisdiction and other vestiges of the past are swept away".[3] As the Model Law sets out certain grounds for refusing recognition and enforcement of an award in arbitral proceedings it would appear that, despite the assertion of certain commentators to the contrary,[4] the common law grounds based on the inherent jurisdiction of the courts no longer exist.[5] However, these grounds for refusing recognition and enforcement of an award set out in the Model Law apply only where the place of arbitration is outside Ireland.[6] Therefore, where Ireland is the place of arbitration it would appear that no grounds whatsoever exist for refusing recognition and enforcement of an award and a party that is unhappy with an award made must apply to the High Court to set aside the award pursuant to the Model Law.[7] The rationale behind this approach is to prevent a party unhappy with an award from having two attempts to frustrate the successful party from enforcing an award, first, by applying to set aside the award and, where unsuccessful, by subsequently attempting to resist recognition and enforcement.

---

[1] See Dowling-Hussey and Dunne, *Arbitration Law* (1st ed, Round Hall, Dublin, 2008) pp 364-369. These grounds applied to awards made under the Arbitration Acts 1954-1998 notwithstanding that no grounds were specified for refusing recognition of awards.

[2] Model Law, Art 5.

[3] Reichert, "Security for Costs in Arbitration – A New Landscape in Ireland" (2010) *Arbitration and ADR Review*, p 130.

[4] Dowling-Hussey and Dunne, "Enforcement of Domestic Arbitral Awards After The Arbitration Act 2010: In with the New, Still with the Old" (2010) *Arbitration and ADR*, p 238.

[5] Model Law, Art 36. These grounds apply whether enforcement is sought by action or by leave of the High Court.

[6] Arbitration Act 2010, s 23(4).

[7] Model Law, Art 34.

***Power of High Court to evaluate foreign law in an application for enforcement of an award*:** Where called upon to evaluate foreign law in the context of an application for recognition and enforcement of an award the High Court will first decide whether even if every question of foreign law was decided in favour of a party resisting recognition and enforcement of an award, it would provide a basis for refusing enforcement of the award. Where the High Court decides that it would provide a basis, it will then have to hear the cross-examination of the foreign lawyers and decide whether as a matter of fact which party's experts are correct in their opinions as to the relevant legal questions. Where it decides to the contrary, then the matter is at an end as even with all of the foreign legal questions decided in favour a party, it would not provide a basis for refusing enforcement.[8]

[1] *Brostrom Tankers AB v Factorias Vulcano SA* [2004] 2 IR 191 which a decision of the High Court (Kelly J) concerning an application for enforcement of an award under the New York Convention. The same reasoning was adopted by the High Court (Finlay Geoghegan J) in the context of an application for enforcement under the Act and Model Law in *Danish Polish Telecommunication Group I/S v Telekomunikacja Polska SA* [2011] IEHC 369.

***Awards rendered pursuant to the Washington Convention*:** The pecuniary obligations imposed by an award rendered pursuant to the Washington Convention are enforceable by leave of the High Court in the same manner as a judgment or order of the High Court.[1] Any person who applies to the High Court for leave to enforce the pecuniary obligations imposed by an award must lodge with his or her application a copy of the award certified in accordance with Art 54(2) of the Washington Convention.[2] Where a stay of an enforcement of an award has been ordered in accordance with Arts 50, 51 or 52 of the Washington Convention, the High Court must stay enforcement of the pecuniary obligations imposed by the award where an application for leave to enforce is made.[3]

[1] Arbitration Act 2010, s 25(5).
[2] Arbitration Act 2010, s 25(6).
[3] Arbitration Act 2010, s 25(7).

24.—New York Convention, Geneva Convention and Geneva Protocol

(1) Subject to this Act—

(a) the New York Convention,

(b) the Geneva Convention, and

(c) the Geneva Protocol,

shall have the force of law in the State.

(2) Subject to this Act, Article II(2) and Article VII(1) of the New York Convention shall be interpreted in accordance with the recommendation adopted by the United Nations Commission on International Trade Law on 7 July 2006 at its thirty-ninth session concerning the interpretation of those Articles.

(3) Subject to this Act, Article II(3) of the New York Convention shall be construed in accordance with Article 8 of the Model Law.

(4) The Minister for Foreign Affairs may by order declare that any state specified in the order is a party to the New York Convention and, while such order is in force, the order shall be evidence that such state is a party to the Convention.

Definitions

'Geneva Convention': Arbitration Act 2010, s 2(1); 'Geneva Protocol': Arbitration Act 2010, s 2(1); 'Model Law': Arbitration Act 2010, s 2(1); 'New York Convention': Arbitration Act 2010, s 2(1).

Notes

***International conventions having the force of law in Ireland*:** Each of the New York Convention[1]; the Geneva Convention[2]; and the Geneva Protocol[3] have the force of law in Ireland.

---

[1] Arbitration Act 2010, s 24(1)(a). The text of the New York Convention is set out at Arbitration Act 2010, sch 2. As this work is concerned only with the Model Law in Ireland, detailed consideration of the New York Convention is outside the scope of this work.

[2] Arbitration Act 2010, s 24(1)(b). The text of the Geneva Convention is set out at Arbitration Act 2010, sch 4. As this work is concerned only with the Model Law in Ireland, detailed consideration of the Geneva Convention is outside the scope of this work.

[3] Arbitration Act 2010, s 24(1)(c). The text of the Geneva Protocol is set out at Arbitration Act 2010, sch 5. As this work is concerned only with the Model Law in Ireland, detailed consideration of the Geneva Protocol is outside the scope of this work.

***The Geneva Convention*:** The Geneva Convention was done on 26 September 1927 at Geneva to provide for the recognition and enforcement of foreign awards. There are currently 35 States which are parties to the Geneva Convention.[1] The Geneva Convention has been superseded by the New York Convention and it only applies where recognition and enforcement of an award made in arbitral proceedings in a non-New York Convention State is sought.

---

[1] Antigua and Barbuda, Austria, Bahamas, Bangladesh, Belgium, Croatia, Czech Republic, Denmark, Estonia, Finland, France, Germany, Greece, India, Ireland, Israel, Italy, Japan, Luxembourg, Malta, Mauritius, Montenegro, Netherlands, New Zealand, Portugal, Romania, Serbia, Slovakia, Spain, Sweden, Switzerland, Thailand, The former Yugoslav Republic of Macedonia, United Arab Emirates, United Kingdom of Great Britain and Northern Ireland.

***The Geneva Protocol*:** The Geneva Protocol was opened on 24 September 1923 at Geneva to provide for the recognition and enforcement of foreign awards. There are currently 41 States which are parties to the Geneva Protocol.[1] The Geneva Protocol has been superseded by the Geneva Convention and the New York Convention and it only

(*Continued*)

applies where recognition and enforcement of an award made in arbitral proceedings in a non-Geneva Convention/non-New York Convention State is sought.

[1] Albania, Antigua and Barbuda, Austria, Bahamas, Bangladesh, Belgium, Brazil, Croatia, Czech Republic, Denmark, Estonia, Finland, France, Germany, Greece, India, Iraq, Ireland, Israel, Italy, Japan, Luxembourg, Malta, Mauritius, Monaco, Montenegro, Netherlands, New Zealand, Norway, Poland, Portugal, Romania, Serbia, Slovakia, Spain, Sweden, Switzerland, Thailand, The former Yugoslav Republic of Macedonia, United Kingdom of Great Britain and Northern Ireland, Zimbabwe.

The New York Convention: The New York Convention was done on 10 June 1958 at New York and provides for the recognition and enforcement of foreign awards. There are currently 146 States which are parties to the New York Convention.[1] An up-to-date list of States which are parties to the New York Convention is kept by UNCITRAL.[2] The Minister for Foreign Affairs may declare by order that any State is a party to the New York Convention and any such order is evidence that the State is a party thereto.[3] No order has yet been promulgated under the Act. The most recent order enacted under the Arbitration Acts 1954-1998 was promulgated in 2000[4] and is now out-of-date.

[1] Afghanistan, Albania, Algeria, Antigua and Barbuda, Argentina, Armenia, Australia, Austria, Azerbaijan, Bahamas, Bahrain, Bangladesh, Barbados, Belarus, Belgium, Benin, Bolivia (Plurinational State of), Bosnia and Herzegovina, Botswana, Brazil, Brunei Darussalam, Bulgaria, Burkina Faso, Cambodia, Cameroon, Canada, Central African Republic, Chile, China, Colombia, Cook Islands, Costa Rica, Côte d'Ivoire, Croatia, Cuba, Cyprus, Czech Republic, Denmark, Djibouti, Dominica, Dominican Republic, Ecuador, Egypt, El Salvador, Estonia, Fiji, Finland, France, Gabon, Georgia, Germany, Ghana, Greece, Guatemala, Guinea, Haiti, Holy See, Honduras, Hungary, Iceland, India, Indonesia, Iran (Islamic Republic of), Ireland, Israel, Italy, Jamaica, Japan, Jordan, Kazakhstan, Kenya, Kuwait, Kyrgyzstan, Lao People's Democratic Republic, Latvia, Lebanon, Lesotho, Liberia, Liechtenstein, Lithuania, Luxembourg, Madagascar, Malaysia, Mali, Malta, Marshall Islands, Mauritania, Mauritius, Mexico, Monaco, Mongolia, Montenegro, Morocco, Mozambique, Nepal, Netherlands, New Zealand, Nicaragua, Niger, Nigeria, Norway, Oman, Pakistan, Panama, Paraguay, Peru, Philippines, Poland, Portugal, Qatar, Republic of Korea, Republic of Moldova, Romania, Russian Federation, Rwanda, Saint Vincent and the Grenadines, San Marino, Saudi Arabia, Senegal, Serbia, Singapore, Slovakia, Slovenia, South Africa, Spain, Sri Lanka, Sweden, Switzerland, Syrian Arab Republic, Thailand, The former Yugoslav Republic of Macedonia, Trinidad and Tobago, Tunisia, Turkey, Uganda, Ukraine, United Arab Emirates, United Kingdom of Great Britain and Northern Ireland, United Republic of Tanzania, United States of America, Uruguay, Uzbekistan, Venezuela (Bolivarian Republic of), Vietnam, Zambia, Zimbabwe.

[2] And is available at UNCITRAL's website: http://www.uncitral.org/uncitral/en/uncitral_texts/arbitration/NYConvention_status.html.

[3] Arbitration Act 2010, s 24(4).

[4] Arbitration Act, 1980 (New York Convention) Order, 2000 (SI No 41 of 2000).

Article II(2) of the New York Convention: Article II(2) of the New York Convention requires an arbitration agreement be in writing and provides that "[t]he term "agreement in writing" shall include an arbitral clause in a contract or an arbitration agreement, signed by the parties or contained in an exchange of letters or telegrams". Article II(2) is to be interpreted in accordance with the recommendation adopted by UNCITARAL on 7 July 2006,[1] which encourages States to recognise "that the circumstances described therein are not exhaustive" in an attempt to include within its definition arbitration agreements concluded or recorded by modern technology such as email. In addition, the recommendation adopted encourages States to adopt the revised Art 7 of the Model Law, which provides for arbitration agreements concluded or recorded by modern technology.[2]

[1] Arbitration Act 2010, s 24(2).
[2] http://www.uncitral.org/uncitral/uncitral_texts/arbitration/2006recommendation.html.

Article VII(1) of the New York Convention: Article VII(1) of the New York Convention concerns the continuing validity of other multilateral or bilateral arbitration treaties and provides that "[t]he provisions of the present Convention shall not affect the validity of multilateral or bilateral agreements concerning the recognition and enforcement of arbitral awards entered into by the Contracting States nor deprive any interested party of any right he may have to avail himself of an arbitral award in the manner and to the extent allowed by the law or the treaties of the country where such award is sought to be relied upon". Article VII(1) is to be interpreted in accordance with the recommendation adopted by UNCITARAL on 7 July 2006,[1] which clarifies that "any interested party" should be allowed "to avail itself of rights it may have, under the law or treaties of the country where an arbitration agreement is sought to be relied upon, to seek recognition of the validity of such an arbitration agreement".[2]

[1] Arbitration Act 2010, s 24(3).
[2] http://www.uncitral.org/uncitral/uncitral_texts/arbitration/2006recommendation.html.

25.—Non-application of provisions of Act to Washington Convention, save in certain circumstances

(1) This Act other than—

(a) sections 11, 14 and 15 , and

(b) section 6, in so far as it gives the force of law to Article 8(1) of the Model Law,

shall not apply to proceedings pursuant to the Washington Convention.

(2) In this section, "award" means an award rendered pursuant to the Washington Convention and includes any decision made—

(a) pursuant to Article 49(2) of that Convention in relation to any question which the Tribunal referred to in that Article had omitted to decide in the award, or in relation to the rectification of any clerical, arithmetical or similar error in the award,

(b) pursuant to Articles 50, 51 and 52 of that Convention, interpreting, revising or annulling the award, and

(c) pursuant to Article 61(2) of that Convention in relation to costs.

(3) Subject to this Act, the Washington Convention shall have the force of law in the State.

(4) The Minister for Finance may discharge any obligations of the Government arising under Article 17 of the Washington Convention and any sums required for this purpose; and any administrative expenses incurred by the Minister for Finance as a result of acceptance by the State of the Washington Convention shall be paid out of moneys provided by the Oireachtas.

(5) The pecuniary obligations imposed by an award shall, by leave of the High Court, be enforceable in the same manner as a judgment or order of the High Court to the same effect and, where leave is so given, judgment may be entered for the amount due or, as the case may be, the balance outstanding under the award.

(6) Any person who applies to the High Court under subsection (5) for leave to enforce the pecuniary obligations imposed by an award shall lodge with his or her application a copy of the award certified in accordance with Article 54(2) of the Washington Convention.

(7) Where an application is made to the High Court pursuant to subsection (5), the High Court shall, in any case where enforcement of an award has been stayed, whether provisionally or otherwise, in accordance with Articles 50, 51 or 52 of the Washington Convention, stay enforcement of the pecuniary obligations imposed by the award and may, in any case where an application has been made in accordance with any of those Articles which, if granted, might result in a stay on the enforcement of the award, stay enforcement of the pecuniary obligations imposed by the award.

Definitions

'Government': Interpretation Act 2005, sch, pt 1; 'High Court': Interpretation Act 2005, sch, pt 1; 'Oireachtas': Interpretation Act 2005, sch, pt 1; 'Model Law': Arbitration Act 2010, s 2(1); 'Washington Convention': Arbitration Act 2010, s 2(1).

Notes

The Washington Convention has the force of law: The Washington Convention was opened for signature on 18 March 1965 at Washington, DC and has the force of law in Ireland.[1] The Washington Convention established the International Centre for the Settlement of Investment Disputes (ICSID) and gives private individuals and corporations who are investors in a foreign State the right to bring legal proceedings against that foreign State before an international arbitral tribunal.

[1] Arbitration Act 2010, s 25(3). The text of the Washington Convention is set out at Arbitration Act 2010, sch 3. As this work is concerned only with the Model Law in Ireland, detailed consideration of the Washington Convention is outside the scope of this work.

Applicability of certain provisions of the Act to proceedings pursuant to the Washington Convention: As the Washington Convention is a self-contained international convention providing for its own rules, not all of the provisions of the Act are necessary for proceedings commenced under the Washington Convention. As such, only the following provisions of the Act apply to proceedings commenced pursuant to the Washington Convention:

1. Section 11, which provides that the determination of a court in any application to refer pending civil proceedings to arbitration pursuant to Art 8 of the Model Law or any determination by the High Court in relation to application to recognise or enforce an award pursuant to the Washington Convention is final;
2. Section 14, which provides that, unless otherwise agreed by the parties, an arbitral tribunal may direct that a party to an arbitration agreement or a witness give evidence on oath or affirmation;
3. Section 15, which provides that the rules concerning High Court assistance in the taking of evidence are applicable for arbitral proceedings which take place outside Ireland as well as an arbitration which take place in Ireland; and
4. Section 6 in so far as it adopts Art 8(1) of the Model Law for arbitral proceedings which take place in Ireland. Article 8(1) of the Model Law provides that a court before which an action is brought in a matter the subject matter of an arbitration agreement must, on request of a party, refer the dispute to arbitration.[1]

[1] Arbitration Act 2010, s 25(1).

Enforcement of pecuniary obligations pursuant to the Washington Convention: Enforcement of the pecuniary obligations of an award rendered pursuant to the Washington Convention may be sought by leave of the High Court. Where enforcement is granted, the pecuniary obligations of the award have effect as a judgment of the High Court.[1] Where an unsuccessful party does not meet its obligations under an award then the successful party may seek to enforce the award by leave of the High Court by originating notice of motion[2] grounded upon affidavit.[3] A respondent may deliver a replying affidavit within seven days of the service by the moving party of the originating notice of motion upon the said respondent.[4] Any replying affidavit must set out concisely the grounds relied upon by the respondent to resist the moving party's claim for the reliefs set out in the originating notice of motion.[5] The moving party is at liberty to file a further affidavit replying to any matter raised by a respondent in a replying affidavit within seven days after the service upon the moving party of the respondent's replying affidavit.[6] A copy of the award must be lodged with the application to enforce its pecuniary obligations.[7] Any person who applies to the High Court for leave to enforce the pecuniary obligations imposed by an award must lodge with his or her application a copy of the award certified in accordance with Art 54(2) of the Washington Convention.[8] Where a stay of an enforcement of an award has been ordered in accordance with Arts 50, 51 or 52

(*Continued*)

of the Washington Convention, the High Court must stay enforcement of the pecuniary obligations imposed by the award where an application for leave to enforce is made.[9]

[1] Arbitration Act 2010, s 25(5).
[2] Rules of the Superior Courts, Ord 56, r 3(1)(l).
[3] Rules of the Superior Courts, Ord 56, r 6(2).
[4] Rules of the Superior Courts, Ord 56, r 6(4).
[5] Rules of the Superior Courts, Ord 56, r 6(5).
[6] Rules of the Superior Courts, Ord 56, r 6(6).
[7] Arbitration Act 2010, s 25(6).
[8] Arbitration Act 2010, s 25(6).
[9] Arbitration Act 2010, s 25(7).

26.—Survival of agreement and authority of arbitral tribunal in event of death

(1) An arbitration agreement shall not be discharged by the death of any party thereto, either as respects the deceased or any other party, but shall in such an event be enforceable by or against the personal representatives of the deceased.

(2) The authority of an arbitral tribunal shall not be revoked by the death of any party by whom he or she was appointed.

(3) Nothing in this section shall affect the operation of any enactment or rule of law by virtue of which any right of action is extinguished by the death of a person.

Definitions

'arbitration agreement': Arbitration Act 2010, s 2(1) and Model Law, Art 7(1) (Option I); 'arbitral tribunal': Model Law, Art 2(b).

Notes

Survival of an arbitration agreement upon death of a party: This section provides that an arbitration agreement survives the death of a party and is enforceable by, or against, the personal representative of the deceased,[1] subject to any other rule of law by which a right of action is extinguished by the death of person. A similar provision existed under the Arbitration Acts 1954-1998.[2] However, while the death of a party may have no effect on the commencement or continuation of arbitral proceedings, in practical terms it is likely that pending arbitral proceedings will be adjourned upon the death of a party to permit the personal representative of the deceased to evaluate the benefit of continuing to prosecute or defend the arbitral proceedings. Commentators have noted that:

> "In the event that one of the parties to the arbitration dies there will not necessarily be any practical effect on the course of the arbitration at all. It may be appropriate to adjourn the reference for an agreed period but

(*Continued*)

the party who passed away remains perfectly entitled through their legal personal representatives to make their claim or to defend an action taken against them. Though there is no legal bar on a party who is personal representative of a deceased claimant from pursuing the action, it could be the case that they will not wish to do so. The personal representatives of the claimant will have to consider the value of the claim, likelihood for success and potential liability for costs and consider whether it is the best interests of the estate to proceed".[3]

[1] Arbitration Act 2010, s 26(1).
[2] Arbitration Act 1954, s 10.
[3] Dowling-Hussey and Dunne, *Arbitration Law* (1st ed, Thomson Round Hall, Dublin, 2008) pp 160-161.

***No revocation of an arbitral tribunal's authority by the death of a party or a third party*:** Where an arbitral tribunal is appointed by a third party such as the president of arbitral institution, it is not specified whether the authority of the arbitral tribunal is revoked by the death of the third party. However, a pragmatic interpretation of the section suggests that an arbitral tribunal's authority will not be revoked in those circumstances. A similar provision under English arbitration legislation uses the term 'person' rather than 'party' in order to clarify that the appointment of an arbitral tribunal by a third party will not be revoked by the death of the third party.[1]

[1] The English Arbitration Act 1996, s 26(2).

Rules of law by which a right of action is extinguished by the death of person: Under Irish law, the only rights of action that are extinguished by the death of a person are breach of promise to marry; defamation; seduction or for inducing one spouse to leave or remain apart from the other; criminal conversation;[1] and claims for compensation under the Workmen's Compensation Act 1934.[2] All other rights of action survive for the benefit of,[3] and subsist against,[4] the estate of a deceased person. Actions against the estate of a deceased person must be commenced within the relevant limitation period for the cause of action or within the period of two years after his death, whichever period first expires.[5]

[1] Civil Liability Act 1961, s 6(a).
[2] *ibid*, s 6(b).
[3] *ibid*, s 7(1).
[4] *ibid*, s 8(1).
[5] *ibid*, s 9(2)(b).

***Mandatory nature of the section*:** This section is mandatory in nature and the parties may not circumvent its effect by agreeing otherwise.

27.—Provisions in event of bankruptcy

(1) Where an arbitration agreement forms part of a contract to which a bankrupt is a party, the agreement shall, if the assignee or trustee in bankruptcy does not disclaim the contract, be enforceable by or against him or her insofar as it relates to any dispute arising out of, or in connection with, such a contract.

(2) Where—

(a) a person who has been adjudicated bankrupt had, before the commencement of the bankruptcy, become a party to an arbitration agreement, and

(b) any matter to which the agreement applies requires to be determined in connection with or for the purposes of the bankruptcy proceedings, and

(c) the case is one to which subsection (1) does not apply,

then, any other party to the agreement or the assignee or, with the consent of the committee of inspection, the trustee in bankruptcy, may apply to the court having jurisdiction in the bankruptcy proceedings for an order directing that the matter in question shall be referred to arbitration in accordance with the agreement and that court may, if it is of the opinion that having regard to all the circumstances of the case, the matter ought to be determined by arbitration, make an order accordingly.

(3) In this section "assignee" means the Official Assignee in Bankruptcy.

Definitions

'arbitration': Arbitration Act 2010, s 2(1) and Model Law, Art 2(a); 'arbitration agreement': Arbitration Act 2010, s 2(1) and Model Law, Art 7(1) (Option I); 'court': Model Law, Art 2(c).

Notes

Disclaimer of contracts in bankruptcy: Where a person is adjudicated bankrupt, his or her property, including contracts entered into before bankruptcy, vests in either the Official Assignee[1] (who is a full-time officer of the High Court)[2] or a trustee in bankruptcy chosen by the bankrupt's creditors.[3] In practice, a trustee in bankruptcy is rarely appointed.[4] Following appointment, an Official Assignee must attempt to realise the property vested for the benefit of the bankrupt's creditors. However, where property is onerous or unprofitable its realisation may not benefit the creditors and the Official Assignee[5] may instead apply to the court with jurisdiction in the bankruptcy proceedings to disclaim the property. Where the Official Assignee applies to disclaim a contract, the court will determine whether the contract is to be disclaimed or not having regard the circumstances of the case.[6] Where the Official Assignee does not disclaim a contract, it is enforceable by or against the Official Assignee.

This section provides that matrix contracts containing arbitration agreements are to be treated like any other contract in the event of a party's bankruptcy.[7] Where an Official Assignee does not disclaim a contract, it continues to be enforceable by or against the

(*Continued*)

Official Assignee.[8] Where an Official Assignee disclaims the matrix contract containing the arbitration agreement, in the event that a matter arises which requires determination in connection with the bankruptcy proceedings, any party to the arbitration agreement or the Official Assignee may apply to the court with jurisdiction in the bankruptcy proceedings for an order referring a matter to arbitration.[9] In determining whether to refer the matter to arbitration, the court should have regard to all the circumstances of a case.[10]

---

[1] Bankruptcy Act 1988, s 44(1).

[2] Court (Supplemental Provisions) Act 1961, sch 8, para 9.

[3] Bankruptcy Act 1988, s 111.

[4] See Sanfey & Holohan, *Bankruptcy Law and Practice* (2nd ed, Round Hall, Dublin, 2010) at p 110 where it is stated that "in the 100 years since their introduction, the [trustee in bankruptcy procedures] have been used a handful of times, and that in recent years they have been ignored".

[5] Bankruptcy Act 1988, s 56(1).

[6] For a general discussion on disclaimer of contracts in bankruptcy, see Forde & Simms, *Bankruptcy Law* (1st ed, Round Hall, Dublin, 2009) pp 111-114.

[7] Arbitration Act 2010, s 27(1). A similar provision existed at Arbitration Act 1954, s 11.

[8] Arbitration Act 2010, s 27(1).

[9] Arbitration Act 2010, s 27(2).

[10] *ibid.*

Disclaimer of contracts containing arbitration agreements in corporate insolvency: The Act only provides for the disclaimer of a matrix contract containing an arbitration agreement in bankruptcy and does not provide for the effect of a corporate party's insolvency on a contract containing an arbitration agreement. However, the provisions of the Companies Acts 1963-2009 provide, *inter alia*, that a liquidator may apply to disclaim onerous property in a winding up[1] and provide that an examiner may repudiate certain contracts in an examinership.[2] It must be noted that neither provision makes specific reference to a matrix contract containing an arbitration agreement.

---

[1] Companies Act 1963, s 290.

[2] Companies (Amendment) Act 1990, s 20.

28.—Full applicability to State parties

This Act shall apply to an arbitration under an arbitration agreement to which a State authority is a party.

Definitions

'arbitration': Arbitration Act 2010, s 2(1) and Model Law, Art 2(a); 'arbitration agreement': Arbitration Act 2010, s 2(1) and Model Law, Art 7(1) (Option I); 'State authority': Arbitration Act 2010, s 2(1).

Notes

***Definition of State authority*:** This section provides that the Act applies to an arbitration agreement that a State authority is a party to.[1] The Act gives 'State authority' a wide definition[2] and includes "a body established by or under any enactment, and financed wholly or partly, whether directly or indirectly, by moneys provided, or loans made or guaranteed, by a Minister of the Government or the issue of shares held by or on behalf of any Minister of the Government". This provision was not included in the Arbitration Acts 1954-1998 and has the effect of specifying that State-sponsored bodies fall within the definition of 'State authority'.

[1] Arbitration Act 2010, s 28.
[2] Arbitration Act 2010, s 2(1).

***No State prerogative or immunity from suit*:** The State of Ireland is a juristic person, which is liable vicariously for the acts of its servants or agents. The former royal prerogative of immunity from suit from its citizens, which existed under Irish law prior to independence did not survive the enactment of the Constitution of the Irish Free State 1922 and has not been vested or continued by the Constitution of Ireland 1937.[1]

[1] *Byrne v Ireland* [1972] 1 IR 241.

29.—Application of Act to arbitrations under other Acts

(1) This Act, other than the excluded provisions, shall apply to every arbitration under any other Act as if the arbitration were pursuant to an arbitration agreement and as if that other Act were an arbitration agreement, except in so far as this Act is inconsistent with that other Act or with any rules or procedure authorised or recognised under that other Act.

(2) The enactments specified in column (2) of Schedule 6 are amended to the extent specified in that Schedule.

(3) In subsection (3) of section 496 of the Merchant Shipping Act 1894, the reference to legal proceedings shall be construed as including a reference to arbitration.

(4) In this section, "excluded provisions" means subsections (2) and (3), subsection (3) of section 8, sections 17, 26, 27, 30 and 31 and Articles 12 and 13.

Definitions

'arbitration': Arbitration Act 2010, s 2(1) and Model Law, Art 2(a); 'arbitration agreement': Arbitration Act 2010, s 2(1) and Model Law, Art 7(1) (Option I).

Notes

***Arbitrations under other Irish legislation*:** Where Irish legislation other than the Act provides for the compulsory resolution of a dispute by arbitration it is known as a 'statutory arbitration'. A statutory arbitration is not really an arbitration at all as it is not premised on the consensual agreement of the parties to submit a dispute to arbitration, which is a fundamental feature of arbitration. Instead, the legislation merely requires a dispute arising over a right created under the legislation to be resolved by a tribunal other than the courts and that process is labelled 'arbitration'.[1] This section expressly provides that the provisions of the Act, other than certain excluded provisions, apply to statutory arbitrations. Commentators have identified the following non-exhaustive list of Irish legislation providing for statutory arbitration:

"• Wildlife Act 1976 and the Wildlife (Amendment) Act 2000;
- Derelict Sites Act 1990;
- National Lottery Act 1986;
- Bankruptcy Act 1988;
- Patents Act 1992;
- Merchant Shipping (Salvage and Wreck) Act 1993;
- Statistics Act 1993;
- Roads Act 1993;
- Dublin Docklands and Development Authority Act 1997;
- Credit Union Act 1997;
- Universities Act 1997;
- Air Navigation and Transport (Amendment) Act 1998;
- Copyright Act 2000 [*sic*];
- Transport (Railway Infrastructure) Act 2001;
- Industrial Designs Act 2001;
- Communication Regulation Act 2002;
- Broadcasting (Major Events Television Coverage)(Amendment) Act 2005".[2]

---

[1] Interestingly, the *travaux préparatoires* (of which Irish courts are permitted to take judicial notice when interpreting provisions of the Model Law) suggest that only 'consensual arbitration' based on the agreement of the parties should fall within the scope of the Model Law. UNCITRAL First Working Group Report, A/CN.9/216, para 17.

[2] Dowling-Hussey and Dunne, *Arbitration Law* (1st ed, Thomson Round Hall, Dublin, 2008) p 55.

***Excluded provisions*:** Although the Act generally applies to statutory arbitrations, the following excluded provisions do not apply:

1. Section 8(3), which enshrines the principle of competence-competence and provides that where the parties have an arbitration agreement any disputes as to the validity of the arbitration agreement must be submitted to arbitration;
2. Section 29(2), which provides for certain amendments to existing legislation consequential on the enactment of the Act;
3. Section 29(3), which provides that the reference to 'legal proceedings' in Merchant Shipping Act 1894, s 496(3) includes arbitral proceedings;
4. Section 30, which provides that the provisions of the Act are not applicable to arbitration agreements in relation to employment disputes and trade disputes and which also provides that s 18 of the Act does not apply to an arbitration conducted by a property arbitrator under s 2 of the Property Values (Arbitration and Appeals) Act 1960;
5. Section 31, which provides that a consumer is not bound by an arbitration agreement where the value of the claim is less than €5,000, unless the term in the contract containing the arbitration agreement has been individually negotiated;
6. Article 12 of the Model Law, which provides that an arbitrator must disclose any circumstances likely to give rise to justifiable doubts to his impartiality or independence; and
7. Article 13 of the Model Law, which provides for a challenge procedure if a party to arbitral proceedings believes that justifiable doubts to an arbitrator's impartiality or independence exist.[1]

[1] Arbitration Act 2010, s 29(4).

***Consequential amendments to other legislation*:** The following legislation has been amended as a consequence of the enactment of the Act:

1. Section 77 of the Statute of Limitations 1957 has been amended with the deletion of "or orders, after the commencement of an arbitration, that the arbitration shall cease to have effect with respect to the dispute referred". It now reads:

   > "—Where the Court orders that an award be set aside, the Court may further order that the period between the commencement of the arbitration and the date of the order of the Court shall be excluded in computing the time fixed by this Act or any other limitation enactment for the commencement of proceedings (including arbitration) with respect to the dispute referred."

2. Section 17 of the Landlord and Tenant (Ground Rents) Act 1967 has been amended with the substitution of "Sections 21 and 23 of the Arbitration Act 2010

(*Continued*)

(and Articles 13 and 14 of the Model Law (within the meaning of the Arbitration Act 2010) as given the force of law in the State by that Act" for "Sections 29, 35, 36, 37 and 41 of the Arbitration Act, 1954". It now reads:

"—(1) If any dispute, question or difficulty arises in regard to the acquisition of the fee simple or any other interest in land under this Act, the purchase price thereof, the apportionment of such purchase money payable in respect of such acquisition or of a rent under or for the purposes of this Act, costs or expenses incurred under this Act, compliance by a person with a provision of this Act or any other matter arising under this Act (other than sections 25 to 30 of this Act), any person concerned may apply to the county registrar for the area in which the land to which the application relates is situate to have the matter determined by his arbitration and the county registrar shall make such award as justice shall require.

(2) Without prejudice to the generality of subsection (1) of this section, a county registrar may, in an arbitration under this Act, make an award in relation to land—

(a) determining the person (if any) entitled to acquire the fee simple therein under this Act,

(b) determining the purchase price to be paid in respect of the acquisition,

(c) determining the person or persons entitled to receive the purchase money in respect of the acquisition and the amount which each person is entitled to receive,

(d) determining if a person is entitled to have a rent apportioned under section 5 or 11 of this Act, and

(e) apportioning (whether under the said section 5 or 11 or otherwise for the purposes of this Act) any rent payable in respect of land part of which is land the fee simple in which is being acquired under this Act.

(3) A county registrar shall have, for the purpose of and in relation to an arbitration under this Act, the same power of making orders in respect of—

(a) security for costs,

(b) discovery and inspection of documents and interrogatories,

(c) the giving of evidence by affidavit,

(d) examination on oath of any witness,

(*Continued*)

as the Court has for the purpose of and in relation to any action or matter in that court.

(4) Whenever it appears to a county registrar for any county that he cannot properly deal with a matter falling to be determined by his arbitration under this Act by reason of the fact that he has a personal interest therein or such personal knowledge of the facts or of the parties as might prejudice his determination of the matter, he shall nominate the county registrar for an adjoining county to hear and determine the matter and, upon such nomination, the matter may be heard and determined accordingly.

(5) Sections 21 and 23 of the Arbitration Act 2010 (and Articles 13 and 14 of the Model Law (within the meaning of the Arbitration Act 2010) as given the force of law in the State by that Act shall not apply in relation to an arbitration under this Act."

3. Section 74 of the Patents Act 1992 has been amended with the deletion of "section 35 of the Arbitration Act 1954 (which relates to the statement of cases by arbitrators for the decision of the Court), shall not apply to the arbitration; but". It now reads:

"—(1) On any appeal from any order made by the Controller in pursuance of an application under section 70 or 72 the Attorney General shall be entitled to appear and be represented.

(2) Where an application is opposed and either—

(a) the parties consent; or

(b) the proceedings require a prolonged examination of documents or any scientific or local investigation which cannot, in the opinion of the Controller, conveniently be made before him,

the Controller may at any time order the whole proceedings, or any question or issue of fact arising therein, to be referred to an arbitrator agreed on by the parties, or, in default of agreement, appointed by the Controller.

(3) Where the whole proceedings are referred under this section, unless the parties otherwise agree before the award of the arbitrator is made, an appeal to the Court shall lie from the award.

(4) Where a question or issue of fact is referred under this section, the arbitrator shall report his findings to the Controller."

4. Section 367 of the Copyright and Related Rights Act 2000 has been amended with the substitution of "request the court under section 9 of the Arbitration Act 2010 to decide on the termination of the mandate of that arbitrator" for "apply to the court

(*Continued*)

for the removal of that arbitrator under section 24 of the Arbitration Act, 1954,". It now reads:

"—(1) In the case of a dispute referred to the Controller under this Act, the Controller may at any time—

(a) where the parties to the dispute consent, or

(b) where a matter requires any prolonged examination of documents or other investigation requiring specialist knowledge which could not be made by him or her,

order the matter to be referred to an arbitrator agreed by the parties or, in the absence of such agreement, appointed by the Controller.

(2) The Controller shall decide whether or not to refer a dispute to arbitration no later than 3 months after the dispute has been referred to the Controller.

(3) The arbitrator shall make his or her award within 3 months of the reference from the Controller, or within such further period of time as may be agreed with the Controller.

(4) The award made by an arbitrator in a case referred to him or her under this section shall, where the parties consent to the reference, be final and binding on the parties.

(5) An appeal from an award made by an arbitrator pursuant to a reference under this section to which the parties to the dispute did not consent shall lie to the High Court and the High Court may make such order confirming, annulling or varying the award of the arbitrator as it thinks fit.

(6) Subject to subsection (7), a decision of the High Court under this section shall be final and may not be appealed.

(7) By leave of the High Court, an appeal from a decision of the High Court under this section shall lie to the Supreme Court on a question of law.

(8) In any reference to an arbitrator under this section, the Controller on giving notice to the parties to the dispute shall have the same power to request the court under section 9 of the Arbitration Act 2010 to decide on the termination of the mandate of that arbitrator, as if he or she had been a party to the arbitration.

(9) Nothing in subsection (8) shall affect the rights of the parties to the arbitration.

(10) For the avoidance of doubt, in the event of an arbitrator being removed under subsection (8), a second or subsequent arbitrator may be appointed to arbitrate the dispute in accordance with this section."

30.—Exclusion of certain arbitrations

(1) This Act shall not apply to—

(a) an arbitration under an arbitration agreement providing for the reference to, or the settlement by, arbitration of any question relating to the terms or conditions of employment or the remuneration of any employees, including persons employed by or under the State or local authorities, or

(b) an arbitration under section 70 of the Industrial Relations Act 1946.

(2) Section 18 shall not apply to an arbitration conducted by a property arbitrator appointed under section 2 of the Property Values (Arbitration and Appeals) Act 1960.

Definitions

'arbitration': Arbitration Act 2010, s 2(1) and Model Law, Art 2(a); 'arbitration agreement': Arbitration Act 2010, s 2(1) and Model Law, Art 7(1) (Option I).

Notes

Non-application of the Act to certain arbitrations: This section provides that the Act has no application to an arbitration agreement relating to an employment dispute[1] and has no application to an arbitration concerning 'trade disputes' under s 70 of the Industrial Relations Act 1946.[2] Although the Act does not apply, a 'private' arbitration may still be conducted outside the remit of the Act and the High Court has an inherent jurisdiction to refer pending civil proceedings to arbitration where an arbitration agreement exists, notwithstanding that the Act, and consequently the Model Law, do not apply.[3] In the event that a private arbitration is conducted, any award made must be enforced by action.[4]

---

[1] Arbitration Act 2010, s 30(1)(a).

[2] Arbitration Act 2010, s 30(1)(b).

[3] *Re Via Net Works (Ireland) Ltd* [2002] 2 IR 47, where the Supreme Court (Keane CJ) cited with approval a passage from the House of Lords' (as it then was) decision in *Channel Group v Balfour Beatty Ltd* [1993] AC 334 which stated: "that those who make agreements for the resolution of disputes must show good reasons for departing from them, but also with the interests of the orderly regulation of international commerce, that having promised to take their complaints to the experts and if necessary to the arbitrators, that is where the appellants should go". However, where Model Law applies, the courts have no inherent jurisdiction to act. In this regard, the Model Law, Art 5 provides that "[i]n matters governed by this Law, no court shall intervene except where so provided in this Law".

[4] For a discussion of arbitration of employment disputes see Stewart, *Arbitration: Commentary and Sources* (1st ed, First Law, Dublin, 2003) pp 251-261.

Definition of "relating to the terms or conditions of employment" and of a "trade dispute": Although there is no Irish case-law on what is meant by the term "relating to the terms and conditions of employment", commentators have noted that it should be given a wide interpretation.[1]

Section 70 of the Industrial Relations Act 1946 provides that where a "trade dispute" occurs or is apprehended, the court in which the dispute is pending, with the consent of all the parties concerned, may refer the dispute to arbitration. The term "trade dispute' means any dispute or difference between employers and workers or between workers and workers connected with the employment or non-employment, or the terms of the employment, or with the conditions of employment, of any person.[2]

---

[1] Forde, *Arbitration Law and Practice* (1st ed, Round Hall, Dublin, 1994) pp 18-19; and Dowling-Hussey and Dunne, *Arbitration Law* (1st ed, Thomson Round Hall, Dublin, 2008) pp 51-52.
[2] Industrial Relations Act 1946, s 3.

Arbitrations conducted by a property arbitrator: The Property Values (Arbitration and Appeals) Act 1960 permits the appointment of property arbitrators to value lands compulsorily purchased under certain legislation.[1] This section provides that s 18 of the Act does not apply to an arbitration conducted under the Property Values (Arbitration and Appeals) Act 1960.[2] However, all other provisions of the Act continue to apply.

---

[1] The Finance (1909-10) Act 1910; the Acquisition of Land (Assessment of Compensation) Act 1919; and the Arterial Drainage Act 1945.
[2] Arbitration Act 2010, s 30(2).

31.—Arbitration agreements and small claims, etc.

(1) Subject to subsection (2), a party to an arbitration agreement who is a consumer shall not be bound (unless he or she otherwise agrees at any time after the dispute has arisen) by an arbitration agreement where—

(a) the agreement between the parties contains a term which has not been individually negotiated concerning the requirement to submit to arbitration disputes which may arise, and

(b) the dispute which has arisen between the parties to the agreement involves a claim for an amount not exceeding €5,000.

(2) For the avoidance of doubt, a reference in this section to a consumer shall not include an amateur sportsperson who, in his or her capacity as such, is a party to an arbitration agreement that contains a term concerning the requirement to submit to arbitration.

Definitions

'arbitration': Arbitration Act 2010, s 2(1) and Model Law, Art 2(a); 'arbitration agreement': Arbitration Act 2010, s 2(1) and Model Law, Art 7(1) (Option I); 'consumer': Arbitration Act 2010, s 2(1).

Notes

***Non-application of arbitration agreements to consumers*:** This section provides that a consumer is not bound by an arbitration agreement where the value of the claim is less than €5,000.00, unless it has been individually negotiated.[1] However, it appears that where a dispute arises, a consumer is entitled to commence civil proceedings notwithstanding the existence of an arbitration agreement and the non-consumer counterparty will not be entitled to rely upon the Model Law, which requires pending civil proceedings to be referred to arbitration.[2]

[1] Arbitration Act 2010, s 31(1).
[2] Model Law, Art 8.

***Continued applicability of arbitration agreements to non-consumers*:** While a consumer is not bound by an arbitration agreement where the value of the claim is less than €5,000.00, unless the arbitration agreement was individually negotiated, it appears that a non-consumer counterparty continues to be bound by the arbitration agreement. Where a dispute arises and a non-consumer counterparty commences civil proceedings then the consumer may request that the court refer the parties to arbitration.[1] Therefore, it would be prudent for the non-consumer to ascertain from the consumer whether or not the dispute should be resolved by arbitration before commencing proceedings.

[1] Model Law, Art 8.

***Value of the claim is less than €5,000.00*:** It is not specified how, when or by who the value of the claim that the consumer asserts is less than €5,000.00 is to be ascertained. Some commentators have criticised the imposition of a monetary limit and have suggested that a blanket protection for all consumers would have been more beneficial.[1] However, it may be that in the event that a consumer commences civil proceedings over a matter which is the subject of an arbitration agreement, a non-consumer counterparty may assert that its liability may not exceed €5,000.00, irrespective of the claim pleaded.

[1] Hutchinson, "Legislative Comment – The new Irish Arbitration Act" (2010) *International Arbitration Law Review* 13(2).

***Individually negotiated*:** A term is not individually negotiated where it has been drafted in advance and where the consumer has not been able to influence its substance.[1] The onus of proof is on the non-consumer to demonstrate that a term was individually negotiated.[2]

[1] European Communities (Unfair Terms in Consumer Contracts) Regulations 1995 (SI No 27 of 1995), reg 3(4).
[2] *ibid*, reg 3(6).

***Status of amateur sportspersons*:** An amateur sportsperson, who in that capacity is party to an arbitration agreement, is not a consumer simply because he or she is an amateur.[1] Therefore, an amateur sportsperson who is party to an arbitration agreement must submit any dispute that may arise to arbitration.

[1] Arbitration Act 2010, s 31(2).

Part 3

Reference to Arbitration Where Proceedings Pending Before Court

32.—Power of High Court and Circuit Court to adjourn proceedings to facilitate arbitration

(1) Without prejudice to any provision of any other enactment or rule of law, the High Court or the Circuit Court may at any time whether before or during the trial of any civil proceedings before it—

(a) if it thinks it appropriate to do so, and

(b) the parties to the proceedings so consent,

by order adjourn the proceedings to enable the parties to consider whether any or all of the matters in dispute might be determined by arbitration.

(2) Where a court makes an order under subsection (1), the adjournment shall be for such period as the court thinks fit.

(3) The parties to the proceedings shall, on or before the expiry of the period referred to in subsection (2), inform the court hearing the civil proceedings concerned whether or not agreement has been reached between the parties that any or all of the matters in dispute should be dealt with by arbitration.

(4) Where such agreement has been reached, the agreement shall be treated as an arbitration agreement for the purposes of this Act.

(5) The court, in respect of an agreement referred to in subsection (4)—

(a) where the agreement relates to all of the matters in dispute, shall by order provide for the discontinuance of the proceedings and may make such order as to the costs of the proceedings as it thinks fit, or

(b) where the agreement relates to part but not all of the matters in dispute, may make such order as to the discontinuance of the proceedings as it thinks fit.

(6) Where no agreement has been reached the court may make such order as it thinks fit in relation to the continuance of the proceedings.

(7) This section is in addition to and not in substitution for any power of a court to adjourn civil proceedings before it.

Definitions

'arbitration': Arbitration Act 2010, s 2(1) and Model Law, Art 2(a); 'arbitration agreement': Arbitration Act 2010, s 2(1) and Model Law, Art 7(1) (Option I); 'court': Model Law, Art 2(c); 'Circuit Court': Interpretation Act 2005, sch, pt 1; 'High Court': Interpretation Act 2005, sch, pt 1.

Notes

Power of High Court and Circuit Court to adjourn pending proceedings to refer disputes to arbitration: This section provides that the High Court and the Circuit Court are permitted to adjourn pending civil proceedings to enable the parties to consider whether the matters in dispute may instead be referred to arbitration.[1] However, as this power requires the consent of all the parties,[2] its benefits seem negligible. Where parties wish for a dispute to be referred to arbitration, they may simply enter into a 'submission' arbitration agreement in the first instance rather than commence civil proceedings. Commentators have noted that "[i]t certainly seems unlikely that we will see many adjournment applications to facilitate arbitration during a trial, as by the time a case gets a trial date and the hearing begins any advantage the arbitration process may have in terms of an expedited hearing will have been lost".[3] This power is relevant only in the uncommon scenario where after civil proceedings are commenced the parties agree that arbitration is the more appropriate method for resolving their dispute.

---

[1] Arbitration Act 2010, s 32(1)(a).
[2] Arbitration Act 2010, s 32(1)(b).
[3] Shanley and Murphy, "Update on the Progress of the Arbitration Bill 2008" (2010) *Arbitration and ADR Review*, p 9.

Power to adjourn limited to the High Court and the Circuit Court: Although the term 'court' is used in this section, the power to adjourn pending civil proceedings to enable the parties to consider whether the matters in dispute may instead be referred to arbitration is expressly limited to the High Court and the Circuit Court.[1] Neither the Supreme Court nor the District Court enjoys a similar power to adjourn pending civil proceedings.

---

[1] Model Law, Art 2(c) defines the term 'court' as "a body or organ of the judicial system of a State", which includes the Supreme Court and the District Court.

No power to impose cost penalties: The High Court and the Circuit Court are not permitted to impose cost penalties upon parties who refuse to refer the matters in dispute to arbitration when invited to do so.[1] This is in contrast with the power of the Supreme Court and the High Court to impose cost penalties[2] where a party refuses to participate in any mediation or conciliation when invited to do so.[3]

---

[1] Hutchinson, "Legislative Comment – The new Irish Arbitration Act" (2010) *International Arbitration Law Review* 13(2).2
[2] Rules of the Superior Courts, Ord 99, r 1B, as inserted by The Rules of the Superior Court (Mediation and Conciliation) Regulations 2010 (SI No 502 of 2010). For a discussion on the power of the Supreme Court and the High Court to impose cost penalties where a party refuses or otherwise fails to participate in any mediation or conciliation ADR in the Commercial Court, see Mansfield, "The cost implications for refusing to avail of ADR in civil litigation in the Superior Courts" (2011) *Commercial Law Practitioner* p 8.
[3] Rules of the Superior Courts, Ord 56A, r 2(1), as inserted by The Rules of the Superior Court (Mediation and Conciliation) Regulations 2010 (SI No 502 of 2010).

Other court powers to adjourn pending civil proceedings: The power conferred on the High Court and the Circuit Court to adjourn pending civil proceedings to enable the parties to consider whether the matters in dispute may instead be referred to arbitration is expressly in addition to any other existing court powers to adjourn pending civil proceedings. Other court powers to adjourn pending civil proceedings include:

1. The power of the High Court to adjourn pending proceedings in its Commercial list to consider whether those proceedings should be referred to mediation, conciliation or arbitration;[1]
2. The power of the High Court, Circuit Court and the District Court to adjourn personal injuries proceedings to direct that the parties meet to discuss and attempt to settle the action under what is referred to as a 'mediation conference';[2]
3. The power of the Circuit Court to adjourn proceedings to invite the parties to use mediation, conciliation, arbitration or other dispute resolution process to settle or determine the proceedings or issue;[3] and
4. The power of the Supreme Court and the High Court to adjourn proceedings to invite the parties to use mediation or conciliation, and, where the parties consent, to refer pending proceedings to mediation or conciliation.[4]

---

[1] Rules of the Superior Courts, Ord 63A, r 6(1)(xiii), as inserted by the Rules of the Superior Courts (Commercial Proceedings) Regulations 2004 (SI No 2 of 2004). For a discussion on alternative dispute resolution in the Commercial Court see Fenelon in Dowling, The Commercial Court (1st ed, Thomson Round Hall, Dublin, 2007) pp 255-295.

[2] Civil Liability and Courts Act 2004, s 15.

[3] Circuit Court Rules, Ord 19A, r 7(1), as inserted by the Circuit Court Rules (Case Progression) General) Regulations 2009 (SI No 539 of 2009).

[4] Rules of the Superior Courts, Ord 56A, r 2(1) as inserted by The Rules of the Superior Court (Mediation and Conciliation) Regulations 2010 (SI No 502 of 2010).

Schedule 1

Text of UNCITRAL Model Law on International Commercial Arbitration

Chapter I

General Provisions

Chapter IV A

Interim Measures and Preliminary Orders

Chapter V

Conduct of Arbitral Proceedings

(As adopted by the United Nations Commission on International Trade Law on 21 June 1985, with amendments as adopted by that Commission on 7 July 2006)

Chapter I

General Provisions

Article 1.—Scope of application

(1) This Law applies to international commercial arbitration, subject to any agreement in force between this State and any other State or States.

(2) The provisions of this Law, except articles 8, 9, 17 H, 17 I, 17 J, 35 and 36, apply only if the place of arbitration is in the territory of this State.

(3) An arbitration is international if:

(a) the parties to an arbitration agreement have, at the time of the conclusion of that agreement, their places of business in different States; or

(b) one of the following places is situated outside the State in which the parties have their places of business:

(i) the place of arbitration if determined in, or pursuant to, the arbitration agreement;

(ii) any place where a substantial part of the obligations of the commercial relationship is to be performed or the place with which the subject matter of the dispute is most closely connected; or

(c) the parties have expressly agreed that the subject matter of the arbitration agreement relates to more than one country.

(4) For the purposes of paragraph (3) of this article:

(a) if a party has more than one place of business, the place of business is that which has the closest relationship to the arbitration agreement;

(b) if a party does not have a place of business, reference is to be made to his habitual residence.

(5) This Law shall not affect any other law of this State by virtue of which certain disputes may not be submitted to arbitration or may be submitted to arbitration only according to provisions other than those of this Law.

Definitions

'arbitration': Arbitration Act 2010, s 2(1) and Model Law, Art 2(a); 'arbitration agreement': Arbitration Act 2010, s 2(1) and Model Law, Art 7(1) (Option I).

Notes

***The Model Law*:** The Model Law means the law as adopted by the United Nations Commission on International Trade Law on 21 June 1985, with amendments as adopted by that Commission at its thirty-ninth session on 7 June 2006. While the Model Law has no legislative force on its own, it is designed to serve as a template for national arbitration legislation. The Model Law has been drafted with flexibility in mind permitting States which adopt the Model Law, or which use it as a template for arbitration legislation, to complete the detail without departing from the spirit of the Model Law.[1]

Although the Act purports to adopt the provisions of the Model Law, in full, for arbitral proceedings where Ireland is the place of arbitration,[2] Art 2 A of the Model Law is not included in the text of the Model Law as set out at schedule 1 to the Act.[3] The effect of this omission most likely means that Art 2 A is not included in the Act. However, in practice, the omission of Art 2 A is unlikely to present a difficulty as commentators have noted that the provisions of Art 2 A are "little more than hortatory".[4]

---

[1] Brekoulakis and Shore in Mistelis, *Concise International Arbitration, UNCITRAL Model Law* (1st ed, Kluwer Law International, Alphen aan den Rijn, 2010) p 584.

[2] Arbitration Act 2010, s 6.

[3] Model Law, Art 2 A is entitled 'International origin and general principles' and provides that: "(1) In the interpretation of this Law, regard is to be had to its international origin and to the need to promote uniformity in its application and the observance of good faith. (2) Questions concerning matters governed by this Law which are not expressly settled in it are to be settled in conformity with the general principles on which this Law is based".

[4] Brekoulakis and Shore in Mistelis, *Concise International Arbitration, UNCITRAL Model Law* (1st ed, Kluwer Law International, Alphen aan den Rijn, 2010) p 591. Furthermore, it has been noted that Arbitration Act 2010, s 8 already encourages a uniform interpretation of the Model Law, which is the principle promoted by Model Law, Art 2 A. See Walsh, "2006 UNCITRAL Model Law: Are States Adopting the Law in Letter and Spirit?" (2010) *Arbitration and ADR Review* p 215.

***The adoption of the Model Law for both international commercial arbitrations and domestic arbitrations*:** Although the Model Law itself provides that it applies only to international commercial arbitrations,[1] the Act adopts the Model Law both for international commercial arbitrations[2] and for domestic arbitrations (which are any arbitrations other than international commercial arbitrations) where Ireland is the place of arbitration.[3] Therefore, the only legislative distinction between an international commercial arbitration and a domestic arbitration concerns a party's ability to demand the taxation of costs, which is applicable only in a domestic arbitration.[4]

---

[1] Model Law, Art 1(1).

[2] Arbitration Act 2010, s 6(a).

[3] Arbitration Act 2010, s 6(b).

[4] Arbitration Act 2010, s 21(4).

***Circumstances where an arbitration is an international commercial arbitration*:** An arbitration is an international commercial arbitration where:

1. At least one of the parties to an arbitration agreement has its place of business outside Ireland;[1]
2. A substantial part of the obligations of the parties' commercial relationship is to be performed outside Ireland or the place with which the subject matter of the dispute is most closely connected is outside Ireland;[2] or
3. The parties have expressly agreed that the subject matter of the arbitration agreement relates to more than one State.[3]

---

[1] Model Law, Art 1(3)(a); and (b)(i). Where a party has more than one place of business, Model Law, Art 1(4)(a) provides that its place of business for the purpose of arbitral proceedings or potential arbitral proceedings is the one which has the closest relationship to an arbitration agreement. Where a party does not have a place of business, Model Law, Art 1(4)(b) provides that its habitual residence will be deemed its place of business.

[2] Model Law, Art 1(3)(b)(ii).

[3] Model Law, Art 1(3)(c).

***Extraterritorial effect of the Act and the Model Law*:** Arbitral proceedings are governed by the law of the place of arbitration[1] and it is for each State to promulgate laws to govern the conduct of arbitrations within its own territory.[2] In Ireland, the law governing the conduct of arbitration is the Act, which adopts and supplements the Model Law.[3] However, like most Irish domestic law, the Act and consequently, the Model Law have limited extraterritorial effect. Only the following provisions of the Model Law apply to arbitral proceedings where the place of arbitration is outside Ireland:

1. Article 8, which requires an Irish court before which an action is brought in a matter that is the subject of an arbitration agreement must be referred to arbitration, unless the arbitration agreement is null and void, inoperative or incapable of being performed, irrespective of where the place of arbitration or potential place of arbitration is or will be;
2. Articles 9 and 17 J, which permit an Irish court to grant interim measures either before or during arbitral proceedings, irrespective of where the place of arbitration is or potential place of arbitration will be;
3. Article 17 H, which requires an Irish court to recognise and enforce an interim measure ordered by an arbitral tribunal as binding, irrespective of where the place of arbitration is;
4. Article 17 I, which provides certain grounds for refusing recognition and enforcement of the interim measure, irrespective of where the place of arbitration is;

(*Continued*)

5. Article 27, which provides that an arbitral tribunal, or a party with the approval of an arbitral tribunal, may request assistance in the taking of evidence in arbitral proceedings from the competent court of the place of arbitration, irrespective of where the place of arbitration is;[4]

6. Article 35, which requires an Irish court to recognise and enforce an award ordered by an arbitral tribunal as binding, irrespective of where the place of arbitration was; and

7. Article 36, which provides certain grounds for refusing recognition and enforcement of the award as set out in Art 36, irrespective of where the place of arbitration was.[5]

---

[1] Blackaby, Partasides, Redfern and Hunter, *Redfern and Hunter on International Arbitration* (5th ed, Oxford University Press, Oxford, 2009) p 164.
[2] *ibid*, p 175.
[3] Arbitration Act 2010, s 6.
[4] Arbitration Act 2010, s 15. Without the extension of the High Court's remit by this provision of the Act, Model Law, Art 27 would only apply where Ireland is the place of arbitration.
[5] Model Law, Art 1(2).

The concept of arbitrability: The Model Law expressly reserves the concept of 'arbitrability' or whether certain disputes are capable of resolution by arbitration to domestic law.[1] Where a dispute is not capable of being resolved by arbitration, national courts are relived from the obligation to recognise and enforcement arbitration agreements to resolve that dispute.[2] Commentators have noted that the concept of arbitrability "rests on the notion that some matters so pervasively involve public rights, or interests of third parties, which are the subjects of uniquely governmental authority, that agreements to resolve such disputes by "private" arbitration should not be given effect".[3] The following categories of disputes are incapable of resolution by arbitration under Irish law:

1. The prosecution of criminal offences, which the Constitution of Ireland requires to be tried in the courts and, other than for non-minor offences, requires trial by jury;[4]

2. Disputes concerning the grant[5] or revocation[6] of patents and trade marks, which are matters of public law to be resolved either by the Controller of Patents, Designs and Trade Marks or by the High Court;[7] and

3. Disputes concerning contracts whose objects are illegal or contrary to public policy.[8] Although there is some debate[9] whether an arbitration agreement is invalid in circumstances where the object of the matrix contract of which it forms a part of is illegal or is contrary to public policy, it is likely that any award made in arbitral proceedings will not be enforceable.[10]

(*Continued*)

In addition to those categories of disputes which are incapable of resolution by arbitration, the availability of arbitration is permitted, but limited, for the following categories of disputes:

1. Disputes involving a consumer where the value of a claim is less than €5,000.00, unless the arbitration agreement contained in the matrix contract has been individually negotiated;[11]
2. Landlord and tenant disputes within the under the Residential Tenancies Act 2004 which must be resolved by the Private Residential Tenancies Board, unless the tenant consents to the dispute being referred to arbitration after the time a dispute arises;[12] and
3. Employment disputes and arbitrations conducted under s 70 of the Industrial Relations Act 1946, to which, although capable of resolution by arbitration, the provisions of the Act and, consequently, the Model Law do not apply.[13]

---

[1] Model Law, Art 1(5). For a discussion of the concept of 'arbitrability' in international commercial arbitration, see Born, *International Commercial Arbitration* (1st ed, Kluwer Law International, Alphen aan den Rijn, 2009) p 767.

[2] *ibid*, p 767.

[3] *ibid*, p 768.

[4] Constitution of Ireland, Art 38.

[5] Patents Act 1992, s 7.

[6] *ibid*, s 57.

[7] For a discussion on the arbitrability of patents and trade marks, see Blessing, "Arbitrability of Intellectual Property Disputes" (1996) *Arbitration International* p 200.

[8] *Soleimany v Soleimany* [1999] QB 785, where the English Court of Appeal stated at p 797 that the courts should "not recognise an agreement between ... highwaymen to arbitrate their difference any more than it would recognise the original agreement to split the proceeds".

[9] Born, *International Commercial Arbitration* (1st ed, Kluwer Law International, Alphen aan den Rijn, 2009) pp 755-759.

[10] Dowling-Hussey and Dunne, *Arbitration Law* (1st ed, Thomson Round Hall, Dublin, 2008) pp 43–45.

[11] Arbitration Act 2010, s 31(1).

[12] Residential Tenancies Act 2004, s 90.

[13] Arbitration Act 2010, s 30(1).

Article 2.—Definitions and rules of interpretation

For the purposes of this Law:

(a) "arbitration" means any arbitration whether or not administered by a permanent arbitral institution;

(b) "arbitral tribunal" means a sole arbitrator or a panel of arbitrators;

(c) "court" means a body or organ of the judicial system of a State;

(d) where a provision of this Law, except article 28, leaves the parties free to determine a certain issue, such freedom includes the right of the parties to authorize a third party, including an institution, to make that determination;

(e) where a provision of this Law refers to the fact that the parties have agreed or that they may agree or in any other way refers to an agreement of the parties, such agreement includes any arbitration rules referred to in that agreement;

(f) where a provision of this Law, other than in articles 25(a) and 32(2)(a), refers to a claim, it also applies to a counter-claim, and where it refers to a defence, it also applies to a defence to such counter-claim.

Definitions

'arbitration': Arbitration Act 2010, s 2(1) and Model Law, Art 2(a); 'arbitral tribunal': Model Law, Art 2(b); 'court': Model Law, Art 2(c).

Notes

***Interpretation of the Act*:** This section provides definitions of certain terms used in the Model Law[1] and provides for rules of interpretation for the Model Law.[2]

---

[1] Model Law, Art 2(a); (b); and (c).
[2] Model Law, Art 2(d); (e); and (f).

***Definition of 'arbitration'*:** The definition of 'arbitration' merely provides clarification that an arbitration includes both an *ad hoc* arbitration and an institutional arbitration. It does not explain what the term means nor does it describe what constitutes an arbitration. This is deliberate and follows the approach adopted by much other arbitration legislation worldwide, including the Act.[1]

The *travaux préparatoires* (of which Irish courts are permitted to take judicial notice when interpreting provisions of the Model Law)[2] suggest that only 'consensual arbitration' based on the agreement of the parties should fall within the scope of the Model Law and that 'compulsory arbitration' required by statute should fall outside its scope.[3] However, the Act provides that the Model Law, other than Arts 12 and 13, applies to Irish legislation providing for the compulsory resolution of disputes by arbitration within Ireland,[4] which is known as 'statutory arbitration'.

---

[1] Arbitration Act 2010, s 2(1). A full discussion of the meaning of 'arbitration' is included at Arbitration Act 2010, s 2(1).
[2] Arbitration Act 2010, s 8(1).
[3] UNCITRAL First Working Group Report, A/CN.9/216, para 17.
[4] Arbitration Act 2010, s 29. A full discussion of 'statutory arbitrations' is included at Arbitration Act 2010, s 29.

***Definition of 'arbitral tribunal'*:** The definition of 'arbitral tribunal' merely provides clarification that an arbitral tribunal includes both a single arbitrator and a panel of arbitrators. In Ireland, an arbitral tribunal shall consist of a single arbitrator, unless the parties agree otherwise.[1] Although both the Act and the Model Law also use the term 'arbitrator' to provide clarification that certain provisions apply not only to an arbitral tribunal but also to an arbitrator as a constituent of an arbitral tribunal, it is not defined in either the Act or the Model Law.[2] The *travaux préparatoires* (of which Irish courts are permitted to take judicial notice when interpreting provisions of the Model Law)[3] suggest that the definition of 'arbitral tribunal' is included in the Model Law to avoid potential misunderstanding in some languages where the word 'tribunal' is used to describe what in the English language would be termed a 'court' (*i.e.*, a body of the judicial system of a State).[4]

---

[1] Arbitration Act 2010, s 13.
[2] Each of Arbitration Act 2010, ss 13; and 22; and Model Law, Arts 10; 11; 12; 13; 14; and 15 use the term 'arbitrator'.
[3] Arbitration Act 2010, s 8(1).
[4] UNCITRAL Seventh Secretarial Note, A/CN.9/264, Art 2, para 1.

***Definition of 'court'*:** The definition of 'court' is self-explanatory. In Ireland, the definition of 'court' includes the Supreme Court; the High Court; the Circuit Court; and the District Court. However, it is the High Court that exercises the functions of arbitration assistance and supervision for the purposes of the Act and the Model Law.[1] The *travaux préparatoires* (of which Irish courts are permitted to take judicial notice when interpreting provisions of the Model Law)[2] suggest that the definition of 'court' is included in the Model Law to avoid potential misunderstanding in some languages where the word 'tribunal' is used to describe what in the English language would be termed a 'court' (*i.e.*, a body of the judicial system of a State).[3]

---

[1] Arbitration Act 2010, s 9.
[2] Arbitration Act 2010, s 8(1).
[3] UNCITRAL Seventh Secretarial Note, A/CN.9/264, Art 2, para 1.

***Rules of interpretation*:** The rules of interpretation provided by the Model Law seek to ensure that the Model Law is interpreted consistently by States adopting its provisions. These rules provide that:

1. Where the Model Law permits the parties to determine a certain issue, the parties may authorise a third party such as an arbitral institution to make the determination on their behalf.[1] The only exception to this rule is the choice of substantive law applicable to a dispute, which may be determined by the parties[2] but may not be determined by a third party on the parties' behalf;[3]

2. Where the parties choose particular arbitration rules to govern arbitral proceedings, the rules are incorporated by reference into the arbitration agreement and apply where the Model Law permits the parties to determine a certain issue.[4] The choice

(*Continued*)

of arbitration rules to govern arbitral proceedings is common practice in international commercial arbitration;[5] and

3. Any reference in the Model Law to a claim includes a reference to a counter-claim and any reference to a defence includes a reference to a defence to a counter-claim.[6] This provision envisages that both claim and any counter-claim be prosecuted within the same set of arbitral proceedings. The only exceptions to this rule are that an arbitral tribunal is not required to terminate arbitral proceedings where a respondent fails to communicate its statement of counter-claim[7] and an arbitral tribunal is not required to terminate arbitral proceedings where a respondent withdraws its counter-claim.[8]

---

[1] Model Law, Art 2(d).
[2] Model Law, Art 28.
[3] Model Law, Art 2(d).
[4] Model Law, Art 2(e).
[5] Binder, *International Commercial Arbitration and Conciliation in UNCITRAL Model Law Jurisdictions* (3rd ed, Sweet & Maxwell, London, 2010) p 44.
[6] Model Law, Art 2(f).
[7] Model Law, Art 25(a).
[8] Model Law, Art 32(2)(a).

***Other definitions*:** Both the Act and the Model Law provide the following other definitions of terms used in the Model Law:

1. The Act provides clarification that an 'award' includes both a partial award and a final award;[1] and

2. The Act and the Model Law together define an 'arbitration agreement' as an agreement by the parties to submit to arbitration all or certain disputes which have arisen or which may arise between them in respect of a defined legal relationship, whether contractual or not, and may be in the form of an arbitration clause in a contract or in the form of a separate agreement.[2]

---

[1] Arbitration Act 2010, s 2(1).
[2] Arbitration Act 2010, s 2(1); and Model Law, Art 7(1) (Option I).

Article 2 A.—International origin and general principles

[…]

Notes

Although the Act purports to adopt the provisions of the Model Law in full for arbitral proceedings where Ireland is the place of arbitration,[1] Art 2 A of the Model Law is not included in the text of the Model Law as set out at sch 1 to the Act.[2] The effect of this omission most likely means that Art 2 A is not included in the Act. However, in practice,

(Continued)

the omission of Art 2 A is unlikely to present a difficulty as commentators have noted that the provisions of Art 2 A are "little more than hortatory".[3]

---

[1] Arbitration Act 2010, s 6.

[2] Model Law, Art 2 A is entitled 'International origin and general principles' and provides that: "(1) In the interpretation of this Law, regard is to be had to its international origin and to the need to promote uniformity in its application and the observance of good faith. (2) Questions concerning matters governed by this Law which are not expressly settled in it are to be settled in conformity with the general principles on which this Law is based".

[3] Brekoulakis and Shore in Mistelis, *Concise International Arbitration, UNCITRAL Model Law* (1st ed, Kluwer Law International, Alphen aan den Rijn, 2010) p 591. Furthermore, it has been noted that Arbitration Act 2010, s 8 already encourages a uniform interpretation of the Model Law, which is the principle promoted by Model Law, Art 2 A. See Walsh, "2006 UNCITRAL Model Law: Are States Adopting the Law in Letter and Spirit?" (2010) *Arbitration and ADR Review* p 215.

Article 3.—Receipt of written communications

(1) Unless otherwise agreed by the parties:

(a) any written communication is deemed to have been received if it is delivered to the addressee personally or if it is delivered at his place of business, habitual residence or mailing address; if none of these can be found after making a reasonable inquiry, a written communication is deemed to have been received if it is sent to the addressee's last-known place of business, habitual residence or mailing address by registered letter or any other means which provides a record of the attempt to deliver it;

(b) the communication is deemed to have been received on the day it is so delivered.

(2) The provisions of this article do not apply to communications in court proceedings.

Definitions

'court': Model Law, Art 2(c).

Notes

***Receipt of written communications*:** This article provides that a written communication is deemed to have been received on the day it was delivered to a respondent if delivered to the respondent personally delivery; to the respondent's place of business, habitual residence or postal address; or if any of those places cannot be found after reasonable inquiry by sending it by pre-paid registered post or by any other form of recorded delivery service addressed to the respondent at his or her last known place of business, habitual residence or postal address.[1] In the context of arbitral proceedings, international case-law decided under the Model Law has held that the term 'written communications' includes communications between the parties[2] and communications by an arbitral tribunal to the parties.[3]

---

[1] Model Law, Art 3(1)(a).

(Continued)

[2] CLOUT CASE 20 – Hong Kong/High Court of Hong Kong: *Fung Sang Trading Ltd v Kai Sun Sea Products and Food Company Ltd* (29 October 1991).

[3] CLOUT CASE 29/CLOUT Case 369 – Canada/Ontario Court of Justice: *Kanto Yakin Kogyo Kabushiki-Kaisha v Can-Eng Manufacturing Ltd* (30 January 1992).

Use of electronic communications: Although neither the Model Law nor the *travaux préparatoires* (of which Irish courts are permitted to take judicial notice when interpreting provisions of the Model Law)[1] specify what constitutes a 'written communication' some commentators[2] have suggested that the term must be interpreted in accordance with the provisions of Art 7(4) of the Model Law, which provides that the 'writing' requirement of an arbitration agreement is met:

> "by an electronic communication if the information contained therein is accessible so as to be useable for subsequent reference: "electronic communication" means any communication that the parties make by means of data messages; "data message" means information generated, sent, received or stored by electronic, magnetic, optical or similar means, including but not limited to, electronic data interchange (EDI), electronic mail, telegram, telex or telecopy".[3]

However, this interpretation ignores the use of the terms 'delivered ... personally' and 'registered letter' both of which suggest that the use of a tangible document. Further, the fact that UNCITRAL at its thirty-ninth session on 7 July 2006 chose to amend the provisions of Art 7(4) of the Model Law to include reference to 'electronic communication' but left the provisions relating to receipt of written communications contained at Art 4 unchanged suggest that the use of an electronic communication should not be permitted in the absence of the express agreement of the parties. Similarly, while the Act refers to the receipt of written communications it does not include reference to an electronic communication.[4] For the avoidance of doubt, where the parties wish to avail of the use of electronic communications to communicate between each other and with the arbitral tribunal they should expressly agree to do so.[5]

---

[1] Arbitration Act 2010, s 8(1).

[2] Binder, *International Commercial Arbitration and Conciliation in UNCITRAL Model Law Jurisdictions* (3rd ed, Sweet & Maxwell, London, 2010) pp 52-53.

[3] Model Law, Art 7(4) (Option I).

[4] Arbitration Act 2010, s 7(2).

[5] Although under Irish law information will not generally be denied legal effect solely on the grounds that it is in electronic form, an exception exists for the rules, practices and procedures of a court or tribunal, which includes an arbitral tribunal. Electronic Commerce Act 2000, s 10(1)(d).

Meaning of 'reasonable inquiry': A written communication must be delivered to an addressee's place of business, habitual residence or mailing address, unless none of these addresses can be ascertained after 'reasonable inquiry'. Neither the Model Law nor the *travaux préparatoires* (of which Irish courts are permitted to take judicial notice when interpreting provisions of the Model Law)[1] specify what constitutes reasonable inquiry.

(*Continued*)

Although international case-law decided under the Model Law on what constitutes reasonable inquiry is limited, the delivery of written communications to all known addresses of a company within a jurisdiction has been held to satisfy the requirements of this article and has been held to permit an arbitral tribunal to proceed to make an award in the absence of a respondent.[2] However, some proof of reasonable inquiry must be demonstrated.[3]

---

[1] Arbitration Act 2010, s 8(1).
[2] CLOUT CASE 384 – Canada/Ontario Court of Justice: *Skorimpex Foreign Trade Co v Lelovic Co* (26 April 1991).
[3] CLOUT CASE 402 – Germany/Highest Regional Court of Bavaria: *4Z Sch 50/99* (16 March 2000).

***Date of receipt*:** This article creates a legal fiction that a written communication is deemed received on the day it is delivered.[1] This has an identical effect to the 'postal rule' in Irish contract law.[2]

---

[1] Model Law, Art 3(1)(b).
[2] For a discussion of the 'postal rule' at Irish law, see McDermott, *Contract Law* (1st ed, Butterworth (Ireland) Ltd, Dublin, 2001) pp 44-49.

***Non-applicability to communications in court proceedings*:** The rules set out in this article apply to arbitral proceedings only. These rules do not apply to High Court[1] proceedings in connection with arbitral proceedings.[2] Service of communication in High Court proceedings in connection with arbitral proceedings are governed by the Rules of the Superior Courts[3] which require personal service of originating court documents (such as an originating notice of motion required to commence an application to the High Court to fulfil its supervisory functions in connection with arbitral proceedings)[4] and service of all other documents by registered prepaid post to the residence or place of business of the person to be served or the place of business of the solicitor (if any) acting for him in the proceedings to which the document relates.[5]

Court proceedings to be served within the European Union are governed by Council Regulation (EC) No 1393/2007 on the service in Member States of judicial and extrajudicial documents in civil and commercial matters (service of documents),[6] which requires each European Union Member State to designate transmitting and receiving agencies for the service of documents. A party wishing to serve a document lodges copies of the document to the transmitting agency in its home Member State and the documents are then transmitted to the receiving agency in the Member State in which the party to whom the document is addressed is resident.[7] Court proceedings in countries that are not in the European Union but are signatories of the Hague Convention on the Service Abroad of Judicial and Extrajudicial Documents in Civil and Commercial Matter[8] are governed by that convention, which requires each signatory State to designate a central authority for the transmission and receipt of documents.[9] A party wishing to serve a

(*Continued*)

document lodges copies of the document to the central authority in its home State and the documents are then transmitted to the central authority in the State in which the party to whom the document is addressed is resident.[10]

---

[1] Arbitration Act 2010, s 9 and Model Law, Art 6.

[2] Model Law, Art 3(2).

[3] For a discussion of service of documents in Irish High Court proceedings, see Delany and McGrath, *Civil Procedure in the Superior Courts* (3rd ed, Round Hall Thomson Reuters, Dublin, 2012) pp 209-225.

[4] Rules of the Superior Courts, Ord 9, r 16.

[5] Rules of the Superior Courts, Ord 121(2).

[6] EC No 1393/2007, effect to which is given in Ireland by Rules of the Superior Courts, Ord 11D.

[7] Rules of the Superior Courts, Ord 11D, r 3(1).

[8] 71 States and one regional economic integration organisation are currently signatories to the Hague Convention. They are: Albania, Argentina, Australia, Austria, Belarus, Belgium, Bosnia and Herzegovina, Brazil, Bulgaria, Canada, Chile, China, Costa Rica, Croatia, Cyprus, Czech Republic, Denmark, Ecuador, Egypt, Estonia, European Union, Finland, France, Georgia, Germany, Greece, Hungary, Iceland, India, Ireland, Israel, Italy, Japan, Jordan, Korea, Republic of, Latvia, Lithuania, Luxembourg, Malaysia, Malta, Mauritius, Mexico, Monaco, Montenegro, Morocco, Netherlands, New Zealand, Norway, Panama, Paraguay, Peru, Philippines, Poland, Portugal, Romania, Russian Federation, Serbia, Slovakia, Slovenia, South Africa, Spain, Suriname, Sweden, Switzerland, The former Yugoslav Republic of Macedonia, Turkey, Ukraine, United Kingdom of Great Britain and Northern Ireland, United States of America, Uruguay, Venezuela (Bolivarian Republic of). An up-to-date list of States which are parties is kept by The Hague Conference on Private International Law and is available at its website: http://www.hcch.net/index_en.php?act=states.listing.

[9] The Hague Convention was concluded on 15 November 1965 and the text of which is available at: http://www.hcch.net/index_en.php?act=conventions.text&cid=17. Effect is given to the Hague Convention in Ireland by Rules of the Superior Courts, Order 11E.

[10] Rules of the Superior Courts, Ord 11E, r 3(1).

Article 4.—Waiver of right to object

A party who knows that any provision of this Law from which the parties may derogate or any requirement under the arbitration agreement has not been complied with and yet proceeds with the arbitration without stating his objection to such non-compliance without undue delay or, if a time-limit is provided therefor, within such period of time, shall be deemed to have waived his right to object.

Definitions

'arbitration': Arbitration Act 2010, s 2(1) and Model Law, Art 2(a); 'arbitration agreement': Arbitration Act 2010, s 2(1) and Model Law, Art 7(1) (Option I).

Notes

***Waiver of right to object to non-compliance with procedural requirements*:** The principle of party autonomy, which permits the parties to agree the procedural requirements of arbitral proceedings, is a fundamental feature of arbitration.[1] To give effect to the parties' agreement, arbitral proceedings are required to comply with parties' chosen procedural requirements or, in the absence of the parties' agreement, the default procedural requirements of the Model Law. Where Ireland is the place of arbitration an award made in arbitral proceedings that does not comply with the agreement of the parties or the default provisions of the Model Law will be liable to be set aside where Ireland is the place of arbitration.[2]

However, this article provides that where one party knows that some element of arbitral proceedings does not comply with procedural requirements but does not promptly object, that party waives its right to object at a later stage in the arbitral proceedings or in court proceedings to set aside an award.[3] This waiver prevents a party who is aware of non-compliance with certain procedural requirements from 'hedging-its-bets' by acquiescing in the continuance of the arbitral proceedings in the hope of an award favourable to its interests but in the knowledge that if the award is unfavourable, it will be liable to be set aside by the High Court.[4] The *travaux préparatoires* (of which Irish courts are permitted to take judicial notice when interpreting provisions of the Model Law)[5] suggest this waiver is based on the common law doctrine of estoppel[6] and on the similar civil law doctrine of *venire contra factum proprium*.[7] The waiver only applies where the following four conditions are met:

1. That non-compliance is with an arbitration agreement or with non-mandatory provisions of the Model Law;
2. That the waiving party has knowledge of non-compliance;
3. That the waiving party fails to object without undue delay; and
4. That the waiving party proceeds with the arbitration.[8]

---

[1] Blackaby, Partasides, Redfern and Hunter, *Redfern and Hunter on International Arbitration* (5th ed, Oxford University Press, Oxford, 2009) p 365.

[2] Model Law, Art 34(2)(a)(iv). Or, where Ireland is not the place of arbitration, an award will be liable to have recognition and enforcement thereof refused Ireland under Model Law, Art 36(1)(a)(iv).

[3] Model Law, Art 4.

[4] Brekoulakis and Shore in Mistelis, *Concise International Arbitration, UNCITRAL Model Law* (1st ed, Kluwer Law International, Alphen aan den Rijn, 2010) p 593.

[5] Arbitration Act 2010, s 8(1).

[6] For a full discussion on the doctrine of estoppel, see Delany, *Equity and the Law of Trust in Ireland* (4th ed, Thomson Round Hall, Dublin, 2007) pp 708-748.

[7] UNCITRAL Seventh Secretariat Note, A/CN.9/264, Art 4, para 1.

[8] Holtzmann and Neuhaus, *A Guide to the UNCITRAL Model Law on International Commercial Arbitration* (1st ed, Kluwer Law and Taxation Publishers, The Hague, 1989) pp 196-200.

Non-compliance with an arbitration agreement or with non-mandatory provisions of the Model Law: The waiver of a right to object applies only to procedural requirements agreed to by the parties in an arbitration agreement or, in the absence of the parties' agreement, to the default provisions of the Model Law, which are non-mandatory in nature. The *travaux préparatoires* (of which Irish courts are permitted to take judicial notice when interpreting provisions of the Model Law)[1] suggest that here is no waiver of a right to object to non-compliance with the mandatory provisions of the Model Law, as the mandatory provisions protect interests that are fundamental to arbitration and must apply in all arbitral proceedings.[2]

The Model Law does not specify which of its provisions are mandatory and which are non-mandatory. Commentators have noted that no jurisdiction that has adopted the Model Law has provided a full list of its mandatory and non-mandatory provisions.[3] However, some commentators[4] have noted that a provision of the Model Law is non-mandatory where an express freedom is provided to the parties[5] or where a default rule is provided but it is stated that the parties may agree otherwise.[6]

---

[1] Arbitration Act 2010, s 8(1).

[2] UNCITRAL Seventh Secretariat Note, A/CN.9/264, Art 4, para 2. A similar principle existed at common law where an ouster of the jurisdiction of the courts in an arbitration agreement was void as being contrary to public policy. See *Czarnikow v Roth, Schmidt & Co* [1922] 2 KB 478, which is a decision of the English Court of Appeal. The decision in *Czarnikow* v *Roth, Schmidt & Co* has received judicial approval in Ireland in *Uniform Construction Ltd v Cappawhite Contractors Ltd* [2007] IEHC 295; and *John Mowlem Construction Ltd t/a Irishenco Construction v Dublin City Council* [2009] IEHC 225.

[3] Binder, *International Commercial Arbitration and Conciliation in UNCITRAL Model Law Jurisdictions* (3rd ed, Sweet & Maxwell, London, 2010) p 57.

[4] Holtzmann and Neuhaus, *A Guide to the UNCITRAL Model Law on International Commercial Arbitration* (1st ed, Kluwer Law and Taxation Publishers, The Hague, 1989) p 198.

[5] See, for example, Model Law, Arts 10(1); 11(2); 13(1); 19(1); 20(1); and 22(1).

[6] See, for example, Model Law, Arts 3(1); 17(1); 17 B(1); 21; 23(2); 24; 25; 26(1); 26(2); 29; and 33(2).

The waiving party has knowledge of non-compliance: In order to waive its right to object later in the arbitral proceedings or in subsequent court proceedings, a party must have known of the non-compliance with the procedural requirements and must have not objected; actual knowledge of non-compliance is required.[1] The *travaux préparatoires* (of which Irish courts are permitted to take judicial notice when interpreting provisions of the Model Law)[2] suggest that the broader formulation permitting constructive knowledge that a party "knows or ought to have known" of non-compliance was not included in the Model Law as it was thought that it would cause ambiguity.[3] However, commentators have noted that the deletion of the formulation knowledge "probably did not alter

(*Continued*)

practical effect of the knowledge requirement ... the existence of knowledge, like any other fact, would not have to be proved directly in all cases. Rather, knowledge may often be proved by proof of circumstances from which such knowledge may be inferred".[4]

---

[1] Model Law, Art 4.
[2] Arbitration Act 2010, s 8(1).
[3] UNCITRAL Commission Report, A/40/17, Art 4, para 54.
[4] Holtzmann and Neuhaus, *A Guide to the UNCITRAL Model Law on International Commercial Arbitration* (1st ed, Kluwer Law and Taxation Publishers, The Hague, 1989) p 199.

***The waiving party fails to object without undue delay*:** In order to waive its right to object later in the arbitral proceedings or in subsequent court proceedings, a party must have failed to object to the non-compliance with the procedural requirements within any time limits contained in an arbitration agreement or provided by the Model Law[1] or, where no time limits exist, without undue delay.[2] Neither the Model Law nor the *travaux préparatoires* (of which Irish courts are permitted to take judicial notice when interpreting provisions of the Model Law)[3] specify what is meant by 'undue delay' but international case-law decided under the Model Law has held it to require that a party object either at the next scheduled oral hearing or raise its objections in its next written submissions.[4]

---

[1] Examples of time limits include Model Law, Art 13(2), which provides that a challenge to an arbitrator is made within 15 days of knowledge of the composition of arbitral tribunal or within 15 days of knowledge of the circumstances giving rise to the grounds for challenge; and Model Law, Art 16(2), which provides that plea that an arbitral tribunal does not have jurisdiction must not be raised later than the submission of the statement of defence.
[2] Model Law, Art 4.
[3] Arbitration Act 2010, s 8(1).
[4] CLOUT Case 659 – Germany/Highest Regional Court of Naumburg: *10 Sch 08/01* (21 February 2002); and CLOUT Case 780 – Egypt/Cairo Regional Center for International Commercial Arbitration: *No 312/2002* (28 November 2004).

***The waiving party proceeds with the arbitration*:** In order to waive its right to object later in the arbitral proceedings or in subsequent court proceedings, a party must proceed with the arbitral proceedings.[1] The *travaux préparatoires* (of which Irish courts are permitted to take judicial notice when interpreting provisions of the Model Law)[2] suggest that acts of proceeding include appearing at a hearing or communication with the arbitral tribunal or the other party.[3] However, where a party knows of non-compliance with procedural requirements it should actively object rather than simply decline to participate further as an arbitral tribunal may continue arbitral proceedings and make an award in circumstances where a party fails to participate in arbitral proceedings.[4]

---

[1] Model Law, Art 4.
[2] Arbitration Act 2010, s 8(1).
[3] UNCITRAL Seventh Secretariat Note, A/CN.9/264, Art 4, para 5.
[4] Model Law, Art 25(c).

Article 5.—Extent of court intervention

In matters governed by this Law, no court shall intervene except where so provided in this Law.

Definitions

'court': Model Law, Art 2(c).

Notes

***The relationship between arbitration and the courts*:** In Ireland, public policy dictates "that parties should be encouraged as far as possible to settle their disputes without recourse to [the courts]".[1] Arbitration, being "an effective way of obtaining a final and binding decision on a dispute or series of disputes, without reference to a court of law"[2] promotes that public policy.[3] However, as a private means of resolving a dispute, arbitration is dependent on the underlying support of the courts to prevent a party from sabotaging arbitral proceedings and arbitration is dependent on the courts to enforce awards made.[4] It has been noted that:

> "[Arbitration] is a fundamentally consensual means of dispute resolution: unless the parties have agreed to arbitrate, there can be no valid arbitral determination of their rights. In turn, an agreement to arbitrate has binding effect only by virtue of a complex framework of national and international law, ultimately enforced via national courts. Equally, an arbitral award has binding effect, and can be recognised and enforced, only be virtue of this same legal framework".[5]

The relationship between arbitration and the courts requires a delicate balancing act as, although arbitration requires the courts to fulfil certain supervisory functions to protect the effectiveness of arbitration, too much interference by the courts will render arbitration redundant as a way of resolving disputes without reference to the courts. The Act and the Model Law achieves this balance through two provisions which safeguard the fundamental principles of arbitration:

1. Where the parties' chosen dispute resolution mechanism is arbitration, effect must be given to their choice and any dispute must be referred to arbitration[6]; and
2. The High Court is permitted to intervene in arbitral proceedings only where it is expressly authorised to do so under the provisions of either the Act[7] or of the Model Law.[8]

---

[1] *Greencore Group plc v Murphy* [1995] 3 IR 520 at 525.

[2] Blackaby, Partasides, Redfern and Hunter, *Redfern and Hunter on International Arbitration* (5th ed, Oxford University Press, Oxford, 2009) p 2.

[3] Notwithstanding the stated public policy of encouraging parties to settle disputes without recourse to the courts, there are limits upon the parties' freedom of choice to arbitrate disputes. The concept of 'arbitrability' dictates that only certain types of disputes are capable of being resolved by arbitration. See Blackaby, Partasides, Redfern and Hunter, *Redfern and Hunter on International Arbitration* (5th ed, Oxford University Press, Oxford, 2009) pp 439-440.

(*Continued*)

[4] Blackaby, Partasides, Redfern and Hunter, *Redfern and Hunter on International Arbitration* (5th ed, Oxford University Press, Oxford, 2009) p 439.
[5] Born, *International Commercial Arbitration Vol. 1* (1st ed, Kluwer Law International, Alphen aan den Rijn, 2009) p 90.
[6] Model Law, Art 8.
[7] Arbitration Act 2010, s 6.
[8] Model Law, Art 5.

Permitted intervention by the High Court: This article provides that court intervention is permitted "where so provided by [the Model Law]". In Ireland, the provisions of the Model Law are supplemented by the Act.[1] Other than applications to refer pending civil proceedings to arbitration, which are heard in the court in which the proceedings themselves are commenced,[2] all other court intervention permitted under this Act and the Model Law is to be performed by the High Court.[3] The High Court is permitted to intervene:

1. To provide interim protection before or during arbitral proceedings;[4]
2. To appoint an arbitrator or arbitrators in the absence of agreement of the parties;[5]
3. To appoint an arbitrator or arbitrators where there has been a failure in the agreement of the parties;[6]
4. To decide on a challenge to the appointment of an arbitrator;[7]
5. To appoint an arbitrator where there has been a failure or an impossibility in an arbitrator who had been appointed acting;[8]
6. To rule on the jurisdiction of an arbitral tribunal where requested to do so by a party within 30 days of the arbitral tribunal's own ruling;[9]
7. To recognise interim measures issued by an arbitral tribunal;[10]
8. To refuse to recognise interim measures issued by an arbitral tribunal;[11]
9. To order interim measures in relation to arbitral proceedings;[12]
10. To assist in the taking evidence at the request of an arbitral tribunal or a party;[13]
11. To recognise and enforce an award where Ireland was not the place of arbitration;[14]
12. To refuse to recognise and enforce an award where Ireland was not the place of arbitration;[15]
13. To enforce an award where Ireland was the place of arbitration;[16] or
14. To enforce the pecuniary obligations of an award rendered pursuant to the Washington Convention.[17]

Unless the Act or the Model Law expressly provides that the parties may agree otherwise, any agreement of the parties which purports to oust the supervisory functions of the High Court is likely to be void as being contrary to public policy.[18]

---

[1] Arbitration Act 2010, s 6.
[2] Model Law, Art 8.

(*Continued*)

[3] Arbitration Act 2010, s 9(1).
[4] Model Law, Art 9 and Arbitration Act 2010, s 10(1).
[5] Model Law, Art 11(3).
[6] Model Law, Art 11(4).
[7] Model Law, Art 13(3).
[8] Model Law, Art 14.
[9] Model Law, Art 16(3).
[10] Model Law, Art 17 H.
[11] Model Law, Art 17 I.
[12] Model Law, Art 17 J.
[13] Model Law, Art 27 and Arbitration Act 2010, s 10(1).
[14] Model Law, Art 35.
[15] Model Law, Art 36.
[16] Arbitration Act 2010, s 23(1).
[17] Arbitration Act 2010, s 25(5).
[18] *Czarnikow v Roth, Schmidt & Co* [1922] 2 KB 478, which is a decision of the English Court of Appeal where the parties had agreed that they would not invoke the special case stated procedure under the English Arbitration Act 1889, s 7 after an award was issued by the arbitral tribunal. This agreement was held to be an ouster of the jurisdiction of the courts and was void as being contrary to public policy. Scrutton LJ stated at p 488 that: "Arbitrators, unless expressly otherwise authorized, have to apply the laws of England ... This is done in order that the Courts may insure the proper administration of the law by inferior tribunals. In my view to allow English citizens to agree to exclude this safeguard for the administration of the law is contrary to public policy. There must be no Alsatia in England where the King's writ does not run". The decision in *Czarnikow v Roth, Schmidt & Co* has received judicial approval in Ireland in *Uniform Construction Ltd v Cappawhite Contractors Ltd* [2007] IEHC 295; and *John Mowlem Construction Ltd t/a Irishenco Construction v Dublin City Council* [2009] IEHC 225.

***Matters governed by the Model Law*:** The restricted nature of court intervention only applies to matters governed by the Model Law.[1] Court intervention in matters outside the Model Law, which commentators have noted may include a general or residual power to supervise arbitral proceedings, is governed by domestic law.[2] Where the Model Law is silent on a matter, the question arises as to what the effect of its silence is. The *travaux préparatoires* (of which Irish courts are permitted to take judicial notice when interpreting provisions of the Model Law)[3] acknowledge that silence might imply any of three results: first, it could mean that the matter was not a matter governed by the Model Law and that a court could therefore intervene in accordance with its domestic law; second, it could mean that the matter is a matter governed by the Model Law and that court intervention is not permitted; or, finally, it could mean that the drafters of the Model Law simply did not consider the matter all.[4] Where the Model Law is silent, the *travaux préparatoires* suggest that a matter may be governed by the Model Law either "expressly or impliedly"[5] and that whether, in fact, a matter is governed by the Model Law must be determined on a case-by-case basis in accordance with the normal rules of statutory interpretation.[6] However, the *travaux préparatoires* also suggest a non-exhaustive list of matters not governed by the Model Law[7],

(*Continued*)

which has been added to be commentators.[8] In Ireland certain of these matters are expressly governed by the Act. The matters listed in the *travaux préparatoires* and added to by commentators as being outside the Model Law include:

1. The capacity of parties to conclude an arbitration agreement;
2. The impact of State immunity, which in Ireland is expressly governed by the Act;[9]
3. The contractual or other relations between parties and an arbitral tribunal or an arbitral institution;
4. The fixing of fees and costs and requests for deposits or security;
5. Consolidation of arbitral proceedings, which in Ireland is expressly governed by the Act;[10]
6. The period of time for the enforcement of arbitral awards;
7. The role of courts prior to the selection of the place of arbitration;
8. The liability of arbitrators for misconduct, which in Ireland is expressly governed by the Act;[11]
9. The competence of a court to execute a request to assist in the taking of evidence and the rules according to which it does so, which in Ireland is expressly governed by the Act;[12] and
10. The concept of 'arbitrability' or whether certain disputes are capable of resolution by arbitration.[13]

International case-law decided under the Model Law has held that judicial intervention into arbitration should be restricted[14] and where the Model Law (or arbitration legislation giving effect to provisions of the Model Law) expressly provides for a matter then a court is prohibited from asserting broader powers of inherent jurisdiction going beyond the limited powers of interference provided by the Model Law.[15] Commentators have expressed similar views and have noted that "[t]his means that unless the High Court has been accorded a specific role by the [Model Law], then it cannot intervene; inherent jurisdiction and other vestiges of the past are swept away".[16] However, where the Model Law does not provide for a matter, a court may apply domestic law, including, potentially, its inherent jurisdiction to decide the matter.[17]

---

[1] Model Law, Art 5.

[2] Holtzmann and Neuhaus, *A Guide to the UNCITRAL Model Law on International Commercial Arbitration* (1st ed, Kluwer Law and Taxation Publishers, The Hague, 1989) p 216.

[3] Arbitration Act 2010, s 8(1).

[4] UNCITRAL Sixth Secretariat Note (U.K. Comments), A/CN.9/263/ADD.2, paras 22-25.

[5] UNCITRAL Seventh Secretariat Note, A/CN.9/264, Art 5, para 4.

[6] UNCITRAL Commission Report, A/40/17, Art 5, para 61.

[7] UNCITRAL Seventh Secretariat Note, A/CN.9/264, Art 5, para 5.

[8] Holtzmann and Neuhaus, *A Guide to the UNCITRAL Model Law on International Commercial Arbitration* (1st ed, Kluwer Law and Taxation Publishers, The Hague, 1989) p 218.

[9] Arbitration Act 2010, s 28.

(Continued)

[10] Arbitration Act 2010, s 16.
[11] Arbitration Act 2010, s 22.
[12] Arbitration Act 2010, s 10.
[13] Model Law, Art 1(5) expressly reserves the concept of arbitrability to domestic law.
[14] CLOUT Case 16 – Canada/British Columbia Court of Appeal: *Quintette Coal Ltd v Nippon Steel Corp* (24 October 1990).
[15] CLOUT Case 513 – Canada/Alberta Court of Queen's Bench: *Western Oil Sands Inc v Allianz Insurance Co* (2 February 2004).
[16] Reichert, "Security for Costs in Arbitration – A New Landscape in Ireland" (2010) *Arbitration and ADR Review*, p 130.
[17] CLOUT Case 450/CLOUT Case 601 – Hong Kong/High Court of Hong Kong: *Owners of the M/V Fu Ning Hai v Whistler International Ltd, Charters of the M/V Fu Ning Hai* (24 May 1999).

Article 6.—Court or other authority for certain functions of arbitration assistance and supervision

The functions referred to in articles 11(3), 11(4), 13(3), 14, 16(3) and 34(2) shall be performed by ... [Each State enacting this model law specifies the court, courts or, where referred to therein, other authority competent to perform these functions.]

Definitions

'court': Model Law, Art 2(c); 'Model Law': Arbitration Act 2010, s 2(1).

Notes

***Designation of a specific court*:** This article provides that a State adopting the Model Law must designate a specific court or courts to fulfil certain supervisory functions. The designated court in Ireland is the High Court.[1]

The *travaux préparatoires* (of which Irish courts are permitted to take judicial notice when interpreting provisions of the Model Law)[2] suggest that the rationale for requiring that a State adopting the Model Law to designate a specific court or courts to fulfil certain supervisory functions is to aid foreign parties in locating the competent court and, more importantly, to encourage specialisation by the designated court in the field of arbitration.[2]

---

[1] Arbitration Act 2010, s 9(1).
[2] Arbitration Act 2010, s 8(1).
[3] UNCITRAL Seventh Secretarial Note, A/CN.9/264, Art 6, para 2.

***Supervisory functions of the High Court to be performed by the President of the High Court or his nominee*:** All supervisory functions in connection with arbitral proceedings under the Act and the Model Law are to be performed by the President of the High Court or his nominee.[1] At present, the High Court's supervisory functions are performed in the Chancery list or in the Commercial list where a matter has been adopted into it.

[1] Arbitration Act 2010, s 9(3).

***Supervisory functions to be fulfilled by the High Court*:** The High Court's[1] supervisory functions under the Model Law are:

1. To appoint an arbitrator or arbitrators in the absence of agreement of the parties;[2]
2. To appoint an arbitrator or arbitrators where there has been a failure in the agreement of the parties;[3]
3. To decide on a challenge to the appointment of an arbitrator;[4]
4. To appoint an arbitrator where there has been a failure or an impossibility in an arbitrator who had been appointed acting;[5] and
5. To rule on the jurisdiction of an arbitral tribunal where requested to do so by a party within 30 days of the arbitral tribunal's own ruling.[6]

In addition, the High Court's supervisory functions under the Act are:

1. To provide interim protection before or during arbitral proceedings;[7]
2. To recognise interim measures issued by an arbitral tribunal;[8]
3. To refuse to recognise and enforce interim measures issued by an arbitral tribunal;[9]
4. To order interim measures in relation to arbitral proceedings;[10]
5. To assist in the taking evidence at the request of an arbitral tribunal or a party;[11]
6. To recognise and enforce an arbitral award where Ireland was not the place of arbitration;[12] and
7. To refuse to recognise and enforce an arbitral award where Ireland was not the place of arbitration.[13]

[1] Arbitration Act 2010, s 9(1)(a).
[2] Model Law, Art 11(3).
[3] Model Law, Art 11(4).
[4] Model Law, Art 13(3).
[5] Model Law, Art 14.
[6] Model Law, Art 16(3).

(*Continued*)

[7] Arbitration Act 2010, s 9(1)(b); and Model Law, Art 9.
[8] Arbitration Act 2010, s 9(1)(c); and Model Law, Art 17 H.
[9] Arbitration Act 2010, s 9(1)(c); and Model Law, Art 17 I.
[10] Arbitration Act 2010, s 9(1)(c); and Model Law, Art 17 J.
[11] Arbitration Act 2010, s 9(1)(c); and Model Law, Art 27.
[12] Arbitration Act 2010, s 9(1)(c); and Model Law, Art 35.
[13] Arbitration Act 2010, s 9(1)(c); and Model Law, Art 36.

Chapter II

Arbitration Agreement

Option I

Article 7.—Definition and form of arbitration agreement

(1) "Arbitration agreement" is an agreement by the parties to submit to arbitration all or certain disputes which have arisen or which may arise between them in respect of a defined legal relationship, whether contractual or not. An arbitration agreement may be in the form of an arbitration clause in a contract or in the form of a separate agreement.

(2) The arbitration agreement shall be in writing.

(3) An arbitration agreement is in writing if its content is recorded in any form, whether or not the arbitration agreement or contract has been concluded orally, by conduct, or by other means.

(4) The requirement that an arbitration agreement be in writing is met by an electronic communication if the information contained therein is accessible so as to be useable for subsequent reference;

"electronic communication" means any communication that the parties make by means of data messages;

"data message" means information generated, sent, received or stored by electronic, magnetic, optical or similar means, including, but not limited to, electronic data interchange (EDI), electronic mail, telegram, telex or telecopy.

(5) Furthermore, an arbitration agreement is in writing if it is contained in an exchange of statements of claim and defence in which the existence of an agreement is alleged by one party and not denied by the other.

(6) The reference in a contract to any document containing an arbitration clause constitutes an arbitration agreement in writing, provided that the reference is such as to make that clause part of the contract.

Option II

[...]

Definitions

'arbitration': Arbitration Act 2010, s 2(1) and Model Law, Art 2(a); 'arbitration agreement': Arbitration Act 2010, s 2(1) and Model Law, Art 7(1)(Option 1).

Notes

***Definition of 'arbitration agreement'*:** The Model Law provides for two distinct definitions of the term 'arbitration agreement', either of which can be adopted by a State enacting the provisions of the Model Law: Option I, which requires an arbitration agreement to in writing; and Option II, which does not.[1] Both Options I and Option II provide that an arbitration agreement can relate to existing or future disputes resulting in no distinction being made between a submission agreement to refer an existing dispute to arbitration and an arbitration clause to refer any future disputes that may arise between the parties to arbitration.[2] In Ireland, the Act has adopted Option I of the Model Law resulting in a requirement that an arbitration agreement be in writing.[3] This requirement is consistent with the arbitration legislation of most arbitration regimes worldwide.[4]

---

[1] Model Law, Art 7.

[2] Roth in Weigand, *Practitioner's Handbook on International Commercial Arbitration, UNCITRAL Model Law on International Commercial Arbitration* (2nd ed, Oxford University Press, Oxford, 2009) pp 983-984.

[3] Arbitration Act 2010, s 2(1).

[4] See, for example, the English Arbitration Act 1996, s 5; the German ZPO, s 1031; the Singapore Arbitration Act 1996, s 4(3); and the US Federal Arbitration Act, 9 USC, s 2. Arbitration statutes that do not include a formal requirement for a written arbitration agreement include the New Zealand Arbitration Act 1996, 1st sch, Art 7(1); and the Swedish Arbitration Act (SFS 1999:116), Art 1. Similarly, the New York Convention, Art II provides that contracting States are only required to recognise and enforce arbitral awards issued in other contracting States where an arbitration agreement is made in writing.

***Requirement that an arbitration agreement be in writing*:** Option I of the Model Law requires an arbitration agreement to be in writing.[1] However, an arbitration agreement will be deemed to be in writing where its content is recorded in any form, whether or not it has been concluded orally, by conduct, or by other means.[2] Similarly, an arbitration agreement will be deemed to be in writing where it is recorded by an electronic communication;[3] where it is contained in an exchange of statements of claim and defence in which the existence of an agreement is alleged by one party and not denied by the other;[4] or where a written agreement to arbitration is incorporated by reference into a contract.[5] The purpose of the requirement that an arbitration agreement be in writing is to meet the formal requirements of the New York Convention concerning recognition and enforcement of foreign awards[6] and to provide manifest proof of consent to the arbitration agreement.[7]

In Ireland, the courts have traditionally adopted a liberal approach to whether or not an arbitration agreement is in writing. Irish case-law decided under the Arbitration Acts 1954-1998[8] has held that an arbitration agreement may be incorporated by reference into a matrix contract[9] and has held that an agreement to arbitrate based on the business dealings between the parties, business realties or a standard form contract may constitute a valid arbitration agreement.[10] In a seminal case decided under the Act and the Model Law,[11] while the High Court held that on the facts presented no valid arbitration agreement

(*Continued*)

existed in circumstances where a subcontract containing an arbitration agreement was sent to a party but the subcontract was never concluded, it was nevertheless stated that:

> "[i]t is ... unnecessary for a party seeking to establish the existence of an arbitration agreement to prove that a particular contract was executed or signed but rather what is required by statute is that the arbitration agreement be in writing. It is possible for the agreement to arbitrate to be concluded orally or by the conduct of the parties or by other means provided the content of the arbitration agreement is recorded in any form".[12]

A similarly liberal approach, as to whether or not an arbitration agreement is in writing, is evident from international case-law decided under the Model Law. For example, it has been held that an arbitration agreement does not require a signature;[13] that pre-contractual negotiations can be used as evidence of a purported arbitration agreement where a document has not been signed;[14] and that an arbitration agreement may be incorporated on the reverse of a standard form contract provided that the contract was expressly made subject to the terms and conditions set forth on its reverse notwithstanding that only the face of the document was faxed to the other party.[15] However, international case-law has held that some evidence of a written document must be produced for the requirement that an arbitration agreement be in writing to be met[16] and that the mere assertion in a party's own documents of the existence of a valid arbitration agreement will be insufficient to prove its conclusion through an exchange of documents.[17]

---

[1] Model Law, Art 7(2) (Option I).

[2] Model Law, Art 7(3) (Option I).

[3] Model Law, Art 7(4) provides that an arbitration agreement will be deemed to be in writing where it is recorded by an electronic communication on condition that the information contained therein is accessible so as to be useable for subsequent reference.

[4] Model Law, Art 7(5) (Option I).

[5] Model Law, Art 7(6) (Option I).

[6] The New York Convention, Art II(2).

[7] Brekoulakis and Shore in Mistelis, *Concise International Arbitration, UNCITRAL Model Law* (1st ed, Kluwer Law International, Alphen aan den Rijn, 2010) p 596.

[8] Arbitration Act 1954, s 2(1) required an arbitration agreement to be in writing.

[9] *Sweeney v Mulcahy* [1993] ILRM 289.

[10] *McCrory Scaffolding v McInerney Contruction Ltd* [2004] 3 IR 592; and *Lynch Roofing Systems (Ballaghaderreen) Ltd v Christopher Bennett & Son (Construction) Ltd* [1999] 2 IR 450.

[11] *Barnmore Demolition and Civil Engineering Ltd v Alandale Logistics Ltd*, unreported, High Court (Feeney J), 11 November 2010.

[12] *ibid.*, at 4.

[13] CLOUT Case 365 – Canada/Saskatchewan Court of Queen's: *Schiff Food Products Inc v Naber Seed & Grain Co Ltd* (1 October 1996).

[14] CLOUT Case 40 – Hong Kong/High Court of Hong Kong: *Pacific International Lines (PTE) Ltd & Another v Tsinlien Metals and Minerals Co Ltd* (30 July 1992).

[15] CLOUT Case 671 – Hong Kong/High Court of Hong Kong: *Landale Development Ltd v Zhen Heng Development Ltd* (12 January 1990).

[16] CLOUT Case 64 – Hong Kong/High Court of Hong Kong: *H Small Ltd v Goldroyce Garment Ltd* (13 May 1994).

[17] CLOUT Case 670 – Germany/Highest Regional Court of Cologne: *9 Sch 16/02* (22 July 2002).

***An oral agreement to arbitrate*:** At common law, an oral agreement to arbitrate was enforceable as a contract, and a 'private' arbitration could be conducted even if arbitration legislation did not apply to a resulting arbitration[1] and the High Court had an inherent jurisdiction to refer pending civil proceedings to arbitration where an arbitration agreement exists.[2] However, the *travaux préparatoires* (of which Irish courts are permitted to take judicial notice when interpreting provisions of the Model Law)[3] suggest that no parallel arbitration regime may exist alongside the Model Law[4] and, therefore, it is uncertain whether or not an oral agreement to arbitrate will continue to be enforceable as a contract in Ireland following the adoption of the Model Law.[5] This uncertainty is more a theoretical than a practical concern as the purported existence of oral arbitration agreements is unlikely to arise with any frequency not least due to the difficulty in proving their existence.

---

[1] Most arbitration legislation requires an arbitration agreement to be in writing. See Dowling-Hussey and Dunne, *Arbitration Law* (1st ed, Thomson Round Hall, Dublin, 2008) p 90.

[2] *Re Via Net Works (Ireland) Ltd* [2002] 2 IR 47, where the Supreme Court (Keane CJ) cited with approval a passage from the House of Lords' (as it then was) decision in *Channel Group v Balfour Beatty Ltd* [1993] AC 334 which stated: "that those who make agreements for the resolution of disputes must show good reasons for departing from them, but also with the interests of the orderly regulation of international commerce, that having promised to take their complaints to the experts and if necessary to the arbitrators, that is where the appellants should go". However, where Model Law applies, the courts have no inherent jurisdiction to act. In this regard, Model Law, Art 5 of the Model Law provides that "[i]n matters governed by this Law, no court shall intervene except where so provided in this Law".

[3] Arbitration Act 2010, s 8(1).

[4] UNCITRAL Third Working Group Report, A/CN.9/233, Art II [Model Law, Art 7 in the final text], para 66.

[5] Arbitration Act 2010, s 6.

***Capacity to enter into an arbitration agreement*:** Whether a party has capacity to enter into an arbitration agreement is not covered by the Model Law, which the *travaux préparatoires* (of which Irish courts are permitted to take judicial notice when interpreting provisions of the Model Law)[1] confirm was a deliberate approach.[2] Therefore, the normal rules of contract law apply to determine whether or not a party has capacity to enter into an arbitration agreement.[3] In Ireland minors; intoxicated persons; and those suffering from mental illness do not typically have capacity to enter into a binding contract.[4]

---

[1] Arbitration Act 2010, s 8(1).

[2] UNCITRAL First Working Group Report, A/CN.9/216, para 28.

[3] Brekoulakis and Shore in Mistelis, *Concise International Arbitration, UNCITRAL Model Law* (1st ed, Kluwer Law International, Alphen aan den Rijn, 2010) p 598.

[4] For a discussion on contractual capacity in Ireland, see McDermott, *Contract Law* (1st ed, Butterworth (Ireland) Ltd, Dublin, 2001) pp 887-915.

***Non-signatory parties to an arbitration agreement*:** The circumstances under which a non-signatory may be party to an arbitration agreement is not covered by the Model Law. Therefore, the normal rules of contract law apply to determine whether or not a legal person, although a non-signatory, is really a party to an arbitration.[1] As some commentators have noted the question of a non-signatory party to an arbitration agreement arise:

> "when an individual or a legal entity which is not a [signatory] to the arbitration agreement wishes to join in the arbitration as one of the claimants – or, more usually, is brought unwillingly into the arbitration as one of the respondents. A common example is that of a claimant with a dispute under contract between itself and the subsidiary of a major international corporation. The contract contains an arbitration [agreement], and so arbitration can be compelled against the subsidiary company; but the claimant would very much like to bring the parent company into the arbitration, so as it improve its chances of being paid, if it succeeds in its claim".[2]

Although much reference is made to the 'extension' of an arbitration agreement in circumstances where a non-signatory to the agreement is joined as a party to arbitral proceedings, as commentators have noted, this terminology "appears inaccurate"[3] as the arbitration agreement is not being extended. Rather the true parties to arbitration agreement are correctly identified.[4] Theories by which a non-signatory may be regarded as a true party to an arbitration agreement include agency; alter ego; implied consent; the 'group of companies doctrine'; estoppel; beneficiary law; guarantee, subrogation; succession; ratification; and assumption.[5]

---

[1] Born, *International Commercial Arbitration* (1st ed, Kluwer Law International, Alphen aan den Rijn, 2009) p 1138.

[2] Blackaby, Partasides, Redfern and Hunter, *Redfern and Hunter on International Arbitration* (5th ed, Oxford University Press, Oxford, 2009) p 38. For a recent example of the problem of a non-signatory party, see *Dallah Real Estate Co v The Ministry of Religious Affairs of Pakistan* [2011] 1 AC 763, which is a decision of the UK Supreme Court. In that case the claimant, a Saudi company, approached the Pakistan Ministry of Religious Affairs with a proposal to provide accommodation in Mecca to pilgrims from Pakistan conducting the Hajj. Following negotiations, the claimant and the government of Pakistan signed a memorandum of understanding under which the claimant agreed to acquire the land, build accommodation suitable for pilgrims and lease it to the government of Pakistan. However, the government of Pakistan had established a trust as a convenient vehicle for the project. Negotiations between the claimant and the government of Pakistan continued and culminated with an agreement between the claimant and the trust. The government of Pakistan was not expressed to be a party to the agreement, nor did it sign it in any capacity. The agreement contained an arbitration agreement. After the trust failed to meet its obligation under the agreement the claimant commenced arbitral proceedings against the Pakistan Ministry of Religious Affairs. Applying French law, the arbitral tribunal found that the Pakistan Ministry of Religious Affairs was a proper party to the arbitration agreement and issued an award in favour of the claimant. However, when the claimant sought to recognise and enforce the award in England, the English High Court found that as a matter of French law the Pakistan Ministry of Religious Affairs was not a proper party to the arbitration agreement and refused recognition and enforcement of the award. This decision was upheld by the English Court of Appeal and subsequently the UK Supreme Court. The decision is controversial and has generated much debate by commentators.

(*Continued*)

[3] Born, *International Commercial Arbitration* (1st ed, Kluwer Law International, Alphen aan den Rijn, 2009) p 1139.

[4] *ibid*, p 1139.

[5] *ibid*, pp 1137-1138. For a discussion on each of these theories in the context of international arbitration, see Born, *International Commercial Arbitration* (1st ed, Kluwer Law International, Alphen aan den Rijn, 2009) pp 1137-1210.

Article 8.—Arbitration agreement and substantive claim before court

(1) A court before which an action is brought in a matter which is the subject of an arbitration agreement shall, if a party so requests not later than when submitting his first statement on the substance of the dispute, refer the parties to arbitration unless it finds that the agreement is null and void, inoperative or incapable of being performed.

(2) Where an action referred to in paragraph (1) of this article has been brought, arbitral proceedings may nevertheless be commenced or continued, and an award may be made, while the issue is pending before the court.

Definitions

'arbitration': Arbitration Act 2010, s 2(1) and Model Law, Art 2(a); 'arbitration agreement': Arbitration Act 2010, s 2(1) and Model Law, Art 7(1) (Option 1); 'award': Arbitration Act 2010, s 2(1); 'court': Model Law, Art 2(c).

Notes

Requirement that courts in which civil proceedings are commenced must refer parties to arbitration and its extraterritorial effect: To promote certainty and party autonomy, mature legal systems support dispute resolution mechanisms chosen by parties to an agreement.[1] Furthermore, it has long been Irish public policy that "parties should be encouraged as far as possible to settle their disputes without recourse to litigation".[2] Where civil proceedings are commenced in a matter which is the subject of an arbitration agreement, the provisions of the Model Law require the court in which the litigation is commenced to decline jurisdiction and, upon request, refer the parties to arbitration, unless it finds that the agreement is null and void, inoperative or incapable of being performed.[3] This requirement applies irrespective of where the place of arbitration, or the potential place of arbitration, is or will be.[4]

---

[1] Born, *International Commercial Arbitration Vol. 1* (1st ed, Kluwer Law International, Alphen aan den Rijn, 2009) p 90.

[2] *Greencore Group plc v Murphy* [1995] 3 IR 520 at 525.

[3] Model Law, Art 8(1). Whether a matter is 'subject of an arbitration agreement' must be given a broad interpretation. See *Gulliver v Brady & ors t/a Matheson Ormsby Prentice* [2003] IESC 68 where the Supreme Court held that the phrases "in relation to" and "arising out of" contained in an arbitration agreement must be given a broad meaning. See also *Ashville Investments Ltd v Elmer Contractors Ltd* [1989] QB 488, where the English Court

(*Continued*)

of Appeal similarly held that the phrase "in connection with" contained in an arbitration agreement should be given a broad meaning. A matter may be subject of an arbitration agreement even where the dispute involves the alleged breach of certain statutory rights. See *Re Via Net Works (Ireland) Ltd* [2002] 2 IR 47; and *Fulham Football Club (1987) Ltd v Richards* [2012] 1 All ER 414, which is a decision of the English Court of Appeal.

[4] Model Law, Art 1(2).

'Null and void, inoperative or incapable of being performed': Although a court need not refer the parties to arbitration where it finds that the arbitration agreement is 'null and void, inoperative or incapable of being performed',[1] neither the text of the Model Law nor the *travaux préparatoires* (of which Irish courts are permitted to take judicial notice when interpreting provisions of the Model Law)[2] provide any guidance on the meaning of the term.[3] However, international case-law decided under the Model Law has held arbitration agreements to be invalid only in very limited circumstances, such as where the arbitration agreement provided that one of the parties was to act as an arbitrator;[4] or where a party was rendered insolvent and unable to afford to commence arbitral proceedings as a result of the other parties' actions.[5] In contrast, international case-law has held arbitration agreements to be valid where the parties agreed to refer a dispute to a non-existent arbitral tribunal;[6] where an arbitral institution agreed by the parties no longer exists;[7] and where one party alleges that the arbitration agreement was rescinded or superseded.[8] International case-law has also held that where one party has alleged that an arbitration agreement has been revoked then there must be demonstrable evidence of the purported revocation.[9]

[1] Model Law, Art 8(1).

[2] Arbitration Act 2010, s 8(1).

[3] Holtzmann and Neuhaus, *A Guide to the UNCITRAL Model Law on International Commercial Arbitration* (1st ed, Kluwer Law and Taxation Publishers, The Hague, 1989) p 305.

[4] CLOUT Case 66 – Canada/Superior Court of Quebec: *Jean Charbonneau v Les Industries AC Davie Inc* (14 March 1991).

[5] CLOUT Case 404 – Germany/Supreme Court: *III ZR 33/00* (14 September 2000). However, English case-law has held that while the financial position of a party is a relevant consideration, it is not a decisive consideration when determining whether a stay of litigation should be granted to permit a matter to be referred to arbitration. See *Fakes v Taylor Woodrow Construction Ltd* [1973] QB 436 and *Goodman v Winchester & Alton Railway plc* [1985] 1 WLR 141, which are both decisions of the English Court of Appeal.

[6] CLOUT Case 871 – Germany/Highest Regional Court of Karlsruhe: *1 U 232/06* (4 April 2007).

[7] CLOUT Case 509 – Canada/Ontario Court of Appeal: *Dalimpex Ltd v Janicki; Agros Trading Spolka ZOO v Dalimpex Ltd* (30 May 2003).

[8] CLOUT Case 522 – Hong Kong/High Court of Hong Kong: *Paladin Agricultural Ltd & Others v Excelsior Hotel (Hong Kong) Ltd* (6 March 2001); CLOUT CASE 525 – Hong Kong/High Court of Hong Kong: *Daily Win Engineering Ltd v The Incorporated Owners of Greenwood Terrace* (7 June 2001); and CLOUT CASE 706 – Hong Kong/High Court of Hong Kong: *Fustar Chemicals Ltd v Sinochem Liaoning Hong Kong Ltd* (5 June 1996).

[9] CLOUT Case 370 – Zimbabwe/Harare High Court: *Bitumat Ltd v Multicom Ltd* (31 May 2000).

***Reference to arbitration requires a stay of litigation rather that a dismissal*:** The text of the Model Law does not specify whether a court-ordered reference to arbitration requires a mandatory stay of civil proceedings or whether it requires the litigation to be dismissed in its entirety. As commentators have noted, the courts in all leading common law systems typically stay litigation commenced in violation of a valid arbitration agreement, while the courts of many civil law jurisdictions simply decline jurisdiction over arbitrable disputes.[1] The Act, albeit in passing, clarifies that Irish litigation commenced in violation of a valid arbitration agreement will be subject of a mandatory stay and will not be dismissed in its entirety,[2] as was recently noted by the High Court:

> "Paragraph 1 of Article 8 [of the Model Law] has the same objective as [section] 5 of the Arbitration Act 1980, namely, to make it mandatory for a court to compel the parties to an arbitration agreement to engage in the arbitral process as a means to resolving their dispute or disputes ... it is interesting to note that the terminology used in [section 11 of the Act], where it is provided that there shall be no appeal from "any court determination of a *stay application* ... "" (*emphasis added*).[3]

---

[1] Born, *International Commercial Arbitration Vol. 1* (1st ed, Kluwer Law International, Alphen aan den Rijn, 2009) pp 1026-1027.

[2] Arbitration Act 2010, s 11(a).

[3] *Osmond Ireland On Farm Business Ltd v McFarland* [2010] IEHC 295.

***Requirement that a party request that an action be referred to arbitration and the time limit for doing so*:** Notwithstanding the existence of a valid arbitration agreement, international case-law suggests that a court cannot act *ex officio* and unilaterally refer a dispute to arbitration;[1] a party must request that the court do so.[2] The party's request is required to be made not later than when submitting its first statement on the substance of the dispute in the action pending before a court. International case-law decided under the Model Law has held that the time limit will be strictly enforced and where a statement of defence is filed without containing a request for arbitration, the right to arbitration is waived.[3]

In Ireland, a party serving a defence to plenary proceedings will waive its right to request that the dispute be referred to arbitration, unless the defence contains a request for arbitration. It is also likely that the filing of an affidavit in defence to summary proceedings will be regarded as "a first statement on the substance of the dispute", unless that party makes clear that the affidavit is filed without prejudice to the entitlement to refer the matter to arbitration. Indeed, this was the position[4] under an analogous provision of the Arbitration Acts 1954-1998, which required an application to refer pending civil proceedings to arbitration to be brought before "delivering any pleadings or taking any other step".[5] In the context of that analogous provision the Supreme Court cited with approval *Halsbury's Laws of England*,[6] which stated that:

> "Steps in the proceedings have been held to include: the filing of an affidavit in opposition to a summons for summary judgment, service of a defence, and an application to the court for leave to serve interrogatories, or for a stay pending the

(*Continued*)

giving of security for costs, or for an extension of time for serving a defence, or for an order of discovery, or for an order for further and better particulars. The following have been held not to be steps: acts preliminary to the issue of proceedings, a request in correspondence for an extension of time for serving a defence, the filing of affidavits in answer to an application by the plaintiff for the appointment of a receiver, transferring a summons into counsel's list, applying to strike out a defective statement of claim, resisting an application for an interlocutory injunction by putting in evidence and appearing in court, and applying for a stay on grounds other than that the dispute was subject to an arbitration payment".[7]

---

[1] CLOUT Case 508 – Canada/Ontario Superior Court of Justice: *United Laboratories, Inc v Abraham* (8 October 2002); and CLOUT Case 657 – Croatia/High Commercial Court: *Pž-7481/03* (27 April 2004).

[2] Model Law, Art 8(1).

[3] CLOUT Case 181 – Canada/British Columbia Supreme Court: *Queensland Sugar Corp v "The Hanjin Jedda"* (24 March 1995); and CLOUT Case 621 – Canada/British Columbia Supreme Court: *Robert Wall and ors v Scott's Hospitality (BC) Inc* (6 March 1990).

[4] *Gleeson v Grimes & anor* [2007] 4 IR 417; and *Dublin Docklands Development Authority v Jermyn Street Ltd & anor* [2010] IEHC 217.

[5] Arbitration Act 1980, s 5(1).

[6] 4th edition, reissue, Volume 2 at paragraph 627.

[7] *O'Dwyer v Boyd* [2002] IESC 54 at p 13.

***The appropriate standard of judicial review*:** Before a court refers a matter to arbitration, a valid arbitration agreement must exist.[1] Where there is no valid arbitration agreement there can be no arbitration and the parties to a dispute are entitled to resolve their differences by commencing civil proceedings. While this concept is straightforward, in practice its application is less simple. Where one party to an action asserts that a valid arbitration agreement exists, which another party denies, the question arises as to whether the existence of a purported arbitration agreement should be decided by the courts or whether an arbitral tribunal should be constituted to make that decision.[2] When attempting to answer this question a court in which civil proceedings are commenced is presented with a dilemma: refer the parties to arbitration for an arbitral tribunal to decide on the validity of the purported arbitration agreement and risk wasting time, money and other resources in arbitral proceedings which are challenged by one of the parties; or make a decision on its validity and risk permitting a party who is bound by the arbitration agreement, but who no longer wants to arbitrate, the opportunity to seek the intervention of the courts merely to delay the commencement or progression of arbitral proceedings.[3]

Although competing provisions of the Model Law provide both arbitral tribunals[4] and the courts[5] with parallel powers to decide whether a valid arbitration agreement exists, where litigation is commenced, the court in which the litigation is pending is entitled to make the decision.[6] However, the Model Law is silent on the standard of judicial review to be applied by the court.[7] International case-law has typically held that one of two standards of judicial review applies:[8]

(*Continued*)

1. Full judicial review, which requires the court to make a final determination on the existence of an arbitration agreement[9]; or
2. *Prima facie* judicial review, which requires the court to refer the matter to the arbitral tribunal for determination where a party establishes a *prima facie* case for the existence of an arbitration agreement.[10]

In a seminal case decided under the provisions of the Act and the Model Law,[11] the High Court declined to set out definitively the appropriate standard of judicial review to be applied as it held that under either standard the defendant had failed to establish that a valid arbitration agreement had been concluded. However, the High Court seemed to favour full judicial review of the existence of a valid arbitration agreement stating that "there appears to be a particularly strong case for the argument that any review as to the existence of the arbitration agreement should be on the basis of full judicial consideration as ... such a stay would in effect be a finding in favour of the existence of a valid arbitration clause".[12] Furthermore, commentators have noted that the courts in a majority of jurisdictions that apply the Model Law or arbitration statutes based-on the Model Law interpret it to require full judicial review, stating that "the weight of better-reasoned national court authority in UNCITRAL Model Law jurisdictions has interpreted Article 8(1) as permitting full judicial consideration (rather than *prima facie* review) in either all or some cases involving interlocutory challenges to the existence, validity, or legality of the arbitration agreement".[13]

---

[1] An arbitration agreement can take the form of a submission agreement, which is made after a dispute has arisen, or, more commonly, of an arbitration clause, which is made prior to dispute but governs any future disputes that may arise. See Blackaby, Partasides, Redfern and Hunter, *Redfern and Hunter on International Arbitration* (5th ed, Oxford University Press, Oxford, 2009) p 15.

[2] Brekoulakis and Shore in Mistelis, *Concise International Arbitration, UNCITRAL Model Law* (1st ed, Kluwer Law International, Alphen aan den Rijn, 2010) p 602.

[3] Bachand, "Does Article 8 of the Model Law Call for Full or Prima Facie Review of the Arbitral Tribunal's Jurisdiction?" (2006) 22 *Arbitration International* 463.

[4] Model Law, Art 16(1).

[5] Model Law, Art 8(1).

[6] However, some commentators have criticised this situation stating that the provisions of the Model Law leave "too much room for national legislatures to confuse the issue of who decides first in terms of the validity of a purported [arbitration agreement], thereby permitting the courts to ride in the saddle while [arbitral] tribunals trudge behind on foot". Brekoulakis and Shore in Mistelis, *Concise International Arbitration, UNCITRAL Model Law* (1st ed, Kluwer Law International, Alphen aan den Rijn, 2010) p 602.

[7] Brekoulakis and Shore in Mistelis, *Concise International Arbitration, UNCITRAL Model Law* (1st ed, Kluwer Law International, Alphen aan den Rijn, 2010) p 602.

[8] However, in *Dell Computer Corp v Union des consommateurs* [2007] 2 SCR 801, the Supreme Court of Canada suggested a third, hybrid standard of judicial review where a challenge to an arbitral tribunal's jurisdiction should be resolved first by the arbitral tribunal in accordance with the competence-competence principle unless the challenge is based solely on a question of law where full judicial review applies. Where the challenge requires production and review of factual evidence, courts should refer the case to arbitration, unless there are mixed questions of law and fact requiring only superficial consideration of documentary evidence in the record. It remains to be seen if other national courts apply this hybrid standard of judicial review.

(*Continued*)

[9] See CLOUT Case 70 – Canada/Federal Court of Appeal: *Nanisivik Mines Ltd and Zinc Corporation of America v Canarctic Shipping Co Ltd* (10 February 1994); CLOUT Case 706 – Hong Kong/High Court of Hong Kong: *Fustar Chemicals Ltd v Sinochem Liaoning Hong Kong Ltd* (5 June 1996); and *Yawata Ltd v Powell* [2000] DCR 334 (Wellington District Court).

[10] See CLOUT Case 20 – Hong Kong/High Court of Hong Kong: *Fung Sang Trading Ltd v Kai Sun Sea Products and Food Company Ltd* (29 October 1991); CLOUT Case 127 – Bermuda/Supreme Court of Bermuda: *Re Skandia International Insurance Company and Mercantile & General Reinsurance Company & ors* (21 January 1994); CLOUT Case 509 – Canada/Ontario Court of Appeal: *Dalimpex Ltd v Janicki; Agros Trading Spolka ZOO v Dalimpex Ltd* (30 May 2003); and CLOUT Case 1074 – Hong Kong/High Court of Hong Kong: *Ocean Park Corporation v Proud Sky Co Ltd* (28 November 2007).

[11] *Barnmore Demolition and Civil Engineering Ltd v Alandale Logistics Ltd*, unreported, High Court (Feeney J), 11 November 2010. For a discussion of the standard of review after the decision in *Barnmore Demolition and Civil Engineering Ltd v Alandale Logistics Ltd*, see Gibson and Shanley, "Existence of an Arbitration Agreement – The High Court Considers the Applicable Standard of Review" (2010) *Arbitration and ADR Review* p 270.

[12] *ibid*, at 8.

[13] Born, *International Commercial Arbitration Vol. 1* (1st ed, Kluwer Law International, Alphen aan den Rijn, 2009) p 885.

***No requirement for there to be facts in dispute*:** Under an analogous provision of the Arbitration Acts 1954-1998, the Irish courts were permitted to decline to refer pending civil proceedings to arbitration where "there [was] not in fact any dispute between the parties with regard to the matter agreed to be referred".[1] Case-law decided under the Arbitration Acts 1954-1998 has held that the mere denial of an obligation by a party was not sufficient to place facts in dispute.[2]

In contrast, the text of the Model Law does not require that there be facts in dispute before a court refers a matter to arbitration. That a matter is the subject of an arbitration agreement and not that there is a factual dispute between the parties is the critical issue. However, it is axiomatic that there must be a dispute to resolve before there can be an arbitration over a matter. While some early international case-law decided under the Model Law has held that where a party has no arguable defence a court should refuse to refer proceedings to arbitration,[3] the modern view is that the term 'dispute' should be interpreted broadly to include the situation where one party to an arbitration agreement has made a claim or has taken an issue that the other party denies or refuses to admit, whether or not there is any answer to the claim in fact or in law.[4] Where the parties have bargained for arbitration, any claim should be resolved by arbitration, irrespective of the strength or weakness of the defence to the claim. To achieve this end, it is likely that future Irish courts will consider the formulation of what constitutes a dispute as set out by the English High Court:

"1. The word 'dispute' ... should be given its normal meaning. It does not have some special or unusual meaning conferred upon it by lawyers.

2. Despite the simple meaning of the word 'dispute', there has been much litigation over the years as to whether or not disputes existed in particular situations. This litigation has not generated any hard-edged legal rules as to what is or is not a dispute. However, the accumulating judicial decisions have produced helpful guidance.

(*Continued*)

3. The mere fact that one party (whom I shall call 'the claimant') notifies the other party (whom I shall call 'the respondent') of a claim does not automatically and immediately give rise to a dispute. It is clear, both as a matter of language and from judicial decisions, that a dispute does not arise unless and until it emerges that the claim is not admitted.

4. The circumstances from which it may emerge that a claim is not admitted are Protean. For example, there may be an express rejection of the claim. There may be discussions between the parties from which objectively it is to be inferred that the claim is not admitted. The respondent may prevaricate, thus giving rise to the inference that he does not admit the claim. The respondent may simply remain silent for a period of time, thus giving rise to the same inference.

5. The period of time for which a respondent may remain silent before a dispute is to be inferred depends heavily upon the facts of the case and the contractual structure. Where the gist of the claim is well known and it is obviously controversial, a very short period of silence may suffice to give rise to this inference. Where the claim is notified to some agent of the respondent who has a legal duty to consider the claim independently and then give a considered response, a longer period of time may be required before it can be inferred that mere silence gives rise to a dispute.

6. If the claimant imposes upon the respondent a deadline for responding to the claim, that deadline does not have the automatic effect of curtailing what would otherwise be a reasonable time for responding. On the other hand, a stated deadline and the reasons for its imposition may be relevant factors when the court comes to consider what is a reasonable time for responding.

7. If the claim as presented by the claimant is so nebulous and ill-defined that the respondent cannot sensibly respond to it, neither silence by the respondent nor even an express non-admission is likely to give rise to a dispute for the purposes of arbitration or adjudication".[5]

---

[1] Arbitration Act 1980, s 5(1).

[2] *Campus and Stadium Ireland Development Ltd v Dublin Waterworld Ltd* [2006] 2 IR 181, where the High Court (Kelly J) declined to refer a dispute concerning non-payment of rent to arbitration where there were no facts in dispute that would justify the court making such an order and where the defendant had merely denied its obligation under the contract between the parties.

[3] CLOUT Case 738 – Hong Kong/Supreme Court of Hong Kong: *Chung Kiu Development Ltd v Sung Foo Kee Ltd* (4 July 1995).

[4] *Halki Shipping Corporation v Sopex Oils Ltd* [1998] 1 WLR 726, where the English Court of Appeal stayed summary proceedings in respect of demurrage claimed as a result of a failure to load and discharge a vessel where the defendant merely denied the claim. Swinton Thomas LJ stated that: "[i]n my judgment if a party has refused to pay a sum which is claimed or has denied that it is owing then in the ordinary use of the English language there is a dispute between the parties".

[5] *AMEC Civil Engineering Ltd v Secretary of State for Transport* [2004] EWCA 2339 (TCC), which is a decision of the English High Court. This decision was upheld on appeal and the propositions were expressly endorsed by the English Court of Appeal in *Collins (Contractors) Ltd v Baltic Quay Management (1994) Ltd* (2004) 99 ConLR 1. where it was held that a dispute exists once it is reasonably inferred that a claim is not admitted.

***No requirement to refer to arbitration a dispute over the effect of an award*:** Where the parties are not in agreement over the effect of an award and one party commences civil proceedings to enforce that award, there is no requirement for a court, in which enforcement is sought, to refer the dispute to arbitration. In a recent case decided under the Model Law the High Court stated that "article 8(1) has no application ... where the arbitration has taken place, the proceedings which are before the [High Court] are proceedings to enforce the arbitration award and the parties are not *ad idem* as to the effect of the award".[1]

[1] *CIE v Spencer Dock Development Company Ltd* [2011] IEHC 185, where neither the applicant nor respondent sought relief contemplated by the Act or the Model Law. The applicant sought an order directing the respondents to comply with an award rather than enforce the award and the respondent in oral submissions sought to refer any new dispute created by the application to arbitration under Model Law, Art 8. The High Court (Laffoy J) rejected the applicant's application and also held that the Model Law, Art 8 can have no application after arbitral proceedings have taken place but where the parties are not *ad idem* as to the effect of an award. While not formally ordering that the award be remitted to the arbitral tribunal Laffoy J indicated that the parties should accept the arbitral tribunal's invitation to make further submissions to it.

Article 9.—Arbitration agreement and interim measures by court

It is not incompatible with an arbitration agreement for a party to request, before or during arbitral proceedings, from a court an interim measure of protection and for a court to grant such measure.

Definitions

arbitration agreement': Arbitration Act 2010, s 2(1) and Model Law, Art 7(1) (Option I); 'court': Model Law, Art 2(c).

Notes

***Courts' power to order interim measures in support of arbitral proceedings*:** National courts have the same powers to order interim measures in respect of arbitral proceedings as they do in any civil proceedings pending before it, irrespective of where the arbitral proceedings are taking place.[1] In Ireland, the court of competent jurisdiction exercising the power to order interim measures in support of arbitral proceedings is the High Court.[2] Although the term 'interim relief' under Irish law typically refers to urgent injunctive relief sought on an *ex parte* basis to maintain the status quo for a short period until an interlocutory application is heard,[3] in arbitration, the term 'interim measures' has a broader meaning and includes injunctive relief, which under Irish law would be classified as both 'interim' and 'interlocutory' relief.[4]

[1] Model Law, Art 17 J.

[2] Arbitration Act 2010, s 9(1)(c).

(*Continued*)

[3] Kirwan, *Injunctions Law & Practice* (1st ed, Thomson Round Hall, Dublin, 2008) p 240.
[4] *Shelbourne Hotel Holdings Ltd v Torriam Hotel Operating Company Ltd* [2010] 2 IR 52. Model Law, Art 17(2) defines an 'interim measure' as "any temporary measure … by which, at any time prior to the issuance of the award by which the dispute is finally decided, the arbitral tribunal orders a party to: (a) Maintain or restore the status quo pending determination of the dispute; (b) Take action that would prevent, or refrain from taking action that is likely to cause current or imminent harm or prejudice to the arbitral process itself; (c) Provide a means of preserving assets out of which a subsequent award may be satisfied; or (d) Preserve evidence that may be relevant and material to the resolution of the dispute".

***Provisions of the Model Law supplemented by the Act*:** The provisions of the Model Law have been supplemented by the Act,[1] which, *inter alia*, provides that the High Court has the same powers to order interim measures of protection in respect of arbitral proceedings as it does in civil proceedings.

A full discussion on the provisions governing the grant of interim measures of protection by the High Court is contained at s 10 of the Act.

[1] Arbitration Act 2010, s 10.

***Concurrent jurisdiction of the High Court and an arbitral tribunal to grant interim measures of protection*:** Both the High Court[1] and an arbitral tribunal[2] are permitted to grant interim measures of protection. While the High Court may grant interim measures before and during arbitral proceedings,[3] it is axiomatic that an arbitral tribunal may only grant interim measures after arbitral proceedings are commenced. Although some international case-law suggests that where an arbitral tribunal has been constituted it is the correct forum from which a party should seek interim measures of protection,[4] the better view which is evident from most international case-law decided under the Model Law[5] and commentators[6] is that both national courts and an arbitral tribunal have concurrent jurisdiction.

[1] Arbitration Act 2010, s 10 (1) and Model Law, Art 9.
[2] Model Law, Art 17(1).
[3] Arbitration Act 2010, s 10 (1) and Model Law, Art 9.
[4] CLOUT Case 386 – Canada/Ontario Court of Justice: *ATM Compute GmbH v DY 4 Systems, Inc* (8 June 1995).
[5] See CLOUT Case 71 – Canada/British Columbia Supreme Court: *Trade Fortune Inc v Amagalmated Mill Supplies Ltd* (25 January 1994); and CLOUT Case 353 – Canada/British Columbia Supreme Court: *TLC Multimedia Inc v Core Curriculum Technologies Inc* (6 July 1998).
[6] Brekoulakis and Shore in Mistelis, *Concise International Arbitration, UNCITRAL Model Law* (1st ed, Kluwer Law International, Alphen aan den Rijn, 2010) p 606.

Chapter III

Composition of Arbitral Tribunal

Article 10.—Number of arbitrators

(1) The parties are free to determine the number of arbitrators.

(2) Failing such determination, the number of arbitrators shall be three.

Notes

The default number of arbitrators: The Act amends the default number of arbitrators from three to one[1] in order to minimise the costs of arbitral proceedings as it is axiomatic that it is cheaper to appoint a single arbitrator rather than three.[2] In addition, the amendment to the default number of arbitrators ensures consistency with existing arbitration practice in Ireland as the default number of arbitrators under the Arbitration Acts 1954-1998 was one.[3] This is of particular importance as the Act applies to many arbitration agreements that were formed prior to its enactment[4] and it would be undesirable to impose increased costs associated with a three arbitrator arbitral tribunal on parties that had entered into an arbitration agreement when the default number of arbitrators was one.[5]

---

[1] Arbitration Act 2010, s 13.

[2] Arbitration Bill 2008: Second Hearing before Dáil, Dáil Debate, 19 November 2008 (statement of Dermot Ahern, the then Minister for Justice, Equality and Law Reform).

[3] Arbitration Act 1954, s 14.

[4] Arbitration Act 2010, s 3(1).

[5] Arbitration Bill 2008: Second Hearing before Dáil, Dáil Debate, 19 November 2008 (statement of Dermot Ahern, the then Minister for Justice, Equality and Law Reform).

Applicability to international commercial arbitration: The Act amends the default number of arbitrators from three to one both for international commercial arbitrations and for 'domestic' arbitrations.[1] In theory, the Act is inconsistent with international practice where the typical number of arbitrators is three, unless the quantum of the dispute is small.[2] However, in practice, the departure from the provisions of the Model Law is unlikely to present a difficulty[3] as most international commercial arbitrations are conducted under the auspices of an arbitral institution and will typically adopt that arbitral institution's rules on the composition of an arbitral tribunal.[4]

---

[1] Arbitration Act 2010, s 13.

[2] Blackaby, Partasides, Redfern and Hunter, *Redfern and Hunter on International Arbitration* (5th ed, Oxford University Press, Oxford, 2009) p 250.

[3] Of course, it would have been possible for the Oireachtas to adopt the provisions of the Model Law without amendment for international commercial arbitrations and to draw a distinction has been drawn between international commercial arbitrations and 'domestic' arbitrations as was done in relation to 'taxation of costs' by Arbitration Act 2010, s 21(4).

[4] Even where international commercial arbitrations are *ad hoc* and not conducted under the auspices of an arbitral institution the parties may agree on the number of arbitrators required to constitute an arbitral tribunal.

Provisions of the Model Law superseded by the Act: As the provisions of the Model Law have been superseded by the Act,[1] a full discussion on the provisions governing the commencement of arbitral proceedings is contained at s 13 of the Act.

[1] Arbitration Act 2010, s 13.

Article 11.—Appointment of arbitrators

(1) No person shall be precluded by reason of his nationality from acting as an arbitrator, unless otherwise agreed by the parties.

(2) The parties are free to agree on a procedure of appointing the arbitrator or arbitrators, subject to the provisions of paragraphs (4) and (5) of this article.

(3) Failing such agreement,

(a) in an arbitration with three arbitrators, each party shall appoint one arbitrator, and the two arbitrators thus appointed shall appoint the third arbitrator; if a party fails to appoint the arbitrator within thirty days of receipt of a request to do so from the other party, or if the two arbitrators fail to agree on the third arbitrator within thirty days of their appointment, the appointment shall be made, upon request of a party, by the court or other authority specified in article 6;

(b) in an arbitration with a sole arbitrator, if the parties are unable to agree on the arbitrator, he shall be appointed, upon request of a party, by the court or other authority specified in article 6.

(4) Where, under an appointment procedure agreed upon by the parties,

(a) a party fails to act as required under such procedure, or

(b) the parties, or two arbitrators, are unable to reach an agreement expected of them under such procedure, or

(c) a third party, including an institution, fails to perform any function entrusted to it under such procedure,

any party may request the court or other authority specified in article 6 to take the necessary measure, unless the agreement on the appointment procedure provides other means for securing the appointment.

(5) A decision on a matter entrusted by paragraph (3) or (4) of this article to the court or other authority specified in article 6 shall be subject to no appeal. The court or other authority, in appointing an arbitrator, shall have due regard to any qualifications required of the arbitrator by the agreement of the parties and to such considerations as are likely to secure the appointment of an independent and impartial arbitrator and, in the case of a sole or third arbitrator, shall take into account as well the advisability of appointing an arbitrator of a nationality other than those of the parties.

Definitions

'arbitration': Arbitration Act 2010, s 2(1) and Model Law, Art 2(a); 'court': Model Law, Art 2(c).

Notes

***Arbitrators' nationality*:** Unless otherwise agreed by the parties, no person can be precluded from acting as an arbitrator because of his or her nationality.[1] The *travaux préparatoires* (of which Irish courts are permitted to take judicial notice when interpreting provisions of the Model Law)[2] suggest this provision was enacted to overcome bias on the part of some national legislators that had enacted arbitration legislation precluding foreigners from acting as arbitrators.[3] However, the parties themselves may agree that nationals of certain States may or may not be appointed as arbitrators and, in practice, frequently do so.[4] In an international commercial arbitration it is "usual practice ... to appoint a sole arbitrator (or a presiding arbitrator) of a different nationality from that of the parties to the dispute".[5] Furthermore, the rules of many arbitral institutions encourage or require a sole or presiding arbitrator to be of a different nationality from the parties.[6]

---

[1] Model Law, Art 11(1).

[2] Arbitration Act 2010, s 8(1).

[3] UNCITRAL Seventh Secretariat Note, A/CN.9/264, Art 11, para 1.

[4] In the recent English case of *Jivraj v Hashwani* [2011] UKSC 40, the UK Supreme Court held that arbitrators are not employees for the purposes of UK equality legislation. If they arbitrators were held to be employees then the parties' agreement that nationals of certain States may, or may not, be appointed as arbitrators would constitute discrimination for the purposes of that legislation. The claimant and the respondent established a joint venture for the purposes of property investment. It was a term of the agreement that any dispute between the parties arising out of the venture should be referred to three arbitrators, one of whom was to be appointed by each party and all of whom were to be respected members of the Ismaili community. After a dispute arose, the claimant wrote to the respondent asserting a claim for payment under the agreement and calling on him to appoint an arbitrator while simultaneously identifying as the claimant's purported appointee as arbitrator a person who was not a member of the Ismaili community. The respondent disputed the validity of that appointment and the claimant applied for an order confirming the appointment, contending, that the provision restricting eligibility for appointment to members of the Ismaili community constituted discrimination on religious grounds, contrary to UK equality laws. At first instance, the English High Court held that arbitrators were not employees and, consequently, UK equality legislation did not apply to them. On appeal, the English Court of Appeal overturned the English High Court decision held that arbitrators were employees and that the restriction of eligibility for appointment as an arbitrator to members of the Ismaili community constituted unlawful discrimination. The English Court of Appeal decision had caused great concern amongst UK arbitration practitioners who believed it jeopardised their position as a centre for international commercial arbitration. The controversy caused by the various decisions in *Jivraj v Hashwani* is irrelevant in an Irish context as there is no provision under Irish law which would prevent parties to an arbitration agreement from specifying that nationals of certain States may, or may not, be appointed as arbitrators.

(*Continued*)

[5] See Blackaby, Partasides, Redfern and Hunter, *Redfern and Hunter on International Arbitration* (5th ed, Oxford University Press, Oxford, 2009) pp 261-262, where it is noted that "this insistence on neutral nationality sometimes produces curious results. In particular, it may lead to a situation where the law applicable to the merits of the dispute is that of one or other of the parties (a situation that is by no means uncommon); but the sole or presiding arbitrator will not be qualified or experienced in that system of law".

[6] See Blackaby, Partasides, Redfern and Hunter, *Redfern and Hunter on International Arbitration* (5th ed, Oxford University Press, Oxford, 2009) p 262. Examples of institutional rules which reflect this preference include: ICC Rules, Art 9.5; LCIA Rules, Art 6.1; and UNCITRAL Rules, Art 6.4.

***Procedure for the appointment of an arbitral tribunal to be determined by the parties*:** The principle of party autonomy is enshrined in the Model Law and it dictates that where the parties agree on a procedure for the appointment an arbitrator or an arbitral tribunal, it must be followed.[1] Where there is a failure to follow an agreed procedure, a party may apply to the High Court[2] for necessary measures to be taken to appoint an arbitral tribunal.[3] A decision of the High Court to take necessary measures to appoint an arbitrator or an arbitral tribunal cannot be appealed.[4] Where the High Court appoints an arbitrator it must have due regard to any qualifications required of the arbitrator by the agreement of the parties and to such considerations as are likely to secure the appointment of an independent and impartial arbitrator.[5] International case-law decided under the Model Law has held that where a national court exercises the power to appoint it should go out of its way to ensure that no sense of grievance is felt however that attitude might appear to others.[6]

---

[1] Model Law, Art 11(2).

[2] Arbitration Act 2010, s. 9(1)(a); and Model Law, Art 6.

[3] Model Law, Art 11(4).

[4] Model Law, Art 11(5).

[5] Model Law, Art 11(5).

[6] CLOUT Case 20 – Hong Kong/High Court of Hong Kong: *Fung Sang Trading Ltd v Kai Sun Sea Products and Food Co Ltd* (29 October 1991).

***Default procedure for the appointment of an arbitral tribunal*:** In the absence of an agreed procedure for the appointment of an arbitral tribunal, the following default rules for the appointment of an arbitral tribunal apply:

1. Where an arbitration agreement provides for three arbitrators, each party must appoint one arbitrator, and the two party-appointed arbitrators must appoint the third arbitrator. Where a party fails to appoint an arbitrator within 30 days of receipt of a request to do so from the other party, or if the two party-appointed arbitrators fail to agree on the third arbitrator within 30 days of their appointment, a party can request that the High Court[1] appoint an arbitrator.[2] International case-law suggests that after the expiry of the 30-day period a party's right to appoint an arbitrator transfers irrevocably to the national court;[3] and

(*Continued*)

2. Where an arbitration agreement provides for one arbitrator, if the parties are unable to agree on an arbitrator, a party can request that the High Court[4] appoint an arbitrator.[5]

This article provides for appointment of an arbitrator by the High Court in the case of deadlock.[6] Application to the High Court is an unsatisfactory and undesirable outcome not least because a major attraction of arbitration is that it allows the parties to submit a dispute to a decision-maker of their own choice rather than allow such choice to be exercised on their behalf.[7] Therefore, the parties to an arbitration agreement should agree on a fallback procedure for appointment of an arbitrator, such as appointment by a third party,[8] in order to avoid the delay, expense and uncertainty occasioned by the necessity of applying to the High Court in the case of deadlock.[9]

---

[1] Arbitration Act 2010, s 9(1)(a); and Model Law, Art 6.

[2] Model Law, Art 11(3)(a).

[3] CLOUT Case 563 – Germany/Highest Regional Court of Baveria: *4 Z SchH 9/01* (16 January 2002).

[4] Arbitration Act 2010, s 9(1)(a); and Model Law, Art 6.

[5] Model Law, Art 11(3)(b).

[6] Model Law, Art 11(3).

[7] Blackaby, Partasides, Redfern and Hunter, *Redfern and Hunter on International Arbitration* (5th ed, Oxford University Press, Oxford, 2009) p 251.

[8] The president or chairman of professional bodies such as the Law Society of Ireland or the Bar Council of Ireland is often required to appoint an arbitrator where the parties cannot otherwise agree on appointment. See Dowling-Hussey and Dunne, *Arbitration Law* (1st ed, Thomson Round Hall, Dublin, 2008) p 63.

[9] Blackaby, Partasides, Redfern and Hunter, *Redfern and Hunter on International Arbitration* (5th ed, Oxford University Press, Oxford, 2009) p 251.

Article 12.—Grounds for challenge

(1) When a person is approached in connection with his possible appointment as an arbitrator, he shall disclose any circumstances likely to give rise to justifiable doubts as to his impartiality or independence. An arbitrator, from the time of his appointment and throughout the arbitral proceedings, shall without delay disclose any such circumstances to the parties unless they have already been informed of them by him.

(2) An arbitrator may be challenged only if circumstances exist that give rise to justifiable doubts as to his impartiality or independence, or if he does not possess qualifications agreed to by the parties. A party may challenge an arbitrator appointed by him, or in whose appointment he has participated, only for reasons of which he becomes aware after the appointment has been made.

Notes

***Conflicts of interest in arbitration*:** Impartiality and independence are the fundamental to the legality and integrity of arbitration.[1] In order to ensure an arbitrator's compliance with the principles of impartiality and independence, this article seeks to prevent certain

(*Continued*)

conflicts of interest from arising that may fetter an arbitrator's impartiality or independence.[2] Rather than provide an exhaustive list of specific circumstances situations where an arbitrator may not act, this article seeks to ensure compliance with these principles by requiring a person approached as a prospective arbitrator to disclose certain circumstances which may give rise to a conflict of interest. Following disclosure, the parties are then permitted to challenge an arbitrator if they believe that the circumstances disclosed raise justifiable doubts to an arbitrator's impartiality or independence.[3]

---

[1] Roth in Weigand, *Practitioner's Handbook on International Commercial Arbitration, UNCITRAL Model Law on International Commercial Arbitration* (2nd ed, Oxford University Press, Oxford, 2009) p 1010.
[2] Model Law, Art 12(1).
[3] Model Law, Art 12(2).

***Duty to disclose certain conflicts of interest*:** A person approached as a prospective arbitrator must disclose all circumstances that give rise to justifiable doubts to his or her impartiality or independence. An ongoing duty to disclose any new facts or circumstances that give rise to justifiable doubts to his or her impartiality or independence continues throughout the arbitration.[1] Although this article does not specify the method of disclosure or to whom it should be made, in practice the disclosure is made to the person who approached a prospective arbitrator.[2] Where new facts or circumstances arise after an arbitrator's appointment that may give rise to a conflict of interest, the disclosure is made to the parties.[3] The disclosure must be sufficient detailed to inform the recipient about the potential conflict and to enable a decision to be made about whether to challenge the appointment of the arbitrator.

---

[1] Model Law, Art 12(1).
[2] Blackaby, Partasides, Redfern and Hunter, *Redfern and Hunter on International Arbitration* (5th ed, Oxford University Press, Oxford, 2009) p 269. Person who may approach an arbitrator include parties and third parties designated by the parties to appoint an arbitral tribunal such as an arbitral institution or a professional body.
[3] Roth in Weigand, *Practitioner's Handbook on International Commercial Arbitration, UNCITRAL Model Law on International Commercial Arbitration* (2nd ed, Oxford University Press, Oxford, 2009) p 1011.

***International Bar Association Guidelines on Conflicts of Interest in International Arbitration*:** This article does not specify what circumstances raise justifiable doubts of impartiality or independence and this vagueness led to varying standards of disclosure and uncertainty about what exactly needs to be disclosed by a prospective arbitrator. In an attempt to harmonise disclosure of potential conflicts in an international context, the International Bar Association has developed 'Guidelines on Conflicts of Interest in International Arbitration'.[1] The IBA Guidelines aim to provide "a common set of principles that would address concrete situations and thus avoid the risk of arbitrators from different cultures applying a radically different standard of disclosure upon appointment".[2] The IBA

(*Continued*)

Guidelines detail common circumstances that may potentially be considered as conflicts of interest. These circumstances form a non-exhaustive list, which has been divided into four colour groups depending on the perceived seriousness of the conflict:

1. A Non-Waivable Red List containing circumstances where a conflict of interest of such sufficient magnitude arises that a prospective arbitrator must not act even where none of the parties object;[3]
2. A Waivable Red List containing circumstances where a conflict of interest arises and a prospective arbitrator may act but only with the express consent of all the parties;[4]
3. An Orange List containing circumstances where a potential conflict of interest arises. The prospective arbitrator must disclose details of the facts and circumstances in order to permit the parties to choose whether or not to challenge the prospective arbitrator.[5] Although conflicts which fall within the Orange List require disclosure by an arbitrator, no guidance is given on whether or not he or she should act; and
4. A Green List containing circumstances where no conflict of interest arises and where, consequently, there is no duty to disclose.[6]

The advantage of the IBA Guidelines is that a precise list of factual circumstances makes a prospective arbitrator's disclosure rule-based rather than subjective. However, the IBA Guidelines are non-exhaustive and potential conflicts of interest may arise that are not specified.[7] For an international commercial arbitration, commentators have noted that the IBA Guidelines have gained general acceptance as a non-binding set of principles which most arbitrators seek to comply[8] and "whilst the [IBA Guidelines] may not be directly cited they are nonetheless present in the minds of the deciding authorities when reaching decisions on concepts of independence and impartiality".[9] It remains to be seen whether the IBA Guidelines are appropriate for a domestic arbitration (which is any arbitration other than an international commercial arbitration) where Ireland is the place of arbitration as Ireland's small, relatively close-knit legal and business community make it likely that prior relationships exist between prospective arbitrators and parties.

---

[1] The IBA Guidelines are available at the IBA's website: http://www.ibanet.org/ENews_Archive/IBA_July_2008_ENews_ArbitrationMultipleLang.aspx.

[2] Blackaby, Partasides, Redfern and Hunter, *Redfern and Hunter on International Arbitration* (5th ed, Oxford University Press, Oxford, 2009) p 270. At p 270 the authors of *Redfern and Hunter on International Arbitration* provide an anecdotal example of the radically different cultures of disclosure "where an American co-arbitrator made three pages of disclosures, including references to congresses where he had been present with counsel for one of the parties, whereas the other European arbitrator did not consider it relevant to disclose that he spent most summer vacations with counsel to the party that appointed him".

[3] The Non-Waivable Red List concerns situations where the prospective arbitrator has direct links to one of the parties.

[4] The Waivable Red List concerns situations where there is a relationship between the prospective arbitrator and the dispute; where the prospective arbitrator has direct or indirect interest in the dispute; and where the prospective arbitrator has a relationship with one of the parties or their counsel.

(*Continued*)

[5] The Orange List concerns situations where the prospective arbitrator has performed previous services for one of the parties or has had previous involvement in the proceedings; where the prospective arbitrator is performing current services for one of the parties; where the prospective arbitrator has a relationship with one of the other arbitrators (if the arbitral tribunal consists of more than one arbitrator) or one of the parties' counsel; where the prospective arbitrator has a relationship with one of the parties or others involved in the arbitral proceedings; and certain other circumstances which may give rise to justifiable doubts to the prospective arbitrator's impartiality or independence.

[6] The Green List concerns situations where the prospective arbitrator has previously expressed legal opinions; where the prospective arbitrator has previously provided service against one of the parties; where the prospective arbitrator is providing certain current services for one of the parties; where the prospective arbitrator has contacts with another arbitrator (if the arbitral tribunal consists of more than one arbitrator) or one of the parties' counsel; and where the prospective arbitrator has contacts with one of the parties.

[7] See, for example, *ASM Shipping Ltd of India v TTMI Ltd of England* [2006] 2 All ER (Comm) 122, where the English High Court expressed the view that the IBA Guidelines "do not purported to be a comprehensive list" and held that an arbitrator ought to have recused himself notwithstanding that his previous relationship with one of the parties did not consist of circumstances contained on the IBA's Red List.

[8] Blackaby, Partasides, Redfern and Hunter, *Redfern and Hunter on International Arbitration* (5th ed, Oxford University Press, Oxford, 2009) p 271.

[9] *ibid*, p 272.

***Grounds for challenge—impartiality and independence*:** A party may challenge an arbitrator where circumstances give rise to justifiable doubts over his or her impartiality or independence. Impartiality has been defined as the "test for the lack of impermissible bias in the mind of the arbitrator towards a party of the subject-matter in dispute".[1] Independence refers to the relationship between an arbitrator and the parties and indicates prior personal, social or business contact between them.[2]

A party must demonstrate 'justifiable doubts' to an arbitrator's impartiality or independence for a challenge to be successful. Whether circumstances give rise to 'justifiable doubts' on behalf of a party is an objective test and challenges must be determined on a case-by-case basis.[3] Commentators have noted that the Model Law envisages a stern test to diminish the opportunities for a party to disrupt arbitral proceedings through unmeritorious challenges.[4] International case-law decided under the Model Law has held challenges sustained where an arbitrator's public comments on arbitral proceedings showed bias.[5] International case-law has held challenges rejected where an arbitrator would have been called as a witness in the proceedings;[6] where the arbitrator and one of the parties had participated in an economic relationship via a public limited partnership;[7] and where allegations of bias were alleged against an arbitral tribunal on the basis of criticism of a party's submissions.[8]

[1] Donahey, "The Independence and Neutrality of Arbitrators" (1992) 4 *Journal of International Arbitrators* 32 cited with approval in Binder, *International Commercial Arbitration and Conciliation in UNCITRAL Model Law Jurisdictions* (3rd ed, Sweet & Maxwell, London, 2010) p 184.

(*Continued*)

[2] Binder, *International Commercial Arbitration and Conciliation in UNCITRAL Model Law Jurisdictions* (3rd ed, Sweet & Maxwell, London, 2010) p 184.
[3] Gearing, "'A judge in his own cause?' – actual or unconscious bias of arbitrators" (2000) *International Arbitration Law Review* 3(2) pp 46-51.
[4] Brekoulakis and Shore in Mistelis, *Concise International Arbitration, UNCITRAL Model Law* (1st ed, Kluwer Law International, Alphen aan den Rijn, 2010) p 610.
[5] CLOUT Case 902 – Germany/Regional Court of Munich: *2 OH 1728/01* (27 June 2002).
[6] CLOUT Case 785 – Egypt/Cairo Regional Center for International Commercial Arbitration: *No 51/1994* (25 March 1996).
[7] CLOUT Case 665 – Germany/Highest Regional Court of Naumberg: *10 SchH 3/01* (19 December 2001).
[8] CLOUT Case 1062 – Germany/Highest Regional Court of Cologne: *9 Sch(H) 22/03* (2 April 2004).

***Irish case-law on conflicts of interest under the Arbitration Acts 1954-1998*:** Irish case-law decided under the provisions of the Arbitration Acts 1954-1998[1] will also be of assistance to future Irish courts called upon to adjudicate on conflicts of interest. However, it must be cautioned that under the provisions of the Arbitration Acts 1954-1998, Irish courts have required a party alleging a lack of impartiality or independence to demonstrate "a good arguable case on the merits to establish that a right minded person with full knowledge of the facts would have been led to conclude that there was a real likelihood of bias".[2] Challenges in reported Irish case-law were invariably rejected, including, where an arbitrator had previously provided services to an associated company of one of the parties;[3] where an arbitrator had previously arbitrated a dispute involving an associated company of one of the parties;[4] where disparaging comments were made about a witness;[5] and where it was alleged that an arbitrator prejudged certain arguments made by a party.[6] Some commentators have asserted that the decisions of the Irish courts indicates a wariness of upholding challenges that may result in disqualifying a large number of arbitrators out of what is a relatively small pool, particularly as prior relationships are likely to exist in Ireland's small business and legal community.[7]

[1] Arbitration Act 1954, s 37 prohibited 'misconduct' on the part of an arbitrator which was interpreted to include accepting an appointment where a pre-existing relationship between the arbitrator and one of the parties created a conflict of interest. Arbitration Act 1954, s 39(1)(b) permitted the High Court to remove an arbitrator who was not impartial.
[2] *Bord na Móna v John Sisk & Son Ltd*, unreported, High Court (Blayney J) 31 May 1990 at 11.
[3] *ibid.*
[4] *Tobin Twomey Services Ltd v Kerry Foods Ltd (No 3)* [1999] 3 IR 483.
[5] *JJ Rhatigan & Co Ltd v Paragon Contracting Ltd & Roughan* [2009] IEHC 117.
[6] *McCarthy v Keane & ors,* unreported, High Court (Lavan J), 24 July 2003.
[7] Carey and Gallagher "Impartiality of arbitrators: English and Irish law contrasted" (2006) *International Arbitration Law Review* 9(6).

***Grounds for challenge — a failure to possess agreed qualifications*:** An arbitrator may be challenged where he or she does not possess qualifications agreed on by the parties. Qualifications agreed by the parties may include professional credentials or designated nationality. This ground is straightforward and will merely require a factual analysis of whether or not an arbitrator possesses the qualifications agreed.[1]

[1] Holtzmann and Neuhaus, *A Guide to the UNCITRAL Model Law on International Commercial Arbitration* (1st ed, Kluwer Law and Taxation Publishers, The Hague, 1989) pp 388-389.

***Challenge where an arbitral tribunal consists of a single arbitrator only*:** In practice, challenges to an arbitrator occur more frequently where an arbitrator has been appointed by one of the parties as it is sometimes perceived that the arbitrator will act favourably to the party that appointed him or her instead of acting impartially and independently. Challenges to single arbitrators or a presiding arbitrator are less common.[1] However, an arbitrator is only to be appointed by one of the parties where the arbitral tribunal consists of three or more arbitrators. An arbitral tribunal in Ireland will consist of a single arbitrator, unless otherwise agreed by the parties.[2] Therefore, the appointment of an arbitrator by each of the parties is likely to be relatively rare and it remains to be seen whether a systematic practice of challenging a single arbitrator develops in Ireland.

[1] Blackaby, Partasides, Redfern and Hunter, *Redfern and Hunter on International Arbitration* (5th ed, Oxford University Press, Oxford, 2009) p 273.
[2] Arbitration Act 2010, s 13.

***Challenge to a party's own appointee*:** A party may only challenge an arbitrator that it appointed where the grounds for challenge arose after the appointment or where the party only became aware of the grounds for challenge after the appointment.[1]

[1] Model Law, Art 12(2).

Article 13.—Challenge procedure

(1) The parties are free to agree on a procedure for challenging an arbitrator, subject to the provisions of paragraph (3) of this article.

(2) Failing such agreement, a party who intends to challenge an arbitrator shall, within fifteen days after becoming aware of the constitution of the arbitral tribunal or after becoming aware of any circumstance referred to in article 12(2), send a written statement of the reasons for the challenge to the arbitral tribunal. Unless the challenged arbitrator withdraws from his office or the other party agrees to the challenge, the arbitral tribunal shall decide on the challenge.

(3) If a challenge under any procedure agreed upon by the parties or under the procedure of paragraph (2) of this article is not successful, the challenging party may request, within thirty days after having received notice of the decision rejecting the challenge, the court or other

authority specified in article 6 to decide on the challenge, which decision shall be subject to no appeal; while such a request is pending, the arbitral tribunal, including the challenged arbitrator, may continue the arbitral proceedings and make an award.

Definitions

'arbitral tribunal': Model Law, Art 2(b); 'court': Model Law, Art 2(c).

Notes

***Procedure for challenge to an arbitrator to be determined by the parties*:** The principle of party autonomy is enshrined in the Model Law and it dictates that where the parties agree on a procedure for challenge to an arbitrator, it must be followed.[1] The parties' agreement includes an agreement to conduct an arbitration under the auspices of an arbitral institution, whose rules will typically provide a procedure for challenge.[2] However, the parties may not exclude the power of the High Court[3] to review any decision rejecting a challenge to an arbitrator.[4]

---

[1] Model Law, Art 13(1).

[2] See, for example, the International Chamber of Commerce's Rules of Arbitration, Art 14.2, which provides that a party seeking to challenge an arbitrator must do so within 30 days of the date of notification of the appointment or within 30 days of when the party became aware of the circumstances giving rise to the challenge. The challenge must be made in writing. The International Chamber of Commerce Court will adjudicate on the challenge after the arbitrator, other party and other members of arbitral tribunal (if any) have been afforded an opportunity to comment; the London Court of International Arbitration's Arbitration Rules, Art 10.4, which provides that a party seeking to challenge an arbitrator must do so within 15 days of the date of notification of the appointment or within 15 days of when the party became aware of the circumstances giving rise to the challenge. The challenge must be made in writing. The London Court of International Arbitration Court will adjudicate on the challenge within 15 days; and the International Center for Dispute Resolution, Art 8, which provides that a party seeking to challenge an arbitrator must do so within 15 days of the date of notification of the appointment or within 15 days of when the party became aware of the circumstances giving rise to the challenge. Commentators have noted that decisions by arbitral institutions on challenges are "generally preferable to decisions by national courts on challenge applications, because they are resolved very expeditiously (which minimizes possible delays or uncertainties to the proceeding) by person with substantial experience in such matters (which makes decisions more reliable and predictable)". Born, *International Commercial Arbitration* (1st ed, Kluwer Law International, Alphen aan den Rijn, 2009) pp 1553-1554.

[3] Arbitration Act 2010, s 9(1)(a) and Model Law, Art 6.

[4] Model Law, Art 13(3). A similar principle existed at common law where an ouster of the jurisdiction of the courts in an arbitration agreement was void as being contrary to public policy. See *Czarnikow v Roth, Schmidt & Co* [1922] 2 KB 478, which is a decision of the English Court of Appeal. The decision in *Czarnikow v Roth, Schmidt & Co* has received judicial approval in Ireland in *Uniform Construction Ltd v Cappawhite Contractors Ltd* [2007] IEHC 295; and *John Mowlem Construction Ltd t/a Irishenco Construction v Dublin City Council* [2009] IEHC 225.

Default procedure for challenge to an arbitrator: In the absence of an agreed procedure for challenge, this article provides for default rules for challenge to an arbitrator. A party seeking to challenge an arbitrator is to apply initially to the arbitral tribunal within 15 days after becoming aware of the constitution of an arbitral tribunal or within 15 days of when the party became aware of the circumstances giving rise to the challenge. The challenge must be made in writing and, unless the challenged arbitrator withdraws, the arbitral tribunal adjudicates on the challenge.[1] The *travaux préparatoires* (of which Irish courts are permitted to take judicial notice when interpreting provisions of the Model Law)[2] suggest the entire arbitral tribunal *including* the challenged arbitrator is to adjudicate on the challenge.[3]

[1] Model Law, Art 13(2).
[2] Arbitration Act 2010, s 8(1).
[3] UNCITRAL Fifth Working Group Report, A/CN.9/246, Art 13, para 38.

Challenge to an arbitral tribunal consisting of a single arbitrator: The *travaux préparatoires* also suggest that where an arbitral tribunal consists of a single arbitrator there is no need for an arbitrator who refuses to resign to adjudicate on the challenge as the refusal to withdraw constitutes an implicit rejection of the challenge.[1] An arbitral tribunal in Ireland will consist of a single arbitrator, unless the parties agree otherwise.[2]

[1] UNCITRAL Commission Report, A/40/17, Art 13, para 129.
[2] Arbitration Act 2010, s 13.

Final decision on a challenge to an arbitrator to be exercised by the High Court and the procedure for challenge: A party cannot invoke the jurisdiction of the High Court until it has exhausted all previously available remedies for challenge.[1] However, where a challenge is rejected by an arbitral tribunal, the challenging party may apply to the High Court[2] for a final decision on the challenge within 30 days after having received notice of the arbitral tribunal's decision rejecting the challenge.[3] There is no appeal from a decision of the High Court on a challenge to an arbitrator.[4] An arbitral tribunal may continue arbitral proceedings and may even make an award while an application to the High Court to decide on the challenge is pending,[5] which serves to limit the disruption and delay occasioned by unmeritorious challenges.

Application to the High Court is made in a summary matter by way of originating notice of motion grounded on affidavit.[6] An application must be entitled in the matter of the arbitral proceedings to which it relates and in the matter of the Act.[7] An application must name as respondent the other party to the arbitral proceedings.[8] An arbitrator or arbitral tribunal should not be joined as a party to any application to the High Court to fulfil its supervisory functions in connection with arbitral proceedings.[9] However, Irish case-law has held that an error in procedure may not be fatal to an application to the High Court for it to fulfil its supervisory functions.[10]

[1] Brekoulakis and Shore in Mistelis, *Concise International Arbitration, UNCITRAL Model Law* (1st ed, Kluwer Law International, Alphen aan den Rijn, 2010) p 611.

(*Continued*)

[2] Arbitration Act 2010, s 9(1)(a); and Model Law, Art 6.
[3] Model Law, Art 13(3).
[4] Model Law, Art 13(3).
[5] Model Law, Art 13(3).
[6] Rules of the Superior Courts, Ord 56, r 3(1).
[7] Rules of the Superior Courts, Ord 56, r (2)1.
[8] Rules of the Superior Courts, Ord 56, r 2(1).
[9] *FBD Insurance plc v Connors* [2011] IEHC 184.
[10] *ibid*, where the applicant commenced an application by special summons rather than originating notice of motion. The High Court (Laffoy J) held that it was appropriate to hear the application notwithstanding the defect in the procedure adopted, particularly as the respondents offered no opposition to the approach adopted.

Article 14.—Failure or impossibility to act

(1) If an arbitrator becomes *de jure* or *de facto* unable to perform his functions or for other reasons fails to act without undue delay, his mandate terminates if he withdraws from his office or if the parties agree on the termination. Otherwise, if a controversy remains concerning any of these grounds, any party may request the court or other authority specified in article 6 to decide on the termination of the mandate, which decision shall be subject to no appeal.

(2) If, under this article or article 13(2), an arbitrator withdraws from his office or a party agrees to the termination of the mandate of an arbitrator, this does not imply acceptance of the validity of any ground referred to in this article or article 12(2).

Definitions

'court': Model Law, Art 2(c).

Notes

***Termination of an arbitrator's mandate due to failure or impossibility to act*:** An arbitrator's mandate terminates where an arbitrator becomes *de facto* or *de jure* unable to perform his or her functions or fails to act without undue delay and either the arbitrator withdraws from office or the parties agree to terminate his or her mandate.[1] A party may apply to the High Court[2] to terminate the arbitrator's mandate where it alleges that an arbitrator is unable to perform his or her functions or fails to act without undue delay but where the arbitrator refuses to withdraw or where the other party does not agree to terminate his or her mandate.[3] Although no definition is provided of when an arbitrator becomes '*de facto* or *de jure* unable to perform,' the *travaux préparatoires* (of which Irish courts are permitted to take judicial notice when interpreting provisions of the Model Law)[4] suggest that controversy surrounding these circumstances will rarely arise as the

(*Continued*)

factual occurrence of a failure will be "so self-evident".[5] Similarly, no definition is provided of what constitutes a failure to act 'without undue delay'. The *travaux préparatoires* also suggest that when judging whether an arbitrator failed to act without undue delay the following considerations may be relevant:

> "Which action was expected or required of him in the light of the arbitration agreement and the specific procedural situation? If he has not done anything in this regard, has the delay been so inordinate as to be unacceptable in the light of the circumstances, including technical difficulties and the complexity of the case? If he has done something and acted in a certain way, did his conduct fall clearly below the standard of what may reasonably be expected from an arbitrator? Amongst the factors influencing the level of expectations are the ability to function efficiently and expeditiously and any special competence or other qualifications required of the arbitrator by agreement of the parties".[6]

---

[1] Model Law, Art 14(1).
[2] Arbitration Act 2010, s 9(1)(a); and Model Law, Art 6.
[3] Model Law, Art 15(1).
[4] Arbitration Act 2010, s 8(1).
[5] UNCITRAL Seventh Secretariat Note, A/CN.9/264, Art 14, para 1.
[6] UNCITRAL Seventh Secretariat Note, A/CN.9/264, Art 14, para 4.

***Non-acceptance by an arbitrator of the validity of grounds for challenge*:** The withdrawal of an arbitrator from office or the parties' agreement to terminate his or her mandate does not imply acceptance by the arbitrator of the validity of the grounds for termination by the arbitrator.[1] The *travaux préparatoires* (of which Irish courts are permitted to take judicial notice when interpreting provisions of the Model Law)[2] suggest that this protection is designed to facilitate withdrawal by an arbitrator or consent to termination by the parties in order to prevent lengthy controversies while preserving an arbitrator's reputation.[3] In addition, commentators have noted that an arbitrator's withdrawal "cannot be used as evidence for his liability if one of the parties sues him for damages for any act or omission as an arbitrator".[4] In Ireland this provision is superfluous as an arbitrator enjoys a complete immunity from civil liability.[5]

---

[1] Model Law, Art 14(2).
[2] Arbitration Act 2010, s 8(1).
[3] UNCITRAL Seventh Secretariat Note, A/CN.9/264, Art 14 *bis*, para 1.
[4] Brekoulakis and Shore in Mistelis, *Concise International Arbitration, UNCITRAL Model Law* (1st ed, Kluwer Law International, Alphen aan den Rijn, 2010) p 612.
[5] Arbitration Act 2010, s 22.

***Non-mandatory nature of the provisions for termination of an arbitrator's mandate*:** While the Model Law does not expressly provide that the parties may agree to alternative procedures for termination of an arbitrator's mandate due to failure or impossibility to act,[1] the *travaux préparatoires* (of which Irish courts are permitted to take judicial notice when interpreting provisions of the Model Law)[2] suggest that the parties are not precluded "from varying the grounds which would give rise to the termination of the mandate or from entrusting a third person or institution with deciding on such termination".[3] The failure of the Model Law to expressly provide that the provisions concerning termination of an arbitrator's mandate are non-mandatory has been criticised by some commentators.[4]

---

[1] Which is in contrast to the provisions of the Model Law concerning the number of arbitrators; the appointment of arbitrators; and the challenge procedure which all expressly provide that the parties can agree alternative procedures. See Model Law, Arts 10; 11; and 13.

[2] Arbitration Act 2010, s 8(1).

[3] UNCITRAL Commission Report, A/40/17, Art 14, para 136.

[4] Binder, *International Commercial Arbitration and Conciliation in UNCITRAL Model Law Jurisdictions* (3rd ed, Sweet & Maxwell, London, 2010) p 206.

***Waiver of right to object to an arbitrator's failure of impossibility to act*:** Where a party becomes aware that an arbitrator is *de facto* or *de jure* unable to perform his or her functions or fails to act without undue delay and that party does not demand termination of the arbitrator's mandate, it waives its right to object later in the proceedings.[1]

---

[1] Model Law, Art 4.

Article 15.—Appointment of substitute arbitrator

Where the mandate of an arbitrator terminates under article 13 or 14 or because of his withdrawal from office for any other reason or because of the revocation of his mandate by agreement of the parties or in any other case of termination of his mandate, a substitute arbitrator shall be appointed according to the rules that were applicable to the appointment of the arbitrator being replaced.

Notes

***Appointment of a substitute arbitrator*:** Where the mandate of an arbitrator is terminated, this article provides that a substitute arbitrator will be appointed according to the rules that were applicable to the appointment of the original arbitrator.[1] This does not mean that the substitute arbitrator need be appointed in the same way as the original arbitrator but only that the same set of rules should apply. For example, where a party had not appointed an original arbitrator thereby requiring the original arbitrator to be appointed by the High Court and the appointed arbitrator subsequently resigned, the party would enjoy the right to appoint a substitute arbitrator and only where it again failed to exercise its right, would the High Court act.[2]

---

[1] Model Law, Art 15.

[2] Holtzmann and Neuhaus, *A Guide to the UNCITRAL Model Law on International Commercial Arbitration* (1st ed, Kluwer Law and Taxation Publishers, The Hague, 1989) p 465.

***Termination of an arbitrator's mandate*:** An arbitrator's mandate terminates where:

1. A party challenges an arbitrator's impartiality or independence and the arbitrator withdraws from office—the other party agrees to the challenge—or the challenges is upheld by either the arbitral tribunal (in the first instance) or the High Court[1] (where the arbitral tribunal rejects the challenge);[2]

2. An arbitrator becomes unable to perform his or her functions or fails to act without undue delay and the arbitrator withdraws; the parties agree to terminate the his or her mandate; or the High Court[3] terminates the arbitrator's mandate;[4]

3 An arbitrator otherwise withdraws from office.[5] The *travaux préparatoires* (of which Irish courts are permitted to take judicial notice when interpreting provisions of the Model Law)[6] suggest that an arbitrator need not show cause to withdraw from office;[7] or

4. The parties otherwise agree to revoke an arbitrator's mandate.[8] The parties need not show cause where it is agreed to revoke an arbitrator's mandate. The *travaux préparatoires* suggest that justification for this is "the consensual nature of arbitration which gives the parties unrestricted freedom to agree on the termination of the mandate of an arbitrator".[9]

In addition, the mandate of the entire arbitral tribunal terminates with the termination of arbitral proceedings.[10]

---

[1] Arbitration Act 2010, s 9(1)(a); and Model Law, Art 6.
[2] Model Law, Art 13.
[3] Arbitration Act 2010, s. 9(1)(a); and Model Law, Art 6.
[4] Model Law, Art 14(1).
[5] Model Law, Art 15.
[6] Arbitration Act 2010, s 8(1).
[7] UNCITRAL Seventh Secretariat Note, A/CN.9/264, Art 15, para 3.
[8] Model Law, Art 15.
[9] UNCITRAL Seventh Secretariat Note, A/CN.9/264, Art 15, para 2.
[10] Model Law, Art 32(3).

Chapter IV

Jurisdiction of Arbitral Tribunal

Article 16.—Competence of arbitral tribunal to rule on its jurisdiction

(1) The arbitral tribunal may rule on its own jurisdiction, including any objections with respect to the existence or validity of the arbitration agreement. For that purpose, an arbitration clause which forms part of a contract shall be treated as an agreement independent of the other terms of the contract. A decision by the arbitral tribunal that the contract is null and void shall not entail *ipso jure* the invalidity of the arbitration clause.

(2) A plea that the arbitral tribunal does not have jurisdiction shall be raised not later than the submission of the statement of defence. A party is not precluded from raising such a plea by the fact that he has appointed, or participated in the appointment of, an arbitrator. A plea that the arbitral tribunal is exceeding the scope of its authority shall be raised as soon as the matter alleged to be beyond the scope of its authority is raised during the arbitral proceedings. The arbitral tribunal may, in either case, admit a later plea if it considers the delay justified.

(3) The arbitral tribunal may rule on a plea referred to in paragraph (2) of this article either as a preliminary question or in an award on the merits. If the arbitral tribunal rules as a preliminary question that it has jurisdiction, any party may request, within thirty days after having received notice of that ruling, the court specified in article 6 to decide the matter, which decision shall be subject to no appeal; while such a request is pending, the arbitral tribunal may continue the arbitral proceedings and make an award.

Definitions

'arbitration': Arbitration Act 2010, s 2(1) and Model Law, Art 2(a); 'arbitration agreement': Arbitration Act 2010, s 2(1) and Model Law, Art 7(1)(Option 1); 'arbitral tribunal': Model Law, Art 2(b); 'award': Arbitration Act 2010, s 2(1); 'court': Model Law, Art 2(c).

Notes

***The doctrine of 'competence-competence'*:** The doctrine of 'competence-competence' (which is also referred to as 'Kompetenz-Kompetenz' or 'jurisdiction to decide jurisdiction')[1] permits an arbitral tribunal "to consider and to decide disputes concerning [its] own jurisdiction".[2] However, commentators have noted that different legal systems have "attached different degrees of both priority and finality to an arbitral tribunal's exercise of its competence-competence".[3] While this article provides that an arbitral tribunal has power to rule on its own jurisdiction,[4] the power is neither final nor exclusive[5] as the arbitral tribunal's decision is subject to review by the court of competent jurisdiction under the Model Law,[6] which in Ireland is the High Court.[7] The doctrine is intended to permit arbitral proceedings to continue where one party seeks to derail those proceedings by alleging that an arbitral tribunal lacks jurisdiction over the dispute.[8]

---

[1] Born, *International Commercial Arbitration* (1st ed, Kluwer Law International, Alphen aan den Rijn, 2009) p 852.

(*Continued*)

[2] *ibid*, p 853.
[3] *ibid*, pp 853-854.
[4] Model Law, Art 16(1).
[5] Holtzmann and Neuhaus, *A Guide to the UNCITRAL Model Law on International Commercial Arbitration* (1st ed, Kluwer Law and Taxation Publishers, The Hague, 1989) p 479.
[6] Model Law, Art 16(3).
[7] Arbitration Act 2010, s 9(1)(a).
[8] Gaillard and Savage, *Fouchard, Gaillard, Goldman on International Commercial Arbitration* (1st ed, Kluwer Law International, The Hague, 1999) p 401.

***Time limit to object to the jurisdiction of an arbitral tribunal*:** Where a party wishes to object to the jurisdiction of an arbitral tribunal, it must do so not later than at the submission of its statement of defence.[1] Similarly, although this article does not expressly provide for an objection by a party to the jurisdiction of an arbitral tribunal to hear a counter-claim, the *travaux préparatoires* (of which Irish courts are permitted to take judicial notice when interpreting provisions of the Model Law)[2] suggest that the relevant time limit is when a party is required to submit his reply to the counter-claim raised.[3] Where a party wishes to object that the arbitral tribunal is exceeding the scope of its authority in the course of arbitral proceedings, it must do so as soon as possible.[4] International case-law decided under the Model Law has held that the prescribed time limits must be strictly complied with.[5] However, where a party has not been properly informed of the commencement of the arbitral proceedings then the time limits will not apply.[6]

[1] Model Law, Art 16(2).
[2] Arbitration Act 2010, s 8(1).
[3] UNCITRAL Seventh Secretariat Note, A/CN.9/264, Art 16, para 5.
[4] Model Law, Art 16(2).
[5] CLOUT Case 781 – Egypt/Cairo Regional Centre for International Commercial Arbitration: *No 111/1998* (12 July 1999).
[6] CLOUT Case 562 – Germany/Highest Regional Court of Hamburg: *6 Sch 4/01* (8 November 2001).

***The consequences of a failure to object*:** While this article does not expressly provide for the consequences of a party's failure to raise timely objection to jurisdiction or scope of an arbitral tribunal's authority, the *travaux préparatoires* (of which Irish courts are permitted to take judicial notice when interpreting provisions of the Model Law)[1] suggest that "a party who failed to raise the plea as required under article 16(2) should be precluded from raising such objections not only during the later stages of the arbitral proceedings but also in other contexts, in particular, in setting aside proceedings or enforcement proceedings, subject to certain limits such as public policy, including those relating to arbitrability".[2] Similarly, international case-law decided under the Model Law has held that a failure to raise objection before the arbitral tribunal prevents a party from making objection in subsequent enforcement proceedings.[3] International case-law has also held that courts should adopt a limited and deferential role to the jurisdiction of an arbitral tribunal.[4]

[1] Arbitration Act 2010, s 8(1).
[2] UNCITRAL Seventh Secretariat Note, A/CN.9/264, Art 16, para 8.

(*Continued*)

[3] CLOUT Case 29/CLOUT Case 369 – Canada/Ontario Court of Justice: *Kanto Yakin Kogyo Kabushiki-Kaisha v Can-Eng Manufacturing Ltd* (30 January 1992).
[4] CLOUT Case 509 – Canada/Ontario Court of Appeal: *Dalimpex Ltd v Janicki; Agros Trading Spolka ZOO v Dalimpex Ltd* (30 May 2003).

***Form of an arbitral tribunal's ruling on its jurisdiction*:** An arbitral tribunal may decide on its jurisdiction as either a preliminary question or as part of an award on the merits.[1] Where an arbitral tribunal decides that it has jurisdiction to determine the dispute as a preliminary question, a party may seek review of this decision from the court of competent jurisdiction of a State adopting the Model Law, which in Ireland is the High Court,[2] within 30 days of having received notice of the ruling.[3] The parties may not exclude the power of the High Court to review any decision of an arbitral tribunal that it has jurisdiction.[4] Where an arbitral tribunal decision forms part of an award on the merits, a party may seek to set aside the award.[5] International case-law decided under the Model Law has held that the decision of an arbitral tribunal on whether it decides on its jurisdiction as either a preliminary question or as part of an award on the merits is not subject to review.[6]

---

[1] Model Law, Art 16(3).
[2] Arbitration Act 2010, s 9(1)(a).
[3] Model Law, Art 16(3).
[4] See *Czarnikow v Roth, Schmidt & Co* [1922] 2 KB 478, which is a decision of the English Court of Appeal where the parties had agreed that they would not invoke the special case stated procedure under the English Arbitration Act 1889, s 7 after an award was issued by the arbitral tribunal. This agreement was held to be an ouster of the jurisdiction of the courts and was void as being contrary to public policy. The decision in *Czarnikow* v *Roth, Schmidt & Co* has received judicial approval in Ireland in *Uniform Construction Ltd v Cappawhite Contractors Ltd* [2007] IEHC 295; and *John Mowlem Construction Ltd t/a Irishenco Construction v Dublin City Council* [2009] IEHC 225.
[5] Model Law, Art 34.
[6] CLOUT Case 441 – Germany/Highest Regional Court of Cologne: *9 Sch 6/00* (20 July 2000).

***Consequences of an arbitral tribunal's decision that it does not have jurisdiction*:** This article expressly provides that a party may seek review of a decision of an arbitral tribunal where the arbitral tribunal decides that has jurisdiction.[1] However, it is left unspecified whether or not a party may seek review where the arbitral tribunal decides that it does not have jurisdiction. International case-law decided under the Model Law provides conflicting authority on the availability of review of an arbitral tribunal's negative decision on its jurisdiction. The German courts have held that, in theory at least, a party may seek review of a negative decision of an arbitral tribunal on its jurisdiction[2] while the courts of Singapore have held that court review is only permitted where an arbitral tribunal decides that it has jurisdiction.[3] While it is uncertain what approach

(*Continued*)

will be adopted by the High Court, commentators have noted that the better view favours equal court review of both positive and negative decisions of an arbitral tribunal on whether it has jurisdiction, stating: "[i]t would be ironic, and contrary to the purposes of the Model Law and the interests of justice, to provide less judicial review for a wrongful refusal to give any effect to the arbitration agreement, than for a refusal to apply a particular procedural aspect of that agreement".[4]

---

[1] Model Law, Art 16(3).

[2] See CLOUT Case 560 – Germany/Supreme Court: *III ZB 44/01* (6 June 2002), where the German Supreme Court held that while a party may potentially seek review of a negative decision of an arbitral tribunal on its jurisdiction it was required to demonstrate a ground for setting aside an award in order to overturn a decision of an arbitral tribunal on its jurisdiction. Elements of this decision has been criticised by commentators. See Born, *International Commercial Arbitration* (1st ed, Kluwer Law International, Alphen aan den Rijn, 2009) pp 897-898.

[3] CLOUT Case 742 – Singapore/Singapore Court of Appeal: *PT Asuransi Jasa Indonesia (Persero) v Dexia Bank SA* (1 December 2006).

[4] Born, *International Commercial Arbitration* (1st ed, Kluwer Law International, Alphen aan den Rijn, 2009) pp 898–899.

***Power of the courts to decide on an arbitral tribunal's jurisdiction*:** The Model Law provides that where civil proceedings are commenced concerning a dispute which is the subject matter of an arbitration agreement, a court must refer the parties to arbitration unless it finds that the arbitration agreement is null and void, inoperative or incapable of being performed.[1] This, invariably, requires the court in which the civil proceedings are pending to make a determination on the jurisdiction of an arbitral tribunal. As the ability of a court to make a determination on the jurisdiction of an arbitral tribunal operates in parallel to an arbitral tribunal's similar power, it is possible that a court will decide on an arbitral tribunal's jurisdiction before an arbitral tribunal decides itself. In this regard, commentators have noted that:

> "the basic structure of the Model Law is: (a) to permit arbitral tribunals to consider and decide jurisdictional issues in an award (under Article 16), which are (b) subject to very prompt judicial review (under Article 34), but also (c) to permit interlocutory judicial consideration of jurisdictional issues to occur prior to, or in parallel with, any arbitral decision (under Article 8(1)), while (d) the arbitral proceedings continue notwithstanding the jurisdictional challenge (under Article 8(2)). This approach makes it entirely possible that a national court may decide jurisdictional issues before the arbitral tribunal itself does so, and that such judicial decisions may pre-empt the tribunal's jurisdictional decision".[2]

---

[1] Model Law, Art 8(1).

[2] Born, *International Commercial Arbitration* (1st ed, Kluwer Law International, Alphen aan den Rijn, 2009) p 880.

***Separability of an arbitration agreement*:** The doctrine of 'competence-competence' is closely linked to the concept of the separability of an arbitration agreement, which provides that where an arbitration agreement forms part of a matrix contract it must be considered separate from the matrix contract and survives any termination of that contract.[1] Commentators have noted that "it would be entirely self-defeating if a breach of contract or a claim that the contract was voidable was sufficient to terminate the arbitration [agreement] as well; this is one of the situations in which the arbitration [agreement] is most needed".[2] This article provides for the separability of an arbitration agreement from the matrix contract and provides that a decision by an arbitral tribunal that the contract is null and void will not invalidate the arbitration agreement.[3] Similarly, Irish case-law decided under the Arbitration Acts 1954-1998 has held that an arbitration agreement survives any contended termination of a matrix contract.[4] However, it is axiomatic that an arbitral tribunal will only have jurisdiction to determine a dispute where the arbitration agreement itself is valid and binding.[5]

---

[1] Blackaby, Partasides, Redfern and Hunter, *Redfern and Hunter on International Arbitration* (5th ed, Oxford University Press, Oxford, 2009) p 117.

[2] *ibid.*

[3] Model Law, Art 16(1).

[4] *Parkarran Ltd v M & P Construction Ltd* [1996] 1 IR 83; and *Doyle v Irish National Insurance Company* [1998] 1 IR 89.

[5] See *Vee Networks Ltd v Econet Wireless International Ltd* [2005] 1 All ER (Comm) 303, where the English High Court in considering the concept of separability under the English Arbitration Act 1996, stated that an arbitral tribunal "would, because of the separability of the agreement to arbitrate, have jurisdiction conclusively to determine whether the matrix contract was void *ab initio* ... provided always that there was a binding agreement to arbitrate".

***Arbitral proceedings may be commenced while an application to refer proceedings to arbitration is pending*:** Where an application is made by a party to a court to direct that pending civil proceedings referred to arbitration, arbitral proceedings may be commenced or continued and an award may even be made, notwithstanding that the application may be pending before the court.[1]

---

[1] Model Law, Art 8(2).

***Power to determine the jurisdiction of an arbitral tribunal at common law*:** At common law, the courts had an inherent power to make a declaration that an arbitral tribunal has no jurisdiction to hear or determine a claim.[1] However, an arbitral tribunal had no comparative power.[2]

---

[1] *Anglo Irish Banking Corporation v Tolka Structural Engineering* [2005] IEHC 239.

[2] Reichert in Rowley, *Arbitration World* (2nd ed, *European Lawyer Reference*, London, 2006) pp 149–50.

Chapter IV A

Interim Measures and Preliminary Orders

Article 17.—Power of arbitral tribunal to order interim measures

(1) Unless otherwise agreed by the parties, the arbitral tribunal may, at the request of a party, grant interim measures.

(2) An interim measure is any temporary measure, whether in the form of an award or in another form, by which, at any time prior to the issuance of the award by which the dispute is finally decided, the arbitral tribunal orders a party to:

(a) Maintain or restore the status quo pending determination of the dispute;

(b) Take action that would prevent, or refrain from taking action that is likely to cause, current or imminent harm or prejudice to the arbitral process itself;

(c) Provide a means of preserving assets out of which a subsequent award may be satisfied; or

(d) Preserve evidence that may be relevant and material to the resolution of the dispute.

Definitions

'arbitral tribunal': Model Law, Art 2(b); 'award': Arbitration Act 2010, s 2(1).

Notes

Arbitral tribunal's power to grant interim measures in support of arbitral proceedings: Unless otherwise agreed by the parties, an arbitral tribunal has power to grant interim measures in respect of arbitral proceedings.[1] In arbitration the term 'interim measures' has a broader meaning than at Irish law under which it refers only to urgent injunctive relief sought on an *ex parte* basis,[2] and includes injunctive relief, which under Irish law would be classified as both 'interim' and 'interlocutory' relief.[3] The interim measures which may be granted by an arbitral tribunal are:

1. Measures to maintain or restore the status quo pending determination of the dispute;
2. Measures to prevent current or imminent harm or prejudice to the arbitral proceedings themselves;
3. Measures to preserve assets out of which an award may be satisfied; and
4. Measures to preserve evidence that may be relevant and material to the resolution of the dispute.[4]

---

[1] Model Law, Art 17(1).
[2] Kirwan, *Injunctions Law & Practice* (1st ed, Thomson Round Hall, Dublin, 2008) p 240.
[3] *Shelbourne Hotel Holdings Ltd v Torriam Hotel Operating Company Ltd* [2010] 2 IR 52.
[4] Model Law, Art 17(2).

***Arbitral tribunal's power to grant anti-suit injunctions*:** In arbitration, an anti-suit injunction is an order directed against the parties or intended parties to foreign litigation prohibiting the commencement or prosecution of litigation where the matter in dispute is the subject of an arbitration agreement.[1] Although the power to prohibit the commencement or prosecution of foreign litigation brought in violation of an arbitration agreement has long been exercised by courts in certain common law jurisdictions,[2] Irish commentators have noted that "[t]here is a dearth of [modern] case-law in this jurisdiction on anti-suit injunctions".[3] However, it is likely that, as in other common law jurisdictions, an anti-suit injunction may be ordered in appropriate circumstances.[4] However, where a court within the European Union has been seised of civil proceedings within the meaning of Council Regulation (EC) No 44/2001 of 22 December 2000 on Jurisdiction and the Recognition and Enforcement of Judgments in Civil and Commercial Matters (the Brussels Regulation),[5] the court of another European Union Member State cannot order an anti-suit injunction to prohibit the prosecution of foreign litigation, even where the initial civil proceedings have been brought in violation of an arbitration agreement.[6]

The Model Law permits an arbitral tribunal to grant an interim measure to prevent current or imminent harm or prejudice to the arbitral proceedings themselves and the *travaux préparatoires* (of which Irish courts are permitted to take judicial notice when interpreting provisions of the Model Law)[7] suggest that this power should be interpreted as encompassing a power of an arbitral tribunal to order an anti-suit injunction.[8] A similar view has been expressed by commentators who have noted that "[t]here should be little doubt that arbitral tribunals in principle have the power to issue [anti-suit] injunctions".[9] However, commentators have noted that the inclusion of this provision under the Model Law has proved to be controversial.[10]

---

[1] Born, *International Commercial Arbitration* (1st ed, Kluwer Law International, Alphen aan den Rijn, 2009) p 1036.

[2] See *Lett v Lett* [1906] 1 IR 618, where the pre-independence High Court granted an injunction restraining the prosecution of family law proceedings in Argentina in violation of an agreement of the parties not to proceed with the suit. The High Court's decision was upheld on appeal. See also: *Pena Copper Mines Ltd v Rio Tinto Co Ltd* [1911-1913] All ER Rep 209, where the English Court of Appeal enjoined an English company not to proceed with litigation in the Spanish courts in violation of an arbitration agreement. Courts in Australia, Bermuda, Canada, Singapore and the United States have also ordered anti-suit injunctions to prevent a party from commencing or prosecuting foreign litigation. For a discussion on anti-suit injunctions in common law jurisdictions, see Born, *International Commercial Arbitration* (1st ed, Kluwer Law International, Alphen aan den Rijn, 2009) pp 1036-1041.

[3] Kirwan, *Injunctions Law & Practice* (1st ed, Thomson Round Hall, Dublin, 2008) p 68.

[4] Guidelines for what may be considered 'appropriate circumstances' were set out in the case of *Airbus Indus GIE v Patel* [1999] 1 AC 119 where the House of Lords (as it then was) refused to grant an anti-suit injunction as the English forum did not have a sufficient interest in, or connection with, the matter in question to justify such interference. It was held that for an anti-suit injunction to be ordered the party seeking the injunction must demonstrate that: first, the forum in which the anti-suit injunction is sought must have a sufficient interest in, or in connection with the dispute in question; second, the foreign proceedings would cause prejudice to the party seeking the anti-suit injunction; and, finally, the anti-suit injunction would not unfairly deprive the plaintiff in the foreign litigation of a legitimate advantage.

(*Continued*)

[5] EC No 44/2001.

[6] *Allianz SpA v West Tankers Inc* [2009] 1 AC 1138 where the European Court of Justice held that an order restraining a party from commencing or continuing proceedings before a court of another Member State on the ground that those proceedings would be contrary to an arbitration agreement was in violation of the provisions of the Brussels Regulation. The decision has been met with near-universal criticism and it has been proposed by the European Commission that its effect will be neutralised by a proposed amendment to the Brussels Regulation, which includes a specific rule on the relation between arbitration and civil proceedings obliging a court seised of a dispute to stay proceedings where its jurisdiction is contested on the basis of an arbitration agreement.

[7] Arbitration Act 2010, s. 8(1).

[8] UNCITRAL Working Group on Arbitration Report, A/CN.9/589, para 94.

[9] Born, *International Commercial Arbitration* (1st ed, Kluwer Law International, Alphen aan den Rijn, 2009) p 2011.

[10] Binder, *International Commercial Arbitration and Conciliation in UNCITRAL Model Law Jurisdictions* (3rd ed, Sweet & Maxwell, London, 2010) p 244.

***Restrictions on an arbitral tribunal's power to grant interim measures*:** When granting interim measures an arbitral tribunal is subject to restrictions to which courts are not. First, an arbitral tribunal's power to grant interim measures in respect of arbitral proceedings is expressly limited to orders directed to the parties and not to third parties.[1] The *travaux préparatoires* (of which Irish courts are permitted to take judicial notice when interpreting provisions of the Model Law)[2] suggest that the fact that only the parties may be bound "follows from the fact that the arbitral tribunal derives its jurisdiction from the arbitration agreement".[3] In contrast, court-ordered interim measures can be issued against third parties.[4] Second, an arbitral tribunal has no means of enforcing an interim measures granted where it is not honoured by a party.[5] However, despite these restrictions, commentators have noted that the power of an arbitral tribunal to grant interim measures may still be advantageous in arbitral proceedings as "it is in most cases far less complicated to convince the arbitral tribunal, which is solely devoted to the case at hand and which is familiar with the circumstances to issue an interim measure, than a court, which only plays the role of safety net in the background".[6]

---

[1] Model Law, Art 17(2).

[2] Arbitration Act 2010, s 8(1).

[3] UNCITRAL Seventh Secretariat Note, A/CN.9/264, Art 18, para 3 [Model Law, Art 17 in the final text].

[4] Binder, *International Commercial Arbitration and Conciliation in UNCITRAL Model Law Jurisdictions* (3rd ed, Sweet & Maxwell, London, 2010) p 238.

[5] *ibid*, p 236.

[6] *ibid*, pp 238-239.

Arbitral tribunal's power to grant interim measures under the Arbitration Acts 1954-1998: Under the Arbitration Acts 1954-1998 international commercial arbitrations were governed by the Model Law and, consequently, an arbitral tribunal had the power to grant interim measures under Art 17 thereof. However, in a domestic arbitration, which

(*Continued*)

is any arbitration other than an international commercial arbitration) an arbitral tribunal had no express power to grant interim measures. Commentators have noted that an arbitral tribunal could potentially have ordered interim measures to the extent that it could structure the interim measures in the form of an interim award. This approach was far from ideal as difficulties could arise in enforcing an interim measures which preserves the status quo rather than final decides the issues between the parties.[1]

---

[1] Reichert in Rowley, *Arbitration World* (2nd ed, *European Lawyer Reference*, London, 2006) p 155.

***Non-mandatory nature of the article*:** This article is non-mandatory in nature and the parties may circumvent its effect by agreeing otherwise.

Article 17 A.—Conditions for granting interim measures

(1) The party requesting an interim measure under article 17(2)(a), (b) and (c) shall satisfy the arbitral tribunal that:

(a) Harm not adequately reparable by an award of damages is likely to result if the measure is not ordered, and such harm substantially outweighs the harm that is likely to result to the party against whom the measure is directed if the measure is granted; and

(b) There is a reasonable possibility that the requesting party will succeed on the merits of the claim. The determination on this possibility shall not affect the discretion of the arbitral tribunal in making any subsequent determination.

(2) With regard to a request for an interim measure under article 17(2)(d), the requirements in paragraphs (1)(a) and (b) of this article shall apply only to the extent the arbitral tribunal considers appropriate.

Definitions

'arbitral tribunal': Model Law, Art 2(b); 'award': Arbitration Act 2010, s 2(1).

Notes

***Conditions for the grant of interim measures*:** A party seeking an interim measure from an arbitral tribunal must demonstrate that it will suffer harm not adequately reparable by damages if the measure sought is not granted[1] and it must demonstrate that it has a reasonable prospect of success on the merits of a claim.[2] These requirements are similar (albeit listed in reverse order) to the test for injunctive relief under Irish law where a party seeking injunctive relief must demonstrate that there is a *bona fide* question to be tried and that damages would not be an adequate remedy if the injunctive relief is refused.[3]

(*Continued*)

The *travaux préparatoires* (of which Irish courts are permitted to take judicial notice when interpreting provisions of the Model Law)[4] suggest that harm not adequately reparable by damages "was intended to apply to a particular type of harm occurring in a situation where, even at a preliminary stage when all the facts of the dispute were not before the tribunal, it could be shown that the requesting party should be protected against harm that could not be remedied by an award of damages".[5] The *travaux préparatoires* suggest examples of harm not adequately reparable by damages include the loss of a priceless or unique work of art, a business becoming insolvent, essential evidence being lost, an essential business opportunity being lost, or harm being caused to the reputation of a business as a result of a trademark infringement.[6]

---

[1] Model Law, Art 17 A(1)(a).
[2] Model Law, Art 17 A(1)(b).
[3] *Campus Oil Ltd v Minister for Industry and Energy (No 2)* [1983] 1 IR 88.
[4] Arbitration Act 2010, s 8(1).
[5] UNCITRAL Working Group on Arbitration Report, A/CN.9/547, para 86.
[6] *ibid*, para 86.

***Application of conditions only to the extent an arbitral tribunal considers appropriate where preservation of evidence is sought*:** Where the interim measure sought is the preservation of evidence, the requirements that a party demonstrate that it will suffer harm, which is not adequately reparable by damages if the measure sought is not granted and that it demonstrate that it has a reasonable prospect of success on the merits of a claim, applies only to the extent the arbitral tribunal considers appropriate.[1]

---

[1] Model Law, Art 17 A(2).

Article 17 B.—Applications for preliminary orders and conditions for granting preliminary orders

(1) Unless otherwise agreed by the parties, a party may, without notice to any other party, make a request for an interim measure together with an application for a preliminary order directing a party not to frustrate the purpose of the interim measure requested.

(2) The arbitral tribunal may grant a preliminary order provided it considers that prior disclosure of the request for the interim measure to the party against whom it is directed risks frustrating the purpose of the measure.

(3) The conditions defined under article 17 A apply to any preliminary order, provided that the harm to be assessed under article 17 A(1)(a), is the harm likely to result from the order being granted or not.

Definitions

'arbitral tribunal': Model Law, Art 2(b).

Notes

Ex parte interim measures or 'preliminary orders': Unless otherwise agreed by the parties,[1] an arbitral tribunal may grant an interim measure on an *ex parte* basis by way of a 'preliminary order'[2] in circumstances where it is feared that a party against whom an interim measure is granted may frustrate the purpose of the measures if prior disclosure is granted.[3] However, the concept of *ex parte* interim measures is a highly controversial provision of the Model Law as it permits single party contact with an arbitral tribunal, jeopardising equality of treatment, which is a principle enshrined in the Model Law.[4] In addition, as an arbitral tribunal's orders cannot bind third parties and can have no direct coercive effect, where a party fears that an opposing party may frustrate the purpose of the measures if prior disclosure is granted, it may be more prudent to apply to a national court for urgent injunctive relief.[5] For these reasons, some commentators have described the inclusion of a regime for preliminary orders in arbitration by the Model Law as "ill-considered"[6]. Critics of *ex parte* interim measures focus particularly on whether any serious purpose can be achieved by the provision:

> "The basic predicate of the extraordinary grant of ex parte relief is that one party cannot be trusted to conduct itself in compliance with its obligations, and must be legally compelled to take particular (immediate) actions without any opportunity to evade its obligation. Although this rationale has force in domestic litigation contexts (e.g., when funds, which could be transferred abroad, can be frozen), it has no real application where an arbitral tribunal cannot issue immediately-effective coercive relief (e.g., attachment or garnishment of bank accounts)".[7]

---

[1] Model Law, Art 17 B(1).
[2] Model Law, Art 17 B (2).
[3] Model Law, Art 17 B (2).
[4] Model Law, Art 18.
[5] Born, *International Commercial Arbitration* (1st ed, Kluwer Law International, Alphen aan den Rijn, 2009) p 2016.
[6] *ibid*, p 2017. See also Brekoulakis and Shore in Mistelis, *Concise International Arbitration, UNCITRAL Model Law* (1st ed, Kluwer Law International, Alphen aan den Rijn, 2010) p 622.
[7] Born, *International Commercial Arbitration* (1st ed, Kluwer Law International, Alphen aan den Rijn, 2009) pp 2017-2018.

Conditions for the grant of preliminary orders: A party seeking a preliminary order from an arbitral tribunal must demonstrate that it has a reasonable prospect of success on the merits of a claim and must demonstrate that it will suffer harm not adequately reparable by damages if the preliminary order sought is granted or not granted.[1] However, preliminary orders should be contemplated only in exceptional circumstances and leading commentators have noted that preliminary orders should only be granted "where they are clearly required in order to prevent immediate and very grave damage that cannot otherwise be avoided".[2]

---

[1] Model Law, Art 17 B(3).
[2] Born, *International Commercial Arbitration* (1st ed, Kluwer Law International, Alphen aan den Rijn, 2009) p. 2018.

***Non-mandatory nature of the article*:** This article is non-mandatory and the parties may circumvent its effect by agreeing otherwise.

Article 17 C.—Specific regime for preliminary orders

(1) Immediately after the arbitral tribunal has made a determination in respect of an application for a preliminary order, the arbitral tribunal shall give notice to all parties of the request for the interim measure, the application for the preliminary order, the preliminary order, if any, and all other communications, including by indicating the content of any oral communication, between any party and the arbitral tribunal in relation thereto.

(2) At the same time, the arbitral tribunal shall give an opportunity to any party against whom a preliminary order is directed to present its case at the earliest practicable time.

(3) The arbitral tribunal shall decide promptly on any objection to the preliminary order.

(4) A preliminary order shall expire after twenty days from the date on which it was issued by the arbitral tribunal. However, the arbitral tribunal may issue an interim measure adopting or modifying the preliminary order, after the party against whom the preliminary order is directed has been given notice and an opportunity to present its case.

(5) A preliminary order shall be binding on the parties but shall not be subject to enforcement by a court. Such a preliminary order does not constitute an award.

Definitions

'arbitral tribunal': Model Law, Art 2(b); 'award': Arbitration Act 2010, s 2(1); 'court': Model Law, Art 2(c).

Notes

***Requirement to provide notice of a preliminary order immediately*:** An arbitral tribunal must give immediate notice to all parties of its determination in respect of an application for a preliminary order.[1] In addition, the arbitral tribunal must provide an opportunity to a party against whom a preliminary order is directed to present its case at the earliest practicable time.[2] The effect of these provisions is to turn the preliminary order into an *inter partes* application for an interim measure as soon as possible.[3] What constitutes 'immediately' and 'at the earliest practicable time' is not defined by either the Model Law or the *travaux préparatoires* (of which Irish courts are permitted to take judicial notice when interpreting provisions of the Model Law).[4] However, it has been noted by commentators that "in practice, particular attention must be paid to the fact that as soon as the party against whom the measure is directed knows of the preliminary order and the application for the interim measure, there is danger that it may commence actions directed at thwarting the interim measure".[5] After notice of provided to the parties, an arbitral tribunal must decide on any objection to a preliminary order promptly.[6]

[1] Model Law, Art 17 C(1).
[2] Model Law, Art 17 C (2).

(Continued)

[3] Binder, *International Commercial Arbitration and Conciliation in UNCITRAL Model Law Jurisdictions* (3rd ed, Sweet & Maxwell, London, 2010) p 254.
[4] Arbitration Act 2010, s 8(1).
[5] Binder, *International Commercial Arbitration and Conciliation in UNCITRAL Model Law Jurisdictions* (3rd ed, Sweet & Maxwell, London, 2010) p. 254.
[6] Model Law, Art 17 C(3).

***Ex parte preliminary order must expire within 20 days*:** An arbitral tribunal may not extend the *ex parte* phase of the proceedings indefinitely and a preliminary order must expire within 20 days from the date on which it was issued by an arbitral tribunal.[1] The *travaux préparatoires* (of which Irish courts are permitted to take judicial notice when interpreting provisions of the Model Law)[2] refer to the time limit of 20 days as the "drop dead date" within which a preliminary order must be converted into an *inter partes* interim measure.[3] Thereafter, an arbitral tribunal must either grant an interim measure adopting or modifying the preliminary order, after the party against whom the preliminary order is directed has been given notice and an opportunity to present its case or else lift the preliminary order.

[1] Model Law, Art 17 C(4).
[2] Arbitration Act 2010, s 8(1).
[3] UNCITRAL Working Group on Arbitration and Conciliation Report, A/CN.9/569, para 64.

***Preliminary orders are not enforceable*:** Preliminary orders while binding on the parties, are not enforceable by the courts.[1] The *travaux préparatoires* (of which Irish courts are permitted to take judicial notice when interpreting provisions of the Model Law)[2] suggest the need for preliminary orders to be enforceable by the courts "was questioned given the temporary nature of a preliminary order and the fact that it could raise practical difficulties, such as whether notification of the preliminary order to the other party should be deferred until after the order had been enforced by a court. Further, it was said that parties usually honour interim measures out of respect for the arbitrators' authority and a desire not to antagonize them".[3] However, as a result of their unenforceability, it is questionable how effective a preliminary order can be in preventing an opposing party from frustrating the purpose of an interim measure.

[1] Model Law, Art 17 C(5).
[2] Arbitration Act 2010, s 8(1).
[3] UNCITRAL Commission Report, A/61/17, Art 17, para 114.

Article 17 D.—Modification, suspension, termination

The arbitral tribunal may modify, suspend or terminate an interim measure or a preliminary order it has granted, upon application of any party or, in exceptional circumstances and upon prior notice to the parties, on the arbitral tribunal's own initiative.

Definitions

'arbitral tribunal': Model Law, Art 2(b).

Notes

***Arbitral tribunal's power to modify, suspend or terminate an interim measure*:** An arbitral tribunal may modify, suspend or terminate an interim measure or a preliminary order it has granted upon application of any party or, in exceptional circumstances and upon prior notice to the parties, *ex officio* on its own motion.[1] The *travaux préparatoires* (of which Irish courts are permitted to take judicial notice when interpreting provisions of the Model Law)[2] suggest the power of modification, suspension or termination is "necessary to make it possible for the arbitral tribunal to correct the serious consequences of an interim measure, particularly where that measure appeared to have been granted on an erroneous or fraudulent basis".[3] It is intended that in the ordinary course an arbitral tribunal will only modify, suspend or terminate an interim measure or a preliminary order on application of a party. Neither the Model Law nor the *travaux préparatoires* provide any guidance on what represents 'exceptional circumstances' as would permit an arbitral tribunal to act on its own motion. However, the *travaux préparatoires* suggest that great caution should be exercised by an arbitral tribunal acting on its own initiative in deciding to modify, suspend or terminate an interim measure or a preliminary order as "it might be seen as unduly protecting the interests of the other party, thus deviating from the impartiality that should be strictly observed by the arbitral tribunal".[4]

---

[1] Model Law, Art 17 D.
[2] Arbitration Act 2010, s 8(1).
[3] Working Group on Arbitration Report, A/CN.9/545, para 38.
[4] *ibid,* para 37.

***No power to modify court-ordered interim measures*:** An arbitral tribunal may only modify, suspend or terminate an interim measure or a preliminary order it has granted and it cannot modify, suspend or terminate an interim measure ordered by a court. The *travaux préparatoires* (of which Irish courts are permitted to take judicial notice when interpreting provisions of the Model Law)[1] suggest that permitting an arbitral tribunal to review a court-ordered interim measure would be "a contentious matter and [would raise] sensitive issues regarding the role of courts and balancing the role of private arbitral bodies against that of courts".[2]

---

[1] Arbitration Act 2010, s 8(1).
[2] UNCITRAL Working Group on Arbitration Report, A/CN.9/547, para 104.

Article 17 E.—Provision of security

(1) The arbitral tribunal may require the party requesting an interim measure to provide appropriate security in connection with the measure.

(2) The arbitral tribunal shall require the party applying for a preliminary order to provide security in connection with the order unless the arbitral tribunal considers it inappropriate or unnecessary to do so.

Definitions

'arbitral tribunal': Model Law, Art 2(b).

Notes

Arbitral tribunal's power to require the provision of security: An arbitral tribunal may require that a party seeking an interim measure of a preliminary order to provide appropriate security.[1] In contrast to the discretion which an arbitral tribunal enjoys to require the party requesting an interim measure to provide appropriate security, an arbitral tribunal *must* require a party applying for a preliminary order to provide security in connection with the order unless it considers it inappropriate or unnecessary to do so.[2] The *travaux préparatoires* (of which Irish courts are permitted to take judicial notice when interpreting provisions of the Model Law)[3] suggest that circumstances where an arbitral tribunal may consider it inappropriate to require the provision of security include where a party "was in an impecunious state because of action taken by the [other party]".[4] A similar requirement exists under Irish law where a party seeking an injunction generally gives an undertaking as to damages. Although an Irish court cannot compel a party to give an undertaking as to damages, where no undertaking is given a court may refuse to grant injunctive relief.[5]

---

1 Model Law, Art 17 E(1).
2 Model Law, Art 17 E (2).
3 Arbitration Act 2010, s 8(1).
4 UNCITRAL Working Group on Arbitration and Conciliation Report, A/CN.9/569, para 36.
5 See Kirwan, *Injunctions Law & Practice* (1st ed, Thomson Round Hall, Dublin, 2008) pp 226–227.

Article 17 F.—Disclosure

(1) The arbitral tribunal may require any party promptly to disclose any material change in the circumstances on the basis of which the measure was requested or granted.

(2) The party applying for a preliminary order shall disclose to the arbitral tribunal all circumstances that are likely to be relevant to the arbitral tribunal's determination whether to grant or maintain the order, and such obligation shall continue until the party against whom the order has been requested has had an opportunity to present its case. Thereafter, paragraph (1) of this article shall apply.

Definitions

'arbitral tribunal': Model Law, Art 2(b).

Notes

***Continued obligation to disclose material change in circumstances*:** Where an interim measure is granted an arbitral tribunal may require any party promptly to disclose any material change in the circumstances on the basis of which the interim measure was requested or granted.[1] After any such disclosure is made, on the application of a party or, in exceptional circumstances, *ex officio* on its own motion, the arbitral tribunal may modify, suspend or terminate the interim measure.[2]

[1] Model Law, Art 17 F(1).
[2] Model Law, Art 17 D.

***Duty to disclose all circumstances relevant to grant of a preliminary order*:** A party applying for a preliminary order must disclose to the arbitral tribunal all circumstances that are likely to be relevant to the arbitral tribunal's determination to grant or maintain the order. This duty continues until the party against whom the order has been requested has had an opportunity to present its case. The *travaux préparatoires* (of which Irish courts are permitted to take judicial notice when interpreting provisions of the Model Law)[1] suggest that the rationale for this requirement is that an arbitral tribunal does not "have the opportunity to hear from both parties, and therefore an additional burden should be placed on the applicant party to disclose facts that might not help its case but that [may be] relevant to the arbitral tribunal's determination".[2] A similar requirement exists under Irish law where a party making an *ex parte* application is required to act *uberrimae fides* (with the utmost good faith).[3] A party making an application *ex parte* must provide full and frank disclosure, even of facts unhelpful to its position.[4]

[1] Arbitration Act 2010, s 8(1).
[2] UNCITRAL Working Group on Arbitration and Conciliation Report, A/CN.9/573.
[3] See Kirwan, *Injunctions Law & Practice* (1st ed, Thomson Round Hall, Dublin, 2008) p 258.
[4] *Balogun v Minister for Justice* [2002] IEHC 134.

***Sanctions for violation of the duty to disclose*:** The sanctions to be placed on a party that fails to meet its duty to disclose are not specified. However, *travaux préparatoires* (of which Irish courts are permitted to take judicial notice when interpreting provisions of the Model Law)[1] suggest that the typical sanction for a violation of the duty to disclose is "either the suspension or termination of the measure, or the award of damages".[2]

[1] Arbitration Act 2010, s 8(1).
[2] UNCITRAL Working Group on Arbitration Report, A/CN.9/547, para 100.

Article 17 G.—Costs and damages

The party requesting an interim measure or applying for a preliminary order shall be liable for any costs and damages caused by the measure or the order to any party if the arbitral tribunal later determines that, in the circumstances, the measure or the order should not have been granted. The arbitral tribunal may award such costs and damages at any point during the proceedings.

Definitions

'arbitral tribunal': Model Law, Art 2(b).

Notes

***Liability of requesting party for costs and damages*:** A party requesting an interim measure is liable for any costs and damages caused by the measure or the order to any other party where the arbitral tribunal later determines that, in the circumstances, the measure or the order should not have been granted.[1] The *travaux préparatoires* (of which Irish courts are permitted to take judicial notice when interpreting provisions of the Model Law)[2] suggest that "the requesting party be considered strictly liable for damages caused to the responding party by an unjustified measure".[3] A similar requirement exists under Irish law where a party seeking an injunction generally gives an undertaking as to damages. Although an Irish court cannot compel a party to give an undertaking as to damages, where no undertaking is given a court may refuse to grant injunctive relief.[4]

---

[1] Model Law, Art 17 G.
[2] Arbitration Act 2010, s 8(1).
[3] UNCITRAL Working Group on Arbitration Report, A/CN.9/523, para 31.
[4] See Kirwan, *Injunctions Law & Practice* (1st ed, Thomson Round Hall, Dublin, 2008) pp 226-227.

***No liability of arbitral tribunal for costs and damages*:** As the Act provides a complete immunity from civil liability for arbitrators for any act or omission in the course of arbitral proceedings[1] this includes a complete immunity for liability for any costs and damages caused by the grant of an interim measure.

---

[1] Arbitration Act 2010, s 22(1).

Article 17 H.—Recognition and enforcement

(1) An interim measure issued by an arbitral tribunal shall be recognized as binding and, unless otherwise provided by the arbitral tribunal, enforced upon application to the competent court, irrespective of the country in which it was issued, subject to the provisions of article 17 I.

(2) The party who is seeking or has obtained recognition or enforcement of an interim measure shall promptly inform the court of any termination, suspension or modification of that interim measure.

(3) The court of the State where recognition or enforcement is sought may, if it considers it proper, order the requesting party to provide appropriate security if the arbitral tribunal has not already made a determination with respect to security or where such a decision is necessary to protect the rights of third parties.

Definitions

'arbitral tribunal': Model Law, Art 2(b); 'court': Model Law, Art 2(c).

Notes

***Recognition and enforcement of interim measures*:** Upon application of a party, an interim measure issued by an arbitral tribunal must be recognised as binding and must be enforced by court of competent jurisdiction in a State enacting the Model Law, irrespective of the country in which the interim measure was issued.[1] In Ireland, the court of competent jurisdiction for the purposes of recognising and enforcing an interim measure is the High Court.[2] The provisions of the Model Law specify only limited grounds for refusing recognition and enforcement of an interim measure.[3] These grounds are exhaustive and the High Court may only refuse recognition and enforcement of an interim measure for the reasons set out under the Model Law.[4] Recognition and enforcement of an interim measure may not be refused for some reason not specified in the Model Law under the courts' inherent jurisdiction. Commentators have noted that "[t]his means that unless the High Court has been accorded a specific role by the [Model Law], then it cannot intervene; inherent jurisdiction and other vestiges of the past are swept away".[5]

[1] Model Law, Art 17 H(1).

[2] Arbitration Act 2010, s 9(1)(c).

[3] Model Law, Art 17 I; and Model Law, Art 36(1).

[4] Model Law, Art 5.

[5] Reichert, "Security for Costs in Arbitration – A New Landscape in Ireland" (2010) *Arbitration and ADR Review* p 130.

***Duty of party to notify court of termination, suspension or modification of interim measures*:** A party seeking recognition or enforcement of an interim measure must promptly inform the court of any termination, suspension or modification of that interim measure by an arbitral tribunal.[1] However, neither the Model Law nor the *travaux préparatoires* (of which Irish courts are permitted to take judicial notice when interpreting provisions of the Model Law)[2] specify any suggested sanction to be imposed where a party seeking recognition or enforcement of an interim measure fails to inform the court as required.[3] Therefore, any proposed sanction lies with tribunal's ability to conduct the arbitral proceedings in such manner as it considers appropriate.[4]

[1] Model Law, Art 17 H(2).

[2] Arbitration Act 2010, s 8(1).

(*Continued*)

[3] Binder, *International Commercial Arbitration and Conciliation in UNCITRAL Model Law Jurisdictions* (3rd ed, Sweet & Maxwell, London, 2010) pp 267-268.
[4] Model Law, Art 19(2).

***Power of the High Court to order security to be provided in connection with interim measures*:** Where application is made to the High Court,[1] it may, where it considers it proper, order the requesting party to provide appropriate security in connection with an interim measure, either where the arbitral tribunal has not already made a determination with respect to security, or where such a decision is necessary to protect the rights of third parties.[2] No guidance is provided by either the Model Law or the *travaux préparatoires* (of which Irish courts are permitted to take judicial notice when interpreting provisions of the Model Law)[3] as to what the High Court should consider 'proper' when adjudicating on whether security should be provided in connection with an interim measure.

[1] Arbitration Act 2010, s 9(1)(c).
[2] Model Law, Art 17 H(3).
[3] Arbitration Act 2010, s 8(1).

Article 17 I.—Grounds for refusing recognition or enforcement

(1) Recognition or enforcement of an interim measure may be refused only:

(a) At the request of the party against whom it is invoked if the court is satisfied that:

(i) Such refusal is warranted on the grounds set forth in article 36(1)(a)(i), (ii), (iii) or (iv); or

(ii) The arbitral tribunal's decision with respect to the provision of security in connection with the interim measure issued by the arbitral tribunal has not been complied with; or

(iii) The interim measure has been terminated or suspended by the arbitral tribunal or, where so empowered, by the court of the State in which the arbitration takes place or under the law of which that interim measure was granted; or

(b) If the court finds that:

(i) The interim measure is incompatible with the powers conferred upon the court unless the court decides to reformulate the interim measure to the extent necessary to adapt it to its own powers and procedures for the purposes of enforcing that interim measure and without modifying its substance; or

(ii) Any of the grounds set forth in article 36(1)(b)(i) or (ii), apply to the recognition and enforcement of the interim measure.

(2) Any determination made by the court on any ground in paragraph (1) of this article shall be effective only for the purposes of the application to recognize and enforce the interim measure. The court where recognition or enforcement is sought shall not, in making that determination, undertake a review of the substance of the interim measure.

Definitions

'arbitral tribunal': Model Law, Art 2(b); 'court': Model Law, Art 2(c).

Notes

Recognition and enforcement of interim measures: The enforcement of an interim measure applies even where the place of arbitration is outside Ireland.[1] Upon application of a party, an interim measure issued by an arbitral tribunal must be recognised as binding and must be enforced by the court of competent jurisdiction in a State enacting the Model Law, irrespective of the country in which the interim measure was issued.[2] In Ireland, the High Court is the court of competent jurisdiction for the purposes of recognising and enforcing an interim measure.[3] The Model Law specifies only limited grounds for refusing recognition and enforcement of an interim measure.[4] These grounds are exhaustive and the High Court may only refuse recognition and enforcement of an interim measure for the reasons set out under the Model Law.[5] Recognition and enforcement of an interim measure may not be refused for some reason not specified in the Model Law under the courts' inherent jurisdiction. Commentators have noted that "[t]his means that unless the High Court has been accorded a specific role by the [Model Law], then it cannot intervene; inherent jurisdiction and other vestiges of the past are swept away".[6]

---

[1] Model Law, Art 1(2).
[2] Model Law, Art 17 H(1).
[3] Arbitration Act 2010, s 9(1)(c).
[4] Model Law, Art 17 I; and Model Law, Art 36(1).
[5] Model Law, Art 5.
[6] Reichert, "Security for Costs in Arbitration – A New Landscape in Ireland" (2010) *Arbitration and ADR Review* p 130.

Grounds for refusing recognition and enforcement of interim measures: The Model Law specifies nine grounds where the High Court[1] may refuse recognition and enforcement of an interim measure:

1. At the request of the party against whom the interim measure is invoked, that the High Court is satisfied that the party was under some incapacity when entering into the arbitration agreement or the arbitration agreement was not valid under the law to which the parties have subjected it or the law of the country where the interim measure was granted;[2]
2. At the request of the party against whom the interim measure is invoked, that the High Court is satisfied that the party was not given proper notice of the appointment of an arbitrator, or of the arbitral proceedings, or was otherwise unable to present their case;[3]
3. At the request of the party against whom the interim measure is invoked, that the High Court is satisfied that the interim measure deals with a dispute not contemplated by or not falling within the terms of the submission to arbitration,

(*Continued*)

or it contains decisions on matters beyond the scope of the submission to arbitration, provided that, if the decisions on matters submitted to arbitration can be separated from those not so submitted, that part of the interim measure which contains decisions on matters submitted to arbitration may be recognised and enforced;[4]

4. At the request of the party against whom the interim measure is invoked, that the High Court is satisfied that the composition of the arbitral tribunal or the arbitral procedure was not in accordance with the agreement of the parties or, failing the agreement of the parties, that the composition of the arbitral tribunal or the arbitral procedure was not in accordance with the law of the country where the arbitration takes place or under the law of which that interim measures was granted;[5]

5. At the request of the party against whom the interim measure is invoked, that the High Court is satisfied that the arbitral tribunal's decision with respect to the provision of security in connection with the interim measure issued by the arbitral tribunal has not been complied with;[6]

6. At the request of the party against whom the interim measure is invoked, that the High Court is satisfied that the interim measure has been terminated or suspended by the arbitral tribunal or, where so empowered, by the court of the State in which the arbitration takes place or under the law of which that interim measure was granted;[7]

7. That the High Court, *ex officio* on its own motion, finds that the interim measure is incompatible with the powers conferred upon the High Court, unless the High Court decides to reformulate the interim measure to the extent necessary to adapt it to its own powers and procedures for the purposes of enforcing that interim measure and without modifying its substance;[8]

8. That the High Court, *ex officio* on its own motion, finds that the subject-matter of the dispute is incapable of settlement by arbitration under Irish law;[9] or

9. That the High Court, *ex officio* on its own motion, finds that the recognition or enforcement of the award would be contrary to the public policy under Irish law.[10]

The High Court, in determining whether to refuse recognition or enforcement of an interim measure, is not permitted to undertake a review of the substance of the interim measure.[11]

---

[1] Arbitration Act 2010, s 9(1)(c).
[2] Model Law, Art 17 I(1)(a)(i); and Model Law, Art 36(1)(a)(i).
[3] Model Law, Art 17 I(1)(a)(i); and Model Law, Art 36(1)(a)(ii).
[4] Model Law, Art 17 I(1)(a)(i); and Model Law, Art 36(1)(a)(iii).
[5] Model Law, Art 17 I(1)(a)(i); and Model Law, Art 36(1)(a)(iv).
[6] Model Law, Art 17 I(1)(a)(ii).
[7] Model Law, Art 17 I(1)(a)(iii).
[8] Model Law, Art 17 I(1)(b)(i).
[9] Model Law, Art 17 I(1)(b)(ii); and Model Law, Art 36(1)(b)(i).
[10] Model Law, Art 17 I(1)(b)(ii); and Model Law, Art 36(1)(b)(ii).
[11] Model Law, Art 17 I(2).

***Court determination effective only for the purposes of recognising and enforcing interim measures*:** Any determination made by the national court, which in Ireland is the High Court,[1] on any ground for refusing recognition and enforcement of an interim measure is effective only for the purposes of the application to recognise and enforce the interim measure and is not effective to pre-determine the outcome of the arbitral proceedings in their entirety.[2]

[1] Arbitration Act 2010, s 9(1)(c).
[2] Model Law, Art 17 I(2).

***Grounds for refusing recognition and enforcement of an award*:** The provisions concerning grounds for refusing recognition and enforcement of interim measures are based on the grounds for refusing recognition and enforcement of awards.[1] A full discussion on the provisions governing the grounds for refusing recognition and enforcement of awards is contained at Art 36 of the Model Law.

[1] Model Law, Art 36.

Article 17 J.—Court-ordered interim measures

A court shall have the same power of issuing an interim measure in relation to arbitration proceedings, irrespective of whether their place is in the territory of this State, as it has in relation to proceedings in courts. The court shall exercise such power in accordance with its own procedures in consideration of the specific features of international arbitration.

Definitions

'arbitration': Arbitration Act 2010, s 2(1) and Model Law, Art 2(a); 'court': Model Law, Art 2(c).

Notes

***Courts' power to order interim measures in support of arbitral proceedings*:** This article and provides that the national courts have the same powers to order interim measures in respect of arbitral proceedings as they do in any civil proceedings pending before them, irrespective of where the arbitral proceedings are taking place.[1] In Ireland, the court of competent jurisdiction exercising the power to order interim measures in support of arbitral proceedings is the High Court.[2] Although the term 'interim relief' under Irish law typically refers to urgent injunctive relief sought on an *ex parte* basis to maintain the status quo for a short period until an interlocutory application is be heard,[3] in arbitration the term 'interim measures' has a broader meaning and includes injunctive relief, which under Irish law would be classified as both 'interim' and 'interlocutory' relief.[4] This power is reaffirmed by the Act.[5]

[1] Arbitration Act 2010, s 10(1).

(*Continued*)

[2] Arbitration Act 2010, s 9(1)(c).
[3] Kirwan, *Injunctions Law & Practice* (1st ed, Thomson Round Hall, Dublin, 2008) p 240.
[4] *Shelbourne Hotel Holdings Ltd v Torriam Hotel Operating Company Ltd* [2010] 2 IR 52. Model Law, Art 17(2) defines an 'interim measure' as "any temporary measure ... by which, at any time prior to the issuance of the award by which the dispute is finally decided, the arbitral tribunal orders a party to: (a) Maintain or restore the status quo pending determination of the dispute; (b) Take action that would prevent, or refrain from taking action that is likely to cause current or imminent harm or prejudice to the arbitral process itself; (c) Provide a means of preserving assets out of which a subsequent award may be satisfied; or (d) Preserve evidence that may be relevant and material to the resolution of the dispute".
[5] Arbitration Act 2010, s 10(1).

***Test for interim or interlocutory injunctive relief at Irish law*:** Under Irish law the test for whether or not injunction relief will be granted at an interim or interlocutory stage is based on the so-called '*Campus Oil* guidelines'.[1] The *Campus Oil* guidelines comprise a multi-stage test requiring, in summary: first, that there is a *bona fide* question to be tried; second, that damages would not be an adequate remedy for a party if it was refused injunctive relief at an interim or interlocutory stage but was later successful at the trial of the action; and finally, that the balance of convenience favours the granting of the injunction.[2]

[1] Named after the seminal case of *Campus Oil Ltd v Minister for Industry and Energy (No 2)* [1983] 1 IR 88, where the principles established by the House of Lords (as it then was) in determining whether to grant interlocutory relied in *American Cyanamid Co v Ethicon Ltd* [1975] AC 396 were adopted by the Supreme Court.
[2] *Osmond Ireland On Farm Business v McFarland* [2010] IEHC 295, where the High Court (Laffoy J) approved the application of the Campus Oil guidelines in the context of an arbitration.

***High Court's power to order anti-suit injunctions*:** In arbitration, an anti-suit injunction is an order directed against the parties, or intended parties, to foreign litigation prohibiting the commencement or prosecution of litigation where the matter in dispute is the subject of an arbitration agreement.[1] Although the power to prohibit the commencement or prosecution of foreign litigation brought in violation of an arbitration agreement has long been exercised by courts in certain common law jurisdictions,[2] Irish commentators have noted that "[t]here is a dearth of [modern] case-law in this jurisdiction on anti-suit injunctions".[3] However, it is likely that, as in other common law jurisdictions, an anti-suit injunction may be ordered in appropriate circumstances.[4] However, where a court within the European Union has been seised of civil proceedings within the meaning of Council Regulation (EC) No 44/2001 of 22 December 2000 on Jurisdiction and the Recognition and Enforcement of Judgments in Civil and Commercial Matters (the Brussels Regulation),[5] the court of another European Union Member State cannot order an anti-suit injunction to prohibit the prosecution of foreign litigation, even where the initial civil proceedings have been brought in violation of an arbitration agreement.[6]

[1] Born, *International Commercial Arbitration* (1st ed, Kluwer Law International, Alphen aan den Rijn, 2009) p 1036.

(*Continued*)

[2] See *Lett v Lett* [1906] 1 IR 618, where the pre-independence High Court granted an injunction restraining the prosecution of family law proceedings in Argentina in violation of an agreement of the parties not to proceed with the suit. The High Court's decision was upheld on appeal. See also *Pena Copper Mines Ltd v Rio Tinto Co Ltd* [1911-1913] All ER Rep 209, where the English Court of Appeal enjoined an English company not to proceed with litigation in the Spanish courts in violation of an arbitration agreement. Courts in Australia, Bermuda, Canada, Singapore and the United States have also ordered anti-suit injunctions to prevent a party from commencing or prosecuting foreign litigation. For a discussion on anti-suit injunctions in common law jurisdictions, see Born, *International Commercial Arbitration* (1st ed, Kluwer Law International, Alphen aan den Rijn, 2009) pp 1036-1041.

[3] Kirwan, *Injunctions Law & Practice* (1st ed, Thomson Round Hall, Dublin, 2008) p 68.

[4] Guidelines for what may be considered 'appropriate circumstances' were set out in the case of *Airbus Indus GIE v Patel* [1999] 1 AC 119 where the House of Lords (as it then was) refused to grant an anti-suit injunction as the English forum did not have a sufficient interest in, or connection with, the matter in question to justify such interference. It was held that for an anti-suit injunction to be ordered the party seeking the injunction must demonstrate that: first, the forum in which the anti-suit injunction is sought must have a sufficient interest in, or in connection with the dispute in question; second, the foreign proceedings would cause prejudice to the party seeking the anti-suit injunction; and, finally, the anti-suit injunction would not unfairly deprive the plaintiff in the foreign litigation of a legitimate advantage.

[5] EC No 44/2001.

[6] *Allianz SpA v West Tankers Inc* [2009] 1 AC 1138 where the European Court of Justice held that an order restraining a party from commencing or continuing proceedings before a court of another Member State on the ground that those proceedings would be contrary to an arbitration agreement was in violation of the provisions of the Brussels Regulation. The decision has been met with near-universal criticism and it has been proposed by the European Commission that its effect will be neutralised by a proposed amendment to the Brussels Regulation, which includes a specific rule on the relation between arbitration and civil proceedings obliging a court seised of a dispute to stay proceedings where its jurisdiction is contested on the basis of an arbitration agreement.

High Court's power to order interim measures prior to the commencement of arbitral proceedings: As any civil proceedings pending before a court that are the subject of a valid arbitration agreement must be referred to arbitration where a party so requests "not later than when submitting his first statement on the substance of the dispute".[1] It is uncertain whether a party that commences civil proceedings to obtain interim or interlocutory injunctive relief loses its right to have the proceedings referred to arbitration. In particular, where an interim measure is requested from the High Court, it is uncertain whether unconditional documents filed in support or opposition to the interim measures sought are a statement on the substance of the dispute such as to jeopardise a party's ability to request that pending civil proceedings be referred to arbitration.[2] The question must be bifurcated depending on whether it is a plaintiff or a defendant to the injunctive relief that requests that pending proceedings be referred to arbitration. Where a plaintiff has attempted to refer its own proceedings to arbitration, case-law decided under the Arbitration Acts 1954-1998 has held that a plaintiff should not be permitted to issue proceedings and subsequently refer those proceedings to arbitration.[3] The likelihood of an Irish court reaching a similar result under the Model Law is uncertain as the Model Law expressly

(*Continued*)

contemplates court-ordered interim measures[4] and, in matters of extreme urgency, it may be prudent for a potential plaintiff to obtain interim measures from the High Court prior to the commencement of arbitral proceedings in circumstances where the plaintiff is concerned about the possibility of the dissipation of assets or destruction of evidence by the proposed defendant. Where a defendant has attempted to refer proceedings to arbitration, case-law decided under the Arbitration Acts 1954-1998 has held a defendant should be permitted to have proceedings referred to arbitration after interlocutory injunctive relief had been obtained by a plaintiff[5] and it is highly likely that an Irish court would reach a similar result under Model Law.

---

[1] Model Law, Art 8(1).

[2] Where a party makes clear that an affidavit is filed without prejudice to the entitlement to refer arbitration, the entitlement shall not be lost. *Gleeson v Grimes & anor* [2007] 4 IR 417; and *Dublin Docklands Development Authority v Jermyn Street Ltd & anor* [2010] IEHC 217.

[3] *MacCormac Products Ltd v Monaghan Co-Operative Agricultural and Diary Society Ltd* [1988] 1 IR 304, in which the High Court (O'Hanlon J) refused to refer proceedings to arbitration under Arbitration Act 1980, s 5 where the plaintiff sought to refer proceedings that he had commenced. The High Court held that the obtaining of interlocutory injunctive relief was a 'step' in the proceedings notwithstanding that only a plenary summons had been issued.

[4] Model Law, Art 17 J.

[5] *Telenor Invest AS v IIU Nominees Ltd* [1999] IEHC 188 where the plaintiff commenced proceedings and sought interlocutory injunctive relief. The High Court (O'Sullivan J) granted the relief sought and referring the proceedings to arbitration.

Chapter V

Conduct of Arbitral Proceedings

Article 18.—Equal treatment of parties

The parties shall be treated with equality and each party shall be given a full opportunity of presenting his case.

Notes

***Due process in arbitral proceedings*:** This article requires that the parties are treated with equality and are each given a full opportunity of presenting its case. Equal treatment of the parties has long been a fundamental feature of arbitration under Irish law.[1] Together with Art 19, this article has been described as the '*Magna Carta* of Arbitral Procedure' and the *travaux préparatoires* (of which Irish courts are permitted to take judicial notice when interpreting provisions of the Model Law)[2] suggest that its purpose is to set out "fundamental principles of fairness" applicable to arbitral proceedings.[3] Commentators have describes the requirements of this article as "the 'due process' clause of arbitration, akin to similar provisions in national constitutions that establish the requirement of procedural fairness as the indispensible foundation of a system of justice".[4] As the *travaux préparatoires* suggest that the requirement that the parties must be treated with equality and that each party must be given a full opportunity to present its case "should be observed not only by the arbitral tribunal but also by the parties when laying down any rules of procedure",[5] this represents a limitation on the principle of party autonomy. Commentators have noted that where the parties agree one-sided rules of procedure an award made is liable to be set aside or to have recognition and enforcement thereof refused.[6]

Although an arbitral tribunal must ensure that one party is not given an advantage over the other and although an arbitral tribunal must provide reasonable opportunities to each party to present their respective cases, "this does not mean that it must sacrifice all efficiency to accommodate unreasonable procedural demands by a party".[7] International case-law decided under the Model Law has held that the purpose of this article is to protect a party from egregious and injudicious conduct by an arbitral tribunal but it is not intended to protect a party from its own failures or strategic choices and where a party that refuses to participate in arbitral proceedings is deemed to have forfeited the opportunity to be heard.[8] Similarly, where a party alleges a breach of its due process rights as a result of being denied an opportunity to be heard, arid, technical or procedural objections that do not prejudice any party should not be tolerated. Only where the alleged breach of natural justice has surpassed the boundaries of legitimate expectation and propriety, resulting in actual prejudice to a party should a remedy be available.[9] A failure by an arbitral tribunal to conduct arbitral proceedings in a language understandable to a party is not a violation of its due process rights where the party declined the opportunity to engage an interpreter to participate fully in the arbitral proceedings.[10]

[1] *State (Hegarty) v Winters* [1956] 1 IR 320.

[2] Arbitration Act 2010, s 8(1).

(*Continued*)

[3] UNCITRAL Seventh Secretariat Note, A/CN.9/264, Art 19, para 1 [Model Law, Art 18 and Model Law, Art 19 in the final text].
[4] Holtzmann and Neuhaus, *A Guide to the UNCITRAL Model Law on International Commercial Arbitration* (1st ed, Kluwer Law and Taxation Publishers, The Hague, 1989) p 550.
[5] UNCITRAL Fifth Working Group Report, A/CN.9/246, Art 19, para 62 [Model Law, Art 18 and Model Law, Art 19 in the final text].
[6] Holtzmann and Neuhaus, *A Guide to the UNCITRAL Model Law on International Commercial Arbitration* (1st ed, Kluwer Law and Taxation Publishers, The Hague, 1989) p. 551.
[7] Holtzmann and Neuhaus, *A Guide to the UNCITRAL Model Law on International Commercial Arbitration* (1st ed, Kluwer Law and Taxation Publishers, The Hague, 1989) p 551.
[8] CLOUT Case 391 – Canada/Superior Court of Justice: *Re Corporacion Transnacional de Inversiones, SA de CV et al and STET International, SpA et al* (22 September 1999).
[9] CLOUT Case 743 – Singapore/Court of Appeal: *Soh Beng Tee and Co Pte Ltd v Fairmount Development Pte Ltd* (9 May 2007); and CLOUT Case 658 – New Zealand/High Court (Commercial List) Auckland: *Trustees of Rotoaria Forest Trust v Attorney-General* (30 November 1998).
[10] CLOUT Case 559 – Germany/Highest Regional Court of Celle: *8 Sch 3/01* (2 October 2001).

***Mandatory nature of the section*:** This article is mandatory in nature and the parties may not circumvent its effect by agreeing otherwise.

Article 19.—Determination of rules of procedure

(1) Subject to the provisions of this Law, the parties are free to agree on the procedure to be followed by the arbitral tribunal in conducting the proceedings.

(2) Failing such agreement, the arbitral tribunal may, subject to the provisions of this Law, conduct the arbitration in such manner as it considers appropriate. The power conferred upon the arbitral tribunal includes the power to determine the admissibility, relevance, materiality and weight of any evidence.

Definitions

'arbitration': Arbitration Act 2010, s 2(1) and Model Law, Art 2(a); 'arbitral tribunal': Model Law, Art 2(b); 'award': Arbitration Act 2010, s 2(1).

Notes

***Rules of procedure to be determined by the parties*:** This article enshrines the principle of party autonomy and it dictates that where the parties agree on the rules of procedure to be adopted by the arbitral tribunal, they must be followed subject only to the limitation that the mandatory provisions of the Model Law must apply.[1] The *travaux préparatoires* (of which Irish courts are permitted to take judicial notice when interpreting provisions of the Model Law)[2] suggest that the mandatory provisions of the Model Law are those from the parties may not derogate.[3] Together with Art 18, this article has been described as the '*Magna Carta* of Arbitral Procedure' and the *travaux préparatoires* suggest that it is

(*Continued*)

"the most important provision of the [Model Law]" as "[i]t goes a long way towards establishing procedural autonomy by recognizing the parties' freedom to lay down the rules of procedure".[4]

Where Ireland is to be the place of arbitration an award made in arbitral proceedings that does not comply with the agreed rules of procedure will be liable to be set aside.[5] International case-law decided under the Model Law has held that an award will be set aside where there has been that a failure to follow agreed procedures.[6]

---

[1] Model Law, Art 19(1).

[2] Arbitration Act 2010, s 8(1).

[3] Such as Model Law, Art 18; Model Law, Art 23(1); Model Law, Art 24(2); (3); and (4); Model Law, Art 27; Model Law, Art 30(2); Model Law, Art 31(1); (3); and (4); Model Law, Art 32; and Model Law, Art 33(1)-(5). See UNCITRAL Seventh Secretariat Note, A/CN.9/264, Art 19, paras 5-6.

[4] UNCITRAL Seventh Secretariat Note, A/CN.9/264, Art 19, para 1 [Model Law, Art 18 and Model Law, Art 19 in the final text].

[5] Model Law, Art 34(2)(a)(iv). Or, where Ireland is not the place of arbitration an award will be liable to have recognition and enforcement thereof refused in Ireland under Model Law, Art 36(1)(a)(iv).

[6] CLOUT Case 1049 – Canada/Superior Court of Quebec: *Louis Dreyfus SAS v Holding Tusculum BV* (8 December 2008).

***The parties' choice of rules of procedure*:** In a domestic arbitration (which is any arbitration other than an international commercial arbitration) it is likely that any rules of procedure agreed by the parties will be influenced by domestic rules of civil procedure. In Ireland, the appropriate rules of civil procedure are the Rules of the Superior Courts. However, commentators have noted that in an international commercial arbitration, references to domestic rules "will soon confuse and complicate the arbitral procedure".[1] In those circumstances, rather than draft rules of procedure themselves, the parties would be advised to adopt the pre-drafted rules of a major international arbitral institution.[2]

---

[1] Binder, *International Commercial Arbitration and Conciliation in UNCITRAL Model Law Jurisdictions* (3rd ed, Sweet & Maxwell, London, 2010) p 283.

[2] Such as UNCITRAL's Arbitration Rules, the International Chamber of Commerce's Arbitration Rules or the London Court of International Arbitration's Arbitration Rules. See Binder, *International Commercial Arbitration and Conciliation in UNCITRAL Model Law Jurisdictions* (3rd ed, Sweet & Maxwell, London, 2010) pp 283-284.

***Default rules of procedure to be determined by an arbitral tribunal*:** In the absence of agreed rules of procedure, the Model Law provides that an arbitral tribunal may conduct an arbitration in the manner it considers appropriate, which includes the ability to determine the admissibility, relevance, materiality and weight of any evidence.[1] Similarly, an arbitral tribunal may adopt the rules of procedure it considers appropriate where the parties agreed rules of procedure do not touch upon a particular point.[2]

While the parties' agreed rules of procedure are subject only to the limitation that the mandatory provisions of the Model Law are to be applied, an arbitral tribunal may

(*Continued*)

conduct an arbitration in the manner it considers appropriate subject to the limitation that both the mandatory *and* the non-mandatory of the Model Law are to be applied.[3] However, subject to this limitation, the *travaux préparatoires* (of which Irish courts are permitted to take judicial notice when interpreting provisions of the Model Law)[4] suggest that an arbitral tribunal's discretion to conduct arbitral proceedings in the manner it considers appropriate is extensive:

> "Except where the parties have laid down detailed and stringent rules of procedure, including evidence, the discretionary powers of the arbitral tribunal are considerable ... This enables the arbitral tribunal to meet the needs of the particular case and to select the most suitable procedure when organizing the arbitration, conducting individual hearings or other meetings and determining the important specifics of taking and evaluating evidence.
>
> [...] In practical terms, the arbitrators would be able to adopt the procedural features familiar, or at least acceptable, to the parties (and to them). For example, where both parties are from a common law system, the arbitral tribunal may rely on affidavits and order pre-hearing discovery to a greater extent than in a case with parties of civil law tradition, where, to mention another example, the mode of proceedings could be more inquisitorial than adversary. Above all, where the parties are from different legal systems, the arbitral tribunal may be a liberal "mixed" procedure, adopting suitable features from different legal systems and relying on techniques proven in international practice and, for instance, let the parties present their case as they themselves judge best. Such procedural discretion in all these cases seems conducive to facilitating international commercial arbitration, while being forced to apply the "law of the land" where the arbitration happens to take place would present a major disadvantage to any party not used to that particular and possibly peculiar system of procedure and evidence".[5]

International case-law decided under the Model Law has held that, in the absence of the parties' agreed rules of procedure, an arbitral tribunal is 'master of its own procedure' and it should take whatever steps it deems appropriate to ascertain the facts.[6]

---

[1] Model Law, Art 19(2).

[2] Holtzmann and Neuhaus, *A Guide to the UNCITRAL Model Law on International Commercial Arbitration* (1st ed, Kluwer Law and Taxation Publishers, The Hague, 1989) p 565.

[3] Holtzman and Neuhaus, *A Guide to the UNCITRAL Model Law on International Commercial Arbitration* (1st ed, Kluwer Law and Taxation Publishers, The Hague, 1989) p 564.

[4] Arbitration Act 2010, s 8(1).

[5] UNCITRAL Seventh Secretariat Note, A/CN.9/264, Art 19, paras 5-6 [Model Law, Art 18 and Model Law, Art 19 in the final text].

[6] CLOUT Case 618 – Canada/Superior Court of Quebec: *Silverberg and Silverman v C Clarke Hooper plc* (6 February 1990).

Article 20.—Place of arbitration

(1) The parties are free to agree on the place of arbitration. Failing such agreement, the place of arbitration shall be determined by the arbitral tribunal having regard to the circumstances of the case, including the convenience of the parties.

(2) Notwithstanding the provisions of paragraph (1) of this article, the arbitral tribunal may, unless otherwise agreed by the parties, meet at any place it considers appropriate for consultation among its members, for hearing witnesses, experts or the parties, or for inspection of goods, other property or documents.

Definitions

'arbitration': Arbitration Act 2010, s 2(1) and Model Law, Art 2(a); 'arbitral tribunal': Model Law, Art 2(b); 'award': Arbitration Act 2010, s 2(1).

Notes

***Significance of the place of arbitration*:** As hearings and other meetings of the arbitral tribunal need not actually take place at the locale designated as the place of arbitration,[1] the place of arbitration may not seem of particular importance.[2] This is especially true in the context of a domestic arbitration (which is any arbitration other than an international commercial arbitration) where it is axiomatic that the place of arbitration will be Ireland. However, in an international commercial arbitration the place of arbitration is of significance for a variety of reasons including:

1. That the place of arbitration determines what law is to apply as arbitral proceedings are governed by the law of the place of arbitration[3] and it is for each State to promulgate laws to govern the conduct of arbitrations within its own territory.[4] In Ireland, the law governing the conduct of arbitration is the Act, which adopts and supplements the Model Law.[5] However, like most Irish domestic law, the Model Law has limited extraterritorial effect with only certain provisions of the Model Law applying where the place of arbitration is outside Ireland;[6]

2. That the place of arbitration may be a factor in determining whether an arbitration is an 'international commercial arbitration'.[7] Where none of the parties have their place of business in the place of arbitration, an arbitration will be 'international';[8] and

3. That recourse against an award must be sought from the courts of the State of the place of arbitration.[9]

---

[1] Model Law, Art 20(2). The parties may prevent an arbitral tribunal from holding hearings and other meetings at a place other than the locale designated as the place of arbitration.

[2] See Holtzmann and Neuhaus, *A Guide to the UNCITRAL Model Law on International Commercial Arbitration* (1st ed, Kluwer Law and Taxation Publishers, The Hague, 1989) where it is stated at p 592 that "[r]ead in isolation, Article 20 might seem to make little sense: paragraph 1 establishes a procedure for selecting the so-called place of arbitration, but then paragraph 2 provides that the arbitrators may hold hearings, consultations or other meetings elsewhere".

[3] Blackaby, Partasides, Redfern and Hunter, *Redfern and Hunter on International Arbitration* (5th ed, Oxford University Press, Oxford, 2009) p 164.

[4] *ibid*, p 175.

(*Continued*)

[5] Arbitration Act 2010, s 6.
[6] Model Law, Art 1(2).
[7] However, the only legislative distinction between an international commercial arbitration and a domestic arbitration in Ireland concerns a party's ability to demand the taxation of costs, which is only applicable in a domestic arbitration. Arbitration Act 2010, s 21(4).
[8] Model Law, Art 1(3)(b)(i).
[9] Blackaby, Partasides, Redfern and Hunter, *Redfern and Hunter on International Arbitration* (5th ed, Oxford University Press, Oxford, 2009) p 591. This general rule is subject to an exception where the parties to an international commercial arbitration agree to subject the arbitration to the procedural law of a country other than that in which the arbitral proceedings are held.

***Place of arbitration to be determined by the parties*:** The principle of party autonomy is enshrined in the Model Law and it dictates that where the parties agree on the place of arbitration, their choice must be followed.[1]

[1] Model Law, Art 20(1).

***Default place of arbitration to be determined by an arbitral tribunal*:** In the absence of an agreed place of arbitration, this article provides that an arbitral tribunal must determine the place of arbitration having regard to the circumstances of the case, including the convenience of the parties.[1] Commentators have noted that factors an arbitral tribunal should consider as coming within the circumstances of the case include: the geographical proximity to the parties; whether the proposed place of arbitration has adhered to the New York Convention; and whether the State of the proposed place of arbitration has adopted arbitration legislation conducive to international commercial arbitration.[2] However, the same commentators have also noted that the geographic or political inconvenience of a particular place of arbitration may be mitigated by the freedom enjoyed by an arbitral tribunal, unless otherwise agreed by the parties, to hold hearings and to otherwise meet at places other than the place of arbitration.[3]

[1] Model Law, Art 20(1).
[2] Holtzmann and Neuhaus, *A Guide to the UNCITRAL Model Law on International Commercial Arbitration* (1st ed, Kluwer Law and Taxation Publishers, The Hague, 1989) pp 594–595.
[3] *ibid*, p 595.

***Venue of hearings and other meetings of an arbitral tribunal*:** Unless otherwise agreed by the parties, hearings and other meetings of the arbitral tribunal need not actually take place at the locale designated as the place of arbitration.[1] The *travaux préparatoires* (of which Irish courts are permitted to take judicial notice when interpreting provisions of the Model Law)[2] suggest that an arbitral tribunal may meet at places other than the place of arbitration in order to facilitate consultation among its members, to hear witnesses, experts or the parties and to inspect goods, other property or documents.[3] The *travaux*

(*Continued*)

préparatoires suggest that the rationale for permitting an arbitral tribunal to meet at places other than the place of arbitration is "for the sake of convenience of the persons involved and for keeping down the costs of arbitration".[4]

[1] Model Law, Art 20(2).
[2] Arbitration Act 2010, s 8(1).
[3] UNCITRAL Seventh Secretariat Note, A/CN.9/264, Art 20, para 4.
[4] *ibid*, para 3.

Article 21.—Commencement of arbitral proceedings

Unless otherwise agreed by the parties, the arbitral proceedings in respect of a particular dispute commence on the date on which a request for that dispute to be referred to arbitration is received by the respondent.

Definitions

'arbitration': Arbitration Act 2010, s 2(1) and Model Law, Art 2(a).

Notes

***Amendments to the provisions of the Model Law by the Act*:** The Model Law provides that, unless otherwise agreed by the parties, arbitral proceedings commence on the date on which a request for the dispute to be referred to arbitration is received by the respondent.[1] The effect of this article has been superseded by s 7 of the Act, which provides that arbitral proceedings commence on either the date on which the parties to an arbitration agreement agree as being the commencement date or, where no date has been agreed, the date on which a written communication containing a request for the dispute to be referred to arbitration is received by the respondent.[2] Section 7 of the Act clarifies that a request for arbitration must be in written form as this article leaves unspecified whether or not such a request for must be in writing.[3]

[1] Model Law, Art 21.
[2] Arbitration Act 2010, s 7(1).
[3] Binder, *International Commercial Arbitration and Conciliation in UNCITRAL Model Law Jurisdictions* (3rd ed, Sweet & Maxwell, London, 2010) p 295.

***Significance of the commencement of arbitral proceedings and limitation periods for arbitral proceedings*:** The date of commencement of arbitral proceedings is significant for the application of relevant limitation periods, which apply to arbitral proceedings as they do to civil proceedings.[1] The limitation period governing specific arbitral proceedings depends on the substantive nature of the claim but as the substance of most arbitral proceedings concern claims for breach of contract, the limitation period is typically six years.[2]

[1] Statute of Limitations 1957, s 75.
[2] *ibid*, s 11.

Provisions of the Model Law superseded by the Act: As this article has been superseded by the Act,[1] a full discussion on the provisions governing the commencement of arbitral proceedings is contained at s 7 of the Act.

[1] Arbitration Act 2010, s 7(1).

Article 22.—Language

(1) The parties are free to agree on the language or languages to be used in the arbitral proceedings. Failing such agreement, the arbitral tribunal shall determine the language or languages to be used in the proceedings. This agreement or determination, unless otherwise specified therein, shall apply to any written statement by a party, any hearing and any award, decision or other communication by the arbitral tribunal.

(2) The arbitral tribunal may order that any documentary evidence shall be accompanied by a translation into the language or languages agreed upon by the parties or determined by the arbitral tribunal.

Definitions

'arbitral tribunal': Model Law, Art 2(b).

Notes

Choice of language or languages to be determined by the parties: The principle of party autonomy is enshrined in the Model Law and it dictates that where the parties agree on the language or languages to be used in arbitral proceedings, their choice must be followed.[1]

[1] Model Law, Art 22(1).

Default choice of language or languages to be determined by an arbitral tribunal: In the absence of an agreed choice of language or languages to be used in arbitral proceedings, the Model Law provides that an arbitral tribunal must determine the language or languages to be used in arbitral proceedings.[1] In a domestic arbitration (which is any arbitration other than an international commercial arbitration) the choice of language by an arbitral tribunal is unlikely to present a difficult as the English language will normally be chosen.[2]

In an international commercial arbitration language may be an issue of paramount importance where the parties speak different languages.[3] The primary concern is that an arbitral tribunal might choose the language of one party but not of the other.[4] While an arbitral tribunal is permitted to choose the language or languages to be used in arbitral proceedings the parties must be treated with equality and each party must be given a full opportunity to present its case.[5] However, the use of multiple languages adds to the cost

(*Continued*)

of arbitral proceedings and the requirement for equal treatment does not necessarily mean that the language of each party must be adopted by an arbitral tribunal. The *travaux préparatoires* (of which Irish courts are permitted to take judicial notice when interpreting provisions of the Model Law)[6] suggest an arbitral tribunal is not prevented choosing the language of one of the parties to be used in arbitral proceedings where the circumstances of the case suggest it is the most appropriate language.[7] The *travaux préparatoires* also suggest relevant circumstances include "where parties have used only one language in their business dealings, in particular in their contract and their correspondence".[8]

---

[1] Model Law, Art 22(1).
[2] Notwithstanding that the Constitution of Ireland 1937, Art 8(1) provides that "[t]he Irish language as the national language is the first official language" commentators have noted that there is "no public record of an arbitration having been conducted in the Irish language in [Ireland] in recent years". See Dowling-Hussey and Dunne, *Arbitration Law* (1st ed, Thomson Round Hall, Dublin, 2008) p 142, fn 70.
[3] Binder, *International Commercial Arbitration and Conciliation in UNCITRAL Model Law Jurisdictions* (3rd ed, Sweet & Maxwell, London, 2010) p 298.
[4] Holtzmann and Neuhaus, *A Guide to the UNCITRAL Model Law on International Commercial Arbitration* (1st ed, Kluwer Law and Taxation Publishers, The Hague, 1989) p 629.
[5] Model Law, Art 18.
[6] Arbitration Act 2010, s 8(1).
[7] UNCITRAL Seventh Secretariat Note, A/CN.9/264, Art 22, para 4.
[8] *ibid.*

***Translation of documentary evidence*:** Where the documentary evidence relevant to a matter is not in the language or languages agreed by the parties or determined by an arbitral tribunal, an arbitral tribunal is permitted to order that the documentary evidence be accompanied by a translation into the language or languages to be used in arbitral proceedings.[1] The *travaux préparatoires* (of which Irish courts are permitted to take judicial notice when interpreting provisions of the Model Law)[2] suggest "this discretion is appropriate in view of the fact that such documents may be voluminous and only part truly relevant to the dispute".[3]

---

[1] Model Law, Art 22(2).
[2] Arbitration Act 2010, s 8(1).
[3] UNCITRAL Seventh Secretariat Note, A/CN.9/264, Art 22, para 5.

***Language of initial statements*:** In the absence of an agreed language or languages to be used in arbitral proceedings, the Model Law provides that an arbitral tribunal must determine the language or languages to be used in arbitral proceedings.[1] Prior to the determination of the choice of language or languages by an arbitral tribunal, some commentators have noted that the parties should be free to choose the language of their initial statements.[2]

---

[1] Model Law, Art 22(1).
[2] Brekoulakis and Shore in Mistelis, *Concise International Arbitration, UNCITRAL Model Law* (1st ed, Kluwer Law International, Alphen aan den Rijn, 2010) p 629.

Language of civil proceedings exercisable in support of arbitral proceedings: Irrespective of the parties' agreement or an arbitral tribunal's determination of the language or languages to be used in arbitral proceedings, civil proceedings conducted in the Irish courts in support of arbitral proceedings are required to be conducted in either the English language or the Irish language.[1] However, parties are entitled to have civil proceedings conducted in a language that they understand and to have interpreters provided if necessary.[2] Similarly, where a witness has an insufficient grasp of either the English language or the Irish language, evidence may be given in some other language and translated into the English language or the Irish language.[3]

[1] Official Languages Act 2003, s 8(1).
[2] *Mac Aodhain v Ireland* [2010] IEHC 335.
[3] *AG v Joyce and Walsh* [1929] 1 IR 526.

Article 23.—Statements of claim and defence

(1) Within the period of time agreed by the parties or determined by the arbitral tribunal, the claimant shall state the facts supporting his claim, the points at issue and the relief or remedy sought, and the respondent shall state his defence in respect of these particulars, unless the parties have otherwise agreed as to the required elements of such statements. The parties may submit with their statements all documents they consider to be relevant or may add a reference to the documents or other evidence they will submit.

(2) Unless otherwise agreed by the parties, either party may amend or supplement his claim or defence during the course of the arbitral proceedings, unless the arbitral tribunal considers it inappropriate to allow such amendment having regard to the delay in making it.

Definitions

'arbitral tribunal': Model Law, Art 2(c).

Notes

Contents of a statement of claim, defence, counter-claim and defence to a counter-claim: This article provides that a claimant must submit a statement of claim and, subsequently, a respondent must submit its defence within the time agreed by the parties or determined by an arbitral tribunal.[1] Although a claimant need only deliver a request for the dispute to be referred to arbitration to the respondent in order to commence an arbitration,[2] in practice, it is not uncommon for a claimant to submit a full statement of claim when requesting the commencement of arbitral proceedings.[3] However, unless the parties agree otherwise, the only essential contents of a statement of claim are that it must state the facts supporting the claimant's claim, the points at issue and the relief or remedy

(*Continued*)

sought while the only essential contents of a respondent's defence are that it must state its defence to these particulars. The same requirements apply to a counter-claim and a defence to a counter-claim.[4]

The essential contents of a statement of claim, defence, counter-claim and defence to a counter-claim are non-mandatory, at least as regards detail, meaning that the parties may agree to other requirements. The *travaux préparatoires* (of which Irish courts are permitted to take judicial notice when interpreting provisions of the Model Law)[5] suggest that the essential contents are non-mandatory in nature so as not to inhibit the use of rules of arbitral institutions which may contain different formal requirements.[6]

---

[1] Model Law, Art 23(1).
[2] Arbitration Act 2010, s 7(1)(b).
[3] Brekoulakis and Shore in Mistelis, *Concise International Arbitration, UNCITRAL Model Law* (1st ed, Kluwer Law International, Alphen aan den Rijn, 2010) p 632.
[4] Model Law, Art 2(f).
[5] Arbitration Act 2010, s 8(1).
[6] UNCITRAL Seventh Secretariat Note, A/CN.9/264, Art 23, para 2.

***Evidence in support of claim or defence*:** The parties are entitled, but not required, to submit all relevant documents or to at least refer to all relevant documents with their statement of claim or defence, as the case may be.[1] The time at which a party reveals the documents it intends to rely upon will depend on that party's procedural strategy. However, while the *travaux préparatoires* (of which Irish courts are permitted to take judicial notice when interpreting provisions of the Model Law)[2] suggest that these documents are not part of the essential contents of the initial pleadings, a party is not fully at liberty to select the point of time for revealing the documents it intends to rely upon as, unless specific provisions is made in the arbitration agreement, an arbitral tribunal in its general discretion[3] may require a party to submit the documents it intends to rely upon within a certain period of time.[4]

---

[1] Model Law, Art 23(1).
[2] Arbitration Act 2010, s 8(1).
[3] Model Law, Art 19(2).
[4] UNCITRAL Seventh Secretariat Note, A/CN.9/264, Art 23, para 3.

***Amendment of a statement of claim, defence, counter-claim and defence to a counter-claim*:** An arbitral tribunal has discretion whether to permit a party to amend a statement of claim, defence, counter-claim or defence to a counter-claim.[1] The *travaux préparatoires* (of which Irish courts are permitted to take judicial notice when interpreting provisions of the Model Law)[2] suggest that the "major criterion [for the amendment of initial pleadings] would be the extent and the reason for the delay in making the amendment (or

(*Continued*)

supplement)".[3] The *travaux préparatoires* suggest another criterion would be procedural prejudice to the other party such as upsetting the normal course of the proceedings or unduly delaying the final settlement of the dispute.[4] The provisions concerning amendment of the initial pleadings are non-mandatory in nature and the parties may agree other requirements for amendment of the initial pleadings and may permit or prohibit amendment as they see fit.[5]

[1] Model Law, Art 23(2).
[2] Arbitration Act 2010, s 8(1).
[3] UNCITRAL Seventh Secretariat Note, A/CN.9/264, Art 23, para 4.
[4] *ibid*, para 4.
[5] *ibid*, para 6.

Article 24.—Hearings and written proceedings

(1) Subject to any contrary agreement by the parties, the arbitral tribunal shall decide whether to hold oral hearings for the presentation of evidence or for oral argument, or whether the proceedings shall be conducted on the basis of documents and other materials. However, unless the parties have agreed that no hearings shall be held, the arbitral tribunal shall hold such hearings at an appropriate stage of the proceedings, if so requested by a party.

(2) The parties shall be given sufficient advance notice of any hearing and of any meeting of the arbitral tribunal for the purposes of inspection of goods, other property or documents.

(3) All statements, documents or other information supplied to the arbitral tribunal by one party shall be communicated to the other party. Also any expert report or evidentiary document on which the arbitral tribunal may rely in making its decision shall be communicated to the parties.

Definitions

'arbitral tribunal': Model Law, Art 2(c).

Notes

Oral hearings and written proceedings: In accordance with the principle of party autonomy, which is enshrined in the Model Law,[1] where the parties have agreed whether or not arbitral proceedings are to include an oral hearing or whether the arbitral proceedings are to be conducted on the basis of documents only, their agreement must be followed.[2] Where the parties have not agreed whether or not arbitral proceedings are to include an oral hearing, an arbitral tribunal must decide whether or not an oral hearing is appropriate. However, an arbitral tribunal's discretion is limited as, in the absence of the agreement of the parties, where any party so requests, an oral hearing must be held.[3]

(*Continued*)

Objections to an arbitral tribunal's decision to dispense with an oral hearing must be made promptly. International case-law decided under the Model Law has held that where a party failed to request an oral hearing in its next written submission after having being informed of an arbitral tribunal's decision to dispense, it had waived the right to object.[4]

The *travaux préparatoires* (of which Irish courts are permitted to take judicial notice when interpreting provisions of the Model Law)[5] suggest that the decision to permit the parties to agree to dispense with oral hearings was controversial.[6] The objections recorded in the *travaux préparatoires* included that "[t]he underlying philosophy is that the right of a party to request a hearing is of such importance ... that the parties should not be allowed to exclude it by agreement".[7] As a compromise to objections recorded, the *travaux préparatoires* suggest that the requirement under the provisions of the Model Law that parties be treated equally[8] "might in exceptional circumstances provide a compelling reason for holding an oral hearing".[9] However, no guidance is provided on what may constitute exceptional circumstances.

---

[1] Model Law, Art 19(1).
[2] Model Law, Art 24(1).
[3] Model Law, Art 24(1).
[4] CLOUT Case 659 – Germany/Highest Regional Court of Naumburg: *10 Sch 08/01* (21 February 2002).
[5] Arbitration Act 2010, s 8(1).
[6] UNCITRAL Seventh Secretariat Note, A/CN.9/264, Art 24, para 4.
[7] UNCITRAL Seventh Secretariat Note, A/CN.9/264, Art 24, para 4.
[8] Model Law, Art 18.
[9] UNCITRAL Commission Report, A/40/17, Art 4, para 205.

***Advance notice of any hearing and other meetings of an arbitral tribunal*:** An arbitral tribunal must give the parties sufficient advance notice of any hearing and of any meeting of the arbitral tribunal for the purposes of inspection of goods, other property or documents.[1] A party will only be in default as a result of its failure or refusal to appear at a hearing where it has been given advance notice of the scheduled hearing.[2] This requirement is mandatory and an agreement of the parties to shorten the period of notice given to below what is 'sufficient' or to dispense with the requirement altogether will be ineffective. However, as neither the Model Law nor the *travaux préparatoires* (of which Irish courts are permitted to take judicial notice when interpreting provisions of the Model Law)[3] provide any guidance on what period of time is required for sufficient notice, whether the period of time granted by an arbitral tribunal is sufficient must be determined on the facts of each case. The *travaux préparatoires* suggest that this requirement "is fundamental in that it enables the parties to participate effectively in the proceedings and to prepare and present their case".[4]

---

[1] Model Law, Art 24(2).
[2] Model Law, Art 25(c).
[3] Arbitration Act 2010, s 8(1).
[4] UNCITRAL Seventh Secretariat Note, A/CN.9/264, Art 24, para 6.

***Communication of statements, documents and other information*:** All statements, documents or other information supplied to the arbitral tribunal by one party are required to be communicated to the other party.[1] This requirement is to ensure equal treatment of the parties as is required under the Model Law.[2] It is not specified whether it is the parties or an arbitral tribunal who is, in fact, obliged to communicate any statement, report, document or other information. However, the *travaux préparatoires* (of which Irish courts are permitted to take judicial notice when interpreting provisions of the Model Law)[3] suggest the obligation ultimately falls on an arbitral tribunal either to ensure that a party sends a copy to the other party or to itself communicate the statement, report, document or other information to the other party.[4] The *travaux préparatoires* suggest that the requirement "is based upon the essential principle that both parties should have full and equal access to information".[5] In addition, an arbitral tribunal must communicate to the parties any expert report or evidentiary document on which it relies when making its decision on a matter.[6]

[1] Model Law, Art 24(3). A similar principle existed under previous Irish law where it has been held that any communication between an arbitral tribunal and one party only might give rise to the suspicion that justice was not being done. See *State (Hegarty) v Winters* [1956] 1 IR 320.
[2] Model Law, Art 18.
[3] Arbitration Act 2010, s 8(1).
[4] UNCITRAL Seventh Secretariat Note, A/CN.9/264, Art 24, para 9.
[5] *ibid.*
[6] Model Law, Art 24(3).

Article 25.—Default of a party

Unless otherwise agreed by the parties, if, without showing sufficient cause,

(a) the claimant fails to communicate his statement of claim in accordance with article 23(1), the arbitral tribunal shall terminate the proceedings;

(b) the respondent fails to communicate his statement of defence in accordance with article 23(1), the arbitral tribunal shall continue the proceedings without treating such failure in itself as an admission of the claimant's allegations;

(c) any party fails to appear at a hearing or to produce documentary evidence, the arbitral tribunal may continue the proceedings and make the award on the evidence before it.

Definitions

'arbitral tribunal': Model Law, Art 2(c); 'award': Arbitration Act 2010, s 2(1).

Notes

***Default by a party*:** In practice, a party may occasionally fail or refuse to participate in arbitral proceedings. The failure or refusal may be complete and occur from the outset of arbitral proceedings or it may occur during the proceedings.[1] Where a party fails or

(*Continued*)

refuses to participate in arbitral proceedings, this article provides an arbitral tribunal with certain powers to terminate or continue arbitral proceedings as a result of that party's default. The *travaux préparatoires* (of which Irish courts are permitted to take judicial notice when interpreting provisions of the Model Law)[2] suggest that the purpose of these powers is "to provide arbitration with its necessary "teeth"".[3] Where the party in default is the claimant, in order to relieve a respondent from the continuing threat of arbitral proceedings pending against it, an arbitral tribunal must terminate proceedings.[4] In contrast, where the party in default is the respondent, in order to prevent a respondent from impeding arbitral proceedings, an arbitral tribunal must continue the arbitral proceedings without treating the respondent's failure as an admission of the claimant's claims and to ultimately proceed to make an award on the evidence before it.[5] The circumstances where a party is in default are:

1. Where a claimant fails or refuses to deliver a statement of claim without sufficient cause.[6] Although to commence arbitral proceedings a claimant need only deliver a request for the dispute to be referred to arbitration to the respondent,[7] in practice it is not uncommon for a claimant to submit a full statement of claim when requesting the commencement of arbitral proceedings.[8] However, where a full statement of claim is not submitted with the request for arbitration, a claimant must submit a statement of claim within the period of time agreed by the parties or determined by the arbitral tribunal;[9]

2. Where a respondent fails or refuses to submit its defence without sufficient cause.[10] A respondent must submit a defence within the period of time agreed by the parties or determined by the arbitral tribunal;[11] and

3. Where either party fails or refuses to appear at a hearing or fails or refuses to produce documentary evidence.[12] This includes where a party fails or refuses to produce evidence to an expert appointed by an arbitral tribunal when requested to do so by an arbitral tribunal.[13]

---

[1] Blackaby, Partasides, Redfern and Hunter, *Redfern and Hunter on International Arbitration* (5th ed, Oxford University Press, Oxford, 2009) p 524.

[2] Arbitration Act 2010, s 8(1).

[3] UNCITRAL First Secretariat Note, A/CN.9/207, para 80.

[4] Holtzmann and Neuhaus, *A Guide to the UNCITRAL Model Law on International Commercial Arbitration* (1st ed, Kluwer Law and Taxation Publishers, The Hague, 1989) p 698.

[5] *ibid.*

[6] Model Law, Art 25(a).

[7] Arbitration Act 2010, s 7(1)(b).

[8] Brekoulakis and Shore in Mistelis, *Concise International Arbitration, UNCITRAL Model Law* (1st ed, Kluwer Law International, Alphen aan den Rijn, 2010) p 632.

[9] Model Law, Art 23(1).

[10] Model Law, Art 25(b).

[11] Model Law, Art 23(1).

[12] Model Law, Art 25(c).

[13] Model Law, Art 26(1)(b).

'Without sufficient cause': A party will only be in default where it fails to act 'without sufficient cause'. As a safeguard against the arbitrary exercise of an arbitral tribunal's power, the *travaux préparatoires* (of which Irish courts are permitted to take judicial notice when interpreting provisions of the Model Law)[1] suggest that for a party to have failed to act without sufficient cause, it must have been notified in advance of its obligations under the Model Law.[2] In particular, an arbitral tribunal must give the parties advance notice of any hearing that is scheduled.[3] To alleviate the potential harshness which may be occasioned by the application of the default rules by an arbitral tribunal, some commentators have suggested that in practice it may be prudent for an arbitral tribunal to take the initiative and inquire about a party's failure to meet its obligations prior to terminating or continuing arbitral proceedings, as the case may be.[4]

---

1 Arbitration Act 2010, s 8(1).

2 UNCITRAL Seventh Secretariat Note, A/CN.9/264, Art 25, para 2.

3 Model Law, Art 24(2).

4 Brekoulakis and Shore in Mistelis, *Concise International Arbitration, UNCITRAL Model Law* (1st ed, Kluwer Law International, Alphen aan den Rijn, 2010) pp 632-633.

Default of a party to arbitral proceedings under the Arbitration Acts 1954-1998: Decisions under the Arbitration Acts 1954-1998 have permitted an arbitral tribunal to continue arbitral proceedings in the absence of a party that has refused to appear.[1] The Supreme Court noted that:

> "[t]here is to be implied into every agreement establishing a forum for the resolution of disputes that there will be fair procedures. Such are not the prerogative of one side or the other. Just as one side is entitled to the opportunity of stating and making his case, the other is entitled to expedition in the determining of the dispute. It is for the arbitrator to balance one against the other insofar as they affect the timing of his decision. Equally fundamental to the principle of fair procedures is that the arbitrator will only decide what is before him... . To proceed in his absence is not a punishment no more than it is such to make an award in such circumstances".[2]

However, in balancing fair procedures against expediency, case-law decided under the Arbitration Acts 1954-1998 has held that an arbitral tribunal should act reasonably when considering a party's request for an adjournment of hearing date and should not continue arbitral proceedings in the absence of a party where an adjournment would not extend arbitral proceedings to an unreasonable degree.[3]

---

1 *Grangeford Structures Ltd (in liquidation) v SH Ltd* [1990] 2 IR 351, where the Supreme Court refused an application to set aside an award in circumstances where, the defendant's solicitor having walked out in protest when his application for an adjournment was refused, the hearing continued and an award was made. The Supreme Court noted that the arbitrator encountered delay from early on in the arbitral proceedings, most of which he attributed to the defendant.

2 *ibid* at 359 (*per* McCarthy J).

3 *Lennon & anor v Murphy & anor* [2004] IEHC 402; and *FBD Insurance plc v Connors* [2011] IEHC 184.

Article 26.—Expert appointed by arbitral tribunal

(1) Unless otherwise agreed by the parties, the arbitral tribunal

(a) may appoint one or more experts to report to it on specific issues to be determined by the arbitral tribunal;

(b) may require a party to give the expert any relevant information or to produce, or to provide access to, any relevant documents, goods or other property for his inspection.

(2) Unless otherwise agreed by the parties, if a party so requests or if the arbitral tribunal considers it necessary, the expert shall, after delivery of his written or oral report, participate in a hearing where the parties have the opportunity to put questions to him and to present expert witnesses in order to testify on the points at issue.

Definitions

'arbitral tribunal': Model Law, Art 2(c).

Notes

***Appointment of experts by an arbitral tribunal*:** This article, which concerns the appointment of experts by an arbitral tribunal, represents a compromise between the civil law tradition of neutral experts and the common law tradition of party-appointed experts.[1] Unless otherwise agreed by the parties, an arbitral tribunal may appoint experts to report to it on specific issues in order to provide expertise that the arbitral tribunal may lack, such as expertise of a technical or scientific nature.[2] In the course of the arbitral proceedings, the appointed experts may then be cross-examined by the parties and the parties may call their own experts to counter the opinion of the experts appointed by the arbitral tribunal.[3]

[1] Brekoulakis and Shore in Mistelis, *Concise International Arbitration, UNCITRAL Model Law* (1st ed, Kluwer Law International, Alphen aan den Rijn, 2010) p 633.
[2] Model Law, Art 26(1)(a).
[3] Model Law, Art 26(2).

***Parties' cooperation with experts appointed*:** An arbitral tribunal may direct that a party give an expert appointed any relevant information or to produce, or to provide access to, any relevant documents, goods or other property for his inspection.[1] As this duty placed upon the parties is administered via the arbitral tribunal, where a party fails to produce evidence to an expert, an arbitral tribunal may continue the arbitral proceedings and make an award on the evidence before it.[2] Parties are, therefore, advised to cooperate with any experts appointed by an arbitral tribunal.

[1] Model Law, Art 26(1)(b).
[2] Model Law, Art 25(c).

Impartiality and independence of experts appointed: Although not expressly stated, commentators have noted that it is generally accepted that experts appointed by an arbitral tribunal are required to meet standards of impartiality and independence expected of arbitrators under the Model Law.[1] However, it is uncertain whether a party should be permitted to challenge an expert that it feels does not meet the requisite standards. Commentators have expressed divergent views on whether challenge of an expert is appropriate.[2] As neither the Act[3] nor the Model Law expressly provides for the challenge of experts, the conservative view is that no challenge is permitted, particularly as the parties may cross-examine an expert appointed and the parties may call their own experts to counter the opinion of the experts appointed by the arbitral tribunal.[4]

---

[1] Brekoulakis and Shore in Mistelis, *Concise International Arbitration, UNCITRAL Model Law* (1st ed, Kluwer Law International, Alphen aan den Rijn, 2010) p 634.

[2] For commentary in support of the challenge of experts by way of analogous application of the provisions used for the challenge of arbitrators, see Binder, *International Commercial Arbitration and Conciliation in UNCITRAL Model Law Jurisdictions* (3rd ed, Sweet & Maxwell, London, 2010) p 325. For commentary in opposition to the challenge of experts, see Brekoulakis and Shore in Mistelis, *Concise International Arbitration, UNCITRAL Model Law* (1st ed, Kluwer Law International, Alphen aan den Rijn, 2010) p 634.

[3] This is in contrast to the arbitration legislation of certain jurisdictions worldwide which expressly provide for the challenge of experts when adopting the provisions of the Model Law. See, for example, the German ZPO, s 1049(3), which provides that the provisions concerning the challenge of arbitrators "apply mutatis mutandis to an expert appointed by the arbitral tribunal".

[4] Model Law, Art 26(2).

Non-mandatory nature of the article: This article is non-mandatory and the parties may circumvent its effect by agreeing otherwise. Although it may seem unhelpful to permit the parties to prevent an arbitral tribunal from remedying its perceived lack of expertise through the appointment of an expert, the *travaux préparatoires* (of which Irish courts are permitted to take judicial notice when interpreting provisions of the Model Law)[1] suggest the non-mandatory nature of the provision was adopted in recognition of the paramount nature of party autonomy and in recognition of the fact that it will be the parties that ultimately are required to pay for any expert appointed.[2] For similar reasons, an arbitral tribunal should consult with the parties prior to appointing an expert.[3]

---

[1] Arbitration Act 2010, s 8(1).

[2] UNCITRAL Seventh Secretariat Note, A/CN.9/264, Art 26, para 2.

[3] Brekoulakis and Shore in Mistelis, *Concise International Arbitration, UNCITRAL Model Law* (1st ed, Kluwer Law International, Alphen aan den Rijn, 2010) p 633.

Article 27.—Court assistance in taking evidence

The arbitral tribunal or a party with the approval of the arbitral tribunal may request from a competent court of this State assistance in taking evidence. The court may execute the request within its competence and according to its rules on taking evidence.

Definitions

'arbitral tribunal': Model Law, Art 2(b); 'court': Model Law, Art 2(c).

Notes

***Court assistance in taking evidence*:** Although evidence will be crucial for an arbitral tribunal to make an award, commentators have noted that an "arbitral tribunal frequently lacks the power to enforce procedural decisions as regards the taking of evidence, which can range from the calling of a witness to the requirement to produce a document".[1] As a result of this lack of coercive powers of their own, an arbitral tribunal must rely on the coercive power of courts in taking evidence. In this regard this article provides that an arbitral tribunal, or a party with the approval of an arbitral tribunal, may request assistance in the taking of evidence in arbitral proceedings from the court of competent jurisdiction in a State adopting the Model Law, which in Ireland is the High Court.[2] The High Court may then execute the request in accordance with its own rules on the taking of evidence.

---

[1] Binder, *International Commercial Arbitration and Conciliation in UNCITRAL Model Law Jurisdictions* (3rd ed, Sweet & Maxwell, London, 2010) p. 326.
[2] Arbitration Act 2010, s 9(1)(c).

***Prevention of abuse by parties in requesting assistance*:** In order to prevent abuse by parties who might seek assistance in the taking of evidence only for the purpose of delay, this article provides that only an arbitral tribunal, or a party with the approval of an arbitral tribunal, may request assistance in the taking of evidence in arbitral proceedings from a court.[1] The *travaux préparatoires* (of which Irish courts are permitted to take judicial notice when interpreting provisions of the Model Law)[2] suggest that "[t]his restriction may be useful to minimize the possibility of abuse of the court process".[3] Where a request is made, a court has no obligation to provide assistance. International case-law decided under the Model Law has held that a court may refuse to provide assistance where it has reason to believe that the request has been made to delay arbitral proceedings.[4] Similarly, international case-law has also held that a court may refuse to provide assistance where the request has not been made in a timely fashion.[5]

---

[1] Model Law, Art 27.
[2] Arbitration Act 2010, s 8(1).
[3] UNCITRAL Third Secretariat Note, A/CN.9/WG.II/WP.41, para 32.
[4] CLOUT Case 68 – Canada/Federal Court of Canada: *Delphi Petroleum Inc v Derin Shipping and Training Ltd* (3 December 1993).
[5] CLOUT Case 77 – Hong Kong/High Court of Hong Kong: *Vibroflotation AG v Express Builders Co Ltd* (15 August 1994).

***Assistance to foreign arbitrations*:** This article is silent on whether assistance may be given by the court of competent jurisdiction of a State adopting the Model Law to a foreign arbitration. International case-law decided under the Model Law has held that requests for assistance in taking evidence may only be made to courts in the State of the place of arbitration,[1] a view that is shared by commentators.[2] However, in Ireland the Act extends the provisions of the Model Law to foreign arbitrations and clarifies that the High Court may provide assistance in the taking of evidence in arbitral proceedings even where Ireland is not the place of arbitration.[3]

---

[1] CLOUT Case 391 – Canada/Superior Court of Justice: *Re Corporación Transnacional de Inversiones, SA de CV and STE International SpA, et al* (22 September 1999).

[2] Holtzmann and Neuhaus, *A Guide to the UNCITRAL Model Law on International Commercial Arbitration* (1st ed, Kluwer Law and Taxation Publishers, The Hague, 1989) p 738.

[3] Arbitration Act 2010, s 15.

***Nature of the assistance to be offered by the High Court*:** In Ireland, the assistance which may be offered by the High Court is governed by the Rules of the Superior Courts[1] and includes the examination of witnesses and the issue of *subpoenas* for the attendance of witnesses. A request for assistance in the taking of evidence is made *ex parte* to the High Court and must be grounded on affidavit.[2]

The rules governing the examination of witnesses provide:

> "4. The Court may, in any cause or matter where it shall appear necessary, make any order for the examination upon oath before the Court, or any officer of the Court, or any other person, and at any place, of any witness, and may allow the deposition of such witness to be adduced in evidence on such terms (if any) as the Court may direct.
>
> 5. (1) In this rule and in rule 5A:
>
> "the Regulation" means Council Regulation (EC) No 1206/2001 of 28 May 2001 on cooperation between the courts of the Member States in the taking of evidence in civil or commercial matters (OJ L174/1 of 27 June 2001);
>
> "Member State" means a Member State of the European Union with the exception of Denmark.
>
> (2) The Court may, in any case in which the Regulation applies, on the application of any party or of its own motion, order the issue of:
>
> (a) a request, in Form A in the Annex to the Regulation, to the competent court of another Member State to take evidence; or
>
> (b) a request, in Form I in the Annex to the Regulation, to a central body or competent authority, designated by the Member State concerned in accordance with Article 3(3) of the Regulation, to take evidence directly in that Member State.

(*Continued*)

(3) Where an order under this rule is sought by a party, the Court may, before making such an order, require that party to file in the Central Office for consideration by the Court a completed draft of Form A or Form I (as appropriate) in the Annex to the Regulation (including any questions sought to be put to any witness, statement of facts about which any witness is sought to be examined, or documents or objects sought to be inspected by the opposing party), together with a certified translation thereof (where necessary) into the official language referred to in Article 5 of the Regulation, and an undertaking to reimburse without delay any fees or costs referred to in Article 18(2) of the Regulation, and to pay any advance or deposit referred to in Article 18(3) of the Regulation.

(4) Where an order under this rule is made of the Court's own motion, the Court may direct the parties or any of them to reimburse (subject to any order made in that regard by the requested court) any fees or costs referred to in Article 18(2) of the Regulation, and to pay any advance or deposit referred to in Article 18(3) of the Regulation in such shares as it shall direct.

(5) The Court may make such orders and give such directions as seem appropriate for the purposes of Article 12 or Article 17 of the Regulation.

(6) The trial judge may make such order as to fees or costs referred to in Article 18(2) of the Regulation, or as to any costs occasioned by the application of Article 12 or Article 17 of the Regulation as shall seem appropriate, notwithstanding any previous undertaking, order or direction in that regard.

(7) An application under rule 5(2) shall, unless the Court otherwise directs or permits, be made by notice of motion grounded upon an affidavit sworn by or on behalf of the applicant.

5A. (1) If in any case in which the Regulation does not apply the Court orders that a request to examine witnesses shall issue in lieu of a commission, the forms Nos. 1 and 3 in Appendix D, Part II, shall be used for the order and request, respectively.

(2) Where an order is made for the issue of a request to examine a witness or witnesses in any foreign country in which the Regulation does not apply, the following procedure shall be adopted:—

(a) the party obtaining such order shall file in the Central Office an undertaking in the Form No. 2 in Appendix D, Part II.

(b) such undertaking shall be accompanied by —

(i) a request in the Form No. 3 in Appendix D, Part II, with such variations as may be directed in the order for the issue thereof, together with a translation of such request into the language of the country in which the same is to be executed;

(*Continued*)

(ii) a copy of the interrogatories (if any) to accompany the request and a translation thereof;

(iii) a copy of the cross-interrogatories (if any) and a translation thereof.

(3) Where, in any case in which the Regulation does not apply, an order is made for the examination of a witness or witnesses before the Irish Consular authority in any foreign country, such order shall be in the Form No. 4 in Appendix D, Part II.

(4) An application for an order under rule 5A(1) shall, unless the Court otherwise directs or permits, be made by notice of motion grounded upon an affidavit sworn by or on behalf of the applicant.

6. The Court may in any cause or matter, at any stage of the proceedings, order the attendance of any person for the purpose of producing any writings or other documents named in the order which the Court may think fit to be produced; provided that no person shall be compelled to produce under any such order any writing or other document which he could not be compelled to produce at the hearing or trial.

7. Any person wilfully disobeying any order requiring his attendance for the purpose of being examined or producing any document, shall be deemed guilty of contempt of Court, and may be dealt with accordingly.

8. Any person required to attend for the purpose of being examined, or of producing any document, shall be entitled to the like conduct money and payment for expenses and loss of time as upon attendance at a trial in Court.

9. Where any witness or person is ordered to be examined before any officer of the Court, or before any person appointed for the purpose, the person taking the examination shall be furnished by the party on whose application the order was made with a copy of the summons, and pleadings, if any, or with a copy of the documents necessary to inform the person taking the examination of the questions at issue between the parties.

10. The examination shall take place in the presence of the parties, their counsel, solicitors, or agents, and the witnesses shall be subject to cross-examination and re-examination.

11. The depositions taken before an officer of the Court, or before any other person appointed to take the examination, shall be taken down in writing by or in the presence of the examiner, so as to represent as nearly as may be the statement of the witness, and when completed shall be read over to the witness and signed by him in the presence of the parties, or such of them as may think fit to attend. If the witness shall refuse to sign the depositions, the examiner shall sign the same. The examiner may put any question to the witness as to the meaning of any answer, or as to any matter arising in the course of the examination. Any questions which may be objected to shall be taken down by the examiner in the depositions, and he shall state his opinion thereon to the counsel, solicitors, or

(*Continued*)

parties, and shall refer to such statement in the depositions, but he shall not have power to decide upon the materiality or relevancy of any question.

12. If any person duly summoned by *subpoena* to attend for examination shall refuse to attend, or if having attended, he shall refuse to be sworn or to answer any lawful question, a certificate of such refusal, signed by the examiner, shall be filed in the Central Office, and thereupon the party requiring the attendance of the witness may apply to the Court ex parte or on the notice for an order directing the witness to attend, or to be sworn, or to answer any question, as the case may be.

13. If any witness shall object to any question which may be put to him before an examiner, the question so put, and the objection of the witness thereto, shall be taken down by the examiner, and transmitted by him to the Central Office to be there filed, and the validity of the objection shall be decided by the Court.

14. If any case under rules 12 and 13, the Court shall have power to order the witness to pay any costs occasioned by his refusal or objection.

15. When the examination of any witness before any examiner shall have been concluded, the original depositions, authenticated by the signature of the examiner, shall be transmitted by him to the Central Office, and there filed.

16. The person taking the examination of a witness under this Order may, and if need be shall make, a special report to the Court touching such examination, and the conduct or absence of any witness or other person thereon, and the Court may direct such proceedings and make such order as upon the report it may think just.

17. Except where by this Order otherwise provided or directed by the Court no deposition shall be given in evidence at the hearing or trial of the cause or matter without the consent of the party against whom the same may be offered, unless the Court is satisfied that the deponent is dead, or beyond the jurisdiction of the Court, or unable from sickness or other infirmity to attend the hearing or trial, in any of which cases the depositions certified under the hand of the person taking the examination shall be admissible in evidence saving all just exceptions without proof of the signature to such certificate.

18. Any officer of the Court or other person, directed to take the examination of any witness or person, may administer oaths.

19. Any party in any cause or matter may by *subpoena ad testificandum or duces tecum* require the attendance of any witness before an officer of the Court, or other person appointed to take the examination, for the purpose of using his evidence upon any proceeding in the cause or matter in like manner as such witness would be bound to attend and be examined at the hearing or trial; and any party or witness having made an affidavit to be used or which shall be used on any proceeding in the cause or matter shall be bound on being served with such *subpoena* to attend before such officer or person for cross-examination.

(*Continued*)

20. Evidence taken subsequently to the hearing or trial of any cause or matter shall be taken as nearly as may be in the same manner as evidence taken at or with a view to a trial.

21. The practice with reference to the examination, cross-examination, and re-examination of witnesses at a trial shall extend and be applicable to evidence taken in any cause or matter at any stage.

22. The practice of the Court with respect to evidence at a trial, when applied to evidence to be taken before an officer of the Court or other person in any cause or matter after the hearing or trial, shall be subject to any special directions which may be given in any case.

23. No affidavit or deposition filed or made before issue joined in any cause or matter shall without special leave of the Court be received at the hearing or trial thereof, unless within one month after issue joined or within such longer time as may be allowed by special leave of the Court, notice in writing shall have been given by the party intending to use the same to the opposing party of his intention in that behalf.

24. All evidence taken at the hearing or trial of any cause or matter may be used in any subsequent proceedings in the same cause or matter."[3]

The rules governing the issue of *subpoenas* for the attendance of witnesses provide:

"25. Where it is intended to apply for the issue of a *subpoena*, a *praecipe* for that purpose, in the Form No. 1 in Appendix D, Part I, and containing the name or firm and the registered place of business of the solicitor so applying, shall in all cases be delivered and filed at the Central Office.

26. A *subpoena* shall be in one of the Forms Nos. 2 to 5 in Appendix D, Part I.

27. A *subpoena* for the attendance of a witness before the Master or the Examiner may issue from the Central Office upon a note from the Master or Examiner as the case may be.

28. Every *subpoena* other than a *subpoena duces tecum* shall contain three names where necessary or required, but may contain any larger number of names.

29. No more than three persons shall be included in one *subpoena duces tecum*, and the party applying for the same shall be at liberty to apply for a *subpoena* for each person if it shall be deemed necessary or desirable.

30. No *subpoena* shall issue for the production of any record in the custody of the Paymaster-General, or other officer of the State, without an order of the Court; and such officer having the custody of any such record shall not be obliged to remove the same under such order from the depository where same is placed without such order, to be served upon him with the *subpoena duces tecum*.

(*Continued*)

31. Any officer of the Court required to attend with any record or document at any court or place, elsewhere than in Dublin, shall be entitled to require that the solicitor or party desiring his attendance shall deposit with him a sufficient sum of money to answer his just fees, charges and expenses, in respect of such attendance, and undertake to pay any further just fees, charges, and expenses which may not be fully answered by such deposit.

32. In the interval between the issue and service of any *subpoena* the party applying for the same may correct any error in the names of parties or witnesses, and may have it re-sealed upon leaving a corrected *praecipe* for such *subpoena* marked with the words "altered and re-sealed" and signed with the name and registered place of business of the solicitor applying.

33. The service of a *subpoena* shall be effected by delivering a copy thereof, indorsed with the name and address of the solicitor or party issuing the same, and at the same time producing the original.

34. The service of any *subpoena* shall be of no validity if not made within twelve weeks after its date."[4]

---

[1] Rules of the Superior Courts, Ord 56, r 4(4).

[2] Rules of the Superior Courts, Ord 56, r 4(4).

[3] Rules of the Superior Courts, Ord 39, rr 4-24.

[4] Rules of the Superior Courts, Ord 39, rr 25-34.

Chapter VI

Making of Award and Termination of Proceedings

Article 28.—Rules applicable to substance of dispute

(1) The arbitral tribunal shall decide the dispute in accordance with such rules of law as are chosen by the parties as applicable to the substance of the dispute. Any designation of the law or legal system of a given State shall be construed, unless otherwise expressed, as directly referring to the substantive law of that State and not to its conflict of laws rules.

(2) Failing any designation by the parties, the arbitral tribunal shall apply the law determined by the conflict of laws rules which it considers applicable.

(3) The arbitral tribunal shall decide *ex aequo et bono* or as *amiable compositeur* only if the parties have expressly authorized it to do so.

(4) In all cases, the arbitral tribunal shall decide in accordance with the terms of the contract and shall take into account the usages of the trade applicable to the transaction.

Definitions

'arbitral tribunal': Model Law, Art 2(b).

Notes

***Choice of law to be determined by the parties*:** The substantive law is the law an arbitral tribunal applies to the facts of a dispute in order to reach a decision on the rights and duties of the parties.[1] The principle of party autonomy is enshrined in the Model Law and it dictates that an arbitral tribunal must decide a dispute in accordance with the substantive law chosen by the parties.[2] Commentators have noted that "[t]he principle of party autonomy is internationally recognized and prescribed by various institutional arbitration rules. The agreement of the parties is authoritative when determining the law applicable to the substance of the dispute".[3] In practice, the parties' choice of law will generally be expressly made. However, in the absence of an express choice of law it may be implied but this is typically very difficult to prove.[4]

The *travaux préparatoires* (of which Irish courts are permitted to take judicial notice when interpreting provisions of the Model Law)[5] suggest that this article uses the term 'rules of law'[6] to clarify that the parties' choice of law need not be limited to a particular national legal system and can use rules of law elaborated on an transnational level[7] or religious law such as Jewish law or Islamic law. Similarly, the parties may permit an arbitral tribunal to act *ex aequo et bono* or as *amiable compositeur*[8] or they may choose individual provisions from a variety of national legal systems.[9] However, choice of law clauses should be interpreted to avoid applying different laws to different aspects of their contractual relationship.[10]

---

[1] Although in practice they may be the same, the concept of substantive law must be separated from the *lex arbitri*, which is the law governing the procedure of arbitral proceedings. The *lex arbitri* is

(*Continued*)

the law of the place of arbitration. For a discussion on the laws applicable to arbitral proceedings, see Blackaby, Partasides, Redfern and Hunter, *Redfern and Hunter on International Arbitration* (5th ed, Oxford University Press, Oxford, 2009) pp 163-239.

[2] Model Law, Art 28(1).

[3] Böckstiegel, Kröll and Nacimiento, *Arbitration in Germany* (1st ed, Kluwer Law International, Alphen aan den Rijn, 2007) p. 349.

[4] *ibid*, p 351.

[5] Arbitration Act 2010, s 8(1).

[6] UNCITRAL Seventh Secretariat Note, A/CN.9/264, Art 28, para 4.

[7] Law elaborated on a transnational level include the *lex mercatoria* and the UNIDROIT Principles. The UNIDROIT Principles consist of a restatement of the general principles of contract law. They cover the interpretation and performance of contractual obligations and the negotiations leading to the formation of a contract. The aim of the UNIDROIT Principles is to establish a neutral set of rules that may be used throughout the world without any particular bias to one system of law over another. See Blackaby, Partasides, Redfern and Hunter, *Redfern and Hunter on International Arbitration* (5th ed, Oxford University Press, Oxford, 2009) p 222. The full text of the UNIDROIT Principles are available at UNIDROIT's website: http://www.unidroit.org/english/principles/contracts/main.htm.

[8] Model Law, Art 28(3).

[9] Böckstiegel, Kröll and Nacimiento, *Arbitration in Germany* (1st ed, Kluwer Law International, Alphen aan den Rijn, 2007) p 352.

[10] *ibid*, pp 350–351.

***Limitation on the parties' choice of law*:** The parties' choice of law is limited only by the requirement that any choice is not contrary to public policy.[1] Public policy dictates that the parties will not be permitted to override the mandatory rules of law of a country to which all the factual elements of a contract point simply by agreeing to apply some foreign law.[2] For example, the English Court of Appeal refused to enforce an award made under Jewish law where the matrix contract involved a breach of Iranian revenue laws notwithstanding that the illegal purpose of the contract had no effect under Jewish law.[3]

---

[1] Model Law, Art 34(2)(b)(ii).

[2] Blackaby, Partasides, Redfern and Hunter, *Redfern and Hunter on International Arbitration* (5th ed, Oxford University Press, Oxford, 2009) pp 197–198.

[3] *Soleimany v Soleimany* [1999] 1 QB 785.

***Arbitral tribunal to determine choice of law in default of parties' agreement*:** In the absence of a designated choice of law by the parties, an arbitral tribunal must determine the substantive law that it considers applicable to decide a dispute.[1] In contrast to the broad freedom the parties have when the choice of law to decide a dispute, an arbitral tribunal must apply the substantive law determined by conflict of law rules. It has been noted by commentators that "[t]his in effect means that the tribunal may not apply non-national rules of law, as the application of conflict of laws or rules will necessarily lead to

(*Continued*)

the application of the national law of a specific country".[2] This result has been criticised for its inconsistency as "[o]nce the drafters of the Model Law accepted ... the principle that a dispute may be determined by non-national rules in arbitration there is no obvious reason why non-national rules could not also be relied upon by the arbitrators in a dispute that has a truly international character".[3]

In a domestic arbitration (which is any arbitration other than an international commercial arbitration), choice of law will be straightforward and, unless otherwise agreed by the parties, an arbitral tribunal will apply Irish law to the substance of the dispute. In an international commercial arbitration, choice of law is more complicated. While an arbitral tribunal has discretion to determine the substantive law that it considers applicable to decide a dispute, this discretion is limited. The conflict of law rules an arbitral tribunal is required to use to determine the substantive law to be applied must be appropriate to the dispute. Commentators have noted that:

> "The arbitrator's freedom to select the "appropriate" conflicts rule should not be understood to open the door to unfettered discretion. On the contrary, the arbitrators remain obliged to select conflict rules that are "appropriate" in light of the procedural law of the arbitration and parties' arbitration agreement; this is a selection with right answers and wrong answers, and not a purely discretionary matter. For example, an arbitrator cannot select the choice-of-law rules of his home jurisdiction, if it has no connection to the dispute, merely because it is familiar and convenient to him or her.
>
> The freedom granted to arbitrators to select an "appropriate" choice-of-law rule is liberating. It is, however, not the end of analysis, nor a substitute for analysis, but only the entry-way for analysis. There is no general rule or *a priori* rule as to what choice-of-law rules are "appropriate" and the only way to answer this query is by applying a reasoned, predictable analysis to select the best-suited choice-of-law rules".[4]

Depending on the nature of the dispute, the appropriate analysis an arbitral tribunal must conduct to determine the substantive law may involve the application of choice of law rules of all States with a meaningful connection to the dispute; the application of transnational choice of law rules; or the application of choice of law rules of the State must closely connected to the dispute.[5]

---

[1] Model Law, Art 28(2).

[2] Brekoulakis and Shore in Mistelis, *Concise International Arbitration, UNCITRAL Model Law* (1st ed, Kluwer Law International, Alphen aan den Rijn, 2010) p 637.

[3] *ibid*, p 637.

[4] Born, International Commercial Arbitration (1st ed, Kluwer Law International, Alphen aan den Rijn, 2009) p 2135.

[5] For a discussion on the choice of law rules applicable in international commercial arbitrations, see Born, International Commercial Arbitration (1st ed, Kluwer Law International, Alphen aan den Rijn, 2009) pp 2105–2248.

***An arbitral tribunal to act ex aequo et bono or as amiable compositeur*:** Where expressly permitted to do so by the parties, an arbitral tribunal is permitted to act *ex aequo et bono* or as *amiable compositeur*.[1] Although there is no general acceptance as to the exact meaning of the terms '*ex aequo et bono*' or '*amiable compositeur*',[2] the essential feature of both terms "is that arbitrators are not obliged to decide the parties' dispute in accordance with a strict application of legal rules; rather, the arbitrators are expected to decide in light of general notions of fairness, equity and justice".[3] In common law jurisdictions, clauses which permitted an arbitral tribunal to act *ex aequo et bono* or as *amiable compositeur* are typically known as 'equity clauses'. The courts of most common law jurisdictions were traditionally sceptical of such equity clauses.[4] Although there is no direct Irish authority on the validity of equity clauses, some commentators believed that, prior to the commencement of the Act, it was "debatable whether such clauses would be enforceable in [Ireland]".[5]

The *travaux préparatoires* (of which Irish courts are permitted to take judicial notice when interpreting provisions of the Model Law)[6] suggest that the Model Law permitted an arbitral tribunal to act in this manner for a variety of reasons including to ensure that the Model Law did not preclude the use of established features of arbitration practice used in certain legal systems; to reduce the importance of the place of arbitration in international commercial arbitrations; and to ensure that there was no risk of misleading an unwary party since the provision requires express agreement of the parties.[7] Where the parties permit an arbitral tribunal to act *ex aequo et bono* or as *amiable compositeur* certain restrictions apply, namely:

1. That an arbitral tribunal must to decide in accordance with the terms of the contract and an arbitral tribunal must take into account usages of the trade applicable to the contract;[8]
2. That an arbitral tribunal may not infringe the principle of party equality and opportunity to present one's case;[9] and
3. That an arbitral tribunal may not violate public policy.[10]

Where Ireland is the place of arbitration and an arbitral tribunal acts *ex aequo et bono* or as *amiable compositeur* in the absence of an express permission to do so by the parties, an award will be liable to be set aside.[11] However, where an express permission to act in this manner is granted by the parties, commentators have noted that there are very few cases in which a decision made by an arbitral tribunal acting *ex aequo et bono* or as *amiable compositeur* have been set aside.[12]

---

[1] Model Law, Art 28(3).

[2] Brekoulakis and Shore in Mistelis, *Concise International Arbitration, UNCITRAL Model Law* (1st ed, Kluwer Law International, Alphen aan den Rijn, 2010) pp 637-638.

[3] Born, *International Commercial Arbitration* (1st ed, Kluwer Law International, Alphen aan den Rijn, 2009) p 2238. See also Blackaby, Partasides, Redfern and Hunter, *Redfern and Hunter on International Arbitration* (5th ed, Oxford University Press, Oxford, 2009) p 228.

(*Continued*)

[4] *Orion Compania Espanola de Seguros v Belfort Maatschappij Voor Algemeen Verzekeringen* [1962] 2 Lloyd's Rep 257, where the English High Court (Megaw J) stated "it is the policy of law in this country that ... arbitrators must in general apply a fixed and recognisable system of law ... and that they cannot be allowed to apply some different criterion such as the view of the individual arbitrator or umpire on abstract justice or equitable principles". However, in *Eagle Star Insurance Co v Yuval Insurance Co Ltd* [1978] 1 Lloyd's Rep 357, the English Court of Appeal held that the use of an equity clause was entirely reasonable and contained nothing contrary to public policy; and in *Home and Overseas Insurance Co Ltd v Mentor Insurance (UK) Ltd (in liquidation)* [1990] 1 WLR 153, the English Court of Appeal stated that while an equity clause that permitted an arbitral tribunal to determine a dispute solely by reference to what was fair and reasonable may not be valid there was no requirement that an arbitral tribunal apply a fixed and recognisable system of law to determine a dispute.

[5] Dowling-Hussey and Dunne, *Arbitration Law* (1st ed, Thomson Round Hall, Dublin, 2008) p 106.

[6] Arbitration Act 2010, s 8(1).

[7] UNCITRAL Seventh Secretariat Note, A/CN.9/264, Art 28, para 8.

[8] Model Law, Art 28(4).

[9] Model Law, Art 18.

[10] Model Law, Art 34(2)(b)(ii).

[11] Model Law, Art 34(2)(a)(iv). Or, where Ireland is not the place of arbitration, an award will be liable to have recognition and enforcement thereof refused under Model Law, Art 36(1)(a)(iv).

[12] Böckstiegel, Kröll and Nacimiento, *Arbitration in Germany* (1st ed, Kluwer Law International, Aalphen aan den Rijn, 2007) p 361

***Disputes to be decided in accordance with the terms of the contract and the usages of the trade applicable*:** An arbitral tribunal must decide a dispute in accordance with the terms of the parties' contract and must take into account the usages of the trade applicable to the transaction.[1] This requirement is in accordance with general principles of arbitration where the contractual terms of the parties prevail over the default provisions of national arbitration legislation but yield to any mandatory provisions.[2] The requirement to decide a dispute in accordance with the terms of the contract and the usages of the trade applicable is of particular importance where the parties permit an arbitral tribunal to act *ex aequo et bono* or as *amiable compositeur* as, notwithstanding an arbitral tribunal's freedom to decide in light of general notions of fairness, equity and justice, it may not decide the dispute contrary to the contractual terms of the parties.[3]

[1] Model Law, Art 28(4).

[2] Brekoulakis and Shore in Mistelis, *Concise International Arbitration, UNCITRAL Model Law* (1st ed, Kluwer Law International, Alphen aan den Rijn, 2010) p 638.

[3] *ibid.*

Article 29.—Decision-making by panel of arbitrators

In arbitral proceedings with more than one arbitrator, any decision of the arbitral tribunal shall be made, unless otherwise agreed by the parties, by a majority of all its members. However, questions of procedure may be decided by a presiding arbitrator, if so authorized by the parties or all members of the arbitral tribunal.

Definitions

'arbitral tribunal': Model Law, Art 2(b).

Notes

***The principle of majority decision-making*:** Where an arbitral tribunal consists of more than one arbitrator, this article provides that at least a majority of the arbitral tribunal is required to reach a decision.[1] Where there is no majority decision for a single position then an arbitral tribunal must either continue to deliberate until a majority decision is reached or else issue no award.[2] The *travaux préparatoires* (of which Irish courts are permitted to take judicial notice when interpreting provisions of the Model Law)[3] suggest the principle of majority decision-making is more conducive to reaching necessary decisions and final settlement of the dispute than unanimity.[4] However even though unanimity is not required for decision-making, the *travaux préparatoires* also suggest that all arbitrators are required to take part in deliberations or, at least, are required to have had an opportunity to do so.[5]

The provision requiring majority decision-making is non-mandatory and the parties may agree alternative requirements. As an arbitral tribunal in Ireland will consist of a single arbitrator unless the parties agree otherwise,[6] the provision is unlikely to be extensively utilised.

---

[1] Similarly, Model Law, Art 31(1) provides that an award must be signed by at least a majority of the arbitral tribunal.

[2] Holtzmann and Neuhaus, *A Guide to the UNCITRAL Model Law on International Commercial Arbitration* (1st ed, Kluwer Law and Taxation Publishers, The Hague, 1989) p 808.

[3] Arbitration Act 2010, s 8(1).

[4] UNCITRAL Seventh Secretariat Note, A/CN.9/264, Art 29, para 2.

[5] *ibid.*

[6] Arbitration Act 2010, s 13.

***Problems created by the principle of majority decision-making*:** Some commentators believe that the principle of majority decision-making may create a substantial problem where no fall-back position is agreed where a majority decision cannot be reached, as an arbitral tribunal will be required to either continue to deliberate until a majority decision is reached or else issue no award.[1] An alternative approach, suggested by these commentators, would permit a presiding arbitrator to unilaterally reach a decision in the event of deadlock.[2] This approached has been adopted by some arbitral legislation worldwide[3] and by the rules of certain arbitral institutions.[4] However, the *travaux préparatoires* (of which Irish courts are permitted to take judicial notice when interpreting provisions of the Model Law)[5] suggest that this approach was not included in this article as it could lead to depriving arbitrators of 'appropriate influence' on decisions reached[6] and that it may prevent some matters from receiving full consideration.[7]

(Continued)

Advocates of the principle of majority decision-making assert that deadlock rarely occurs in practice.[8] In Ireland, the failure of an arbitral tribunal to reach a majority decision is unlikely to present a difficulty as an arbitral tribunal will consist of a single arbitrator unless the parties agree otherwise.[9] Where the parties do agree otherwise, they should also provide for some fall-back position in the event of deadlock or, alternatively, they should adopt the rules of an arbitral institution containing a fall-back position.

---

[1] Blackaby, Partasides, Redfern and Hunter, *Redfern and Hunter on International Arbitration* (5th ed, Oxford University Press, Oxford, 2009) p 570.

[2] *ibid*, p 571.

[3] The English Arbitration Act 1996, s 20(4); and the Swiss Law on Private International Law, Art 189(2).

[4] The International Chamber of Commerce's Arbitration Rules, Art 31(1); and the London Court of International Arbitration's Arbitration Rules, Art 26.3.

[5] Arbitration Act 2010, s 8(1).

[6] UNCITRAL Commission Report, A/40/17, Art 29, para 244.

[7] UNCITRAL Summary Record, A/CN.9/SR.327, Art 29, para 48.

[8] Holtzmann and Neuhaus, *A Guide to the UNCITRAL Model Law on International Commercial Arbitration* (1st ed, Kluwer Law and Taxation Publishers, The Hague, 1989) p 809, which states that in the first 60 years of the history of the International Chamber of Commerce, its rules permitting a presiding arbitrator to decide alone in the event of deadlock had been used only twice.

[9] Arbitration Act 2010, s 13.

***Obligations on an arbitral tribunal where an arbitrator refuses to take part in a decision*:** In order to prevent possible recourse against an award, where an arbitrator refuses to take part in the decision-making process, it is good practice for an arbitral tribunal to inform the parties of an arbitrator's refusal. German case-law decided under German arbitration legislation based upon the Model Law[1] has permitted an award to be set aside as a result of an arbitral tribunal's failure to notify adequately the parties that an arbitrator was refusing to cooperate in the decision-making process.[2] It must be noted that the German arbitration legislation contains requirements additional to the provisions of the Model Law and it was these requirements that were not met by the arbitral tribunal. As such, the precedential value of this German case-law to a future Irish court called upon to interpret this article is questionable.

---

[1] The German ZPO, s 1052, which is based on Model Law, Art 29 but contains an additional paragraph which states "[i]f an arbitrator refuses to take part in the vote on a decision, the other arbitrators may take the decision without him, unless otherwise agreed by the parties. The parties shall be given advance notice of the intention to make an award without the arbitrator refusing to participate in the vote. In the case of other decisions, the parties shall subsequent to the decision be informed of the refusal to participate in the vote". It was held that one day's notice was inadequate to satisfy the requirement for advance notice where an arbitrator refuses to participate in the vote.

[2] CLOUT Case 662 – Germany/Highest Regional Court of Saarland: *4 Sch 2/02* (29 October 2002).

***Decisions on questions of procedure*:** Although a substantive decision on the merits is required to be reached by least a majority of the arbitral tribunal, either the parties or the arbitral tribunal may delegate questions of procedure to a presiding arbitrator for his or her unilateral decision. The *travaux préparatoires* (of which Irish courts are permitted to take judicial notice when interpreting provisions of the Model Law)[1] suggest unilateral decision-making by a presiding arbitrator is permitted "for the sake of expediency and efficiency".[2] Although this article does not specify what a question of procedure is,[3] the *travaux préparatoires* suggest that it is for an arbitral tribunal to distinguish between substance and procedure.[4]

---

[1] Arbitration Act 2010, s 8(1).
[2] UNCITRAL Fourth Working Group Report, A/CN.9/245, Art XX [*Model Law, Art 29 in the final text*], para 104.
[3] See Blackaby, Partasides, Redfern and Hunter, *Redfern and Hunter on International Arbitration* (5th ed, Oxford University Press, Oxford, 2009) p 570, where the criticism is levied against the provision of UNCITRAL's Arbitration Rules on which Model Law, Art 29 is based.
[4] UNCITRAL Summary Record, A/CN.9/SR.327, Art 29, para 44.

Article 30.—Settlement

(1) If, during arbitral proceedings, the parties settle the dispute, the arbitral tribunal shall terminate the proceedings and, if requested by the parties and not objected to by the arbitral tribunal, record the settlement in the form of an arbitral award on agreed terms.

(2) An award on agreed terms shall be made in accordance with the provisions of article 31 and shall state that it is an award. Such an award has the same status and effect as any other award on the merits of the case.

Definitions

'arbitral tribunal': Model Law, Art 2(b); 'award': Arbitration Act 2010, s 2(1).

Notes

***Settlement of arbitral proceedings*:** As in all forms of dispute resolution, parties to arbitral proceedings may settle a dispute rather than have the arbitral tribunal reach a decision and make an award. Where the parties reach a settlement, this article provides that the arbitral tribunal must terminate the arbitral proceedings.[1] International case-law decided under the Model Law has held that settlement reached after the hearings are closed is still 'during arbitral proceedings' for the purposes of this article and has held that an arbitral tribunal should permit the settlement to stand and terminate the arbitral proceedings.[2]

---

[1] Model Law, Art 30(1).
[2] CLOUT Case 779 – Egypt/Cairo Regional Center for International Commercial Arbitration: *No 497/2006* (17 February 2006).

An award on agreed terms: Where the parties to arbitral proceedings request, an arbitral tribunal may record the terms of settlement as an award on agreed terms.[1] The *travaux préparatoires* (of which Irish courts are permitted to take judicial notice when interpreting provisions of the Model Law)[2] suggest that both parties are required to request that the terms of settlement be recorded in an award on agreed terms and a single party may not unilaterally make a request.[3] An arbitral tribunal has discretion whether or not to record a settlement in the form of an award on agreed terms. Although there is no limit on the discretion of an arbitral tribunal, in practice arbitral tribunals rarely refuse to make an award on agreed terms where requested to do so by the parties. Arbitral tribunals will typically only refuse to make an award on agreed terms where there are well-founded objections to approval of a settlement such as fraud, corruption or violation of applicable laws.[4]

---

[1] Model Law, Art 30(1).

[2] Arbitration Act 2010, s 8(1).

[3] UNCITRAL Commission Report, A/40/17, Art 30, para 250.

[4] Born, *International Commercial Arbitration* (1st ed, Kluwer Law International, Alphen aan den Rijn, 2009) pp 2437–2438.

Reasons for an award on agreed terms: Where the parties settle arbitral proceedings, their settlement agreement is enforceable as a contract.[1] However, where the parties record the settlement as an award on agreed terms, it is enforceable as an award. In a domestic arbitration (which is any arbitration other than an international commercial arbitration), recording a settlement as an award on agreed terms permits a party to enforce by leave of the High Court as well as by commencing a new action for breach of contract.[2] In international commercial arbitrations recording a settlement as an award on agreed terms permits a party to rely on the provisions of the New York Convention[3] to obtain recognition and enforcement in those States which are parties to the New York Convention.[4]

---

[1] Brekoulakis and Shore in Mistelis, *Concise International Arbitration, UNCITRAL Model Law* (1st ed, Kluwer Law International, Alphen aan den Rijn, 2010) p 639.

[2] Arbitration Act 2010, s 23(1).

[3] The text of the New York Convention is silent on whether an award on agreed terms is an 'arbitral award' for the purposes of the New York Convention. However, commentators have noted that the better view is that an award on agreed terms should be regarded as an arbitral award. Born, *International Commercial Arbitration* (1st ed, Kluwer Law International, Alphen aan den Rijn, 2009) pp 2438-2439.

[4] Currently: Afghanistan, Albania, Algeria, Antigua and Barbuda, Argentina, Armenia, Australia, Austria, Azerbaijan, Bahamas, Bahrain, Bangladesh, Barbados, Belarus, Belgium, Benin, Bolivia (Plurinational State of), Bosnia and Herzegovina, Botswana, Brazil, Brunei Darussalam, Bulgaria, Burkina Faso, Cambodia, Cameroon, Canada, Central African Republic, Chile, China, Colombia, Cook Islands, Costa Rica, Côte d'Ivoire, Croatia, Cuba, Cyprus, Czech Republic, Denmark, Djibouti, Dominica, Dominican Republic, Ecuador, Egypt, El Salvador, Estonia, Fiji, Finland, France, Gabon, Georgia, Germany, Ghana, Greece, Guatemala, Guinea, Haiti, Holy

(*Continued*)

See, Honduras, Hungary, Iceland, India, Indonesia, Iran (Islamic Republic of), Ireland, Israel, Italy, Jamaica, Japan, Jordan, Kazakhstan, Kenya, Kuwait, Kyrgyzstan, Lao People's Democratic Republic, Latvia, Lebanon, Lesotho, Liberia, Liechtenstein, Lithuania, Luxembourg, Madagascar, Malaysia, Mali, Malta, Marshall Islands, Mauritania, Mauritius, Mexico, Monaco, Mongolia, Montenegro, Morocco, Mozambique, Nepal, Netherlands, New Zealand, Nicaragua, Niger, Nigeria, Norway, Oman, Pakistan, Panama, Paraguay, Peru, Philippines, Poland, Portugal, Qatar, Republic of Korea, Republic of Moldova, Romania, Russian Federation, Rwanda, Saint Vincent and the Grenadines, San Marino, Saudi Arabia, Senegal, Serbia, Singapore, Slovakia, Slovenia, South Africa, Spain, Sri Lanka, Sweden, Switzerland, Syrian Arab Republic, Thailand, The former Yugoslav Republic of Macedonia, Trinidad and Tobago, Tunisia, Turkey, Uganda, Ukraine, United Arab Emirates, United Kingdom of Great Britain and Northern Ireland, United Republic of Tanzania, United States of America, Uruguay, Uzbekistan, Venezuela (Bolivarian Republic of), Vietnam, Zambia, Zimbabwe. An up-to-date list of States which are parties is kept by UNCITRAL and is available at UNCITRAL's website:http://www.uncitral.org/uncitral/en/uncitral_texts/arbitration/NYConvention_status.html.

***Form of an award on agreed terms*:** An award on agreed terms is required to have the same attributes any other award.[1] It must be made in writing and must be signed by at least a majority of the arbitral tribunal.[2] It must state the date on which and place where it is made[3] and, after it is made, a signed copy must be delivered to each of the parties.[4] However, where an award is made on agreed terms there is no requirement that the reasons for the award be given.[5]

[1] Model Law, Art 30(2).
[2] Model Law, Art 31(1).
[3] Model Law, Art 31(3).
[4] Model Law, Art 31(4).
[5] Model Law, Art 31(2).

***Recourse against an award on agreed terms*:** While some commentators have questioned whether a party may seek recourse against an award on agreed terms,[1] international case-law decided under the Model Law has held that an award on agreed terms is in principle open to challenge, at least where a party alleges that the award violates public policy.[2]

[1] Brekoulakis and Shore in Mistelis, *Concise International Arbitration, UNCITRAL Model Law* (1st ed, Kluwer Law International, Alphen aan den Rijn, 2010) p 640.
[2] CLOUT Case 407 – Germany/Federal Supreme Court: ZB 55/99 (2 November 2000). This case was decided under the German ZPO, s 1053(1), which is based on Model Law, Art 30(1).

Article 31.—Form and contents of award

(1) The award shall be made in writing and shall be signed by the arbitrator or arbitrators. In arbitral proceedings with more than one arbitrator, the signatures of the majority of all members of the arbitral tribunal shall suffice, provided that the reason for any omitted signature is stated.

(2) The award shall state the reasons upon which it is based, unless the parties have agreed that no reasons are to be given or the award is an award on agreed terms under article 30.

(3) The award shall state its date and the place of arbitration as determined in accordance with article 20(1). The award shall be deemed to have been made at that place.

(4) After the award is made, a copy signed by the arbitrators in accordance with paragraph (1) of this article shall be delivered to each party.

Definitions

'arbitration': Arbitration Act 2010, s 2(1) and Model Law, Art 2(a); 'arbitral tribunal': Model Law, Art 2(b); 'award': Arbitration Act 2010, s 2(1).

Notes

***Form and contents of an award*:** This article provides certain mandatory requirements for the form and content of an award. An award must be made in writing and must be signed by at least a majority of the arbitral tribunal.[1] Unless the parties agree otherwise, an award must state the reasons upon which it is based.[2] An award must state the date on which and place where it is made.[3] A signed copy of an award must be delivered to each of the parties.[4] However, there is no standard method of drafting an award. Commentators have noted that "the only essential point is that [an arbitral tribunal] deliver an award which is clear, comprehensive and enforceable".[5]

[1] Model Law, Art 31(1).
[2] Model Law, Art 31(2).
[3] Model Law, Art 31(3).
[4] Model Law, Art 31(4).
[5] Carrigan, "Arbitration Awards: Important New Requirements under the Arbitration Act 2010" (2010) *Arbitration and ADR Review* p 261.

***That an award be made in writing*:** The rationale for the requirement that an award be in writing is to ensure due reflection by the arbitral tribunal and to aid a precise recording of what exactly was decided.[1] It is also to ensure personal attention and responsibility by the arbitral tribunal.[2] That only a majority and not the entire of the arbitral tribunal need sign an award prevents deadlock in circumstances where one arbitrator is unable to sign from stopping the making of an award. The *travaux préparatoires* (of which Irish courts are permitted to take judicial notice when interpreting provisions of the Model Law)[3] suggest this provision is appropriate where an arbitrator dies or becomes physically unable to sign[4] but the *travaux préparatoires* leave unresolved whether it is appropriate that a majority sign in circumstances where an arbitrator to refuse to sign an award because he or she dissents with the decision of the majority.[5] However, commentators[6] believe that the provision should be used in those circumstances, particularly as the Model Law requires only majority decision-making by an arbitral tribunal and not unanimity.[7]

(*Continued*)

In the event that an arbitrator is unable or unwilling to sign an award, it is required that the reason for the omitted signature be stated. International case-law decided under the Model Law has held that the reason for the omitted signature need not be stated in the award.[8] It is uncertain whether a future Irish High Court would adopt a similar approach or whether it would set aside an award signed by a majority of the arbitral tribunal that fails to state the reason for an omitted signature as not being in accordance with the Model Law.[9] However, as the Model Law expressly permits an award to be remitted to an arbitral tribunal in order to permit it remedy a technical omission to eliminate grounds for setting aside the award where court proceedings to set aside have been commenced,[10] it is likely that the power to remit an award would be utilised by the High Court in circumstances where the reason for an omitted was not stated in an award. In addition, the refusal of an arbitrator to sign an award is unlikely to present a practical difficulty in Ireland as, unless the parties agree otherwise, an arbitral tribunal will consist of a single arbitrator.[11]

---

[1] Born, *International Commercial Arbitration* (1st ed, Kluwer Law International, Alphen aan den Rijn, 2009) p 2446.
[2] *ibid*, p 2447.
[3] Arbitration Act 2010, s 8(1).
[4] UNCITRAL Seventh Secretariat Note, A/CN.9/264, Art 31, para 2.
[5] *ibid.*
[6] Brekoulakis and Shore in Mistelis, *Concise International Arbitration, UNCITRAL Model Law* (1st ed, Kluwer Law International, Alphen aan den Rijn, 2010) p 640. Some commentators go as far as to suggest that any country whose law prevents signature of an award by a majority of the arbitral tribunal only is unsuitable for international commercial arbitration. See Blackaby, Partasides, Redfern and Hunter, *Redfern and Hunter on International Arbitration* (5th ed, Oxford University Press, Oxford, 2009) p 553.
[7] Model Law, Art 29. Dissenting opinions are not prohibited by the Model Law and occur in practice. Brekoulakis and Shore in Mistelis, *Concise International Arbitration, UNCITRAL Model Law* (1st ed, Kluwer Law International, Alphen aan den Rijn, 2010) p 640.
[8] CLOUT Case 12 – Canada/Federal Court of Canada (Trial Division): *D Frampton & Co Ltd v Sylvio Thibeault and Navigation Harvey & Frères Inc* (7 April 1988), where a statement by the presiding arbitrator in court annulment proceedings was held to be sufficient.
[9] Model Law, Art 34(2)(a)(iv).
[10] Model Law, Art 34(4).
[11] Arbitration Act 2010, s 13.

That an award be reasoned: Traditionally, arbitral awards in many common law jurisdictions were unreasoned.[1] Unreasoned awards were thought to increase efficiency[2] and prevent challenge to the award.[3] The practice of unreasoned awards was continued by the provisions of the Arbitration Acts 1954-1998 (other than for international commercial arbitrations).[4] However, as arbitration practice developed internationally,[5] reasoned awards were increasingly thought to improve the quality of decisions made.[6] The practice of unreasoned awards in international commercial arbitration became unsustainable and much arbitration legislation worldwide either came to require reasoned awards[7] or came to require reasoned awards, unless the parties agree otherwise.[8] The Model Law follows the

(*Continued*)

latter approach.[9] Where Ireland is the place of arbitration, unless the other parties agree, an award which does not state any reasons upon which it is based, is not in accordance with the Model Law and will be liable to be set aside.[10]

Although some commentators have suggested that basic reasons may be sufficient,[11] it is uncertain how comprehensive and coherent a future Irish High Court will require reasons to be. In Irish case-law decided under the provisions of the Arbitration Acts 1954-1998,[12] an award was set aside on the grounds of misconduct of an arbitral tribunal but at the same time the reasoning of an arbitral tribunal was criticised, *obiter dicta*, as being "laconic to a point well beyond any admirable brevity".[13] However, international case-law decided under the Model Law has held that an award will only be set aside if the reasons provided are totally lacking content, are senseless or are contrary to the decision amounting to a complete lack of reasoning; an incomplete discussion of a party's arguments in the reasoning of an award will not render the award liable to be set aside.[14] Similarly, international case-law has held that an arbitral tribunal cannot be criticised for expressing themselves as commercial men and not as lawyers.[15]

---

[1] Born, *International Commercial Arbitration* (1st ed, Kluwer Law International, Alphen aan den Rijn, 2009) p 2451.

[2] The traditional arguments in favour of unreasoned awards are summarised in Mustill and Boyd, *Commercial Arbitration* (1st ed, Butterworths, London, 1982) at pp 541-542: "First, there was the peculiarly English practice of making awards without reasons. Where the dispute turned on a single short issue of fact, this did no harm. Very often, the arbitrator was chosen for his prestige and experience in a particular trade. His decision was intended to result from a swift and authoritative appreciation of the data placed before him, rather than from a consciously reasoned analysis of the evidence and arguments. Decisions of this kind are not readily explained in writing, particularly by persons whose skills lie in the field of commerce, not language, and the labour required to formulate an explanation would compromise the speed which is essential to this type of arbitration. What the parties wanted was the answer, not the arbitrator's account of how he arrived at it".

[3] This was particularly true in circumstances where the outcome of an award is correct but the reasons incorrect. Hence the practice of arbitral tribunals following the advice which Lord Mansfield is reputed to have given to English judges: "Consider what you consider justice requires, and decide accordingly. But never give your reasons; for your judgment will probably be right, but your reasons will certainly be wrong". Cited in Bingham, "Reasons and Reasons for Reasons" (1988) *4 Arbitration International* p 141.

[4] Dowling-Hussey and Dunne, *Arbitration Law* (1st ed, Thomson Round Hall, Dublin, 2008) pp 56-57. Since the introduction of the Arbitration (International Commercial) Arbitration Act 1998, an international commercial arbitration which has Ireland as its place of arbitration has been governed by the provisions of the Model Law.

[5] The requirement for reasoned awards appears to have had its principal origins in civil law systems. Born, *International Commercial Arbitration* (1st ed, Kluwer Law International, Alphen aan den Rijn, 2009) p 2451, fn 153.

[6] The particular benefits include that the parties are told why they have won or lost; as a safeguard against arbitrariness, private judgment or an irrational splitting of the difference; to guide future conduct; to enable any appellate court to review the decision made; and as a valuable intellectual discipline for the decision maker. See Bingham, "Reasons and Reasons for Reasons" (1988) *4 Arbitration International* p 141.

(*Continued*)

[7] See, for example, the Belgian Judicial Code, Art 1701; and the French New Code of Civil Procedure, Art 1471.

[8] See, for example, the Australian International Arbitration Act 1974, s 16(1); the English Arbitration Act 1996, s 52(4); the German ZPO, s 1054 and 31(2); and the Swiss Law on Private International Law, Art 189(2).

[9] Model Law, Art 31(2).

[10] Model Law, Art 34(2)(a)(iv). Or, where Ireland is not the place of arbitration an award will be liable to have recognition and enforcement thereof refused in Ireland under Model Law, Art 36(1)(a)(iv).

[11] English commentators believe that basic reasons such as "I found that the goods did not correspond to sample" may satisfy the requirement for reasons under the English Arbitration Act 1996, s 52(4). See Mustill and Boyd, *Commercial Arbitration* (2nd ed, 2001 Companion, Butterworths, London, 2001) p 336.

[12] *Galway City Council v Samuel Kingston Construction Ltd & anor* [2010] 3 IR 95.

[13] *ibid,* at 118. The misconduct consisted of an arbitral tribunal reached its conclusions without giving a party the opportunity to present its case and excluded a relevant witness without sufficient reason. Although criticising the reasons given, the Supreme Court (O'Donnell J) stated that the provision by an arbitral tribunal of basic reasons such as the mere preference of one piece of evidence to another is "itself not irrational". Whether reasons of this nature would be sufficient is uncertain and would presumably depend on the nature and complexity of the dispute submitted to arbitration.

[14] CLOUT Case 569 – Germany/Highest Regional Court of Hamburg: *11 Sch 1/01* (8 June 2001).

[15] CLOUT Case 10 – Canada/Superior Court of Quebec: *Navigation Sonamar Inc v Algoma Steamships Ltd* (16 April 1987).

Implied agreement that no reasons be given: Although an agreement of the parties that no reason for an award be given is typically expressly made,[1] the *travaux préparatoires* (of which Irish courts are permitted to take judicial notice when interpreting provisions of the Model Law)[2] suggest that an agreement that no reasons be given may be implied, by, for example, submitting a dispute to an established arbitration system that is known not to contemplate the giving of reasons.[3] Arbitration systems of the 'look-sniff variety' are known not to contemplate the giving of reasons as "there is no room for the giving of reasons: tapioca pellets either are, in the experienced judgment of a trade arbitrator, of fair average quality or they are not; whichever way his opinion goes there is probably not much he can usefully add by way of exegesis".[4]

---

[1] However, case-law decided under Arbitration Acts 1954-1998 has held that an arbitral tribunal may issue a reasoned award, and that the High Court may subsequently consider the reasons given, even where the parties have expressly agreed that no reasons be given or where they have agreed that reasons be given only on a restricted basis. See *John Mowlem Construction Ltd t/a Irishenco Construction v Dublin City Council* [2009] IEHC 225 where the High Court (McKechnie J) at p 17 stated "[the High Court], when considering its supervisory role, is entitled to consider the reasons given by the [arbitral tribunal] for his Award".

[2] Arbitration Act 2010, s 8(1).

[3] UNCITRAL Seventh Secretariat Note, A/CN.9/264, Art 31, para 3.

[4] Bingham, "Reason and Reasons for Reasons" (1988) *4 Arbitration International* p 141, 144.

***That an award state its date*:** The date of an award is of importance in the context of modification of an award and in the context of possible recourse against an award. A request for modification of an award must take place within 30 days of receipt of an award.[1] Application to set aside an award may not be made after three months have elapsed from the date from receipt of an award[2] (on grounds other than public policy).[3] In contrast to the place of an award, which is automatically deemed to have been made at the place of arbitration irrespective of where it was actually signed, the date of an award is determined as a factual act and the award must state the date on which it was actually signed.[4]

[1] Model Law, Art 33, which also provides that an arbitral tribunal may correct a clerical or typographic error in an award *ex officio* or on its own motion within 30 days of the date of an award.

[2] Model Law, Art 34(3).

[3] Arbitration Act 2010, s 12.

[4] Holtzmann and Neuhaus, *A Guide to the UNCITRAL Model Law on International Commercial Arbitration* (1st ed, Kluwer Law and Taxation Publishers, The Hague, 1989) p 839.

***That an award state the place at which it is made*:** In an international commercial arbitration the place of an award is of considerable importance in the context of recourse against an award,[1] which must be sought from the courts of the State of the place of arbitration.[2] The Model Law provides that the parties may agree on the place of arbitration.[3] In the absence of an agreed place of arbitration, the Model Law provides that an arbitral tribunal must determine the place of arbitration having regard to the circumstance of the case, including the convenience of the parties.[4]

Hearings and other meetings of the arbitral tribunal need not actually take place at the locale designated as the place of arbitration.[5] An award is presumed to have been made at the place of arbitration,[6] which the *travaux préparatoires* (of which Irish courts are permitted to take judicial notice when interpreting provisions of the Model Law)[7] suggest is an irrebuttable presumption.[8] The actual place where the hearings took place or where the award was signed is irrelevant.[9] The presumption recognises that the making of an award is a legal act rather than a factual act and modern technology means that an award may be made following deliberations at various places, by telephone or by correspondence.[10] Similar provisions exist in much other arbitration legislation worldwide[11] and the effect of these provisions is to limit the effect of certain international case-law described by commentators as 'idiosyncratic authorities', which hold that an award is not made at the place of arbitration but rather where the hearings took place or where the award was signed.[12]

[1] UNCITRAL Seventh Secretariat Note, A/CN.9/264 para 4.

[2] Blackaby, Partasides, Redfern and Hunter, *Redfern and Hunter on International Arbitration* (5th ed, Oxford University Press, Oxford, 2009) p 591. This general rule is subject to an exception where the parties to an international commercial arbitration agree to subject the arbitration to the procedural law of a country other than that in which the arbitral proceedings are held.

[3] Model Law, Art 20(1).

[4] Model Law, Art 20(1).

(*Continued*)

[5] Model Law, Art 20(2).
[6] Model Law, Art 31(3).
[7] Arbitration Act 2010, s 8(1).
[8] UNCITRAL Seventh Secretariat Note, A/CN.9/264, Art 31, para 5.
[9] Brekoulakis and Shore in Mistelis, *Concise International Arbitration, UNCITRAL Model Law* (1st ed, Kluwer Law International, Alphen aan den Rijn, 2010) p 641.
[10] UNCITRAL Seventh Secretariat Note, A/CN.9/264, Art 31, para 5.
[11] See, for example, the English Arbitration Act 1996, s 53 and the Swiss Law on Private International Law, Art 176.
[12] See, for example, *Hiscox v Outhwaite* [1992] 1 AC 562, where the House of Lords (as it then was) held that an award was made in France, where the arbitral tribunal signed the award, rather than in England, which was the contractual place of arbitration. See also various US federal court decisions including *McGregor & Werner, Inc v Motion Picture Laboratory Technicians Local 780, IATSE*, 806 F2d 1003 (11th Cir 1986); *Motion Picture Laboratory Technicians Local 780, IATSE v McGregor & Werner, Inc*, 804 F2d 16 (2nd Cir 1986); and *City of Naples v Prepakt Concrete Co*, 490 F2d 182 (5th Cir 1974), which have held that domestic awards were made where the hearings were held. For a discussion on these 'idiosyncratic authorities', see Born, *International Commercial Arbitration* (1st ed, Kluwer Law International, Alphen aan den Rijn, 2009) pp 2370-2373.

***Consequences of an award failing to state its date or place*:** Although it is a mandatory requirement that an award states its date and place, international case-law decided under the Model Law has held that a failure to do so may be corrected by an arbitral tribunal and will not necessarily render the award liable to be set aside, at least where it is possible for the missing information to be ascertained by other means.[1] It is uncertain whether a future Irish High Court would follow this approach or whether it would set aside an award that fails to state its date or place as not being in accordance with the Model Law.[2] However, as the Model Law expressly permits an award to be remitted to an arbitral tribunal in order to permit it remedy a technical omission to eliminate grounds for setting aside the award where court proceedings to set aside have been commenced,[3] it is likely that the power to remit an award would be utilised by the High Court in circumstances where its date or place not stated in an award.

[1] Germany/Highest Regional Court of Stuttgart: *1 Sch 22/01* (4 June 2002). Cited in Böckstiegel, Kröll and Nacimiento, *Arbitration in Germany* (1st ed, Kluwer Law International, Aalphen aan den Rijn, 2007) p 391, fn 23 and Brekoulakis and Shore in Mistelis, *Concise International Arbitration, UNCITRAL Model Law* (1st ed, Kluwer Law International, Alphen aan den Rijn, 2010) p 641.
[2] Model Law, Art 34(2)(a)(iv).
[3] Model Law, Art 34(4).

***The delivery of an award to each party*:** A signed copy of an award must be delivered to each of the parties.[1] The date of the receipt of an award determines the time limits for applications to set aside awards[2] (on grounds other than public policy)[3] and for applications for modification of an award.[4] Delivery must be carried out in accordance with the Act[5] and the Model Law.[6] The purpose of requiring delivery to each party is to ensure 'due process'.[7]

[1] Model Law, Art 31(4).
[2] Model Law, Art 34(2)(a).

(*Continued*)

[3] Arbitration Act 2010, s 12.
[4] Model Law, Art 33.
[5] Arbitration Act 2010, s 7(2).
[6] Model Law, Art 3(1).
[7] Brekoulakis and Shore in Mistelis, *Concise International Arbitration, UNCITRAL Model Law* (1st ed, Kluwer Law International, Alphen aan den Rijn, 2010) p 641. However, some commentators believe this requirement to be superfluous as it could already be derived from the Model Law's requirement to treat all parties equally. See Binder, *International Commercial Arbitration and Conciliation in UNCITRAL Model Law Jurisdictions* (3rd ed, Sweet & Maxwell, London, 2010) p 356.

Article 32.—Termination of proceedings

(1) The arbitral proceedings are terminated by the final award or by an order of the arbitral tribunal in accordance with paragraph (2) of this article.

(2) The arbitral tribunal shall issue an order for the termination of the arbitral proceedings when:

(a) the claimant withdraws his claim, unless the respondent objects thereto and the arbitral tribunal recognizes a legitimate interest on his part in obtaining a final settlement of the dispute;

(b) the parties agree on the termination of the proceedings;

(c) the arbitral tribunal finds that the continuation of the proceedings has for any other reason become unnecessary or impossible.

(3) The mandate of the arbitral tribunal terminates with the termination of the arbitral proceedings, subject to the provisions of articles 33 and 34(4).

Definitions

'arbitral tribunal': Model Law, Art 2(b); 'award': Arbitration Act 2010, s 2(1).

Notes

Termination of arbitral proceedings: This article provides that an arbitral tribunal is required to terminate arbitral proceedings where:

1. A 'final' award is ordered.[1] Although not defined in the Model Law, the *travaux préparatoires* (of which Irish courts are permitted to take judicial notice when interpreting provisions of the Model Law)[2] suggest that a 'final' award is an award intended "to settle the dispute in full";[3]

2. A claimant withdraws his claim, unless a respondent objects and the arbitral tribunal recognises a legitimate interest on a respondent's part.[4] The *travaux préparatoires* suggest that the purpose of this provision is to recognise that parties

(*Continued*)

other than the claimant may have an interest in the current arbitral proceedings being pursued such as the reduction of "the risk of harassment by a claimant repeatedly bringing a claim and then withdrawing it";[5]

3. The parties agree on termination;[6] or
4. The arbitral tribunal finds that the continuation of the arbitral proceedings becomes unnecessary or impossible.[7] The Model Law does not specify when the continuation of arbitral proceedings becomes unnecessary or impossible and the *travaux préparatoires* provide little guidance on when arbitral proceedings become unnecessary or impossible other than suggest that it is for an arbitral tribunal in its discretion to determine when to terminate.[8]

In addition to the means of termination provided in this article, the Model Law also provides that an arbitral tribunal must terminate arbitral proceedings:

1. Where a claimant fails to communicate his statement of claim within the designated time period;[9] or
2. Where the parties settle the dispute.[10]

[1] Model Law, Art 32(1).
[2] Arbitration Act 2010, s 8(1).
[3] UNCITRAL First Working Group Report First Draft, A/CN.9/WP.38, Art 25 [*incorporated in part into Model Law, Art 32 in the final text*].
[4] Model Law, Art 32(2)(a).
[5] UNCITRAL Summary Record, A/CN.9/SR.329, Art 32, para 30.
[6] Model Law, Art 32(2)(b).
[7] Model Law, Art 32(2)(c).
[8] UNCITRAL Summary Record, A/CN.9/SR.329, Art 32, para 30.
[9] Model Law, Art 25(a).
[10] Model Law, Art 30(1).

Consequences of termination: Where arbitral proceedings are terminated the arbitral tribunal is *functus officio* and no longer has any mandate to deal with the arbitral proceedings subject to limited exceptions provided by the Model Law.[1] The doctrine of *functus officio* also existed at common law and its rationale is based on "an unwillingness to permit one who is not a judicial officer and who acts informally and sporadically, to re-examine a final decision which he has rendered, because of the potential evil of outside communication and unilateral influence which might affect a new conclusion".[2]

[1] Model Law, Art 32(3).
[2] *McClatchy Newspapers v Central Valley Typo Union No 46*, 686 F2d 731, 734 (9th Cir 1982), which is a US Court of Appeal decision. This decision was cited with approval by the High Court (Gilligan J) in *Redahan v Minister for Education* [2005] 3 IR 64. However, an arbitral tribunal is not *functus officio* until arbitral proceedings are terminated and an arbitral tribunal will be permitted to hear additional evidence until such time; for example, an arbitral tribunal may hear additional evidence after the scheduled oral hearing is completed but before a final award is issued. See *O'Sullivan v Joseph Woodward and Sons Ltd* [1987] 1 IR 255.

Exceptions to the principle of functus officio: The following limited exceptions to the principle that an arbitral tribunal is *functus officio* upon termination of arbitral proceedings exist:

1. That an arbitral tribunal may modify an award by correcting clerical or typographic errors,[1] by interpreting a specific point or part of an award[2] and, unless the parties agree otherwise, by issuing an additional award as to claims presented in the arbitral proceedings but omitted from the award;[3] and

2. That an arbitral tribunal is permitted to resume arbitral proceedings or to take any other action that will eliminate grounds to set aside an award in circumstances where a party has commenced court proceedings to set aside the award and where the court suspends the court proceedings in order to give the arbitral tribunal an opportunity to correct the purported defect in the proceedings.[4]

[1] Model Law, Art 33(1)(a).
[2] Model Law, Art 33(1)(b).
[3] Model Law, Art 33(3).
[4] Model Law, Art 34(4).

Article 33.—Correction and interpretation of award; additional award

(1) Within thirty days of receipt of the award, unless another period of time has been agreed upon by the parties:

(a) a party, with notice to the other party, may request the arbitral tribunal to correct in the award any errors in computation, any clerical or typographical errors or any errors of similar nature;

(b) if so agreed by the parties, a party, with notice to the other party, may request the arbitral tribunal to give an interpretation of a specific point or part of the award.

If the arbitral tribunal considers the request to be justified, it shall make the correction or give the interpretation within thirty days of receipt of the request. The interpretation shall form part of the award.

(2) The arbitral tribunal may correct any error of the type referred to in paragraph (1)(a) of this article on its own initiative within thirty days of the date of the award.

(3) Unless otherwise agreed by the parties, a party, with notice to the other party, may request, within thirty days of receipt of the award, the arbitral tribunal to make an additional award as to claims presented in the arbitral proceedings but omitted from the award. If the arbitral tribunal considers the request to be justified, it shall make the additional award within sixty days.

(4) The arbitral tribunal may extend, if necessary, the period of time within which it shall make a correction, interpretation or an additional award under paragraph (1) or (3) of this article.

(5) The provisions of article 31 shall apply to a correction or interpretation of the award or to an additional award.

Definitions

'arbitral tribunal': Model Law, Art 2(b); 'award': Arbitration Act 2010, s 2(1).

Notes

Correction of clerical or typographic errors or any errors of similar nature: A party may request that an arbitral tribunal modify an award in the form of correction of clerical or typographic errors or any errors of similar nature within 30 days of receipt of the award.[1] Such request must be on notice to the other party. Additionally, an arbitral tribunal may correct such errors on its own initiative within 30 days of the date of the award.[2]

The type of errors which may typically be corrected are "flagrant mathematical errors or typing errors, which would otherwise complicate the execution of the award".[3] Correction of an error must not result in amendment of the content of an award.[4] A similar provision existed under the Arbitration Acts 1954-1998,[5] which permitted an arbitral tribunal to "correct in an award any clerical mistake or error arising from any accidental slip or omission", and case-law decided had interpreted this provision as permitting correction of an award containing numerical or arithmetic errors.[6]

---

[1] Model Law, Art 33(1).
[2] Model Law, Art 33(2).
[3] Binder, *International Commercial Arbitration and Conciliation in UNCITRAL Model Law Jurisdictions* (3rd ed, Sweet & Maxwell, London, 2010) p 370.
[4] Brekoulakis and Shore in Mistelis, *Concise International Arbitration, UNCITRAL Model Law* (1st ed, Kluwer Law International, Alphen aan den Rijn, 2010) p 643.
[5] Arbitration Act 1954, s 28.
[6] *McCaughey v Stringer* [1914] 1 IR 73.

Interpretation of an award: Where the parties agree, an arbitral tribunal may modify an award by providing interpretation of a specific point or part of an award.[1] If permitted to do so, a party must request interpretation within 30 days of receipt of the award,[2] unless an alternative period of time has been agreed to. A request must be on notice to the other party.

The concept of an arbitral tribunal providing interpretation of an award is not common in arbitration legislation worldwide[3] and the *travaux préparatoires* (of which Irish courts are permitted to take judicial notice when interpreting provisions of the Model Law)[4] suggest its inclusion was highly controversial. The objections recorded in the *travaux préparatoires* include that interpretation may "encourage further proceedings and undermine the principle of the finality of the arbitral award"[5] and that it "might be used by the losing party to harass the arbitral tribunal".[6] However, the *travaux préparatoires* suggest that the concept of interpretation has benefits as it permits clarification, which may be necessary in an international commercial arbitration, particularly where an "award might have been written in a language other than the mother-tongue of its drafter, increasing the possibility of ambiguity".[7] By way of compromise, the *travaux préparatoires*

(*Continued*)

suggest that the power of interpretation is included in the Model Law but it will only be applicable where the parties expressly agree to it.[8] As the concept of interpretation was previously alien to Irish arbitration legislation[9] and arbitration practice, it is unlikely that many parties to arbitration agreements will provide an arbitral tribunal with the power of interpretation. Where parties do choose to permit an arbitral tribunal to provide interpretation of an award they would be advised to consider some of its dangers and benefits noted by commentators:

> "When agreeing on allowing the interpretation of an award the parties have to be aware that the result reached might not always provide the hoped-for result and could perhaps give rise to new problems. For example, the tribunal could fail to reach agreement on the appropriate interpretation and problems that up until then had been undiscovered or intentionally avoided could be uncovered. On the other hand, however, one of the parties will nearly always seek the clarification or interpretation of an unclear arbitral award and if the arbitral tribunal does not or cannot fulfil this task, the enforcing court will do so; it is submitted that the tribunal, of course, is better suited to fulfil that task".[10]

[1] Model Law, Art 33(1)(b).
[2] Model Law, Art 33(1).
[3] Brekoulakis and Shore in Mistelis, *Concise International Arbitration, UNCITRAL Model Law* (1st ed, Kluwer Law International, Alphen aan den Rijn, 2010) p 643.
[4] Arbitration Act 2010, s 8(1).
[5] UNCITRAL Summary Record, A/CN.9/SR.329, Art 33, para 40.
[6] UNCITRAL Commission Report, A/40/17, Art 33, para 266.
[7] *ibid*, para 267.
[8] *ibid*, para 268.
[9] Other than for international commercial arbitrations, for which the Model Law has been adopted since the commencement of Arbitration (International Commercial) Act 1998.
[10] Binder, *International Commercial Arbitration and Conciliation in UNCITRAL Model Law Jurisdictions* (3rd ed, Sweet & Maxwell, London, 2010) p 372.

Issuance of an additional award: A party may request that an arbitral tribunal issue an additional award to claims presented in the arbitral proceedings but omitted from the award within 30 days from the receipt of an award.[1] The rationale for the issuance of an additional award is to remedy inadvertence of behalf of an arbitral tribunal.[2] Where an arbitral tribunal considers the request justified, it must make the correction or provide the interpretation within 60 days of the date of the request. An arbitral tribunal has power to extend the period of time within which it is required to issue an additional award.[3] Additional awards are "autonomous and therefore and can be challenged or enforced independently of the main award".[4]

[1] Model Law, Art 33(3).
[2] Brekoulakis and Shore in Mistelis, *Concise International Arbitration, UNCITRAL Model Law* (1st ed, Kluwer Law International, Alphen aan den Rijn, 2010) p 643.
[3] Model Law, Art 33(4).
[4] Brekoulakis and Shore in Mistelis, *Concise International Arbitration, UNCITRAL Model Law* (1st ed, Kluwer Law International, Alphen aan den Rijn, 2010) p 643.

Period of time for modification of an award: Unless the parties have agreed an alternative period of time, a party may request modification of an award in the form of correction, interpretation (where agreed by the parties) or issuance of an additional award within 30 days of receipt of the award. A request must be on notice to the other party. Where an arbitral tribunal considers the request justified, it must make the correction or provide the interpretation within 30 days of receipt of the request[1] or it must issue an additional award within 60 days of the date of the request.[2] Although an arbitral tribunal has no power to extend the period of time within which a party can make a request for a modification or additional award, it has discretion to extend the period of time within which it must issue a modified award.[3] The *travaux préparatoires* (of which Irish courts are permitted to take judicial notice when interpreting provisions of the Model Law)[4] suggest that possible reasons for an arbitral tribunal to extend the period of time include: permitting consultation amongst the arbitrators where an arbitral tribunal consists of more than one arbitrator; permitting additional hearings to be held if required; and permitting the non-requesting party to respond to the request.[5]

[1] Model Law, Art 33(1).
[2] Model Law, Art 33(3).
[3] Model Law, Art 33(4).
[4] Arbitration Act 2010, s 8(1).
[5] UNCITRAL Seventh Secretariat Note, A/CN.9/264, Art 33, para 2.

Form of a modified or additional award: A modified award (whether by way of correction, interpretation or additional award) is required to have the same attributes as any other award.[1] It must be made in writing and must be signed by at least a majority of the arbitral tribunal.[2] It must be reasoned, unless otherwise agreed by the parties.[3] It must state the date on which and place where it is made[4] and, after it is made, a signed copy must be delivered to each of the parties.[5]

[1] Model Law, Art 33(5).
[2] Model Law, Art 31(1).
[3] Model Law, Art 31(2).
[4] Model Law, Art 31(3).
[5] Model Law, Art 31(4).

Mandatory nature of the article: This article is mandatory in nature and the parties may not circumvent its effect by agreeing otherwise, although they may agree on a different period of time within which a request for correction is to made.[1]

[1] Holtzmann and Neuhaus, *A Guide to the UNCITRAL Model Law on International Commercial Arbitration* (1st ed, Kluwer Law and Taxation Publishers, The Hague, 1989) p 890.

Chapter VII

Recourse Against Award

Article 34.—Application for setting aside as exclusive recourse against arbitral award

(1) Recourse to a court against an arbitral award may be made only by an application for setting aside in accordance with paragraphs (2) and (3) of this article.

(2) An arbitral award may be set aside by the court specified in article 6 only if:

(a) the party making the application furnishes proof that:

(i) a party to the arbitration agreement referred to in article 7 was under some incapacity; or the said agreement is not valid under the law to which the parties have subjected it or, failing any indication thereon, under the law of this State; or

(ii) the party making the application was not given proper notice of the appointment of an arbitrator or of the arbitral proceedings or was otherwise unable to present his case; or

(iii) the award deals with a dispute not contemplated by or not falling within the terms of the submission to arbitration, or contains decisions on matters beyond the scope of the submission to arbitration, provided that, if the decisions on matters submitted to arbitration can be separated from those not so submitted, only that part of the award which contains decisions on matters not submitted to arbitration may be set aside; or

(iv) the composition of the arbitral tribunal or the arbitral procedure was not in accordance with the agreement of the parties, unless such agreement was in conflict with a provision of this Law from which the parties cannot derogate, or, failing such agreement, was not in accordance with this Law; or

(b) the court finds that:

(i) the subject-matter of the dispute is not capable of settlement by arbitration under the law of this State; or

(ii) the award is in conflict with the public policy of this State.

(3) An application for setting aside may not be made after three months have elapsed from the date on which the party making that application had received the award or, if a request had been made under article 33, from the date on which that request had been disposed of by the arbitral tribunal.

(4) The court, when asked to set aside an award, may, where appropriate and so requested by a party, suspend the setting aside proceedings for a period of time determined by it in order to give the arbitral tribunal an opportunity to resume the arbitral proceedings or to take such other action as in the arbitral tribunal's opinion will eliminate the grounds for setting aside.

Definitions

'arbitration': Arbitration Act 2010, s 2(1) and Model Law, Art 2(a); 'arbitration agreement': Arbitration Act 2010, s 2(1) and Model Law, Art 7(1)(Option 1); 'arbitral tribunal': Model Law, Art 2(b); 'award': Arbitration Act 2010, s 2(1); 'court': Model Law, Art 2(c); 'months': Interpretation Act 2005, sch, Pt 1.

Notes

Application to set aside an award: Where a party is unhappy with an award made by an arbitral tribunal, the only recourse available to it is to apply to set aside the award.[1] The Model Law provides limited grounds for setting aside an award.[2] The *travaux préparatoires* (of which Irish courts are permitted to take judicial notice when interpreting provisions of the Model Law)[3] suggest that there can be no grounds to set aside an award that are not contained in the Model Law[4] and the *travaux préparatoires* suggest that an "application for setting aside constitutes the exclusive recourse to a court against the award in the sense that it is the only means for actively attacking the award, *i.e.*, initiating proceedings for judicial review".[5] An award may not be set aside for some reason not specified in the Model Law as a result of the courts' inherent jurisdiction. Commentators have noted that "[t]his means that unless the High Court has been accorded a specific role by the [Model Law], then it cannot intervene; inherent jurisdiction and other vestiges of the past are swept away".[6] In Ireland, an application to set aside an award is made to the High Court.[7] The grounds for setting aside an award are bifurcated into:

1. Party grounds to set aside an award, which the party challenging the award must prove;[8] and
2. *Ex officio* grounds, which a court may find on its own motion without the party challenging the award having the burden of proof.[9]

---

[1] Model Law, Art 34(1).
[2] Model Law, Art 34(2).
[3] Arbitration Act 2010, s 8(1).
[4] Seventh Secretarial Note, A/CN.9/264, Art 34, para 6.
[5] UNCITRAL Seventh Secretarial Note, A/CN.9/264, Art 34, para 2.
[6] Reichert, "Security for Costs in Arbitration – A New Landscape in Ireland" (2010) *Arbitration and ADR Review* p 130.
[7] Arbitration Act 2010, s 9(1)(a); and Model Law, Art 6.
[8] Model Law, Art 34(2)(a).
[9] Model Law, Art 34(2)(b).

Party grounds to set aside an award: The Model Law specifies four grounds, which a party challenging an award must prove in order for the High Court to set aside an award:

(*Continued*)

1. That a party to an arbitration agreement was under some incapacity or where an arbitration agreement was not valid under the law to which the parties have subjected it or, failing any indication thereon, the law of Ireland.[1] Whether a party had capacity to enter into an arbitration agreement is not covered by the provisions of the Model Law. Therefore, the normal rules of contract law apply to determine whether or not a party had capacity to enter into the arbitration agreement.[2] In Ireland minors; intoxicated persons; and those suffering from mental illness do not typically have capacity to enter into a binding contract;[3]

2. That the party making the application was not given proper notice of the appointment of an arbitrator or of the arbitral proceedings or was otherwise unable to present its case.[4] The Model Law requires due process in arbitral proceedings and provides that parties must be treated with equality and must be given a full opportunity to present their case.[5] Commentators have noted that the "ground includes both procedural and substantive fairness, and thus it overlaps with the public policy ground".[6] International case-law has held that the requirement for due process is not intended to protect a party from its own failures or strategic choices so that a party that refuses to participate in arbitral proceedings is deemed to have forfeited the opportunity to be heard.[7] Similarly, where a party alleges a breach of its due process rights as a result of being denied an opportunity to be heard, arid, technical or procedural objections that do not prejudice any party should not be tolerated and only where the alleged breach of natural justice has surpassed the boundaries of legitimate expectation and propriety, resulting in actual prejudice to a party, should a remedy be made.[8] International case-law has also held that a failure by an arbitral tribunal to conduct arbitral proceedings in a language understandable to a party is not a violation of its due process rights where the party declined the opportunity to engage an interpreter to participate fully in the arbitral proceedings;[9] and that there is no violation of due process where there is a minor procedural infringement by an arbitral tribunal[10] or where an arbitral tribunal rejects one party's submission.[11] Although not governed by the Model Law, English case law that has held that there was a serious violation of due process where an arbitral tribunal decided an issue that had not been argued by the parties, is also likely to be persuasive for future Irish courts;[12]

3. That the award deals with a dispute not contemplated by or not falling within the terms of the submission to arbitration, or contains decisions on matters beyond the scope of the submission to arbitration.[13] Commentators have noted that "this ground is infrequently invoked, and it is even less frequently accepted by national courts to set an award aside"[14] and international case-law decided under the Model Law has held that this ground is to be narrowly construed;[15] and

4. That the composition of the arbitral tribunal or the arbitral procedure was not in accordance with the agreement of the parties, unless such agreement was in conflict with a provision of the Act and the Model Law from which the parties cannot derogate, or, failing the agreement of the parties, that the composition of the arbitral tribunal or the arbitral procedure was not in accordance with the Act

(*Continued*)

and the Model Law.[16] Commentators have noted that "[t]his can be seen as a catch-all provision for procedural defects under the arbitration agreement or under the Model Law".[17] However, international case-law has held that an award made by an arbitral tribunal consisting of a sole arbitrator, despite the arbitration clause requiring a three-person arbitral tribunal, was not in accordance with the agreement of the parties and was set aside.[18] Similarly, international case-law has held that the refusal of the tribunal to appoint the claimant's nomination for a substitute arbitrator was a procedural error which resulted in an award being set aside.[19]

---

1 Model Law, Art 34(2)(a)(i).

2 Brekoulakis and Shore in Mistelis, *Concise International Arbitration, UNCITRAL Model Law* (1st ed, Kluwer Law International, Alphen aan den Rijn, 2010) p 647.

3 For a discussion on contractual capacity in Ireland, see McDermott, *Contract Law* (1st ed, Butterworth (Ireland) Ltd, Dublin, 2001) pp 887-915.

4 Model Law, Art 34(2)(a)(ii).

5 Model Law, Art 18.

6 Brekoulakis and Shore in Mistelis, *Concise International Arbitration, UNCITRAL Model Law* (1st ed, Kluwer Law International, Alphen aan den Rijn, 2010) p 646.

7 CLOUT Case 391 – Canada/Superior Court of Justice: *Re Corporacion Transnacional de Inversiones, SA de CV et al and STET International, SpA et al* (22 September 1999).

8 CLOUT Case 743 – Singapore/Court of Appeal: *Soh Beng Tee and Co Pte Ltd v Fairmount Development Pte Ltd* (9 May 2007); and CLOUT Case 658 – New Zealand/High Court (Commercial List) Auckland: *Trustees of Rotoaria Forest Trust v Attorney-General* (30 November 1998).

9 CLOUT Case 559 – Germany/Highest Regional Court of Celle: *8 Sch 3/01* (2 October 2001).

10 CLOUT Case 146 – Russian Federation/Moscow City Court: *No court reference/unidentified parties* (10 November 1994).

11 CLOUT Case 457 – Germany/Highest Regional Court of Hamburg: *1 Sch 2/99* (14 May 1999).

12 *OAO Northern Shipping Co v Remolcadores De Marin SL ("The Renmar")* [2007] EWHC 1821 (Comm).

13 Model Law, Art 34(2)(a)(iii).

14 Brekoulakis and Shore in Mistelis, *Concise International Arbitration, UNCITRAL Model Law* (1st ed, Kluwer Law International, Alphen aan den Rijn, 2010) p 647.

15 CLOUT Case 16 – Canada/British Columbia Court of Appeal: *Quintette Coal Ltd v Nippon Steel Corp et al* (24 October 1990).

16 Model Law, Art 34(2)(a)(iv).

17 Binder, *International Commercial Arbitration and Conciliation in UNCITRAL Model Law Jurisdictions* (3rd ed, Sweet & Maxwell, London, 2010) p 383.

18 CLOUT Case 628 – Canada/Alberta Queen's Bench: *Fleming, Fleming and Moran v Space Homes Ltd* (15 January 1985).

19 CLOUT Case 436/CLOUT Case 437 – Germany/Highest Regional Court of Bavaria: *4Z Sch 17/98* (24 February 1999).

Ex officio grounds to set aside an award: The Model Law specifies two grounds, which the High Court may examine *ex officio* on its own motion for setting aside an award. The party challenging an award does not have the burden of proving these *ex officio* grounds:

(*Continued*)

1. That the subject-matter of the dispute is incapable of resolution by arbitration under Irish law.[1] The Model Law expressly reserves the concept of 'arbitrability' or whether a dispute is capable of resolution by arbitration (so-called 'arbitrability') to domestic law.[2] Categories of disputes which are incapable of resolution by arbitration in Ireland include the prosecution of criminal offences;[3] disputes concerning the grant[4] or revocation[5] of patents and trade marks;[6] and disputes concerning contracts whose objects are illegal or contrary to public policy;[7] and

2. That the award is in conflict with public policy.[8] The *travaux préparatoires* (of which Irish courts are permitted to take judicial notice when interpreting provisions of the Model Law)[9] suggest that "[i]n discussing the term "public policy", it was understood that it was not equivalent to the political stance or international policies of a State but comprised the fundamental notions and principles of justice ... Thus, instances such as corruption, bribery or fraud and similar serious cases would constitute a ground for setting aside".[10] International case-law has held that what is meant by the term 'public policy' is to be narrowly interpreted.[11] Public policy is intended to encompass only the rules that ensure the basic principles of a legal system[12] and an award may only be set aside for infringement of public policy where it is contrary to basic legal values, not merely for factual incorrectness.[13] Limited examples of the violation of public policy from international case-law decided under the Model Law has held that where an award was so arbitrary and based on facts so distorted that it would violate generally accepted fundamental judicial principles;[14] where there were allegations of witness intimidation;[15] or where there was an evident lack of impartiality on the part of an arbitral tribunal.[16] In addition, an award that gives effect to a contract that offends European competition law is to be regarded as in violation of public policy in all European Union Member States.[17] Examples from international case-law where it was held that no violation of public policy occurred include where an award required payment in a foreign currency;[18] where there was a minor procedural infringement by an arbitral tribunal;[19] where an incorrect method of calculation was used by an arbitral tribunal in making it award;[20] and where an award enforced a penalty provision in a contract.[21]

---

[1] Model Law, Art 34(2)(b)(i).

[2] Model Law, Art 1(5). For a discussion of the concept of 'arbitrability' in international commercial arbitration, see Born, *International Commercial Arbitration* (1st ed, Kluwer Law International, Alphen aan den Rijn, 2009) p 767.

[3] Constitution of Ireland, Art 38.

[4] Patents Act 1992, s 7.

[5] Patents Act 1992, s 57.

[6] For a discussion on the arbitrability of patents and trade marks, see Blessing, "Arbitrability of Intellectual Property Disputes" (1996) *Arbitration International* p 200.

[7] See *Soleimany v Soleimany* [1999] QB 785, where the English Court of Appeal stated at p 797 that the courts should "not recognise an agreement between ... highwaymen to arbitrate their difference any more than it would recognise the original agreement to split the proceeds".

[8] Model Law, Art 34(2)(b)(ii).

(*Continued*)

[9] Arbitration Act 2010, s 8(1).
[10] UNCITRAL Commission Report, A/40/17, Art 34, para 296-297.
[11] CLOUT Case 391 – Canada/Superior Court of Justice: *Re Corporacion Transnacional de Inversiones, SA de CV et al and STET International, SpA et al* (22 September 1999); and CLOUT Case 599 – Hong Kong/High Court of Hong Kong: *Hebei Import & Export Corp v Polytek Engineering Co Ltd* (9 February 1999).
[12] CLOUT Case 1068 – Croatia/Supreme Court of the Republic of Croatia: *Gž 2/08-2* (30 May 2008).
[13] CLOUT Case 868 – Germany/Highest Regional Court of Bavaria: *4 Z Sch 23/02* (20 March 2003).
[14] CLOUT Case 667 – Germany/Highest Regional Court of Cologne: *9 Sch 19/02* (26 November 2002).
[15] CLOUT Case 687 – Hong Kong/High Court of Hong Kong: *JJ Agro Industries (P) Ltd v Texuna International Ltd* (12 August 1992), where it was alleged by a defendant that its main witness was kidnapped and forced into making a false affidavit in arbitral proceedings. A stay was placed on court enforcement of the award until evidence could be taken regarding the allegations of kidnapping.
[16] CLOUT Case 972 – Spain/Madrid Provincial High Court: *89/2005* (9 May 2005); and CLOUT Case 973 – Spain/Madrid Provincial High Court: *381/2005* (31 March 2005).
[17] *Eco Swiss China Time Ltd v Benetton International N.V.* [1999] Case C-126/97 (European Court of Justice). For a discussion of the effect of the decision of the European Court of Justice in *Eco Swiss China Time Ltd v Benetton International N.V*, see Leonard and Daly, "Eco Swiss – Weakening the UNCITRAL Model Law" (2005) *Irish Journal of European Law* p 259.
[18] CLOUT Case 149 – Russian Federation/Moscow City Court: *No court reference/unidentified parties* (18 September 1995).
[19] CLOUT Case 146 – Russian Federation/Moscow City Court: *No court reference/unidentified parties* (10 November 1994).
[20] CLOUT Case 444 – Germany/Highest Regional Court of Dresden: *11 Sch 08/01* (8 May 2001).
[21] *Amaltal Corp Ltd v Maruha (NZ) Corp Ltd* [2004] 2 NZLR 614 (Court of Appeal of New Zealand).

The grounds to set aside an award are discretionary in nature: The grounds to set aside an award, whether party grounds or *ex officio* grounds, are discretionary not mandatory in nature.[1] As commentators have noted "a court may annul an award if one or more of the [a]rticle 34(2) grounds are satisfied, but the court is not mandatorily required to annul the award, even where one of the grounds applies".[2] However, in most cases the existence of one of the grounds will be sufficient for a court to set aside an award.[3]

---

[1] Model Law, Art 34(2).
[2] Born, *International Commercial Arbitration* (1st ed, Kluwer Law International, Alphen aan den Rijn, 2009) p 2563.
[3] *ibid,* p 2563.

Time limit for setting aside an award: The Model Law provides that a party may apply to set aside an award within three months from the date of receipt of the award. Where an application has been made under Art 33 for correction or interpretation of an award, the time limit commences from the date on which that request had been disposed of by the arbitral tribunal.[1] International case-law decided under the Model Law has held that the time limit is to be strictly enforced and a party will not be permitted to raise new grounds for setting aside an award that were not in its original application outside the three-month time limit.[2]

In Ireland, the Act amends the time limit provided by the Model Law within which a party can apply to set aside an award on public policy grounds from three months from the date of receipt of the award[3] to 56 days from date on which the circumstances giving rise to the application became known or ought reasonably to have become known to the party concerned.[4] The rationale for this amendment is to ensure that a party may seek redress where circumstances giving rise to challenge on public policy grounds become apparent only some time after an award is received.[5]

---

[1] Model Law, Art 34(3).

[2] CLOUT Case 566 – Singapore/Singapore High Court: *ABC Co v XYZ Co Ltd* (8 May 2003); and CLOUT Case 744 – New Zealand/High Court, Wellington Registry: *Downer-Hill Joint Venture v The Government of Fiji* (24 August 2004).

[3] Model Law, Art 34(3).

[4] Arbitration Act 2010, s 12.

[5] Arbitration Bill 2008: Hearing before Select Committee on Justice, Equality, Defence and Women's Rights, Dáil Debate, 23 April 2009 (statement of Dermot Ahern, the then Minister for Justice, Equality and Law Reform).

Waiver of right to apply to set aside an award: International case-law decided under the Model Law has held that a party may waive its right to apply to set aside an award in the following circumstances:

1. Where it has agreed to prohibit any court application other than to enforce an award;[1]
2. Where it failed to make clear its objection to the jurisdiction of an arbitral tribunal as soon as they are known[2] or where it refused to take part in arbitral proceedings;[3] and
3. By estoppel, where it made an assertion during arbitral proceedings that it later seeks to deny.[4]

---

[1] *Noble China Inc v Lei* (1998) 42 OR (3d) 69 (Ontario Court of Justice).

[2] CLOUT Case 148 – Russian Federation/Moscow City Court: *No court reference/unidentified parties* (10 February 1995).

[3] CLOUT Case 391 – Canada/Superior Court of Justice: *Re Corporacion Transnacional de Inversiones, SA de CV et al and STET International, SpA et al* (22 September 1999).

[4] CLOUT Case 448 – Hong Kong/High Court of Hong Kong: *Sam Ming City Forestry Economic Co v Lam Pun Hung Trading as Henry Company* (27 June 2001).

Power of the High Court to remit an award: When asked to set aside an award, the High Court may, where appropriate and so requested by a party, suspend the setting aside proceedings and remit the award to the arbitral tribunal in order to give the arbitral tribunal an opportunity to resume the arbitral proceedings or to take action to eliminate the grounds for setting aside the award.[1] The *travaux préparatoires* (of which Irish courts are permitted to take judicial notice when interpreting provisions of the Model Law)[2] suggest that the power to remit an award "would enable the arbitral tribunal to cure certain defects which otherwise would necessarily lead to the setting aside of the award".[3]

The judicial power to remit an award for the reconsideration of an arbitral tribunal is familiar in an Irish context, as the Arbitration Acts 1954-1998[4] permitted the High Court to remit an award in certain circumstances.[5] It is likely that the High Court will utilise the power to remit an award under the Model Law in order to permit an arbitral tribunal to cure defects in an award. For example, in a recent case decided under the Model Law, the High Court stated, that in circumstances where the parties believed there to be a lack of clarity in an award that "the logical and sensible course for the parties to adopt would be to avail of the [arbitral tribunal's] invitation to make further submission to [it]".[6] However, international case-law has held that the power to remit an award cannot permit an arbitral tribunal to consider a question that had not originally been considered;[7] and has held that power to remit cannot permit an arbitral tribunal to hear fresh evidence on the merits of a matter.[8]

---

[1] Model Law, Art 34(4).

[2] Arbitration Act 2010, s 8(1).

[3] UNCITRAL Commission Report, A/40/17, Art 34, para 306.

[4] Arbitration Act 1954, s 36.

[5] Arbitration Act 1954, s 36. Although the circumstances were not specified under the Arbitration Acts 1954-1998, case-law has held that a court may remit an award where there was a patent error of calculation; where an award was ambiguous or uncertain; where the arbitral tribunal itself sought to rectify an error; and, in certain circumstance, where new evidence had become available. In *Keenan v Shield Insurance Co Ltd* [1988] 1 IR 89, the Supreme Court also stated that the courts possess the power to remit an award at common law. However, some commentators believe this statement to be incorrect. See Simms, "Court intervention in the arbitration process at common law and under the Arbitration Act 1954" (2005) *Commercial Law Practitioner* p 13.

[6] *CIE v Spencer Dock Development Company Ltd* [2011] IEHC 185, where neither the applicant nor respondent sought relief contemplated by the Act or the Model Law. The applicant sought an order directing the respondents to comply with an award rather than enforce the award and the respondent in oral submissions sought to refer any new dispute created by the application to arbitration under Model Law, Art 8. The High Court (Laffoy J) rejected the applicant's application and also held that Model Law, Art 8 can have no application after arbitral proceedings have taken place but where the parties are not *ad idem* as to the effect of an award. While not formally ordering that the award be remitted to the arbitral tribunal the High Court indicated that the parties should accept the arbitral tribunal's invitation to make further submissions to it.

[7] CLOUT Case 12 – Canada/Federal Court of Canada: *D Frampton & Co Ltd v Sylvio Thibeault and Navigation Harvey & Frères Inc* (7 April 1988).

[8] CLOUT Case 391 – Canada/Superior Court of Justice: *Re Corporacion Transnacional de Inversiones, SA de CV et al and STET International, SpA et al* (22 September 1999).

Procedure for setting aside an award: An application made to the High Court to set aside an award is made in a summary manner and must be commenced by originating notice of motion grounded on affidavit.[1] An application must be entitled in the matter of the arbitral proceedings to which it relates and in the matter of the Act.[2] An application must name as respondent the party to the arbitral proceedings.[3] An arbitrator or arbitral tribunal should not be joined as a party to any application to the High Court to fulfil its supervisory functions in connection with arbitral proceedings.[4] However, Irish case-law has held that an error in procedure may not be fatal to an application to the High Court for it to fulfil its supervisory functions.[5]

---

[1] Rules of the Superior Courts, Ord 56, r 3(1).

[2] Rules of the Superior Courts, Ord 56, r (2)1.

[3] Rules of the Superior Courts, Ord 56, r 2(1).

[4] *FBD Insurance plc v Connors* [2011] IEHC 184.

[5] *ibid*, where the applicant commenced an application by special summons rather than originating notice of motion. The High Court (Laffoy J) held that it was appropriate to hear the application notwithstanding the defect in the procedure adopted, particularly as the respondents offered no opposition to the approach adopted.

Chapter VIII

Recognition and Enforcement of Awards

Article 35.—Recognition and enforcement

(1) An arbitral award, irrespective of the country in which it was made, shall be recognized as binding and, upon application in writing to the competent court, shall be enforced subject to the provisions of this article and of article 36.

(2) The party relying on an award or applying for its enforcement shall supply the original award or a copy thereof. If the award is not made in an official language of this State, the court may request the party to supply a translation thereof into such language.

Definitions

'award': Arbitration Act 2010, s 2(1); 'court': Model Law, Art 2(c).

Notes

Recognition and enforcement of an award: This article provides that an award must be recognised as binding[1] and must be enforced by the court of competent jurisdiction in a State enacting the Model Law, irrespective of the country in which the award was issued subject to only limited grounds for refusing recognition and enforcement thereof.[2] In Ireland the court of competent jurisdiction is the High Court.[3] The Model Law specifies limited grounds for refusing recognition and enforcement of an award.[4] These grounds are exhaustive and the High Court may only refuse recognition and enforcement of an award for the reasons set out by the Model Law.[5] Recognition and enforcement of an award may not be refused for some reason not specified in the Model Law under the courts' inherent jurisdiction. Commentators have noted that "[t]his means that unless the High Court has been accorded a specific role by the [Model Law], then it cannot intervene; inherent jurisdiction and other vestiges of the past are swept away".[6]

---

[1] The *travaux préparatoires* suggest the distinction between recognition and enforcement of an award is that "[w]hile an award would be enforced only on application by a party, recognition was an abstract legal effect which could obtain automatically without being requested by a party". UNCITRAL Fifth Working Group Report, A/CN.9/246, Art 35, para 146.

[2] Model Law, Art 35(1).

[3] Arbitration Act 2010, s 9(1)(c).

[4] Model Law, Art 36(1).

[5] Model Law, Art 5.

[6] Reichert, "Security for Costs in Arbitration – A New Landscape in Ireland" (2010) *Arbitration and ADR Review* p 130.

No applicability to arbitral proceedings which took place in Ireland: An award cannot be recognised and enforced pursuant to this article where the arbitral proceedings took place in Ireland.[1] Instead, a party seeking to enforce an award where Ireland was the place of arbitration may do so either by action or by leave of the High Court in the same manner as a judgment of the High Court.[2] An award made where Ireland was the place of arbitration is automatically recognised as binding for all purposes on the parties.[3]

[1] Arbitration Act 2010, s 23(4).
[2] Arbitration Act 2010, s 23(1).
[3] Arbitration Act 2010, s 23(2).

Procedure for enforcing an award: An application made to the High Court to enforce an award pursuant to this article is made in a summary manner by way of originating notice of motion grounded on affidavit.[1] An application must be entitled in the matter of the arbitral proceedings to which it relates and in the matter of the Act.[2] An application must name as respondent the parties to the arbitral proceedings.[3] An arbitrator or arbitral tribunal should not be joined as a party to any application to the High Court to enforce an award.[4] However, Irish case law has held that an error in procedure may not be fatal to an application to the High Court for it to fulfil its supervisory functions.[5]

Where leave to enforce is granted the High Court will enter a judgment "in the terms of the award".[6] Where enforcement of a partial award is sought there must be an order of an arbitral tribunal separately disposing of the partial award.[7]

[1] Rules of the Superior Courts, Ord 56, r 3(1)(k).
[2] Rules of the Superior Courts, Ord 56, r (2)1.
[3] Rules of the Superior Courts, Ord 56, r 2(1).
[4] *FBD Insurance plc v Connors* [2011] IEHC 184.
[5] *ibid*, where the applicant commenced an application by special summons rather than originating notice of motion. The High Court (Laffoy J) held that it was appropriate to hear the application notwithstanding the defect in the procedure adopted, particularly as the respondents offered no opposition to the approach adopted.
[6] Arbitration Act 2010, s 23(1).
[7] *Danish Polish Telecommunication Group I/S v Telekomunikacja Polska SA* [2011] IEHC 369, where the High Court (Finlay Geoghegan J) held that the High Court had no jurisdiction to give leave to enforce a partial award in circumstances where there was no order of the arbitral tribunal separately directing payment of the partial amount sought.

Formal requirements for enforcing an award: A party seeking to enforce an award must supply either an original or a copy of the award and, where an award is made in a language other than in the English language or the Irish language, the High Court may request a translation of the award.[1] As it is not necessary for a party relying on an award to supply a copy of the arbitration agreement, it is uncertain whether case-law decided under the Arbitration Acts 1954-1998 that required a court called upon to enforce an award had to

(*Continued*)

satisfy itself that there was a valid arbitration agreement will be followed under the Act and the Model Law.[2]

[1] Model Law, Art 35(2).

[2] See *Cremer (Peter) GmbH v Co-Operative Molasses Traders Ltd* [1985] ILRM 564, where the Supreme Court (Finlay CJ) stated that a court called upon to enforce an award "must first be satisfied that the document or decision sought to be enforced is, within the meaning of [the Arbitration Acts 1954-1998], an award made in pursuance of an arbitration agreement within the meaning of that [the Arbitration Acts 1954-1998]. In determining that issue the court cannot rely, of course, on any decision reached by the arbitral authority that an arbitration agreement had been reached, nor is it, however, in my view, in any way debarred from reaching a decision on that issue by reason of the existence in the award of a decision by the arbitral authority that an arbitration agreement exists". See also *Kastrup Trae-Aluvinduet A/S v Aluwood Concepts Ltd* [2009] IEHC 577. For a recent example of where a full *de novo* hearing on the existence of a valid arbitration agreement was conducted in the context of an application for recognition and enforcement of an award under the New York Convention see *Dallah Real Estate Co v The Ministry of Religious Affairs of Pakistan* [2011] 1 AC 763, which is a decision of the UK Supreme Court.

Article 36.—Grounds for refusing recognition or enforcement

(1) Recognition or enforcement of an arbitral award, irrespective of the country in which it was made, may be refused only:

(a) at the request of the party against whom it is invoked, if that party furnishes to the competent court where recognition or enforcement is sought proof that:

(i) a party to the arbitration agreement referred to in article 7 was under some incapacity; or the said agreement is not valid under the law to which the parties have subjected it or, failing any indication thereon, under the law of the country where the award was made; or

(ii) the party against whom the award is invoked was not given proper notice of the appointment of an arbitrator or of the arbitral proceedings or was otherwise unable to present his case; or

(iii) the award deals with a dispute not contemplated by or not falling within the terms of the submission to arbitration, or it contains decisions on matters beyond the scope of the submission to arbitration, provided that, if the decisions on matters submitted to arbitration can be separated from those not so submitted, that part of the award which contains decisions on matters submitted to arbitration may be recognized and enforced; or

(iv) the composition of the arbitral tribunal or the arbitral procedure was not in accordance with the agreement of the parties or, failing such agreement, was not in accordance with the law of the country where the arbitration took place; or

(v) the award has not yet become binding on the parties or has been set aside or suspended by a court of the country in which, or under the law of which, that award was made; or

(b) if the court finds that:

(i) the subject-matter of the dispute is not capable of settlement by arbitration under the law of this State; or

(ii) the recognition or enforcement of the award would be contrary to the public policy of this State.

(2) If an application for setting aside or suspension of an award has been made to a court referred to in paragraph (1)(a)(v) of this article, the court where recognition or enforcement is sought may, if it considers it proper, adjourn its decision and may also, on the application of the party claiming recognition or enforcement of the award, order the other party to provide appropriate security.

Definitions

'arbitration': Arbitration Act 2010, s 2(1) and Model Law, Art 2(a); 'arbitration agreement': Arbitration Act 2010, s 2(1) and Model Law, Art 7(1)(Option 1); 'arbitral tribunal': Model Law, Art 2(b); 'award': Arbitration Act 2010, s 2(1); 'court': Model Law, Art 2(c).

Notes

Recognition and enforcement of an award: An award must be automatically recognised as binding and must be enforced by the court of competent jurisdiction in a State enacting the Model Law, irrespective of the country in which the award was issued.[1] In Ireland, the court of competent jurisdiction for the purposes of enforcing an award is the High Court.[2] This article specifies limited grounds for refusing recognition and enforcement of an award.[3] These grounds are exhaustive and the High Court may only refuse recognition and enforcement of an award for the reasons set out by the Model Law.[4] Recognition and enforcement of an award may not be refused for some reason not specified in the Model Law under the courts' inherent jurisdiction. Commentators have noted that "[t]his means that unless the High Court has been accorded a specific role by the [Model Law], then it cannot intervene; inherent jurisdiction and other vestiges of the past are swept away".[5] The grounds for refusing recognition and enforcement of an award are bifurcated into:

1. Party grounds to set aside an award, which require the party challenging the award to prove;[6] and
2. *Ex officio* grounds, which a court may find on its own motion without the party challenging the award having the burden of proof.[7]

Objections similar to those which may be raised in the context of setting aside an award[8] may also be raised in the context of refusing recognition and enforcement of an award.[9] However, since the connection between an award and an enforcing State may be weaker than that between an award and State in which arbitral proceedings took place, arguments for refusing recognition and enforcement may have to overcome an even higher hurdle. The US Supreme Court stated in the context of enforcement proceedings under the New York Convention:

(*Continued*)

"international comity, respect for the capacities of foreign and transnational tribunals, and sensitivity to the need of the international system for predictability in the resolution of disputes require that we enforce the parties' agreement, even assuming that a contrary result would be forthcoming in a domestic context".[10]

[1] Model Law, Art 35(1).
[2] Arbitration Act 2010, s 9(1)(c).
[3] Model Law, Art 36(1).
[4] Model Law, Art 5.
[5] Reichert, "Security for Costs in Arbitration – A New Landscape in Ireland" (2010) *Arbitration and ADR Review* p 130.
[6] Model Law, Art 36(1)(a).
[7] Model Law, Art 36(1)(b).
[8] Model Law, Art 34(2).
[9] Model Law, Art 36(1).
[10] *Mitsubishi Motors Corp v Soler Chrysler-Plymouth Inc* (1985) 473 US 614 at 629.

No applicability to arbitral proceedings which took place in Ireland: As an award cannot be recognised and enforced pursuant to Art 35 of the Model Law where Ireland was the place of arbitration, the grounds for refusal of recognition and enforcement set out in this article also have no effect where Ireland was the place of arbitration.[1] Instead, a party that wishes to take recourse against an award where Ireland was the place of arbitration must apply to set aside the award.[2] Unless set aside, an award made where Ireland was the place of arbitration is automatically recognised as binding for all purposes on the parties.[3]

[1] Arbitration Act 2010, s 23(4).
[2] Model Law, Art 34.
[3] Arbitration Act 2010, s 23(2).

Party grounds for refusing recognition or enforcement of an award: The Model Law specifies five grounds which a party challenging an award is required to prove in order for the High Court to refuse recognition or enforcement of an award:

1. That a party to an arbitration agreement was under some incapacity or where an arbitration agreement was not valid under the law to which the parties have subjected it or, failing any indication thereon, the law of Ireland.[1] Whether a party had capacity to enter into an arbitration agreement is not covered by the provisions of the Model Law. Therefore, the normal rules of contract law apply to determine whether or not a party had capacity to enter into the arbitration agreement.[2] In Ireland minors; intoxicated persons; and those suffering from mental illness do not typically have capacity to enter into a binding contract;[3]

2. That the party making the application was not given proper notice of the appointment of an arbitrator, or of the arbitral proceedings, or was otherwise unable to present its case.[4] The Model Law requires due process in arbitral

(*Continued*)

proceedings and provides that parties must be treated with equality and must be given a full opportunity to present their case.[5] In the context of setting aside an award,[6] commentators have noted that the "ground includes both procedural and substantive fairness, and thus it overlaps with the public policy ground".[7] In international case-law decided under the Model Law an example of a violation of due process in the context of the refusal of recognition or enforcement of an award occurred where a party was never served with a written communication notifying it of arbitral proceedings notwithstanding that service was deemed permissible in the State where the arbitral proceedings took place;[8]

3. That the award deals with a dispute not contemplated by or not falling within the terms of the submission to arbitration or contains decisions on matters beyond the scope of the submission to arbitration.[9] In the context of setting aside an award,[10] commentators have noted that "this ground is infrequently invoked, and it is even less frequently accepted by national courts to set an award aside";[11]

4. That the composition of the arbitral tribunal or the arbitral procedure was not in accordance with the agreement of the parties, unless such agreement was in conflict with a provision of the Act and the Model Law from which the parties cannot derogate, or, failing the agreement of the parties, that the composition of the arbitral tribunal or the arbitral procedure was not in accordance with the Act and the Model Law.[12] In the context of setting aside an award,[13] commentators have noted that "[t]his can be seen as a catch-all provision for procedural defects under the arbitration agreement or under the Model Law".[14] However, international case-law has held that a party must object to irregular constitution of an arbitral tribunal during arbitral proceedings or risk waiving its right to resist recognition or enforcement of an award;[15] and

5. That the award has not yet become binding on the parties or has been set aside or suspended by a court of the State in which the award was made.[16] While a similar provision of the New York Convention[17] has cause judicial debate over whether a court has discretion to enforcement an award which has been set aside in the State in where the arbitral proceedings took place,[18] the *travaux préparatoires* (of which Irish courts are permitted to take judicial notice when interpreting provisions of the Model Law)[19] suggest that "for the sake of certainty and predictability, the court should not be given such discretion and that that interpretation could be made clear using the wording 'shall be refused'".[20] Although some international case-law decided under the Model Law suggests there is discretion for a court called upon to enforce an award that has been set aside in the State in where the arbitral proceedings took place,[21] the better view is that courts are obliged to reject enforcement of an award that has been already set aside or suspended.[22]

---

[1] Model Law, Art 36(1)(a)(i).

[2] Brekoulakis and Shore in Mistelis, *Concise International Arbitration, UNCITRAL Model Law* (1st ed, Kluwer Law International, Alphen aan den Rijn, 2010) p 647.

(*Continued*)

[3] For a discussion on contractual capacity in Ireland, see McDermott, *Contract Law* (1st ed, Butterworth (Ireland) Ltd, Dublin, 2001) pp 887-915.
[4] Model Law, Art 36(1)(a)(ii).
[5] Model Law, Art 18.
[6] Model Law, Art 34(2).
[7] Brekoulakis and Shore in Mistelis, *Concise International Arbitration, UNCITRAL Model Law* (1st ed, Kluwer Law International, Alphen aan den Rijn, 2010) p 646.
[8] CLOUT Case 402 – Germany/Highest Regional Court of Bavaria: *4Z Sch 50/99* (16 March 2000).
[9] Model Law, Art 36(1)(a)(iii).
[10] Model Law, Art 34(2).
[11] Brekoulakis and Shore in Mistelis, *Concise International Arbitration, UNCITRAL Model Law* (1st ed, Kluwer Law International, Alphen aan den Rijn, 2010) p 647.
[12] Model Law, Art 36(1)(a)(iv).
[13] Model Law, Art 34(2).
[14] Binder, *International Commercial Arbitration and Conciliation in UNCITRAL Model Law Jurisdictions* (3rd ed, Sweet & Maxwell, London, 2010) p 383.
[15] CLOUT Case 76 – Hong Kong/High Court of Hong Kong: *China Nanhai Oil Joint Service Corporation, Shenzhen Branch v Gee Tai Holdings Co Ltd* (13 July 1994).
[16] Model Law, Art 36(1)(a)(v).
[17] The New York Convention, Art V(1)(e).
[18] See, for example, *In re Chromalloy Aeroservices* 939 F. Supp 907 (D.D.C. 1996), where a US Federal District Court enforced an award notwithstanding that it had been set aside by an Egyptian court where Egypt was the place of arbitration. The US Federal District Court cited the discretion in the New York Convention that a court "may" refuse enforcement if the award has been set aside and determined that, under US law, as there was a "no appeal" clause in the contract, the award should not have been set aside.
[19] Arbitration Act 2010, s 8(1).
[20] UNCITRAL Third Working Group Report, A/CN.9/233, Art 37 [*Model Law, art 36 in the final text*], para 139.
[21] CLOUT Case 88 – Hong Kong/High Court of Hong Kong: *Nanjing Cereals, Oils and Foodstuffs Import & Export Corporation v Luckmate Commodities Trading Ltd* (16 December 1994).
[22] CLOUT Case 372 – Germany/Highest Regional Court of Rostock: *1 Sch 3/99* (28 October 1999). For an endorsement of this view by commentators, see Brekoulakis and Shore in Mistelis, *Concise International Arbitration, UNCITRAL Model Law* (1st ed, Kluwer Law International, Alphen aan den Rijn, 2010) p 653.

Ex officio grounds for refusing recognition or enforcement of an award: The Model Law specifies two grounds which that the High Court may examine *ex officio* on its own motion in order to refuse recognition and enforcement of an award. The party challenging an award does not have the burden of proving these *ex officio* grounds:

1. That the subject-matter of the dispute is incapable of resolution by arbitration under Irish law.[1] The Model Law expressly reserves the concept of 'arbitrability' or whether a dispute is capable of resolution by arbitration (so-called 'arbitrability') to domestic law.[2] Categories of disputes which are incapable of resolution by

(*Continued*)

arbitration in Ireland include the prosecution of criminal offences;[3] disputes concerning the grant[4] or revocation[5] of patents and trade marks;[6] and disputes concerning contracts whose objects are illegal or contrary to public policy;[7] and

2. That the award is in conflict with public policy.[8] In the context of setting aside an award,[9] the *travaux préparatoires* (of which Irish courts are permitted to take judicial notice when interpreting provisions of the Model Law)[10] suggest that "[i]n discussing the term "public policy", it was understood that it was not equivalent to the political stance or international policies of a State but comprised the fundamental notions and principles of justice. ... Thus, instances such as corruption, bribery or fraud and similar serious cases would constitute a ground for setting aside".[11] International case-law has held that what is meant by the term 'public policy' should be narrowly interpreted.[12] Public policy is intended to encompass only the rules that ensure the basic principles of a legal system[13] and an award may only be set aside for infringement of public policy where it is the result of a procedure which differs from the fundamental principles of procedural law of the State of enforcement in such a way that it cannot be considered the result of a fair and constitutional procedure or because it contains substantial errors touching upon the very foundations of public and economic life.[14] An example of violation of public policy in the context of the refusal of recognition or enforcement of an award occurred where a party was never served with a written communication notifying it of the arbitral proceedings notwithstanding that such service was deemed permissible in the State where the arbitral proceedings took place.[15]

---

[1] Model Law, Art 34(2)(b)(i).

[2] Model Law, Art 1(5). For a discussion of the concept of 'arbitrability' in international commercial arbitration, see Born, *International Commercial Arbitration* (1st ed, Kluwer Law International, Alphen aan den Rijn, 2009) p 767.

[3] Constitution of Ireland, Art 38.

[4] Patents Act 1992, s 7.

[5] Patents Act 1992, s 57.

[6] For a discussion on the arbitrability of patents and trade marks, see Blessing, "Arbitrability of Intellectual Property Disputes" (1996) *Arbitration International* p 200.

[7] See *Soleimany v Soleimany* [1999] QB 785, where the English Court of Appeal stated at p 797 that the courts should "not recognise an agreement between ... highwaymen to arbitrate their difference any more than it would recognise the original agreement to split the proceeds".

[8] Model Law, Art 36(1)(b)(ii).

[9] Model Law, Art 34(2).

[10] Arbitration Act 2010, s 8(1).

[11] UNCITRAL Commission Report, A/40/17, Art 34, para 296-297.

[12] CLOUT Case 391 – Canada/Superior Court of Justice: *Re Corporacion Transnacional de Inversiones, SA de CV et al and STET International, SpA et al* (22 September 1999); and CLOUT Case 599 – Hong Kong/High Court of Hong Kong: *Hebei Import & Export Corp v Polytek Engineering Co Ltd* (9 February 1999).

[13] CLOUT Case 1068 – Croatia/Supreme Court of the Republic of Croatia: *Gž 2/08-2* (30 May 2008).

[14] CLOUT Case 371 – Germany/Highest Regional Court of Bremen: *(2) Sch 4/99* (30 September 1999).

[15] CLOUT CASE 402 – Germany/Highest Regional Court of Bavaria: *4Z Sch 50/99* (16 March 2000).

The grounds to refuse recognition and enforcement of an award are discretionary in nature: The grounds to refuse recognition and enforcement of an award, whether party grounds or *ex officio* grounds, are discretionary not mandatory in nature.[1] However, in most cases the existence of one of the grounds will be sufficient for a court to refuse recognition and enforcement of an award.[2]

[1] Model Law, Art 36(1).

[2] Born, *International Commercial Arbitration* (1st ed, Kluwer Law International, Alphen aan den Rijn, 2009) p 2563, in the context of setting aside an award.

Power of the High Court to evaluate foreign law in an application for enforcement of an award: When called upon to evaluate foreign law in the context of an application for recognition and enforcement of an award the test the High Court will apply requires it to first decide whether even if every question of foreign law was decided in favour of a party, would it provide a basis for refusing enforcement of the award. Where the High Court decides that it would provide a basis it will then have to hear the cross-examination of the foreign lawyers and decide whether as a matter of fact which party's experts are correct in their opinions as to the relevant legal questions. Where it decides to the contrary, then the matter is at an end as even with all of the foreign legal questions decided in favour a party, it would not provide a basis for refusing recognition and enforcement.[1]

[1] *Brostrom Tankers AB v Factorias Vulcano SA* [2004] 2 IR 191, which is a decision of the High Court (Kelly J) of an application for enforcement of an award under the New York Convention. The same reasoning was adopted by the High Court (Finlay Geoghegan J) in the context of an application for enforcement under the Act and the Model Law in *Danish Polish Telecommunication Group I/S v Telekomunikacja Polska SA* [2011] IEHC 369.

Waiver of right to resist recognition and enforcement of an award: International case-law decided under the Model Law has held that a party may waive its right to resist recognition and enforcement of an award in the following circumstances:

1. It has agreed not to oppose enforcement in an arbitration agreement;[1]
2. It refused to take part in arbitral proceedings or otherwise failed to make objection.[2] The High Court has held that in the context of an application for enforcement of an award under the New York Convention that "there is an onus on the party opposing enforcement to prove to the [High Court] that it raised grounds upon which it resists enforcement at the earliest opportunity before the [arbitral tribunal]";[3] and
3. By estoppel, where it participated in an arbitral proceedings without clearly reserving the right to object to an award in circumstances where the jurisdiction of the arbitral tribunal was later challenged.[4]

[1] CLOUT Case 351 – Canada/British Columbia Supreme Court: *Food Services of America Inc v Pan Pacific Specialties Ltd* (24 March 1997).

(*Continued*)

[2] CLOUT Case 436/CLOUT Case 437 – Germany/Highest Regional Court of Bavaria: *4Z Sch 17/98* (24 February 1999).
[3] *Kastrup Trae-Aluvinduet A/S v Aluwood Concepts Ltd* [2009] IEHC 577.
[4] CLOUT Case 76 – Hong Kong/High Court of Hong Kong: *China Nanhai Oil Joint Service Corporation, Shenzhen Branch v Gee Tai Holdings Co Ltd* (13 July 1994).

Arbitral tribunal's power to adjourn a decision pending an application to set aside and to require the provision of security: The High Court, as the Irish court of competent jurisdiction,[1] may adjourn its decision on an application for enforcement of an award where an application has been made to a court of the State in which the award was made to set aside or suspend an award.[2] When requested to adjourn an application for enforcement of an award, the High Court has held that it "must engage in a 'brief consideration' of the material before it and then decide whether [the party seeking to set aside or suspend the award] has demonstrate that it has reasonable grounds or a seriously arguable case for setting aside [the award in the State in which it was made]".[3] In addition, where an adjournment of an application for enforcement of an award is granted, the High Court may order a party to provide appropriate security[4] having regard to the estimate and nature of the assets against which a party may ultimately seek to enforce an award.[5]

[1] Arbitration Act 2010, s 9(1)(c).
[2] Model Law, Art 36(2).
[3] *Danish Polish Telecommunication Group I\S v Telekomunikacja Polska SA* [2011] IEHC 369.
[4] Model Law, Art 36(2).
[5] *Danish Polish Telecommunication Group I\S v Telekomunikacja Polska SA* [2011] IEHC 369.

Schedule 2

Text of 1958 Convention on the Recognition and Enforcement of Foreign Arbitral Awards

Article I

1. This Convention shall apply to the recognition and enforcement of arbitral awards made in the territory of a State other than the State where the recognition and enforcement of such awards are sought, and arising out of differences between persons, whether physical or legal. It shall also apply to arbitral awards not considered as domestic awards in the State where their recognition and enforcement are sought.

2. The term "arbitral awards" shall include not only awards made by arbitrators appointed for each case but also those made by permanent arbitral bodies to which the parties have submitted.

3. When signing, ratifying or acceding to this Convention, or notifying extension under article X hereof, any State may on the basis of reciprocity declare that it will apply the Convention to the recognition and enforcement of awards made only in the territory of another Contracting State. It may also declare that it will apply the Convention only to differences arising out of legal relationships, whether contractual or not, which are considered as commercial under the national law of the State making such declaration.

Article II

1. Each Contracting State shall recognise an agreement in writing under which the parties undertake to submit to arbitration all or any differences which have arisen or which may arise between them in respect of a defined legal relationship, whether contractual or not, concerning a subject matter capable of settlement by arbitration.

2. The term "agreement in writing" shall include an arbitral clause in a contract or an arbitration agreement, signed by the parties or contained in an exchange of letters or telegrams.

3. The court of a Contracting State, when seized of an action in a matter in respect of which the parties have made an agreement within the meaning of this article, shall, at the request of one of the parties, refer the parties to arbitration, unless it finds that the said agreement is null and void, inoperative or incapable of being performed.

Article III

Each Contracting State shall recognise arbitral awards as binding and enforce them in accordance with the rules of procedure of the territory where the award is relied upon, under the conditions laid down in the following articles. There shall not be imposed substantially more onerous conditions or higher fees or charges on the recognition or enforcement of arbitral awards to which this Convention applies than are imposed on the recognition or enforcement of domestic arbitral awards.

ARTICLE IV

1. To obtain the recognition and enforcement mentioned in the preceding article, the party applying for recognition and enforcement shall, at the time of the application, supply:

   (a) The duly authenticated original award or a duly certified copy thereof;

   (b) The original agreement referred to in article II or a duly certified copy thereof.

2. If the said award or agreement is not made in an official language of the country in which the award is relied upon, the party applying for recognition and enforcement of the award shall produce a translation of these documents into such language. The translation shall be certified by an official or sworn translator or by a diplomatic or consular agent.

ARTICLE V

1. Recognition and enforcement of the award may be refused, at the request of the party against whom it is invoked, only if that party furnishes to the competent authority where the recognition and enforcement is sought, proof that:

   (a) The parties to the agreement referred to in article II were, under the law applicable to them, under some incapacity, or the said agreement is not valid under the law to which the parties have subjected it or, failing any indication thereon, under the law of the country where the award was made; or

   (b) The party against whom the award is invoked was not given proper notice of the appointment of the arbitrator or of the arbitration proceedings or was otherwise unable to present his case; or

   (c) The award deals with a difference not contemplated by or not falling within the terms of the submission to arbitration, or it contains decisions on matters beyond the scope of the submission to arbitration, provided that, if the decisions on matters submitted to arbitration can be separated from those not so submitted, that part of the award which contains decisions on matters submitted to arbitration may be recognised and enforced; or

   (d) The composition of the arbitral authority or the arbitral procedure was not in accordance with the agreement of the parties, or, failing such agreement, was not in accordance with the law of the country where the arbitration took place; or

   (e) The award has not yet become binding on the parties, or has been set aside or suspended by a competent authority of the country in which, or under the law of which, that award was made.

2. Recognition and enforcement of an arbitral award may also be refused if the competent authority in the country where recognition and enforcement is sought finds that:

   (a) The subject matter of the difference is not capable of settlement by arbitration under the law of that country; or

   (b) The recognition or enforcement of the award would be contrary to the public policy of that country.

Article VI

If an application for the setting aside or suspension of the award has been made to a competent authority referred to in article V(1)(e), the authority before which the award is sought to be relied upon may, if it considers it proper, adjourn the decision on the enforcement of the award and may also, on the application of the party claiming enforcement of the award, order the other party to give suitable security.

Article VII

1. The provisions of the present Convention shall not affect the validity of multilateral or bilateral agreements concerning the recognition and enforcement of arbitral awards entered into by the Contracting States nor deprive any interested party of any right he may have to avail himself of an arbitral award in the manner and to the extent allowed by the law or the treaties of the country where such award is sought to be relied upon.
2. The Geneva Protocol on Arbitration Clauses of 1923 and the Geneva Convention on the Execution of Foreign Arbitral Awards of 1927 shall cease to have effect between Contracting States on their becoming bound and to the extent that they become bound, by this Convention.

Article VIII

1. This Convention shall be open until 31 December 1958 for signature on behalf of any Member of the United Nations and also on behalf of any other State which is or hereafter becomes a member of any specialised agency of the United Nations, or which is or hereafter becomes a party to the Statute of the International Court of Justice, or any other State to which an invitation has been addressed by the General Assembly of the United Nations.
2. This Convention shall be ratified and the instrument of ratification shall be deposited with the Secretary-General of the United Nations.

Article IX

1. This Convention shall be open for accession to all States referred to in article VIII.
2. Accession shall be effected by the deposit of an instrument of accession with the Secretary-General of the United Nations.

Article X

1. Any State may, at the time of signature, ratification or accession, declare that this Convention shall extend to all or any of the territories for the international relations of which it is responsible. Such a declaration shall take effect when the Convention enters into force for the State concerned.
2. At any time thereafter any such extension shall be made by notification addressed to the Secretary-General of the United Nations and shall take effect as from the ninetieth day after the day of receipt by the Secretary-General of the United Nations of this notification, or as from the date of entry into force of the Convention for the State concerned, whichever is the later.

3. With respect to those territories to which this Convention is not extended at the time of signature, ratification or accession, each State concerned shall consider the possibility of taking the necessary steps in order to extend the application of this Convention to such territories, subject, where necessary for constitutional reasons, to the consent of the Governments of such territories.

Article XI

In the case of a federal or non-unitary State, the following provisions shall apply:

(a) With respect to those articles of this Convention that come within the legislative jurisdiction of the federal authority, the obligations of the federal Government shall to this extent be the same as those of Contracting States which are not federal States;

(b) With respect to those articles of this Convention that come within the legislative jurisdiction of constituent states or provinces which are not, under the constitutional system of the federation, bound to take legislative action, the federal Government shall bring such articles with a favourable recommendation to the notice of the appropriate authorities of constituent states or provinces at the earliest possible moment;

(c) A federal State Party to this Convention shall, at the request of any other Contracting State transmitted through the Secretary-General of the United Nations, supply a statement of the law and practice of the federation and its constituent units in regard to any particular provision of this Convention, showing the extent to which effect has been given to that provision by legislative or other action.

Article XII

1. This Convention shall come into force on the ninetieth day following the date of deposit of the third instrument of ratification or accession.
2. For each State ratifying or acceding to this Convention after the deposit of the third instrument of ratification or accession, this Convention shall enter into force on the ninetieth day after deposit by such State of its instrument of ratification or accession.

Article XIII

1. Any Contracting State may denounce this Convention by a written notification to the Secretary-General of the United Nations. Denunciation shall take effect one year after the date of receipt of the notification by the Secretary-General.
2. Any State which has made a declaration or notification under article X may, at any time thereafter, by notification to the Secretary-General of the United Nations, declare that this Convention shall cease to extend to the territory concerned one year after the date of the receipt of the notification by the Secretary-General.
3. This Convention shall continue to be applicable to arbitral awards in respect of which recognition or enforcement proceedings have been instituted before the denunciation takes effect.

Article XIV

A Contracting State shall not be entitled to avail itself of the present Convention against other Contracting States except to the extent that it is itself bound to apply the Convention.

Article XV

The Secretary-General of the United Nations shall notify the States contemplated in article VIII of the following:

(a) Signatures and ratifications in accordance with article VIII;

(b) Accessions in accordance with article IX;

(c) Declarations and notifications under articles I, X and XI;

(d) The date upon which this Convention enters into force in accordance with article XII;

(e) Denunciations and notifications in accordance with article XIII.

Article XVI

1. This Convention, of which the Chinese, English, French, Russian and Spanish texts shall be equally authentic, shall be deposited in the archives of the United Nations.

2. The Secretary-General of the United Nations shall transmit a certified copy of this Convention to the States contemplated in article VIII.

Schedule 3

Text of 1965 Convention on the Settlement of Investment Disputes between States and Nationals of Other States

Preamble

The Contracting States

Considering the need for international cooperation for economic development, and the role of private international investment therein;

Bearing in mind the possibility that from time to time disputes may arise in connection with such investment between Contracting States and nationals of other Contracting States;

Recognising that while such disputes would usually be subject to national legal processes, international methods of settlement may be appropriate in certain cases;

Attaching particular importance to the availability of facilities for international conciliation or arbitration to which Contracting States and nationals of other Contracting States may submit such disputes if they so desire;

Desiring to establish such facilities under the auspices of the International Bank for Reconstruction and Development;

Recognising that mutual consent by the parties to submit such disputes to conciliation or to arbitration through such facilities constitutes a binding agreement which requires in particular that due consideration be given to any recommendation of conciliators, and that any arbitral award be complied with; and

Declaring that no Contracting State shall by the mere fact of its ratification, acceptance or approval of this Convention and without its consent be deemed to be under any obligation to submit any particular dispute to conciliation or arbitration,

Have agreed as follows:

Chapter I

International Centre for Settlement of Investment Disputes

Section 1

Establishment and Organisation

Article 1

(1) There is hereby established the International Centre for Settlement of Investment Disputes (hereinafter called the Centre).

(2) The purpose of the Centre shall be to provide facilities for conciliation and arbitration of investment disputes between Contracting States and nationals of other Contracting States in accordance with the provisions of this Convention.

Article 2

The seat of the Centre shall be at the principal office of the International Bank for Reconstruction and Development (hereinafter called the Bank). The seat may be moved to another place by decision of the Administrative Council adopted by a majority of two-thirds of its members.

Article 3

The Centre shall have an Administrative Council and a Secretariat and shall maintain a Panel of Conciliators and a Panel of Arbitrators.

Section 2

The Administrative Council

Article 4

(1) The Administrative Council shall be composed of one representative of each Contracting State. An alternate may act as representative in case of his principal's absence from a meeting or inability to act.

(2) In the absence of a contrary designation, each governor and alternate governor of the Bank appointed by a Contracting State shall be *ex officio* its representative and its alternate respectively.

Article 5

The President of the Bank shall be *ex officio* Chairman of the Administrative Council (hereinafter called the Chairman) but shall have no vote. During his absence or inability to act and during any vacancy in the office of President of the Bank, the person for the time being acting as President shall act as Chairman of the Administrative Council.

Article 6

(1) Without prejudice to the powers and functions vested in it by other provisions of this Convention, the Administrative Council shall

(a) adopt the administrative and financial regulations of the Centre;

(b) adopt the rules of procedure for the institution of conciliation and arbitration proceedings;

(c) adopt the rules of procedure for conciliation and arbitration proceedings (hereinafter called the Conciliation Rules and the Arbitration Rules);

(d) approve arrangements with the Bank for the use of the Bank's administrative facilities and services;

(e) determine the conditions of service of the Secretary-General and of any Deputy Secretary-General;

(f) adopt the annual budget of revenues and expenditures of the Centre;

(g) approve the annual report on the operation of the Centre.

The decisions referred to in sub-paragraphs (a), (b), (c) and (f) above shall be adopted by a majority of two-thirds of the members of the Administrative Council.

(2) The Administrative Council may appoint such committees as it considers necessary.

(3) The Administrative Council shall also exercise such other powers and perform such other functions as it shall determine to be necessary for the implementation of the provisions of this Convention.

Article 7

(1) The Administrative Council shall hold an annual meeting and such other meetings as may be determined by the Council, or convened by the Chairman, or convened by the Secretary-General at the request of not less than five members of the Council.

(2) Each member of the Administrative Council shall have one vote and, except as otherwise herein provided, all matters before the Council shall be decided by a majority of the votes cast.

(3) A quorum for any meeting of the Administrative Council shall be a majority of its members.

(4) The Administrative Council may establish, by a majority of two-thirds of its members, a procedure whereby the Chairman may seek a vote of the Council without convening a meeting of the Council. The vote shall be considered valid only if the majority of the members of the Council cast their votes within the time limit fixed by the said procedure.

Article 8

Members of the Administrative Council and the Chairman shall serve without remuneration from the Centre.

Section 3

The Secretariat

Article 9

The Secretariat shall consist of a Secretary-General, one or more Deputy Secretaries-General and staff.

Article 10

(1) The Secretary-General and any Deputy Secretary-General shall be elected by the Administrative Council by a majority of two-thirds of its members upon the nomination of the Chairman for a term of service not exceeding six years and shall be eligible for re-election. After consulting the members of the Administrative Council, the Chairman shall propose one or more candidates for each such office.

(2) The offices of Secretary-General and Deputy Secretary-General shall be incompatible with the exercise of any political function. Neither the Secretary-General nor any Deputy Secretary-General may hold any other employment or engage in any other occupation except with the approval of the Administrative Council.

(3) During the Secretary-General's absence or inability to act, and during any vacancy of the office of Secretary-General, the Deputy Secretary-General shall act as Secretary-General. If there shall be more than one Deputy Secretary-General, the Administrative Council shall determine in advance the order in which they shall act as Secretary-General.

Article 11

The Secretary-General shall be the legal representative and the principal officer of the Centre and shall be responsible for its administration, including the appointment of staff, in accordance with the provisions of this Convention and the rules adopted by the Administrative Council. He shall perform the function of registrar and shall have the power to authenticate arbitral awards rendered pursuant to this Convention, and to certify copies thereof.

Section 4

The Panels

Article 12

The Panel of Conciliators and the Panel of Arbitrators shall each consist of qualified persons, designated as hereinafter provided, who are willing to serve thereon.

Article 13

(1) Each Contracting State may designate to each Panel four persons who may but need not be its nationals.

(2) The Chairman may designate ten persons to each Panel. The persons so designated to a Panel shall each have a different nationality.

Article 14

(1) Persons designated to serve on the Panels shall be persons of high moral character and recognised competence in the fields of law, commerce, industry or finance, who may be relied upon to exercise independent judgment. Competence in the field of law shall be of particular importance in the case of persons on the Panel of Arbitrators.

(2) The Chairman, in designating persons to serve on the Panels, shall in addition pay due regard to the importance of assuring representation on the Panels of the principal legal systems of the world and of the main forms of economic activity.

Article 15

(1) Panel members shall serve for renewable periods of six years.

(2) In case of death or resignation of a member of a Panel, the authority which designated the member shall have the right to designate another person to serve for the remainder of that member's term.

(3) Panel members shall continue in office until their successors have been designated.

Article 16

(1) A person may serve on both Panels.

(2) If a person shall have been designated to serve on the same Panel by more than one Contracting State, or by one or more Contracting States and the Chairman, he shall be deemed to have been designated by the authority which first designated him or, if one such authority is the State of which he is a national, by that State.

(3) All designations shall be notified to the Secretary-General and shall take effect from the date on which the notification is received.

Section 5

Financing the Centre

Article 17

If the expenditure of the Centre cannot be met out of charges for the use of its facilities, or out of other receipts, the excess shall be borne by Contracting States which are members of the Bank in proportion to their respective subscriptions to the capital stock of the Bank, and by Contracting States which are not members of the Bank in accordance with rules adopted by the Administrative Council.

Section 6

Status, Immunities and Privileges

Article 18

The Centre shall have full international legal personality. The legal capacity of the Centre shall include the capacity

(a) to contract;

(b) to acquire and dispose of movable and immovable property;

(c) to institute legal proceedings.

Article 19

To enable the Centre to fulfil its functions, it shall enjoy in the territories of each Contracting State the immunities and privileges set forth in this Section.

Article 20

The Centre, its property and assets shall enjoy immunity from all legal process, except when the Centre waives this immunity.

Article 21

The Chairman, the members of the Administrative Council, persons acting as conciliators or arbitrators or members of a Committee appointed pursuant to paragraph (3) of Article 52, and the officers and employees of the Secretariat

(a) shall enjoy immunity from legal process with respect to acts performed by them in the exercise of their functions, except when the Centre waives this immunity;

(b) not being local nationals, shall enjoy the same immunities from immigration restrictions, alien registration requirements and national service obligations, the same facilities as regards exchange restrictions and the same treatment in respect of travelling facilities as are accorded by Contracting States to the representatives, officials and employees of comparable rank of other Contracting States.

Article 22

The provisions of Article 21 shall apply to persons appearing in proceedings under this Convention as parties, agents, counsel, advocates, witnesses or experts; provided, however, that sub-paragraph (b) thereof shall apply only in connection with their travel to and from, and their stay at, the place where the proceedings are held.

Article 23

(1 The archives of the Centre shall be inviolable, wherever they may be.

(2) With regard to its official communications, the Centre shall be accorded by each Contracting State treatment not less favourable than that accorded to other international organisations.

Article 24

(1) The Centre, its assets, property and income, and its operations and transactions authorised by this Convention shall be exempt from all taxation and customs duties. The Centre shall also be exempt from liability for the collection or payment of any taxes or customs duties.

(2) Except in the case of local nationals, no tax shall be levied on or in respect of expense allowances paid by the Centre to the Chairman or members of the Administrative Council, or on or in respect of salaries, expense allowances or other emoluments paid by the Centre to officials or employees of the Secretariat.

(3) No tax shall be levied on or in respect of fees or expense allowances received by persons acting as conciliators, or arbitrators, or members of a Committee appointed pursuant to paragraph (3) of Article 52, in proceedings under this Convention, if the sole jurisdictional basis for such tax is the location of the Centre or the place where such proceedings are conducted or the place where such fees or allowances are paid.

Chapter II

Jurisdiction of the Centre

Article 25

(1) The jurisdiction of the Centre shall extend to any legal dispute arising directly out of an investment, between a Contracting State (or any constituent subdivision or agency of a Contracting State designated to the Centre by that State) and a national of another Contracting State, which the parties to the dispute consent in writing to submit to the Centre. When the parties have given their consent, no party may withdraw its consent unilaterally.

(2) "National of another Contracting State" means:—

(a) any natural person who had the nationality of a Contracting State other than the State party to the dispute on the date on which the parties consented to submit such dispute to conciliation or arbitration as well as on the date on which the request was registered pursuant to paragraph (3) of Article 28 or paragraph (3) of Article 36, but does not include any person who on either date also had the nationality of the Contracting State party to the dispute; and

(b) any juridical person which had the nationality of a Contracting State other than the State party to the dispute on the date on which the parties consented to submit such dispute to conciliation or arbitration and any juridical person which had the nationality of the Contracting State party to the dispute on that date and which, because of foreign control, the parties have agreed should be treated as a national of another Contracting State for the purposes of this Convention.

(3) Consent by a constituent subdivision or agency of a Contracting State shall require the approval of that State unless that State notifies the Centre that no such approval is required.

(4) Any Contracting State may, at the time of ratification, acceptance or approval of this Convention or at any time thereafter, notify the Centre of the class or classes of disputes which it would or would not consider submitting to the jurisdiction of the Centre. The Secretary-General shall forthwith transmit such notification to all Contracting States. Such notification shall not constitute the consent required by paragraph (1).

Article 26

Consent of the parties to arbitration under this Convention shall, unless otherwise stated, be deemed consent to such arbitration to the exclusion of any other remedy. A Contracting State may require the exhaustion of local administrative or judicial remedies as a condition of its consent to arbitration under this Convention.

Article 27

(1) No Contracting State shall give diplomatic protection, or bring an international claim, in respect of a dispute which one of its nationals and another Contracting State shall have consented to submit or shall have submitted to arbitration under this Convention, unless such other Contracting State shall have failed to abide by and comply with the award rendered in such dispute.

(2) Diplomatic protection, for the purposes of paragraph (1), shall not include informal diplomatic exchanges for the sole purpose of facilitating a settlement of the dispute.

Chapter III

Conciliation

Section 1

Request for Conciliation

Article 28

(1) Any Contracting State or any national of a Contracting State wishing to institute conciliation proceedings shall address a request to that effect in writing to the Secretary-General who shall send a copy of the request to the other party.

(2) The request shall contain information concerning the issues in dispute, the identity of the parties and their consent to conciliation in accordance with the rules of procedure for the institution of conciliation and arbitration proceedings.

(3) The Secretary-General shall register the request unless he finds, on the basis of the information contained in the request, that the dispute is manifestly outside the jurisdiction of the Centre. He shall forthwith notify the parties of registration or refusal to register.

Section 2

Constitution of the Conciliation Commission

Article 29

(1) The Conciliation Commission (hereinafter called the Commission) shall be constituted as soon as possible after registration of a request pursuant to Article 28.

(2) (a) The Commission shall consist of a sole conciliator or any uneven number of conciliators appointed as the parties shall agree.

(b) Where the parties do not agree upon the number of conciliators and the method of their appointment, the Commission shall consist of three conciliators, one conciliator appointed by each party and the third, who shall be the president of the Commission, appointed by agreement of the parties.

Article 30

If the Commission shall not have been constituted within 90 days after notice of registration of the request has been dispatched by the Secretary-General in accordance with paragraph (3) of Article 28, or such other period as the parties may agree, the Chairman shall, at the request of either party and after consulting both parties as far as possible, appoint the conciliator or conciliators not yet appointed.

Article 31

(1) Conciliators may be appointed from outside the Panel of Conciliators, except in the case of appointments by the Chairman pursuant to Article 30.

(2) Conciliators appointed from outside the Panel of Conciliators shall possess the qualities stated in paragraph (1) of Article 14.

Section 3

Conciliation Proceedings

Article 32

(1) The Commission shall be the judge of its own competence.

(2) Any objection by a party to the dispute that that dispute is not within the jurisdiction of the Centre, or for other reasons is not within the competence of the Commission, shall be considered by the Commission which shall determine whether to deal with it as a preliminary question or to join it to the merits of the dispute.

Article 33

Any conciliation proceeding shall be conducted in accordance with the provisions of this Section and, except as the parties otherwise agree, in accordance with the Conciliation Rules in effect on the date on which the parties consented to conciliation. If any question of procedure arises which is not covered by this Section or the Conciliation Rules or any rules agreed by the parties, the Commission shall decide the question.

Article 34

(1) It shall be the duty of the Commission to clarify the issues in dispute between the parties and to endeavour to bring about agreement between them upon mutually acceptable terms. To that end, the Commission may at any stage of the proceedings and from time to time recommend terms of settlement to the parties. The parties shall cooperate in good faith with the Commission in order to enable the Commission to carry out its functions, and shall give their most serious consideration to its recommendations.

(2) If the parties reach agreement, the Commission shall draw up a report noting the issues in dispute and recording that the parties have reached agreement. If, at any stage of the proceedings, it appears to the Commission that there is no likelihood of agreement between the parties, it shall close the proceedings and shall draw up a report noting the submission of the dispute and recording the failure of the parties to reach agreement. If one party fails to appear or participate in the proceedings, the Commission shall close the proceedings and shall draw up a report noting that party's failure to appear or participate.

Article 35

Except as the parties to the dispute shall otherwise agree, neither party to a conciliation proceeding shall be entitled in any other proceeding, whether before arbitrators or in a court of law or otherwise, to invoke or rely on any views expressed or statements or admissions or offers of settlement made by the other party in the conciliation proceedings, or the report or any recommendations made by the Commission.

Chapter IV

Arbitration

Section 1

Request for Arbitration

Article 36

(1) Any Contracting State or any national of a Contracting State wishing to institute arbitration proceedings shall address a request to that effect in writing to the Secretary-General who shall send a copy of the request to the other party.

(2) The request shall contain information concerning the issues in dispute, the identity of the parties and their consent to arbitration in accordance with the rules of procedure for the institution of conciliation and arbitration proceedings.

(3) The Secretary-General shall register the request unless he finds, on the basis of the information contained in the request, that the dispute is manifestly outside the jurisdiction of the Centre. He shall forthwith notify the parties of registration or refusal to register.

Section 2

Constitution of the Tribunal

Article 37

(1) The Arbitral Tribunal (hereinafter called the Tribunal) shall be constituted as soon as possible after registration of a request pursuant to Article 36.

(2) (a) The Tribunal shall consist of a sole arbitrator or any uneven number of arbitrators appointed as the parties shall agree.

(b) Where the parties do not agree upon the number of arbitrators and the method of their appointment, the Tribunal shall consist of three arbitrators, one arbitrator appointed by each party and the third, who shall be the president of the Tribunal, appointed by agreement of the parties.

Article 38

If the Tribunal shall not have been constituted within 90 days after notice of registration of the request has been despatched by the Secretary-General in accordance with paragraph (3) of Article 36, or such other period as the parties may agree, the Chairman shall, at the request of either party and after consulting both parties as far as possible, appoint the arbitrator or arbitrators not yet appointed. Arbitrators appointed by the Chairman pursuant to this Article shall not be nationals of the Contracting State party to the dispute or of the Contracting State whose national is a party to the dispute.

Article 39

The majority of the arbitrators shall be nationals of States other than the Contracting State party to the dispute and the Contracting State whose national is a party to the dispute; provided, however, that the foregoing provisions of this Article shall not apply if the sole arbitrator or each individual member of the Tribunal has been appointed by agreement of the parties.

Article 40

(1) Arbitrators may be appointed from outside the Panel of Arbitrators, except in the case of appointments by the Chairman pursuant to Article 38.

(2) Arbitrators appointed from outside the Panel of Arbitrators shall possess the qualities stated in paragraph (1) of Article 14.

Section 3

Powers and Functions of the Tribunal

Article 41

(1) The Tribunal shall be the judge of its own competence.

(2) Any objection by a party to the dispute that that dispute is not within the jurisdiction of the Centre, or for other reasons is not within the competence of the Tribunal, shall be considered by the Tribunal which shall determine whether to deal with it as a preliminary question or to join it to the merits of the dispute.

Article 42

(1) The Tribunal shall decide a dispute in accordance with such rules of law as may be agreed by the parties. In the absence of such agreement, the Tribunal shall apply the law of the Contracting State party to the dispute (including its rules on the conflict of laws) and such rules of international law as may be applicable.

(2) The Tribunal may not bring in a finding of *non liquet* on the ground of silence or obscurity of the law.

(3) The provisions of paragraphs (1) and (2) shall not prejudice the power of the Tribunal to decide a dispute *ex aequo et bono* if the parties so agree.

Article 43

Except as the parties otherwise agree, the Tribunal may, if it deems it necessary at any stage of the proceedings,

(a) call upon the parties to produce documents or other evidence, and

(b) visit the scene connected with the dispute, and conduct such inquiries there as it may deem appropriate.

Article 44

Any arbitration proceeding shall be conducted in accordance with the provisions of this Section and, except as the parties otherwise agree, in accordance with the Arbitration Rules in effect on the date on which the parties consented to arbitration. If any question of procedure arises which is not covered by this Section or the Arbitration Rules or any rules agreed by the parties, the Tribunal shall decide the question.

Article 45

(1) Failure of a party to appear or to present his case shall not be deemed an admission of the other party's assertions.

(2) If a party fails to appear or to present his case at any stage of the proceedings the other party may request the Tribunal to deal with the questions submitted to it and to render an award. Before rendering an award, the Tribunal shall notify, and grant a period of grace to, the party failing to appear or to present its case, unless it is satisfied that that party does not intend to do so.

Article 46

Except as the parties otherwise agree, the Tribunal shall, if requested by a party, determine any incidental or additional claims or counter-claims arising directly out of the subject-matter of the dispute provided that they are within the scope of the consent of the parties and are otherwise within the jurisdiction of the Centre.

Article 47

Except as the parties otherwise agree, the Tribunal may, if it considers that the circumstances so require, recommend any provisional measures which should be taken to preserve the respective rights of either party.

Section 4

The Award

Article 48

(1) The Tribunal shall decide questions by a majority of the votes of all its members.

(2) The award of the Tribunal shall be in writing and shall be signed by the members of the Tribunal who voted for it.

(3) The award shall deal with every question submitted to the Tribunal, and shall state the reasons upon which it is based.

(4) Any member of the Tribunal may attach his individual opinion to the award, whether he dissents from the majority or not, or a statement of his dissent.

(5) The Centre shall not publish the award without the consent of the parties.

Article 49

(1) The Secretary-General shall promptly dispatch certified copies of the award to the parties. The award shall be deemed to have been rendered on the date on which the certified copies were dispatched.

(2) The Tribunal upon the request of a party made within 45 days after the date on which the award was rendered may after notice to the other party decide any question which it had

omitted to decide in the award, and shall rectify any clerical, arithmetical or similar error in the award. Its decision shall become part of the award and shall be notified to the parties in the same manner as the award. The periods of time provided for under paragraph (2) of Article 51 and paragraph (2) of Article 52 shall run from the date on which the decision was rendered.

Section 5

Interpretation, Revision and Annulment of the Award

Article 50

(1) If any dispute shall arise between the parties as to the meaning or scope of an award, either party may request interpretation of the award by an application in writing addressed to the Secretary-General.

(2) The request shall, if possible, be submitted to the Tribunal which rendered the award. If this shall not be possible, a new Tribunal shall be constituted in accordance with Section 2 of this Chapter. The Tribunal may, if it considers that the circumstances so require, stay enforcement of the award pending its decision.

Article 51

(1) Either party may request revision of the award by an application in writing addressed to the Secretary-General on the ground of discovery of some fact of such a nature as decisively to affect the award, provided that when the award was rendered that fact was unknown to the Tribunal and to the applicant and that the applicant's ignorance of that fact was not due to negligence.

(2) The application shall be made within 90 days after the discovery of such fact and in any event within three years after the date on which the award was rendered.

(3) The request shall, if possible, be submitted to the Tribunal which rendered the award. If this shall not be possible, a new Tribunal shall be constituted in accordance with Section 2 of this Chapter.

(4) The Tribunal may, if it considers that the circumstances so require, stay enforcement of the award pending its decision. If the applicant requests a stay of enforcement of the award in his application, enforcement shall be stayed provisionally until the Tribunal rules on such request.

Article 52

(1) Either party may request annulment of the award by an application in writing addressed to the Secretary-General on one or more of the following grounds:

   (a) that the Tribunal was not properly constituted;

   (b) that the Tribunal has manifestly exceeded its powers;

   (c) that there was corruption on the part of a member of the Tribunal;

   (d) that there has been a serious departure from a fundamental rule of procedure; or

   (e) that the award has failed to state the reasons on which it is based.

(2) The application shall be made within 120 days after the date on which the award was rendered except that when annulment is requested on the ground of corruption such application shall be made within 120 days after discovery of the corruption and in any event within three years after the date on which the award was rendered.

(3) On receipt of the request the Chairman shall forthwith appoint from the Panel of Arbitrators an ad hoc Committee of three persons. None of the members of the Committee shall have been a member of the Tribunal which rendered the award, shall be of the same nationality as any such member, shall be a national of the State party to the dispute or of the State whose national is a party to the dispute, shall have been designated to the Panel of Arbitrators by either of those States, or shall have acted as a conciliator in the same dispute. The Committee shall have the authority to annul the award or any part thereof on any of the grounds set forth in paragraph (1).

(4) The provisions of Articles 41-45, 48, 49, 53 and 54, and of Chapters VI and VII shall apply *mutatis mutandis* to proceedings before the Committee.

(5) The Committee may, if it considers that the circumstances so require, stay enforcement of the award pending its decision. If the applicant requests a stay of enforcement of the award in his application, enforcement shall be stayed provisionally until the Committee rules on such request.

(6) If the award is annulled the dispute shall, at the request of either party, be submitted to a new Tribunal constituted in accordance with Section 2 of this Chapter.

Section 6

Recognition and Enforcement of the Award

Article 53

(1) The award shall be binding on the parties and shall not be subject to any appeal or to any other remedy except those provided for in this Convention. Each party shall abide by and comply with the terms of the award except to the extent that enforcement shall have been stayed pursuant to the relevant provisions of this Convention.

(2) For the purposes of this Section, "award" shall include any decision interpreting, revising or annulling such award pursuant to Articles 50, 51 or 52.

Article 54

(1) Each Contracting State shall recognise an award rendered pursuant to this Convention as binding and enforce the pecuniary obligations imposed by that award within its territories as if it were a final judgement of a court in that State. A Contracting State with a federal constitution may enforce such an award in or through its federal courts and may provide that such courts shall treat the award as if it were a final judgement of the courts of a constituent state.

(2) A party seeking recognition or enforcement in the territories of a Contracting State shall furnish to a competent court or other authority which such State shall have designated for this purpose a copy of the award certified by the Secretary-General. Each Contracting State

shall notify the Secretary-General of the designation of the competent court or other authority for this purpose and of any subsequent change in such designation.

(3) Execution of the award shall be governed by the laws concerning the execution of judgements in force in the State in whose territories such execution is sought.

Article 55

Nothing in Article 54 shall be construed as derogating from the law in force in any Contracting State relating to immunity of that State or of any foreign State from execution.

Chapter V

Replacement and Disqualification of Conciliators and Arbitrators

Article 56

(1) After a Commission or a Tribunal has been constituted and proceedings have begun, its composition shall remain unchanged; provided, however, that if a conciliator or an arbitrator should die, become incapacitated, or resign, the resulting vacancy shall be filled in accordance with the provisions of Section 2 of Chapter III or Section 2 of Chapter IV.

(2) A member of a Commission or Tribunal shall continue to serve in that capacity notwithstanding that he shall have ceased to be a member of the Panel.

(3) If a conciliator or arbitrator appointed by a party shall have resigned without the consent of the Commission or Tribunal of which he was a member, the Chairman shall appoint a person from the appropriate Panel to fill the resulting vacancy.

Article 57

A party may propose to a Commission or Tribunal the disqualification of any of its members on account of any fact indicating a manifest lack of the qualities required by paragraph (1) of Article 14. A party to arbitration proceedings may, in addition, propose the disqualification of an arbitrator on the ground that he was ineligible for appointment to the Tribunal under Section 2 of Chapter IV.

Article 58

The decision on any proposal to disqualify a conciliator or arbitrator shall be taken by the other members of the Commission or Tribunal as the case may be, provided that where those members are equally divided, or in the case of a proposal to disqualify a sole conciliator or arbitrator, or a majority of the conciliators or arbitrators, the Chairman shall take that decision. If it is decided that the proposal is well-founded the conciliator or arbitrator to whom the decision relates shall be replaced in accordance with the provisions of Section 2 of Chapter III or Section 2 of Chapter IV.

Chapter VI

Cost of Proceedings

Article 59

The charges payable by the parties for the use of the facilities of the Centre shall be determined by the Secretary-General in accordance with the regulations adopted by the Administrative Council.

Article 60

(1) Each Commission and each Tribunal shall determine the fees and expenses of its members within limits established from time to time by the Administrative Council and after consultation with the Secretary-General.

(2) Nothing in paragraph (1) of this article shall preclude the parties from agreeing in advance with the Commission or Tribunal concerned upon the fees and expenses of its members.

Article 61

(1) In the case of conciliation proceedings the fees and expenses of members of the Commission as well as the charges for the use of the facilities of the Centre, shall be borne equally by the parties. Each party shall bear any other expenses it incurs in connection with the proceedings.

(2) In the case of arbitration proceedings the Tribunal shall, except as the parties otherwise agree, assess the expenses incurred by the parties in connection with the proceedings, and shall decide how and by whom those expenses, the fees and expenses of the members of the Tribunal and the charges for the use of the facilities of the Centre shall be paid. Such decision shall form part of the award.

Chapter VII

Place of Proceedings

Article 62

Conciliation and arbitration proceedings shall be held at the seat of the Centre except as hereinafter provided.

Article 63

Conciliation and arbitration proceedings may be held, if the parties so agree,

(a) at the seat of the Permanent Court of Arbitration or of any other appropriate institution, whether private or public, with which the Centre may make arrangements for that purpose; or

(b) at any other place approved by the Commission or Tribunal after consultation with the Secretary-General.

Chapter VIII

Disputes between Contracting States

Article 64

Any dispute arising between Contracting States concerning the interpretation or application of this Convention which is not settled by negotiation shall be referred to the International Court of Justice by the application of any party to such dispute, unless the States concerned agree to another method of settlement.

Chapter IX

Amendment

Article 65

Any Contracting State may propose amendment of this Convention. The text of a proposed amendment shall be communicated to the Secretary-General not less than 90 days prior to the meeting of the Administrative Council at which such amendment is to be considered and shall forthwith be transmitted by him to all the members of the Administrative Council.

Article 66

(1) If the Administrative Council shall so decide by a majority of two-thirds of its members, the proposed amendment shall be circulated to all Contracting States for ratification, acceptance or approval. Each amendment shall enter into force 30 days after dispatch by the depositary of this Convention of a notification to Contracting States that all Contracting States have ratified, accepted or approved the amendment.

(2) No amendment shall affect the rights and obligations under this Convention of any Contracting State or of any of its constituent subdivisions or agencies, or of any national of such State arising out of consent to the jurisdiction of the Centre given before the date of entry into force of the amendment.

Chapter X

Final Provisions

Article 67

This Convention shall be open for signature on behalf of States members of the Bank. It shall also be open for signature on behalf of any other State which is a party to the Statute of the International Court of Justice and which the Administrative Council, by a vote of two-thirds of its members, shall have invited to sign the Convention.

Article 68

(1) This Convention shall be subject to ratification, acceptance or approval by the signatory States in accordance with their respective constitutional procedures.

(2) This Convention shall enter into force 30 days after the date of deposit of the twentieth instrument of ratification, acceptance or approval. It shall enter into force for each State which subsequently deposits its instrument of ratification, acceptance or approval 30 days after the date of such deposit.

Article 69

Each Contracting State shall take such legislative or other measures as may be necessary for making the provisions of this Convention effective in its territories.

Article 70

This Convention shall apply to all territories for whose international relations a Contracting State is responsible, except those which are excluded by such State by written notice to the depositary of this Convention either at the time of ratification, acceptance or approval or subsequently.

Article 71

Any Contracting State may denounce this Convention by written notice to the depositary of this Convention. The denunciation shall take effect six months after receipt of such notice.

Article 72

Notice by a Contracting State pursuant to Articles 70 or 71 shall not affect the rights or obligations under this Convention of that State or of any of its constituent subdivisions or agencies or of any national of that State arising out of consent to the jurisdiction of the Centre given by one of them before such notice was received by the depositary.

Article 73

Instruments of ratification, acceptance or approval of this Convention and of amendments thereto shall be deposited with the Bank which shall act as the depositary of this Convention. The depositary shall transmit certified copies of this Convention to States members of the Bank and to any other State invited to sign the Convention.

Article 74

The depositary shall register this Convention with the Secretariat of the United Nations in accordance with Article 102 of the Charter of the United Nations and the Regulations thereunder adopted by the General Assembly.

Article 75

The depositary shall notify all signatory States of the following:

(a) signatures in accordance with Article 67;

(b) deposits of instruments of ratification, acceptance and approval in accordance with Article 73;

(c) the date on which this Convention enters into force in accordance with Article 68;

(d) exclusions from territorial application pursuant to Article 70;

(e) the date on which any amendment of this Convention enters into force in accordance with Article 66; and

(f) denunciations in accordance with Article 71.

Done at Washington in the English, French and Spanish languages, all three texts being equally authentic, in a single copy which shall remain deposited in the archives of the International Bank for Reconstruction and Development which has indicated by its signature below its agreement to fulfil the functions with which it is charged under this Convention.

Schedule 4

Text of 1927 Convention on the Execution of Foreign Arbitral Awards

Article 1

In the territories of any High Contracting Party to which the present Convention applies, an arbitral award made in pursuance of an agreement, whether relating to existing or future differences (hereinafter called "a submission to arbitration") covered by the Protocol on Arbitration Clauses, opened at Geneva on September 24th, 1923, shall be recognised as binding and shall be enforced in accordance with the rules of the procedure of the territory where the award is relied upon, provided that the said award has been made in a territory of one of the High Contracting Parties to which the present Convention applies and between persons who are subject to the jurisdiction of one of the High Contracting Parties.

To obtain such recognition or enforcement, it shall, further, be necessary:

(a) That the award has been made in pursuance of a submission to arbitration which is valid under the law applicable thereto;

(b) That the subject-matter of the award is capable of settlement by arbitration under the law of the country in which the award is sought to be relied upon;

(c) That the award has been made by the Arbitral Tribunal provided for in the submission to arbitration or constituted in the manner agreed upon by the parties and in conformity with the law governing the arbitration procedure;

(d) That the award has become final in the country in which it has been made, in the sense that it will not be considered as such if it is open to *opposition, appel or pourvoi en cassation* (in the countries where such forms of procedure exist) or if it is proved that any proceedings for the purpose of contesting the validity of the award are pending;

(e) That the recognition or enforcement of the award is not contrary to the public policy or to the principles of the law of the country in which it is sought to be relied upon.

Article 2

Even if the conditions laid down in Article 1 hereof are fulfilled, recognition and enforcement of the award shall be refused if the Court is satisfied:

(a) That the award has been annulled in the country in which it was made;

(b) That the party against whom it is sought to use the award was not given notice of the arbitration proceedings in sufficient time to enable him to present his case; or that, being under a legal incapacity, he was not properly represented;

(c) That the award does not deal with the differences contemplated by or falling within the terms of the submission to arbitration or that it contains decisions on matters beyond the scope of the submission to arbitration.

If the award has not covered all the questions submitted to the arbitral tribunal, the competent authority of the country where recognition or enforcement of the award is sought can, if it think fit, postpone such recognition or enforcement or grant it subject to such guarantee as that authority may decide.

Article 3

If the party against whom the award has been made proves that, under the law governing the arbitration procedure, there is a ground, other than the grounds referred to in Article 1 (a) and (c), and Article 2 (b) and (c), entitling him to contest the validity of the award in a Court of Law, the Court may, if it thinks fit, either refuse recognition or enforcement of the award or adjourn the consideration thereof, giving such party a reasonable time within which to have the award annulled by the competent tribunal.

Article 4

The party relying upon an award or claiming its enforcement must supply, in particular:

(1) The original award or a copy thereof duly authenticated, according to the requirements of the law of the country in which it was made;

(2) Documentary or other evidence to prove that the award has become final, in the sense defined in Article 1(d), in the country in which it was made;

(3) When necessary, documentary or other evidence to prove that the conditions laid down in Article 1, paragraph 1 and paragraph 2(a) and (c), have been fulfilled.

A translation of the award and of the other documents mentioned in this Article into the official language of the country where the award is sought to be relied upon may be demanded. Such translation must be certified correct by a diplomatic or consular agent of the country to which the party who seeks to rely upon the award belongs or by a sworn translator of the country where the award is sought to be relied upon.

Article 5

The provisions of the above Articles shall not deprive any interested party of the right of availing himself of an arbitral award in the manner and to the extent allowed by the law or the treaties of the country where such award is sought to be relied upon.

Article 6

The present Convention applies only to arbitral awards made after the coming into force of the Protocol on Arbitration Clauses, opened at Geneva on September 24th, 1923.

Article 7

The present Convention, which will remain open to the signature of all the signatories of the Protocol of 1923 on Arbitration Clauses, shall be ratified.

It may be ratified only on behalf of those Members of the League of Nations and non-Member States on whose behalf the Protocol of 1923 shall have been ratified.

Ratifications shall be deposited as soon as possible with the Secretary-General of the League of Nations, who will notify such deposit to all the signatories.

Article 8

The present Convention shall come into force three months after it shall have been ratified on behalf of two High Contracting Parties. Thereafter, it shall take effect, in the case of each High Contracting Party, three months after the deposit of the ratification on its behalf with the Secretary-General of the League of Nations.

Article 9

The present Convention may be denounced on behalf of any Member of the League or non-Member State. Denunciation shall be notified in writing to the Secretary-General of the League of Nations, who will immediately send a copy thereof, certified to be in conformity with the notification, to all the other Contracting Parties, at the same time informing them of the date on which he received it.

The denunciation shall come into force only in respect of the High Contracting Party which shall have notified it and one year after such notification shall have reached the Secretary-General of the League of Nations.

The denunciation of the Protocol on Arbitration Clauses shall entail, ipso facto, the denunciation of the present Convention.

Article 10

The present Convention does not apply to the Colonies, Protectorates or territories under suzerainty or mandate of any High Contracting Party unless they are specially mentioned.

The application of this Convention to one or more of such Colonies, Protectorates or territories to which the Protocol on Arbitration Clauses, opened at Geneva on September 24th, 1923, applies, can be effected at any time by means of a declaration addressed to the Secretary-General of the League of Nations by one of the High Contracting Parties.

Such declaration shall take effect three months after the deposit thereof.

The High Contracting Parties can at any time denounce the Convention for all or any of the Colonies, Protectorates or territories referred to above. Article 9 hereof applies to such denunciation.

Article 11

A certified copy of the present Convention shall be transmitted by the Secretary-General of the League of Nations to every Member of the League of Nations and to every non-Member State which signs the same.

SCHEDULE 5

TEXT OF 1923 PROTOCOL ON ARBITRATION CLAUSES

1. Each of the Contracting States recognises the validity of an agreement whether relating to existing or future differences between parties subject respectively to the jurisdiction of different Contracting States by which the parties to a contract agree to submit to arbitration all or any differences that may arise in connection with such contract relating to commercial matters or to any other matter capable of settlement by arbitration, whether or not the arbitration is to take place in a country to whose jurisdiction none of the parties is subject.

   Each Contracting State reserves the right to limit the obligation mentioned above to contracts which are considered as commercial under its national law. Any Contracting State which avails itself of this right will notify the Secretary-General of the League of Nations, in order that the other Contracting States may be so informed.

2. The arbitral procedure, including the constitution of the arbitral tribunal, shall be governed by the will of the parties and by the law of the country in whose territory the arbitration takes place.

   The Contracting States agree to facilitate all steps in the procedure which require to be taken in their own territories, in accordance with the provisions of their law governing arbitral procedure applicable to existing differences.

3. Each Contracting State undertakes to ensure the execution by its authorities and in accordance with the provisions of its national laws of arbitral awards made in its own territory under the preceding articles.

4. The tribunals of the Contracting Parties, on being seized of a dispute regarding a contract made between persons to whom Article 1 applies and including an arbitration agreement whether referring to present or future differences which is valid in virtue of the said article and capable of being carried into effect, shall refer the parties on the application of either of them to the decision of the arbitrators.

   Such reference shall not prejudice the competence of the judicial tribunals in case the agreement or the arbitration cannot proceed or becomes inoperative.

5. The present Protocol, which shall remain open for signature by all States, shall be ratified. The ratifications shall be deposited as soon as possible with the Secretary-General of the League of Nations, who shall notify such deposit to all the Signatory States.

6. The present Protocol will come into force as soon as two ratifications have been deposited. Thereafter it will take effect, in the case of each Contracting State, one month after the notification by the Secretary-General of the deposit of its ratification.

7. The present Protocol may be denounced by any Contracting State on giving one year's notice. Denunciation shall be effected by a notification addressed to the Secretary-General of the League, who will immediately transmit copies of such notification to all the other Signatory States and inform them of the date on which it was received. The denunciation shall take effect one year after the date on which it was notified to the Secretary-General, and shall operate only in respect of the notifying State.

8. The Contracting States may declare that their acceptance of the present Protocol does not include any or all of the under-mentioned territories: that is to say, their colonies, overseas possessions or territories, protectorates or the territories over which they exercise a mandate.

   The said States may subsequently adhere separately on behalf of any territory thus excluded. The Secretary-General of the League of Nations shall be informed as soon as possible of such adhesions. He shall notify such adhesions to all Signatory States. They will take effect one month after the notification by the Secretary-General to all Signatory States.

   The Contracting States may also denounce the Protocol separately on behalf of any of the territories referred to above. Article 7 applies to such denunciation.

   A certified copy of the present Protocol will be transmitted by the Secretary-General to all the Contracting States.

Schedule 6

Consequential Amendments to Other Acts

Section 29

Number and Year (1)	Short Title (2)	Provision affected (3)	Amendment (4)
No. 6 of 1957	Statute of Limitations 1957	Section 77	To delete "or orders, after the commencement of an arbitration, that the arbitration shall cease to have effect with respect to the dispute referred".
No. 3 of 1967	Landlord and Tenant (Ground Rents) Act 1967	Section 17	In subsection (5) substitute "*Sections 21* and *23* of the *Arbitration Act 2010* (and Articles 13 and 14 of the Model Law (within the meaning of the *Arbitration Act 2010*) as given the force of law in the State by that Act) for "Sections 29, 35, 36, 37 and 41 of the Arbitration Act, 1954".
No. 1 of 1992	Patents Act 1992	Section 74	In subsection (3) delete "section 35 of the Arbitration Act, 1954 (which relates to the statement of cases by arbitrators for the decision of the Court), shall not apply to the arbitration; but".
No. 28 of 2000	Copyright and Related Rights Act 2000	Section 367	In subsection (8) substitute "request the court under *section 9* of the *Arbitration Act 2010* to decide on the termination of the mandate of that arbitrator" for "apply to the court for the removal of that arbitrator under section 24 of the Arbitration Act, 1954,".

Order: 56

Arbitration: S.I. No.361 of 2010

1. (1) These Rules, which may be cited as the Rules of the Superior Courts (Arbitration) 2010, shall come into operation on the 17th day of August 2010.

   (2) These Rules shall be construed together with the Rules of the Superior Courts.

   (3) The Rules of the Superior Courts as amended by these Rules may be cited as the Rules of the Superior Courts 1986 to 2010.

2. Nothing in these Rules shall:

   (a) affect the validity of any step taken or any other thing done in any proceedings concerning any arbitration initiated before the repeal by section 4 of the Arbitration Act 2010 of the Arbitration Acts 1954 to 1998 (in this Article, the "repeal"), and any such proceedings shall, save where the court in those proceedings otherwise orders, be continued and completed as if these Rules had not been made;

   (b) require that any proceedings, whether or not pending before a court or before an arbitral tribunal at the time of the repeal, in respect of any right, privilege, obligation or liability acquired, accrued or incurred under the Arbitration Acts 1954 to 1998 be taken in accordance with these Rules and any proceedings taken under those Acts in respect of any such right, privilege, obligation or liability may be instituted, continued or enforced as if these Rules had not been made.

3. The Rules of the Superior Courts are amended:

. . . .

   (ii) by the substitution for Orders 56 and Order 56A of the following Order:

"Order 56

Arbitration

I. Preliminary and General

1. In this Order:

"the Act" means the Arbitration Act 2010;

"arbitration" and "arbitration agreement" each has the same meaning as in the Act;

"Model Law" means the UNCITRAL Model Law on International Commercial Arbitration (as adopted by the United Nations Commission on International Trade Law on 21 June 1985, with amendments as adopted by that Commission at its thirty-ninth session on 20 July 2006), the text of which is set out in Schedule 1 to the Act;

"party" includes the personal representative of a deceased party;

unless the context otherwise admits or requires, words and phrases in Part II of this Order have the same meanings as in the Act.

II. Applications to the Court concerning arbitrations

2. (1) Where an arbitration has been commenced, any application pursuant to this Order by a party to such arbitration concerning or affecting such arbitration shall be entitled in the matter of the arbitration to which it relates and in the matter of the Act. Any originating notice of motion in respect of any such application shall name as respondent the other party or parties to the reference. In the case of any application described in paragraph (d), (e) or (i) of sub-rule (1) of rule 3, and in any other case where the Court so directs, notice of the application shall be given to the arbitral tribunal, which shall not be a party to the proceedings.

(2) Where no arbitration has been commenced, any application pursuant to this Order by a person concerning or affecting an intended arbitration shall be entitled in the matter of an intended arbitration and in the matter of the Act. Any originating motion in respect of any such application shall name as respondent the intended other party or parties to the reference.

3. (1) Subject to sub-rules (2) and (3), any application or request to the Court for any of the following orders or reliefs by any party to a reference under an arbitration agreement in relation to an arbitration, or by any person in relation to an intended arbitration, may be made by originating notice of motion:

(a) for any interim measure of protection in relation to an arbitration or an intended arbitration under Article 9 of the Model Law; or

(b) to appoint an arbitrator pursuant to Article 11(3)(a) or 11(3)(b) of the Model Law; or

(c) to take the necessary measure pursuant to Article 11(4) of the Model Law in the event of a failure to act, an inability to reach agreement or a failure to perform a function under an appointment procedure agreed upon by the parties; or

(d) to decide on a challenge to an arbitrator pursuant to Article 13(3) of the Model Law (provided that the application is made within the period prescribed in that Article); or

(e) to decide on the termination of the mandate of an arbitrator pursuant to Article 14(1) of the Model Law; or

(f) to decide on a plea that the arbitral tribunal does not have jurisdiction pursuant to Article 16(3) of the Model Law (provided that the application is made within the period prescribed in that Article); or

(g) to recognise or to recognise and enforce an interim measure issued by an arbitral tribunal in accordance with Article 17 H(1), but subject to the provisions of Article 17 I, of the Model Law; or

(h) to issue any interim measure in relation to arbitration proceedings in accordance with Article 17 J of the Model Law; or

(i) to make an order in accordance with Article 34 of the Model Law (provided, in a case to which section 12 of the Act applies, the application is made within the period prescribed in that section); or

(j) for the leave of the Court to enforce or to enter judgment in respect of an award pursuant to section 23(1) of the Act; or

(k) to enforce an award in accordance with Article 35(1), but subject to the provisions of Articles 35 and 36, of the Model Law; or

(l) to enforce the pecuniary obligations imposed by an award, within the meaning of section 25 of the Act, under that section; or

(m) for any other relief under or in pursuance of the Act, for which provision is not otherwise made in this Order.

(2) Where an order has been made by the Court in proceedings begun by originating notice of motion in accordance with sub-rule (1), any application for any further order or relief mentioned in that sub-rule by any party to the same reference or arbitration may be made by notice of motion in the proceedings commenced by the originating motion referred to in sub-rule (1). In any such case, the provisions of rules 5 and 6 relating to an originating notice of motion shall apply to that notice of motion.

(3) Notwithstanding sub-rule (1), the Court may permit an application mentioned in paragraph (a) or (h) of sub-rule (1) to be made by originating motion ex parte and may hear any such application *ex parte*.

(4) An order on an application ex parte permitted to be made in a case referred to in sub-rule (3) may be made subject to such terms as to costs or otherwise, and subject to such undertaking, if any, as the Court may think just; and any party affected by such order may, within twenty eight days of receipt of notice of the making of such order, move by motion on notice to vary it or set it aside.

(5) An originating notice of motion or originating motion in any application requesting the Court to grant any interim measure of protection in accordance with Article 9 of the Model

Law or to issue any interim measure in accordance with Article 17 J of the Model Law shall specify the particular orders which the Court is requested to make.

4. (1) A request for an order under Article 8(1) of the Model Law or Article II.3 of the New York Convention shall be made by motion in the proceedings concerned and Order 52 shall apply to every such motion.

(2) Where relief by way of interpleader is granted, an application to direct the issue between the claimants to be determined by arbitration in pursuance of section 17 of the Act, may be made by any party at the hearing of the application or proceedings in which such relief is granted or at the conclusion of such hearing.

(3) An application under section 27(2) of the Act shall be by motion in the Bankruptcy proceedings brought in accordance with Part VIII of Order 76.

(4) A request to the Court under Article 27 of the Model Law for assistance in the taking of evidence may be made to the Court *ex parte* grounded on an affidavit and where the Court makes such an order, the provisions of Parts II and III of Order 39 shall apply *mutatis mutandis*.

5. Every originating notice of motion issued pursuant to this Order shall be returnable before, and shall be heard and determined by, the President of the High Court or a Judge of the High Court for the time being nominated by the President to perform the functions of the High Court referred to in section 9(2) of the Act.

6. (1) Subject, in the case of any proceedings which have been entered in the Commercial List, to the provisions of Order 63A and of any order made or direction given by the Court under that Order, the procedure specified in this rule shall apply to proceedings by originating notice of motion in accordance with this Order.

(2) Every originating notice of motion shall be grounded upon an affidavit sworn by or on behalf of the moving party. Each such grounding affidavit shall set out the basis upon which the moving party alleges that the Court has jurisdiction to grant the relief sought in the notice of motion.

(3) Copies of the originating notice of motion and of the grounding affidavit and of any exhibits thereto shall be served upon each respondent and, where required or directed under rule 2(1), shall be delivered to the arbitral tribunal, not later than fourteen days before the date fixed for the hearing of the said motion.

(4) Any respondent may deliver a replying affidavit. Any such replying affidavit shall be filed in the Central Office and a copy served upon the applicant and upon every other respondent within seven days of the service by the applicant of the originating notice of motion and the applicant's grounding affidavit upon the said respondent.

(5) Any replying affidavit shall set out concisely the grounds relied upon by the respondent to resist the applicant's claim for the reliefs set out in the originating notice of motion as against such respondent.

(6) The applicant shall be at liberty to file a further affidavit replying to any matter raised by a respondent in a replying affidavit, which further affidavit shall be filed in the

Central Office and a copy delivered to each respondent within seven days after the service upon the applicant of the respondent's replying affidavit.

(7) An affidavit giving the names and addresses of, and the places and dates of service on, all persons who have been served with the originating notice of motion, grounding affidavit and exhibits (if any) shall be filed before the motion is heard. If any person who ought under this Order to have been served has not been so served, the affidavit shall state that fact and the reason for it.

7. Save where the Court otherwise directs, every application under this Part shall be heard and determined on affidavit.

8. The Court, on the application of any of the parties or of its own motion, may at any time make an order under section 32 of the Act and where such an order is made, the Court may make such consequential, further or other orders or give such directions as the Court considers will facilitate the effective use of that process.

9. An application by a party for an order under rule 8 shall be made by motion to the Court on notice to the opposing party or parties, and shall, unless the Court otherwise orders, be grounded upon an affidavit sworn by or on behalf of the moving party.

10. Save where the Court for special reason to be recited in the Court's order allows, an application for an order under rule 8 shall not be made later than 28 days before the date on which the proceedings are first listed for hearing."

Index

R

S

T

U

V

W